# www.wadsworth.com

*wadsworth.com* is the World Wide Web site for Wadsworth Publishing Company and is your direct source to dozens of online resources.

At *wadsworth.com* you can find out about supplements, demonstration software, and student resources. You can also send e-mail to many of our authors and preview new publications and exciting new technologies.

**wadsworth.com**
Changing the way the world learns®

# Intentional Group Counseling

## A Microskills Approach

**Allen E. Ivey**
University of Massachusetts, Amherst

**Paul B. Pedersen**
University of Alabama at Birmingham

**Mary Bradford Ivey**
Microtraining Associates

**Brooks/Cole**
Thomson Learning™

Australia • Canada • Mexico • Singapore • Spain • United Kingdom • United States

Counseling Editor: *Julie Martinez*
Assistant Editor: *Kerry Dixon*
Editorial Assistant: *Marin Plank*
Marketing Manager: *Caroline Concilla*
Signing Representative: *Jennifer Wilkinson*
Project Editor: *Matt Stevens*
Print Buyer: *Karen Hunt*
Permissions Editor: *Joohee Lee*

Production Service: *Scratchgravel Publishing Services*
Text Designer: *Anne Draus*
Copy Editor: *Patterson Lamb*
Cover Designer: *Andrew Ogus*
Cover Printer: *Malloy Lithographing*
Compositor: *Scratchgravel Publishing Services*
Printer: *Malloy Lithographing*

Printed in the United States of America
1 2 3 4 5 6 7   04 03 02 01 00

For permission to use material from this text, contact
us by
**Web:** http://www.thomsonrights.com
**Fax:** 1-800-730-2215
**Phone:** 1-800-730-2214

**Library of Congress Cataloging-in-Publication Data**
Ivey, Allen E.
    Intentional group counseling : a microskills approach /
Allen E. Ivey, Paul B. Pedersen, Mary Bradford Ivey.
        p.   cm.
    Includes index.
    ISBN 0-534-52651-9 (alk. paper)
    1. Group counseling.   I. Pedersen, Paul, [date]–.
II. Ivey, Mary Bradford.   III. Title.

BF637.C6 .I96   2001
158'.35—dc21                                    00-036109

**Wadsworth/Thomson Learning**
**10 Davis Drive**
**Belmont, CA 94002-3098**
**USA**

For more information about our products, contact us:
**Thomson Learning Academic Resource Center**
**1-800-423-0563**
http://www.wadsworth.com

**International Headquarters**
Thomson Learning
International Division
290 Harbor Drive, 2nd Floor
Stamford, CT 06902-7477
USA

**UK/Europe/Middle East/South Africa**
Thomson Learning
Berkshire House
168-173 High Holborn
London WC1V 7AA
United Kingdom

**Asia**
Thomson Learning
60 Albert Street, #15-01
Albert Complex
Singapore 189969

**Canada**
Nelson Thomson Learning
1120 Birchmount Road
Toronto, Ontario M1K 5G4
Canada

 *This book is printed on*
*acid-free recycled paper.*

# DEDICATION

### To Norma Jean Anderson and Ernest Washington

Norma Jean Anderson was Associate Dean and Professor at the University of Massachusetts, Amherst. Norma Jean and I taught together and facilitated "Black and White in Helping" groups in the late 1960s at the University of Massachusetts. Norma Jean, your warmth and sensitivity are always with me; I learned so much about the world working and being with you. Everybody loves you, and I do too!

Ernest Washington is Professor at the University of Massachusetts, Amherst. The "Ernie and Al" show, our Multicultural Counseling and Therapy course, was a feature at the university for many years. Ernie, you are the ultimate scholar and gentleman, always pushing me to learn something new. You are the good friend who encouraged me to work with children for the first time in your "cultural identity groups." Let's get together for lunch at the "Black Sheep Deli."

**Allen**

### To Paul Torrance and Harold Pepinsky

Paul Torrance was a Professor in Educational Psychology at the University of Minnesota and my first mentor in working with small groups. He made each class an experience in small group dynamics with interactive learning and structured experiences. He demonstrated the importance of cultural and special interest membership for group dynamics long before that became a popular topic in psychology. Paul Torrance is perhaps best known for his work on creativity, for his influence in small group work, and for counseling at the U of M.

Harold Pepinsky was a Professor in Counseling Psychology at Ohio State University who helped guide me toward understanding coalitions in small groups in general and toward counseling in particular. My contacts with him resulted in my design of a Triad Training Model where the counselor and the client form a coalition against the problem. He taught me the importance of "power issues" through coalitions in small group dynamics and counseling.

**Paul**

### To Marge and Kenneth Blanchard

Marge Blanchard is a nationally known author and management consultant who currently serves as Chair of the Board at Blanchard Training and Development, San Diego, California. She is my long-time best friend and mentor. Marge, together, we worked through the challenges and growth opportunities of the women's movement. It was you who encouraged me to continue on toward my doctorate, who provided support through the difficult times, and who joined me in celebrating the victories.

Kenneth Blanchard is known for his bestselling book, *The One-Minute Manager,* and is recognized nationally and internationally for his innovative work in business consulting and training, particularly for situational leadership. He was formerly a faculty member at the University of Massachusetts, Amherst. Ken, you were my doctoral chair, and you are an incredible group and workshop leader. But, most of all, I admire your giving and loving support to people everywhere. You suggested long ago that my dissertation on process observation be published. Well, here it is—finally! Thanks!

**Mary**

# ABOUT THE AUTHORS

**Allen E. Ivey** is Distinguished University Professor (Emeritus), University of Massachusetts, Amherst. He is president of Microtraining Associates, an educational publishing firm. Allen also serves on the Board of Directors of the National Institute for Multicultural Competence. He received his undergraduate degree (Phi Beta Kappa) from Stanford University followed by a year of social work study as a Fulbright Scholar at the University of Copenhagen, Denmark. Allen's doctoral degree was earned at Harvard. Major portions of this book were written while he served as Norman Munn Visiting Scholar at Flinders University, South Australia.

Allen is the author or co-author of more than 25 books and 200 articles and chapters, translated into at least 16 languages. He is the originator of the microskills approach, basic to this book. A past president of the Division of Counseling Psychology of the American Psychological Association, he is a Fellow of APA and a Diplomate of the American Board of Professional Psychology. He is also a Fellow of APA's Society for the Study of Ethnic and Minority Psychology. Allen has spoken widely throughout North American and internationally. A lifetime member of the American Counseling Association, he received their Professional Development Award in 1992.

Allen's first group experience was at the National Training Laboratories (NTL) in Bethel, Maine, followed by experiential work with William Shutz at Esalen in Big Sur, California. In his early group practice, he focused on the "wheel," using groups as a way to facilitate individual therapy from a psychoanalytic frame. Influenced by the writings of Ruth Cohn, he moved to a theme-centered and psychoeducational orientation to groups. Multicultural theory and practice have become increasingly central to his work. He is the co-author with Derald Wing Sue and Paul Pedersen of *A Theory of Multicultural Counseling and Therapy* (Brooks/Cole).

**Paul B. Pedersen** is Professor at the University of Alabama at Birmingham, School of Education, Department of Human Studies and Counseling Program. He has been a faculty member at Syracuse University, University of Hawai'i, University of Minnesota, Nommensen University in Indonesia, and University of Malaya in Malaysia. He received his undergraduate degree and two masters degrees from the University of Minnesota. His Ph.D. is from Claremont Graduate School in California. Portions of this book were written while he was on a Senior Fulbright Grant, teaching at the National Taiwan University in Taiwan.

Paul is the author, editor, or co-author of 34 books, 62 chapters, and 92 articles on various aspects of multicultural counseling and communication. He is a Fellow in Divisions 17, 9, 45, and 52 of the American Psychological Association and an active member of the American Counseling Association. He has been President of the Society for Intercultural Education Training and Research. He has been a Senior Fellow at the East West Center and Principal Investigator for the NIMH project "Developing Interculturally Skilled Counselors" at the University of Hawai'i.

Paul's group training began under Professor Paul Torrance at the University of Minnesota. He was also strongly influenced by Harold Pepinsky from Ohio State University and Clyde Parker at the University of Minnesota. He has organized and run training groups, counseling groups with international students, and workshops in Europe, Asia, Australia, South Africa, and throughout the United States. He has taught group classes at the University of Pittsburgh (Semester at Sea), the University of Alabama at Birmingham, and the University of Hawai'i. He is the author of *Hidden Messages* (Sage Publications), a book that applies group theories to a better understanding of intrapersonal dynamics in each person's multicultural identity.

**Mary Bradford Ivey** is vice president of Microtraining Associates and a former school counselor in the Amherst, Massachusetts, schools. She has served as visiting professor or counselor at Amherst College; University of Massachusetts, Amherst; University of Hawai'i, Manoa; and Keene State University. Mary's undergraduate degree in social work and education is from Gustavus Adolphus College, and she has a master's degree in counseling and guidance from the University of Wisconsin, Madison. She earned her doctorate in organizational development at the University of Massachusetts, Amherst. Mary is also on the Board of Directors of the National Institute for Multicultural Competence. Major portions of this book were written while she served as visiting lecturer at Flinders University, South Australia.

Mary is the author or co-author of eight books, several articles and chapters, and more than ten counseling videotapes, translated into multiple languages. She is co-author, with Allen Ivey, of *Intentional Interviewing and Counseling: Facilitating Multicultural Development,* 4th Edition (Brooks/Cole). She is a nationally certified counselor (NCC) and a licensed mental health counselor, and she holds a certificate in school counseling. She has presented workshops and keynote lectures throughout the world including Australia, Canada, Greater Britain, Germany, Greece, Hong Kong, Iceland, Israel, Mexico, Japan, New Zealand, Portugal, and Sweden. Mary received national recognition in 1988 when her elementary counseling program at the Fort River School was named one of the ten best in the nation at the Christa McAullife Conference. She is also the recipient of the O'hana Award of the American Counseling Association for her work in multicultural counseling in the schools.

Mary's first experience in groups was in a Black/White encounter group led by two National Training Laboratory (NTL) trainers. This was followed by extensive organizational group work with her doctoral chair, Kenneth Blanchard, author of the *One-Minute Manager* and well-known for his work in situational leadership. This combination of experiences led her to a contextual and developmental frame, which was important in her work in the schools. Mary has facilitated many child and adult groups, including unstructured client-centered encounter groups, psychoeducational groups of widely varying types, and culture-centered counseling groups. Her most recent videotape is *Counseling Children: A Microskills Approach,* distributed through Microtraining Associates.

# CONTENTS

# PREFACE

## Why read a skills book for group work?

*Intentional Group Counseling: A Microskills Approach* defines specific skills and strategies for training group leaders. Over the past few years basic introductory texts in group work increasingly have talked about the foundational skills of listening and leading a group. To this date, no text has directly taken the comprehensive microskills approach to the complex process of facilitating groups. Extensive transcripts of groups in action highlight this text throughout.

This book seeks to meet the need for more depth in the foundational microskills and strategies of group leadership. Over the years, we have found that the thoroughly researched microskills approach facilitates an understanding and mastery of group approaches. The specificity of microskills enables both beginners and advanced students to master the complexities of group work at a deeper level.

## For whom is this text intended?

The book is designed to meet two alternative teaching approaches: it can serve as the base for a course in itself, or it may be used in conjunction with one of the many excellent introduction to groups texts currently available. The process observation instruments and detailed transcripts are designed to illustrate many theoretical and practical strategies in action.

Students and professionals who have mastered the concepts of this book succeed more rapidly in coping with advanced group work and theories. This book may also be used in group practicum courses as the applications presented here can be used immediately by students in practice during the coming week in a gradual progression of competencies.

Many students will have encountered the skills approach through study in individual counseling courses. Such experience will facilitate their movement through this book, and they will be able to spend more time on process observation and practice. More time can also be devoted to the influencing skills, conflict management, and alternative approaches to group work. Some instructors may want to use this book with an individual counseling skills course. Although that would cause a demanding schedule, it is a worthwhile possibility with strong students.

This is a practical book designed for beginning group workers in the mental health helping fields—counseling, nursing, psychiatry, psychology, and social work.

The book will also have value in business programs, communication studies, and any field in which group process is important. We have found the microskills concepts useful in supervision, and thus this book may be useful for experienced professionals.

## What are the goals of this text?

By the time the beginning group leader has successfully completed this book, he or she will be able to do the following:

1. Recognize the importance of an ethically based group practice, including the vitality of the multicultural foundation that exists in all group work.
2. Identify and demonstrate basic listening and influencing skills and strategies essential to group process.
3. Learn to help group members focus their comments in a variety of areas balancing the individual, the group, and cultural/environmental context.
4. Conduct a complete theme-centered group session by the time he or she completes Chapter 6 of this text.
5. Utilize several process observation frameworks to look at and classify groups in action.
6. Master the skills of interpersonal influence, including conflict management and confrontation.
7. Understand how microskills and strategies are used in comprehensive and intentional ways among the multiple orientations to group theory and practice.
8. Assess her or his own skills and define a personal orientation to group practice.

## How might this text be useful in teaching?

Special features of this book include:

▲ Sequenced and clear learning activities designed so that students can learn the basics of group facilitation step by step. Each chapter contains multiple exercises for practice.
▲ Transcripts illustrating the concepts, found throughout the book with process commentary on what is occurring in the group.
▲ The positive asset search, which helps ensure a strength orientation to group process and may assist beginning leaders later when they find themselves encountering difficult issues.
▲ Process observation instruments so that students can learn the all-important skill of experienced leaders—observing what is going on around them in the group.
▲ Listening skills with the specifics on how to listen effectively through the basic listening sequence.
▲ Focusing skills to help ensure that group members cover relevant issues in a timely fashion.
▲ Influencing strategies of group work showing how to use structuring, reframing/interpretation, feedback, and related concepts.
▲ Conflict management strategies of challenging and confrontation, presented in depth because handling these difficult issues is particularly important for beginning leaders.

▲ Multicultural issues, which are given special attention throughout this book. *Before You Start,* the introductory section, initiates this process, pointing out that all group work in some way is multicultural.

▲ Children and adolescent group issues, which are examined in all chapters.

▲ Theories and multiple orientations to group practice that are summarized with specifics on how they relate to microskills, focusing, and influencing strategies.

▲ Explanations for beginning students on how to classify skill usage in their own groups. Students will be able to engage in process observation and analysis of their own styles of group leadership.

We have found that both we and our students have enjoyed working with these concepts. All of us can improve our skills as we work together and better understand the specifics of communication in groups. In short, the microskills approach is comfortable and enjoyable to teach, particularly as both student and instructor can see constant improvement in specific and observable aspects of group work.

## What supportive teaching aids are available?

An *Instructional Guide* accompanies this text with suggestions and many exercises for teaching, film and video resources, web links, and multiple choice and essay examination questions. Overhead transparencies are included in the *Instructional Guide.* Visit www.emicrotraining.com for more supportive links and materials.

## Acknowledgments

We would first like to thank the reviewers of drafts of this text for their many helpful comments and suggestions. They include: Cheryl Bartholomew, George Mason University; Paul Blisard, Southwest Missouri State University; Dorothy J. Blum, George Mason University; M. Sylvia Fernandez, Arkansas State University; Elizabeth Kincade, Indiana University of Pennsylvania; Muriel Stockburger, Eastern Kentucky University; Rex Stockton, Indiana University at Bloomington; and Myrna Thompson, Southside Virginia Community College.

Much of the work on the book was completed while Allen and Mary Ivey were serving as visiting professors in psychology at Flinders University, Adelaide, South Australia. Special thanks to Drs. Lia and Zig Kapelis for their encouragement and hospitality during our visit. David Rathman, Chief Executive Officer of Aboriginal Affairs in South Australia, was instrumental in expanding our awareness of cultural difference, and we thank him for the opportunity to work once again with the Indigenous People of Australia. The influence of Liz, Zig, and David has been central in the developmental of this book.

Paul Pedersen served as Fulbright Scholar at the National Taiwan University during much of the writing of this book. He wishes to acknowledge and thank Larry Tyson for helping him "try out" the microskills approach in his group class and thinking through the applications of microskills to group work. Also important is Juanita Turner at the University of Alabama at Birmingham for her help in preparing materials and for her computer expertise. Paul would like to express appreciation to Professor Hwang Kwang Kuo at the National Taiwan University and Professor Wu Jing Ji at the Fulbright Foundation for providing access to the office computers and secretarial support while serving as a Senior Fulbright Scholar in Taiwan, thus making it possible to work on the book from a distance.

We would all like to thank Sherry Lord at Syracuse University for her aid in preparing materials for the book and the *Instructional Guide*.

Multicultural concepts have been supported both in this book and in the past by the Board of Directors of the National Institute of Multicultural Competence—Michael D'Andrea, Executive Officer, and members Patricia Arredondo, Beverly Bryant, Judy Daniels, Allen Ivey, Mary Bradford Ivey, Don C. Locke, Derald Wing Sue, and Thomas Parham. The inspiration of Teresa LaFromboise, Susan Cameron, and Sherlon Pack-Brown is also present here.

There is a long history of microskills work and research, and many students and scholars have participated and defined this area since 1966. Without their work, this book would not have been possible. Several key figures are listed in Allen and Mary Bradford Ivey's 1999 book *Intentional Interviewing and Counseling: Facilitating Client Development in a Multicultural Society,* 4th Edition (Brooks/Cole).

Special recognition and thanks go to two individuals who have contributed to this book directly. Thomas Daniels of Memorial University of Newfoundland, Cornerbrook, has worked with us on microskill issues for many years and provided important feedback. Peter Sherrard of the University of Florida did the basic research work on microskills work in groups. His thought-provoking and innovative approach has inspired us for years, and we are delighted that some of his ideas are at last presented here in print.

Finally, we would like to thank the editorial and production staff at Brooks/Cole. We wish all publishers were as pleasant and professional as this group. Specifically, we especially thank Eileen Murphy, who worked with us in the early stages of this book, and Julie Martinez, who very ably and smoothly took over editorship in the final stages. We have never experienced such a smooth transition in editors. We also acknowledge Jennifer Wilkinson, Marin Plank, Matt Stevens, Patterson Lamb, and Anne Draus for their outstanding work.

We thank you for joining us in this venture of skill-based work in groups. We believe it has immense promise and look forward to working with you as we move together toward the future. Please use the feedback sheet at the end of the book and let us know what you think.

*Allen E. Ivey*
Distinguished University Professor, Emeritus,
    University of Massachusetts, Amherst
President, Microtraining Associates, Inc.
Norman Munn Distinguished Visiting Scholar in
    Psychology, Flinders University, South Australia

*Paul B. Pedersen*
Professor, Counseling Program
Department of Human Studies
University of Alabama at Birmingham
Visiting Fulbright Scholar, National Taiwan University

*Mary Bradford Ivey*
Vice President, Microtraining Associates, Inc.
Visiting Lecturer, Flinders University, South Australia

# Intentional Group Counseling

A Microskills Approach

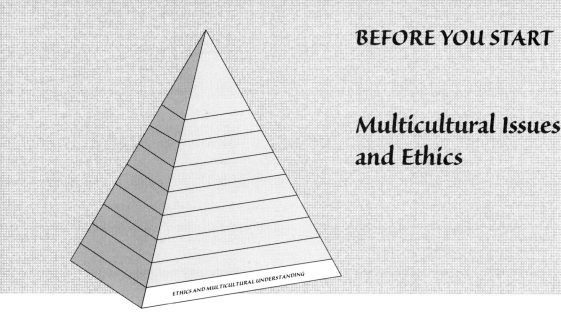

# Multicultural Issues and Ethics

ETHICS AND MULTICULTURAL UNDERSTANDING

As you begin examining the world of group work, two central issues will be critical in your development as a leader: expanding your awareness of multicultural factors and developing a solid ethical understanding.

Multicultural issues are present in every group—and each group is culturally different from all other groups. The word *multicultural* implies many cultures. In each group you experience, you will encounter individuals who have vastly different life experiences from your own. And as the group process goes forward, you will find that a unique microculture for the group evolves.

Group practice needs to begin on the basis of solid ethical understanding. Groups are powerful social vehicles and your leadership can be for good or ill. Professional ethical guidelines for group work are reprinted here so that they are readily available as you work through the many issues presented in this book.

Multicultural and ethical issues join together—each individual is unique and comes from a distinct cultural background. To understand that background, you need to approach it with empathy, which is most often defined as seeing the world through another person's eyes, living in that person's shoes, and feeling his or her emotions. Ethics in group work demands that you continually seek to understand the different and special qualities of the individuals and groups with which you will work. Your first task in understanding the uniqueness and specialness of others, however, is to develop awareness of your own multicultural background.

## OUR MULTICULTURAL HERITAGE

We are all multicultural human beings; our very selfhood and identity are embedded in the language we speak, our gender, our ethnic/racial background, and our individual life path and experience. Because all behaviors are learned and displayed in a cultural context, we bring our own cultural experiences into our group through

1

the manner in which we participate. The multicultures cannot be separated from the individual; they are deeply embedded in our concept of self and others.

The following exercise is one we have used many times to encourage people to think about themselves as multicultural beings. As presented, it is focused on you and your multicultural world, but it also is an exercise that you can readily adapt in your own work. Group members who complete the questions below and tell stories of their cultural backgrounds will develop information that can fill several group sessions.

Work through the list and think about how these factors influence who you are, the opportunities you have, where you can live, and how others react to you. Consider how these factors lead you to think, feel, and behave in certain ways—and how they influence others' reactions to you.

As you work through this list, feel free not to share any issue that you would prefer to keep private. This list is to enable you to think about the multicultures that help make you the person you are. Do you have a single multicultural identity or do you have multiple multicultural identities?

### Family context

Describe the nature of your family or families both past and present—nuclear, extended, divorce/remarriage, single parent, adoptive, gay/lesbian/heterosexual. Your family experience is your introduction to and foundation for the multicultures in which you grow and develop. Almost all of the multicultural dimensions discussed below are affected by your family context.

_____

_____

_____

_____

### Social systems context

What language(s) do you speak? _____

What is your gender? _____

Your ethnicity and race? _____

Religion and spirituality? _____

### Demographic context

Age? _____

Sexual orientation? _____

National origin? _____

Region of the nation? _____

Community of origin and present community? _____

### Status context

Past and present socioeconomic background? _____

Education? _____

Key group affiliations? _____
(living groups, fraternities, social groups, athletics)

### Life experience context

Have you encountered major physical issues? _____

Have you encountered major emotional issues? _____

Have you experienced discrimination or prejudice? _____

What trauma(s) have you experienced in life? _____
(rape, divorce, accident, war, serious illness, family)

Important experiences of family members? _____

Other important issues _____

The above identities can be considered your multicultural background. Put them all together and it becomes immediately apparent that all group work is culturally bound. Our way of thinking and behaving—even the way we respond emotionally—is deeply affected by each of these factors.

Each of these identities (and others) will become the most important at varying times in the group. At one point, race or ethnicity may be the predominant multicultural issue for an individual or group. At the next, gender may take precedence. Then, as a group member shares a war or rape assault experience, trauma may take precedence. Depending on what occurs in the group context, any one of our multiple identities may become the most salient.

Two vital questions for your work as a group leader arise. The first is, How does your life experience affect the way you view the world? If we are to be empathic and understanding of others, we first need to understand our own worldview—our way of making sense of what we see. The second question, perhaps even more important, is, How do we become aware of biases and prejudices we may have? Corey (1995, p. 27) comments:

> . . . because of the power group counselors possess, it is possible to use this power to stifle group members instead of empowering them. Being aware of your personal biases is the first step toward guarding against unethical practices in your own group work.

However, if you are confident in yourself and have personal power as a group leader, you are more likely to use the power of leadership in an affirming manner. Corey (2000, p. 29) adds,

> Personal power involves self-confidence and awareness of one's influence on others. If group leaders do not have a sense of power in their own lives . . . it is difficult for them to facilitate members' movement toward empowerment.

The list of multicultural issues also creates a picture of what is dominant and powerful in the larger culture and what represents a minority. Historically, in the United States and Canada, dominance belongs to those who speak English, are male, White of European descent, Christian, heterosexual, young to early middle-aged, able bodied, of middle or upper class, and who have been fortunate enough to avoid major life trauma. However, virtually no one moves through life in a constant state of power and privilege.

Many White people in North America may not give much thought to being White or think consciously about the privilege they may enjoy because of power dynamics in a sometimes racist society. McIntosh (1989) terms this *White privilege.* Men and heterosexuals may not think of gender and sexual orientation as issues because they enjoy many privileges of society that are not always open to others. With each case of dominance, central privileges and entitlements may be expected.

Consider the characteristics of White privilege above as a summary of power and dominance. Where do you personally stand in the power hierarchy? What are your personal feelings and thoughts about the concept of dominance and privilege as presented here? Positions of power and dominance deeply affect possible biases that we may have as those issues play themselves out in other multicultural areas. List below your areas of privilege.

_____

_____

_____

_____

_____

_____

_____

_____

_____

_____

Revisit your list and reflect on how these multiple dimensions or identities affect you as a multicultural being. What is your unique path as a family member, a group member, a person-in-community, and a person in a particular geographic location? How will group members different from you think about you? Write below several perceptions others might have of you as a group leader because of your multicultural background.

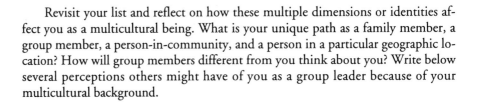

_____

_____

_____

_____

_____

_____

_____

_____

_____

_____

Full awareness and realization of our multicultural being moves us away from stereotyping ourselves and others, for clearly each of us is one of a kind, different, and special. When we bring all this multicultural individuality into a group, these differences often underlie what people think and say in the group. There is an ethical imperative to learn about the multicultural context of group process. The American Counseling Association (ACA) (1995, A.5.b) *Code of Ethics* comments:

> Counselors are aware of their own values, attitudes, beliefs, and behaviors and how these apply in a diverse society, and avoid imposing values on clients.

## THE ETHICS OF GROUP WORK

The Association for Specialists in Group Work has developed a comprehensive set of guidelines, "Ethical Guidelines for Group Counselors," reprinted here in its entirety. It is important that you read and discuss these guidelines as you start thinking about your work in groups. You will also want to refer to them frequently as you encounter various issues in this book or in the suggested practice exercises following each chapter.

The full "Ethical Guidelines for Group Counselors" are presented on pages 11–18. The following pages (6–10) provide summary comments discussing the immediate implications of these guidelines for you in the early stages of your work as a group leader. *Intentional Group Counseling: A Microskills Approach* contains many practical exercises to increase and build your skills as a leader. As such, you will want to review the guidelines frequently so that ethical standards become an integral part of your awareness and your leadership style. You will also find a "Sample Group Contract" that may be useful in screening group members for your early practice sessions. Be open to seeking supervision and consultation as you enter the beginning stages of learning group work and even as an experienced professional years from now. Ethical challenges will be with you throughout your professional life.

## 1. Orientation and Providing Information

As a beginning group leader, you may be asking volunteers to work with you as you practice group skills. The first ethical guideline stresses the importance of sharing with your members what to expect from the group, the group goals, and the potential risks of group membership. One route toward this objective is for you to develop a written handout for potential group members as part of the prescreening process. In addition, you will need to go over key informational points as you initiate the group.

Risks are always present in any group. Be sure you have supervision and backup to help you with any issues that may arise. You can help prevent problems by using the positive asset search emphasized in this book and focusing on member and group efficacy and abilities. Group members tend to feel more secure if you focus on their strengths, particularly in the early phases of the group.

Another important rule to share early with any group is the "right to pass" and not say anything or not to participate in a certain exercise. Group pressure can force some people to talk when they would rather be silent and merely observe. On the other hand, as you develop trust among the group, some members may become too open in their self-disclosures and you will want to work to help them keep certain issues to themselves.

It is important that you share your experiential background as a beginning leader with your volunteer group members.

## 2. Screening of Members

We strongly suggest that you prescreen members of your group individually before the group begins. Issues for screening are defined clearly in Section 1 of the "Guidelines," Orientation. The key issues for prescreening are informing the members about the nature of the group and its potential risks, your own level of experience, general policies of the group, and issues of confidentiality.

Part of screening includes providing the potential group member with a group contract that both you and the member sign. One example of such a contract is offered on the following page.

If you are working with volunteers or friends, you may feel particularly awkward in asking whether they are drug users or whether they have been in psychotherapy (see "Ethical Guidelines," 1.h). A way to handle this issue is to say that anyone who has these issues should likely not volunteer for your group. At times, individual prescreening will not be possible; on these occasions a prescreening group session as described in the "Ethical Guidelines" may be used.

## 3. Confidentiality

As a beginning leader, you do not have professional qualifications that permit legal confidentiality. Your group needs to know this as you simultaneously stress that they should disclose only the information they are comfortable in sharing. You must maintain confidentiality yourself, but you cannot guarantee confidentiality from the group members present. Group members are strongly encouraged to "keep what is said here in our session *in the group*."

## Sample Group Contract

| Group members will | The leader(s) will |
|---|---|
| 1. Attend all sessions and be there when the group starts and recognize that participation is central to group success. | 1. Be prepared for each session and start the group on time as agreed. |
| 2. Keep information within the group and not discuss what occurs with others, even family and close friends. | 2. Maintain group confidentiality within legal limits. Notify group members about supervision arrangements. |
| 3. Participate and share as openly as possible and not dominate others. | 3. Support group members and ensure that all have space and time within the group session. |
| 4. Listen to others and not interrupt. | 4. Listen to others and not interrupt. |
| 5. Treat all members with respect, even when differing strongly with what they say. | 5. Treat all members with respect, even when differing strongly with what they say. |
| 6. Reserve the right to "pass" and not comment or participate in an exercise. | 6. Respect the right of any member to "pass" and not comment or participate in an exercise if they so wish. |
| 7. Recognize the need to expect referral to external services if concerns develop during the group that are beyond the scope of the group and the leader's experience. | 7. Arrange for appropriate supervision and have a plan to assist members who may ask for or need special help beyond the scope of the group. |
| 8. Consult with appropriate individuals if undergoing counseling or therapy with another person or group. This is to be done before entering the group. Appropriate permission needs to be obtained from both other professionals and this group leader. | 8. Recognize the importance of coordinating all group work with other professionals who may be counseling or conducting therapy with an individual in the group. |
| 9. Raise additional questions that may occur now or during the group. | 9. Answer to the best of one's ability all questions and/or seek assistance in providing the answer. |

_____     _____
Signature of Group Member          Signature of Leader

Date _____     Date _____

In school situations and with minors, most states require you to obtain parental permission before engaging in group work. Consult with your supervisor carefully on this issue.

We recommend videotaping or audiotaping your practice with groups as often as possible, but this must be done only with prior consent of group members and, if you are working with minors, parental consent as well. Inform group members that you may be showing the video or audiotape to your supervisor and that you might transcribe certain information for supervision purposes. If at any point an individual is uncomfortable with the taping process, the equipment should be turned off immediately. Usually, you can turn it on again after discussion of the problematic topic is completed. One guideline for recording is especially important: if you are relaxed and comfortable with recording equipment, your participants will be also. If you are worried about the equipment, expect them to be concerned as well.

## 4. Voluntary/Involuntary Participation

## 5. Leaving a Group

## 6. Coercion and Pressure

## 7. Imposing Counselor Values

## 8. Equitable Treatment

These five dimensions of the guidelines are important and relatively self-explanatory. In different ways, they all focus on group members' rights. As a beginning leader, you will want to ensure that participation is voluntary, that members are free to leave a group at any time, that you avoid imposing personal biases on the group, and that you treat all members equally. Multicultural understanding speaks particularly to the last two issues.

## 9. Dual Relationships

The issue of dual relationships is a particularly important one for professional group workers and it is equally important for beginners. A dual relationship occurs when you are a group leader and at the same time have some other special interest in the group or its members For example, even in your early work in groups you have considerable power as you learn about group members. Ideally, you will do all your practice exercises and group work with those with whom you are not acquainted.

In a beginning group course, however, you are very likely to be forced into several dual relationships. You will probably engage in group exercises in a workshop or class with friends and acquaintances. When you work with people you know who have volunteered to participate in a group with you, you are obviously in a potentially complex dual relationship.

In short, dual relationships cannot be fully avoided. When they do occur, the nature of the dual relationship and its problems need to be part of prescreening and discussed early in the first group.

## 10. Use of Techniques

*Intentional Group Counseling: A Microskills Approach* is very much oriented to techniques and strategies. You will find that the group practice exercises are designed so that you will have constant supervision by your group leader or instructor throughout the course of study. The readings and exercises are structured to provide training before you engage in leading a group on your own. We have attempted to include multicultural commentaries and examples throughout. The movement of theory to practice is inherent in the design of this book.

## 11. Goal Development
## 14. Evaluation and Follow-up

Goals and evaluation are placed together here because we consider the achievement of group or personal goals to be perhaps the best follow-up and evaluation. As part of prescreening and the initial stage of a group, clear goals for both the group and for each member need to be established. These can and likely should be revised as the group progresses over time. With less structured groups (e.g., person-centered, psychoanalytic), the prescreening becomes even more important as goal development tends to be an evolving aspect of these groups and goals are not usually well defined at the beginning.

Process observation is an important part of evaluation, and you will find a number of process observation instruments and exercises throughout this book. The way a group moves over time can be evaluated in multiple ways and you will find it very helpful to have several strategies in mind to observe what is happening in your group.

One purpose of group work is to facilitate personal growth and development. You will want to observe degrees of individual change in your work as a group leader. And you will also need to be aware of those who remain where they are. The Observation of Change Scale, presented in Chapter 7, provides a systematic way to organize in your mind individual and group movement and change. You will want to add other follow-up evaluation measures of group work as you gain further experience.

## 12. Consultation

Consultation and supervision is essential for the beginning group worker and equally important to the experienced professional. We all have room to learn and grow. As stated earlier, inform your participants about the nature of consultation and supervision before the group begins. At times, you may want to report results of consultation sessions with your participants.

## 13. Termination from the Group

Termination is a point of concern primarily for professionals. In group therapy particularly, some members may stay longer than they need to, thus developing a dependency on the group. The leader may have become dependent on that group member as a good and helpful participant—and perhaps as a financial contributor as well. If the individual does not need the group, help him or her terminate in a timely fashion.

## 15. Referrals

Group work cannot solve all problems or issues. You may need to refer a group member for individual counseling or therapy or to community agencies for specialized help. For example, a group member may profit from referral for financial advice from a community agency; for religious counseling from a pastor, rabbi, priest, or other spiritual source; for medical services for possible physical issues; or for help on college selection from a school counselor. You need to be knowledgeable not only about group practice, but also about the services of other community agencies that may be able to assist those in your group.

## 16. Professional Development

Simply put, there is no end to one's development as a group leader. There is always something new to learn. The effective beginner and the competent experienced professional both need further study and learning. An important part of professional development is participating in a wide number of groups yourself.

Multicultural and ethical principles and understanding will form the basis of a lifelong learning plan.

Let us begin . . .

*Allen, Paul, and Mary*

## REFERENCES

American Counseling Association. (1995). *Code of ethics and standards of practice.* Alexandria, VA: Author.

Corey, G. (1995). *Theory & Practice of Group Counseling* (3rd ed.). Pacific Grove, CA: Brooks/Cole.

Corey, G. (2000). *Theory & Practice of Group Counseling* (4th ed.). Pacific Grove, CA: Brooks/Cole.

McIntosh, P. (1989, July/August). White privilege: Unpacking the invisible knapsack. *Peace and Freedom,* pp. 8–10.

## Ethical Guidelines for Group Counselors

| Preamble | One characteristic of any professional group is the possession of a body of knowledge, skills, and voluntarily, self-professed standards for ethical practice. A Code of Ethics consists of those standards that have been formally and publicly acknowledged by the members of a profession to serve as the guidelines for professional conduct, discharge of duties, and the resolution of moral dilemmas. By this document, the Association for Specialists in Group Work (ASGW) has identified the standards of conduct appropriate for ethical behavior among its members.

The Association for Specialists in Group Work recognizes the basic commitment of its members to the Ethical Standards of its parent organization, the American Association for Counseling and Development (AACD) and nothing in this document shall be construed to supplant that code. These standards are intended to complement the AACD standards in the area of group work by clarifying the nature of ethical responsibility of the counselor in the group setting and by stimulating a greater concern for competent group leadership.

The group counselor is expected to be a professional agent and to take the processes of ethical responsibility seriously. ASGW views *ethical process* as being integral to group work and views group counselors as *ethical agents*. Group counselors, by their very nature in being responsible and responsive to their group members, necessarily embrace a certain potential for ethical vulnerability. It is incumbent upon group counselors to give considerable attention to the intent and context of their actions because the attempts of counselors to influence human behavior through group work always have ethical implications.

The following ethical guidelines have been developed to encourage ethical behavior of group counselors. These guidelines are written for students and practitioners, and are meant to stimulate reflection, self-examination, and discussion of issues and practices. They address the group counselor's responsibility for providing information about group work to clients and the group counselor's responsibility for providing group counseling services to clients. A final section discusses the group counselor's responsibility for safeguarding ethical practice and procedures for reporting unethical behavior. Group counselors are expected to make known these standards to group members. |

| Ethical Guidelines | 1. *Orientation and Providing Information:* Group counselors adequately prepare prospective or new group members by providing as much information about the existing or proposed group as necessary.

▲ Minimally, information related to each of the following areas should be provided.
  a. Entrance procedures, time parameters of the group experience, group participation expectations, methods of payment (where appropriate), and termination procedures are explained by the group counselor as appropriate to the level of maturity of group members and the nature and purpose(s) of the group.
  b. Group counselors have available for distribution, a professional disclosure statement that includes information on the group counselor's qualifications

**(continued)** |

**Ethical Guidelines for Group Counselors (continued)**

and group services that can be provided, particularly as related to the nature and purpose(s) of the specific group.

c. Group counselors communicate the role expectations, rights, and responsibilities of group members and group counselor(s).

d. The group goals are stated as concisely as possible by the group counselor including *whose* goal it is (the group counselor's, the institution's, the parent's, the law's, society's, etc.) and the role of group members in influencing or determining the group's goal(s).

e. Group counselors explore with group members the risks of potential life changes that may occur because of the group experience and help members explore their readiness to face these possibilities.

f. Group members are informed by the group counselor of unusual or experimental procedures that might be expected in their group experience.

g. Group counselors explain, as realistically as possible, what services can and cannot be provided within the particular group structure offered.

h. Group counselors emphasize the need to promote full psychological functioning and presence among group members. They inquire from prospective group members whether they are using any kind of drug or medication that may affect functioning in the group. They do not permit any use of alcohol and/or illegal drugs during group sessions and they discourage the use of alcohol and/or drugs (legal or illegal) prior to group meetings which may affect the physical or emotional presence of the member or other group members.

i. Group counselors inquire from prospective group members whether they have ever been a client in counseling or psychotherapy. If a prospective group member is already in a counseling relationship with another professional person, the group counselor advises the prospective group member to notify the other professional of their participation in the group.

j. Group counselors clearly inform group members about the policies pertaining to the group counselor's willingness to consult with them between group sessions.

k. In establishing fees for group counseling services, group counselors consider the financial status and the locality of prospective group members. Group members are not charged fees for group sessions where the group counselor is not present and the policy of charging for sessions missed by a group member is clearly communicated. Fees for participating as a group member are contracted between group counselor and group member for a specified period of time. Group counselors do not increase fees for group counseling services until the existing contracted fee structure has expired. In the event that the established fee structure is inappropriate for a prospective member, group counselors assist in finding comparable services of acceptable cost.

2. *Screening of Members:* The group counselor screens prospective group members (when appropriate to their theoretical orientation). Insofar as possible, the counselor selects group members whose needs and goals are compatible with the goals of the group, who will not impede the group process, and whose well-being will not be jeopardized by the group experience. An orientation to the group (i.e., ASGW Ethical Guideline #1) is included during the screening process.

▲ Screening may be accomplished in one or more ways, such as the following:
  a. Individual interview
  b. Group interview of prospective group members
  c. Interview as part of a team staffing
  d. Completion of a written questionnaire by prospective group members.

3. *Confidentiality:* Group counselors protect members by defining clearly what confidentiality means, why it is important, and the difficulties involved in enforcement.
  a. Group counselors take steps to protect members by defining confidentiality and the limits of confidentiality (i.e., when a group member's condition indicates that there is clear and imminent danger to the member, others, or physical property, the group counselor takes reasonable personal action and/or informs responsible authorities).
  b. Group counselors stress the importance of confidentiality and set a norm of confidentiality regarding all group participants' disclosures. The importance of maintaining confidentiality is emphasized before the group begins and at various times in the group. The fact that confidentiality cannot be guaranteed is clearly stated.
  c. Members are made aware of the difficulties involved in enforcing and ensuring confidentiality in a group setting. The counselor provides examples of how confidentiality can nonmaliciously be broken to increase members' awareness, and helps to lessen the likelihood that this breach of confidence will occur. Group counselors inform group members about the potential consequences of intentionally breaching confidentiality.
  d. Group counselors can only ensure confidentiality on their part and not on the part of the members.
  e. Group counselors video or audio tape a group session only with the prior consent and the members' knowledge of how the tape will be used.
  f. When working with minors, the group counselor specifies the limits of confidentiality.
  g. Participants in a mandatory group are made aware of any reporting procedures required of the group counselor.
  h. Group counselors store or dispose of group member records (written, audio, video, etc.) in ways that maintain confidentiality.
  i. Instructors of group counseling courses maintain the anonymity of group members whenever discussing group counseling cases.

4. *Voluntary/Involuntary Participation:* Group counselors inform members whether participation is voluntary or involuntary.
  a. Group counselors take steps to ensure informed consent procedures in both voluntary and involuntary groups.
  b. When working with minors in a group, counselors are expected to follow the procedures specified by the institution in which they are practicing.
  c. With involuntary groups, every attempt is made to enlist the cooperation of the members and their continuance in the group on a voluntary basis.
  d. Group counselors do not certify that group treatment has been received by members who merely attend sessions, but did not meet the defined group

*(continued)*

**Ethical Guidelines for Group Counselors (continued)**

expectations. Group members are informed about the consequences for failing to participate in a group.

5. *Leaving a Group:* Provisions are made to assist a group member to terminate in
an effective way.
   a. Procedures to be followed for a group member who chooses to exit a group
      prematurely are discussed by the counselor with all group members either
      before the group begins, during a prescreening interview, or during the initial
      group session.
   b. In the case of legally mandated group counseling, group counselors inform
      members of the possible consequences for premature self-termination.
   c. Ideally, both the group counselor and the member can work cooperatively to
      determine the degree to which a group experience is productive or counter-
      productive for that individual.
   d. Members ultimately have a right to discontinue membership in the group,
      at a designated time, if the predetermined trial period proves to be un-
      satisfactory.
   e. Members have the right to exit a group, but it is important that they be made
      aware of the importance of informing the counselor and the group members
      prior to deciding to leave. The counselor discusses the possible risks of leav-
      ing the group prematurely with a member who is considering this option.
   f. Before leaving a group, the group counselor encourages members (if appro-
      priate) to discuss their reasons for wanting to discontinue membership in the
      group. Counselors intervene if other members use undue pressure to force a
      member to remain in the group.

6. *Coercion and Pressure:* Group counselors protect member rights against physical
threats, intimidation, coercion, and undue peer pressure insofar as is reasonably
possible.
   a. It is essential to differentiate between *therapeutic pressure* that is part of any
      group and *undue pressure,* which is not therapeutic.
   b. The purpose of a group is to help participants find their own answer, not to
      pressure them into doing what the group thinks is appropriate.
   c. Counselors exert care not to coerce participants to change in directions which
      they clearly state they do not choose.
   d. Counselors have a responsibility to intervene when others use undue pressure
      or attempt to persuade members against their will.
   e. Counselors intervene when any member attempts to act out aggression in a
      physical way that might harm another member or themselves.
   f. Counselors intervene when a member is verbally abusive or inappropriately
      confrontive to another member.

7. *Imposing Counselor Values:* Group counselors develop an awareness of their own
values and needs and the potential impact they have on the interventions likely
to be made.
   a. Although group counselors take care to avoid imposing their values on mem-
      bers, it is appropriate that they expose their own beliefs, decisions, needs, and
      values, when concealing them would create problems for the members.
   b. There are values implicit in any group, and these are made clear to potential
      members before they join the group. (Examples of certain values include:

expressing feelings, being direct and honest, sharing personal material with others, learning how to trust, improving interpersonal communication, and deciding for oneself.)

   c. Personal and professional needs of group counselors are not met at the members' expense.

   d. Group counselors avoid using the group for their own therapy.

   e. Group counselors are aware of their own values and assumptions and how these apply in a multicultural context.

   f. Group counselors take steps to increase their awareness of ways that their personal reactions to members might inhibit the group process and they monitor their countertransference. Through an awareness of the impact of stereotyping and discrimination (i.e., biases based on age, disability, ethnicity, gender, race, religion, or sexual preference), group counselors guard the individual rights and personal dignity of all group members.

8. *Equitable Treatment:* Group counselors make every reasonable effort to treat each member individually and equally.

   a. Group counselors recognize and respect differences (e.g., cultural, racial, religious, lifestyle, age, disability, gender) among group members.

   b. Group counselors maintain an awareness of their behavior toward individual group members and are alert to the potential detrimental effects of favoritism or partiality toward any particular group member to the exclusion or detriment of any other member(s). It is likely that group counselors will favor some members over others, yet all group members deserve to be treated equally.

   c. Group counselors ensure equitable use of group time for each member by inviting silent members to become involved, acknowledging nonverbal attempts to communicate, and discouraging rambling and monopolizing of time by members.

   d. If a large group is planned, counselors consider enlisting another qualified professional to serve as a co-leader for the group sessions.

9. *Dual Relationships:* Group counselors avoid dual relationships with group members that might impair their objectivity and professional judgment, as well as those that are likely to compromise a group member's ability to participate fully in the group.

   a. Group counselors do not misuse their professional role and power as group leader to advance personal or social contacts with members throughout the duration of the group.

   b. Group counselors do not use their professional relationship with group members to further their own interests either during the group or after the termination of the group.

   c. Sexual intimacies between group counselors and members are unethical.

   d. Group counselors do not barter (exchange) professional services with group members for services.

   e. Group counselors do not admit their own family members, relatives, employees, or personal friends as members to their groups.

   f. Group counselors discuss with group members the potential detrimental effects of group members engaging in intimate inter-member relationships outside of the group.

*(continued)*

## Ethical Guidelines for Group Counselors (continued)

g. Students who participate in a group as a partial course requirement for a group course are not evaluated for an academic grade based upon their degree of participation as a member in a group. Instructors of group counseling courses take steps to minimize the possible negative impact on students when they participate in a group course by separating course grades from participation in the group and by allowing students to decide what issues to explore and when to stop.

h. It is inappropriate to solicit members from a class (or institutional affiliation) for one's private counseling or therapeutic groups.

10. *Use of Techniques:* Group counselors do not attempt any technique unless trained in its use or under supervision by a counselor familiar with the intervention.

    a. Group counselors are able to articulate a theoretical orientation that guides their practice, and they are able to provide a rationale for their interventions.

    b. Depending upon the type of an intervention, group counselors have training commensurate with the potential impact of a technique.

    c. Group counselors are aware of the necessity to modify their techniques to fit the unique needs of various cultural and ethnic groups.

    d. Group counselors assist members in translating in-group learnings to daily life.

11. *Goal Development:* Group counselors make every effort to assist members in developing their personal goals.

    a. Group counselors use their skills to assist members in making their goals specific so that others present in the group will understand the nature of the goals.

    b. Throughout the course of a group, group counselors assist members in assessing the degree to which personal goals are being met, and assist in revising any goals when it is appropriate.

    c. Group counselors help members clarify the degree to which the goals can be met within the context of a particular group.

12. *Consultation:* Group counselors develop and explain policies about between-session consultation to group members.

    a. Group counselors take care to make certain that members do not use between-session consultations to avoid dealing with issues pertaining to the group that would be dealt with best in the group.

    b. Group counselors urge members to bring the issues discussed during between-session consultations into the group if they pertain to the group.

    c. Group counselors seek out consultation and/or supervision regarding ethical concerns or when encountering difficulties which interfere with their effective functioning as group leaders.

    d. Group counselors seek appropriate professional assistance for their own personal problems or conflicts that are likely to impair their professional judgment and work performance.

    e. Group counselors discuss their group cases only for professional consultation and educational purposes.

    f. Group counselors inform members about policies regarding whether consultation will be held confidential.

13. *Termination from the Group:* Depending upon the purpose of participation in the group, counselors promote termination of members from the group in the most efficient period of time.

a. Group counselors maintain a constant awareness of the progress made by each group member and periodically invite the group members to explore and reevaluate their experiences in the group. It is the responsibility of group counselors to help promote the independence of members from the group in a timely manner.

14. *Evaluation and Follow-up:* Group counselors make every attempt to engage in ongoing assessment and to design follow-up procedures for their groups.
   a. Group counselors recognize the importance of ongoing assessment of a group, and they assist members in evaluating their own progress.
   b. Group counselors conduct evaluation of the total group experience at the final meeting (or before termination), as well as ongoing evaluation.
   c. Group counselors monitor their own behavior and become aware of what they are modeling in the group.
   d. Follow-up procedures might take the form of personal contact, telephone contact, or written contact.
   e. Follow-up meetings might be with individuals, or groups, or both to determine the degree to which: (i) members have reached their goals, (ii) the group had a positive or negative effect on the participants, (iii) members could profit from some type of referral, and (iv) as information for possible modification of future groups. If there is no follow-up meeting, provisions are made available for individual follow-up meetings to any member who needs or requests such a contact.

15. *Referrals:* If the needs of a particular member cannot be met within the type of group being offered, the group counselor suggests other appropriate professional referrals.
   a. Group counselors are knowledgeable of local community resources for assisting group members regarding professional referrals.
   b. Group counselors help members seek further professional assistance, if needed.

16. *Professional Development:* Group counselors recognize that professional growth is a continuous, ongoing, developmental process throughout their career.
   a. Group counselors maintain and upgrade their knowledge and skill competencies through educational activities, clinical experiences, and participation in professional development activities.
   b. Group counselors keep abreast of research findings and new developments as applied to groups.

*Safeguarding Ethical Practice and Procedures for Reporting Unethical Behavior*

The preceding remarks have been advanced as guidelines which are generally representative of ethical and professional group practice. They have not been proposed as rigidly defined prescriptions. However, practitioners who are thought to be grossly unresponsive to the ethical concerns addressed in this document may be subject to a review of their practices by the AACD Ethics Committee and ASGW peers.

▲ For consultation and/or questions regarding these ASGW Ethical Guidelines or group ethical dilemmas, you may contact the Chairperson of the ASGW Ethics Committee. The name, address, and telephone number of the current ASGW Ethics Committee Chairperson may be acquired by telephoning the AADC office in Alexandria, Virginia, at 703/823–9800.

**(continued)**

**Ethical Guidelines for Group Counselors (continued)**

▲ If a group counselor's behavior is suspected as being unethical, the following procedures are to be followed:

a. Collect more information and investigate further to confirm the unethical practice as determined by the ASGW Ethical Guidelines.

b. Confront the individual with the apparent violation of ethical guidelines for the purposes of protecting the safety of any clients and to help the group counselor correct any inappropriate behaviors. If satisfactory resolution is not reached through this contact then:

c. A complaint should be made in writing, including the specific facts and dates of the alleged violation and all relevant supporting data. The complaint should be included in an envelope marked "CONFIDENTIAL" to ensure confidentiality for both the accuser(s) and the alleged violator(s) and forward to all of the following sources:

1. The name and address of the Chairperson of the state Counselor Licensure Board for the respective state, if in existence.

2. The Ethics Committee c/o The President, American Association for Counseling and Development, 5999 Stevenson Avenue, Alexandria, Virginia 22304.

3. The name and address of all private credentialing agencies in which the alleged violator maintains or holds professional membership. Some of these include the following:

National Board for Certified Counselors, Inc.
5999 Stevenson Avenue
Alexandria, Virginia 22304

National Council for Credentialing of Career Counselors
c/o NBCC
5999 Stevenson Avenue
Alexandria, Virginia 22304

National Academy for Certified Clinical Mental Health Counselors
5999 Stevenson Avenue
Alexandria, Virginia 22304

Commission on Rehabilitation Counselor Certification
162 North State Street
Suite 317
Chicago, Illinois 60601

American Association for Marriage and Family Therapy
1717 K Street, N. W., Suite 407
Washington, D.C. 20006

American Psychological Association
1200 Seventeenth Street, N. W.
Washington, D.C. 20036

American Group Psychotherapy Association, Inc.
25 East 21st Street, 6th Floor
New York, New York 10010

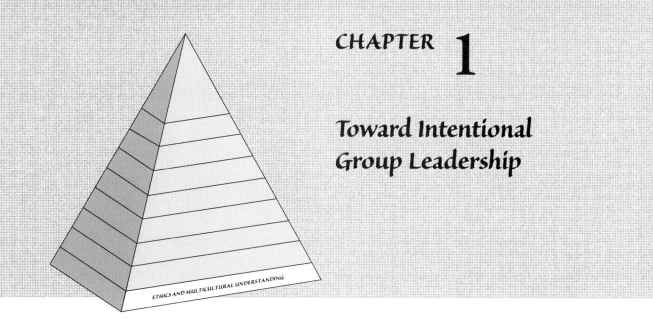

## CHAPTER 1

# Toward Intentional Group Leadership

ETHICS AND MULTICULTURAL UNDERSTANDING

## INTRODUCTION AND GOALS OF THIS BOOK

The power and importance of groups in our lives cannot be denied. We exist as individuals only if we are in relation to others. Whether it is our family, early peer groups and friends, or community, much of our uniqueness comes from being with and learning from others. Human development occurs in a group context.

Group counseling, group therapy, and a variety of structured groups help us see ourselves as selves-in-relation. Effective group work provides an opportunity for us to engage each other at a deeper level, to learn who we are and how we are seen by others, and to discover new skills and knowledge. You will find your experience as a group leader and group member profound and helpful.

The major goal of *Intentional Group Counseling: A Microskills Approach* is to demystify groups and make what occurs clearer and more specific. The book is designed to help you build concrete and observable leadership skills and strategies enabling you to understand what is happening in groups and to make things happen as well. As you develop the microskills of intentional group leadership, you will be asked to examine your own style of group leadership and to move toward your own theory of group practice.

In this book, you will have the opportunity to accomplish the following objectives of understanding and mastery:

▲ Become skilled in process observation. Part of becoming an effective group leader is developing the ability to observe and identify multiple aspects of group functioning.
▲ Develop specific intervention skills and strategies of group leadership and integrate these skills into many orientations to groups.

▲ Engage in leading your own groups in practice sessions in which you can take some risks in a safe setting.

▲ Generate your own conception of the skills and strategies that make the most sense to you in your own practice as a group leader.

▲ Use these together to become an intentional group leader who can empower group members to become more fully themselves and also able to relate to others and society more effectively.

## INTENTIONAL GROUP LEADERSHIP

Intentionality is a major objective of this book. If you master the basic skills of observation and intervention, you will have multiple possibilities for action when faced even with the most difficult leadership challenge. Intentionality means that you are able to flex with changing situations, develop creative new responses, and constantly increase your repertoire of skills and strategies with groups. Intentionality can be expanded with the idea of cultural intentionality—the ability to work with many varying types of people with widely varying multicultural backgrounds.

By mastering the basic skills of observation and intervention, you will be able to predict with some accuracy the influence of any intervention you may use. As an instance, if you ask a group an open question (Chapter 3), expect them to respond with more words than if your question were closed. If you focus on feelings and the here and now group experience (Chapter 2), your group members will likely do the same. A classic study of group leaders' style and their interventions revealed that group members tend to follow the specific microskill interventions of the leader (Sherrard, 1973). Equally important, Sherrard noted that what members do influences what the leader will do next. Related studies over time support this idea (Crouch, Bloch, & Wanlass, 1994; Kaul & Bednar, 1994). In effect, you can predict what your group members are likely to do in response to your leadership style.

Intentionality means being ready for whatever happens, being able anticipate the results of your interventions. But intentionality also demands full awareness that what you expect may not happen, as each person and group is different from all others. Sherrard also found that group members did not always follow the leader as anticipated. At these times, the intentional leader flexes and draws on other skills and strategies—the ability to recover from surprise and the inevitable errors we all make is a central dimension of intentionality.

Your major task in this book is to expand your possibilities for intentional leadership in groups and start the process of defining your own conception of your theory and practice in group work. There is extensive research on the skills and strategies of this book—over 400 data-based studies (Daniels & Ivey, in press; Ivey & Daniels, 1999). This research clearly suggests that helpers skilled with multiple interventions can make a significant difference in the lives of those whom they would help.

The word *leadership* implies action and direction. You as group leader are indeed in charge of your group. Whereas each group will take on a unique life of its own, the way you structure and guide the group will deeply affect what happens. And, in turn, whatever happens in the group influences you as well, how you feel as a person, and how you respond. Group work is an interactional process in which we are all affected by what occurs for any one member.

## THE GROUP CONTEXT

Developmentally, our first group is the family and extended family. Much of our thinking about self and how we relate in later groups can be tied to our family history. Important group issues such as power, authority, and responsibility play themselves out first in the family of origin. This is not a book about family counseling or family therapy, but let us recall that it is from our families that we gain so much of our identity.

The community context of friend and peer groups, school, spiritual, leisure time groups (scouting, sports, music), and others define our next level of group interaction. These experiences are vital in developing our sense of personal identity and enable us to interact with others in daily life. In community groups, we develop important assumptions and beliefs about ourselves. In turn, these internalized messages manifest themselves throughout life in many groups in which we participate—work, family, and community.

Each of us has learned habits—ways of thinking and behaving acquired from our past experiences—and we all have different paths through life. Participating in groups helps us discover ourselves more completely and how our habits of living are perceived by others. Group membership teaches us things about ourselves and our style that we didn't know before.

At a societal and cultural level, we are members of many different groups at the same time. We have racial and ethnic identities, we are men or women, we have a sexual orientation, and we are part of many other multicultural aspects of life. As we move from one group to another, while our inner core may be stable, the way we behave often depends on the nature of the group in which we currently find ourselves. Are you the same person in a family group as in a peer group at a party? Or do you find your persona changing as you move from home to school to time with your friends to a quiet spiritual retreat?

Small wonder that the helping fields are giving increased attention to group counseling and therapy. Studying group interaction provides us with an opportunity to see ourselves both as individuals and as group members. Many believe that group work is the method of choice for human growth and change. *The individual develops within a family in a community setting.* These groups and their interaction with us teach us about both our cultural identity and our individuality. Each identity is unique, shared with some groups, but not all, and universal in that all humanity has similar experiences. Our individuality and our commonality with others comes from ourselves, our family, and the many groups in our communities.

As a person,

*You are unique.* We cannot and must not stereotype any individual. No one has the same experience and life process that you do.

*You share common experiences with other group members.* Even though we are distinct individuals, we nonetheless share mutual experiences with others and we all experience pain and joy that stay with us for a lifetime. None of us is alone. You may live in the same neighborhood and attend the same school or church, synagogue, or mosque as others. You may have endured an alcoholic family or rape, or been part of the Vietnam or Gulf wars. You have a similar multicultural background with many people due to your race, ethnicity, gender, or other characteristics.

*You share universal humanity with all.* Regardless of how different we are, we are all human beings. We all need relationships, we all learn in groups, and we all experience pain and joy. None of us is alone. You are not alone.

It is in this context of individual uniqueness, shared experience, and universal humanity that group work becomes so important. In the process of effective, intentional group leadership and facilitation, you can help people discover themselves at new levels of awareness. Individual counseling and therapy are, of course, of vital importance, but there is nothing like group experience to help an individual discover herself or himself in relation to others.

## TYPES OF GROUPS

We are raised in families and communities of varying types, but we are all constantly in many types of groups. Similarly, there are many varieties of groups and you will find it fascinating to discover which ones you enjoy most and which are the most challenging. Perhaps you will even find that some types of groups don't appeal to you.

*Group work* is a broad professional practice that refers to the giving of help or the accomplishment of tasks in a group setting. It involves the application of group theory and process by a capable professional practitioner to assist an interdependent collection of people to reach their mutual goals, which may be personal, interpersonal, or task-related in nature. (ASGW, 1991)

Within each type of group with which you will work, you will find that similar group process dimensions and interactions occur. This is so whether the group is extremely structured and organized or if it is unstructured and open. Groups may be organized into three main types (see Box 1.1), but note the considerable overlap among them. All of the groups at times may involve personal, interpersonal, and task-related issues.

*Structured groups* tend to have preset agendas and frequently may use formal instructional plans. These groups often have the task of imparting specific information to members, such as information about careers, sexual disease prevention, managing time, how to write a resume, and many other topics. In addition, task groups are often oriented toward solving a particular problem in the school, business, or community. These task groups may be compared to and are related to structured psychoeducational groups in which the purpose is to enable members to learn more information about themselves in a structured way. You may have experienced values clarification sessions or character/moral education in which you

**Box 1.1**    *Overlap Among Structured Groups, Group Counseling, and Group Therapy*

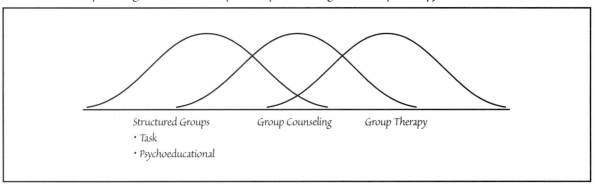

work through highly structured exercises to learn more precisely how your behavior relates to understanding your underlying values and beliefs. Training in communication skills, assertiveness, and stress management are other possibilities you will find with structured psychoeducational groups.

*Group counseling* has as its major purpose the exploration of normal developmental issues and concerns. Less structured than those discussed above, group counseling nonetheless often follows relatively predictable patterns. Theme-centered topical groups, stressed in Chapters 5 and 6, are a prime example of a counseling group. A special topic is selected and the group meets to explore issues around that topic. Theme-centered groups might involve high school students meeting to discuss their feelings and ideas about sexuality, eating concerns, drugs, or alcohol. Gay teenage students gathering together to share experiences and support each other is another illustration. The common thread is that people who share a concern or problem get together to work through issues and plan for the future. In a similar fashion, people suffering from AIDS, cancer, or the loss of a child may benefit from group counseling around their special interest or theme. The concerns they deal with in such groups are indeed powerful and intense, but they deal with these matters as a normal part of life.

Prominent among group counseling systems is the interpersonally oriented group, also known as person-centered. These groups tend to be quite unstructured. The leader is there to support the group as it finds its own direction. Personal growth is usually a major goal of these groups. The focus is on exploring internal processes with minimal attention to issues outside the group. These groups are considered particularly effective for helping group leaders understand themselves and group process in general. Interpersonal and person-centered groups were influenced in the early stages by the unstructured encounter and T-groups (*T* for training).

Another type of group counseling occurs in consciousness-raising groups in which men or women, people with disabilities, or members of a racial or ethnic group gather to share their experiences with social oppression and to band together to work against sexism, discrimination against those with handicaps, or racism. Rape survivor groups often start as support groups and end up with consciousness raising of the surrounding "rape culture."

With children, you will find counseling groups focusing on "banana splits" (children of divorce), living in an alcoholic home, moving groups (in which children are scheduled to leave the school at the end of the year for a new setting), and friendship groups in which children learn to work on their issues together.

As counseling groups move toward depth discussion, particularly in their later stages as trust has been developed, they often begin to overlap with psychotherapy groups, discussed below.

*Group psychotherapy* is focused on people with severe psychological or psychiatric distress. The issue in these groups is therapeutic and aimed at helping patients return to normal functioning. Rape survivors often may start their group experiences focusing on severe trauma. Adolescents with complex eating disorders or serious delinquency problems may find benefit in group psychotherapy and searching for the roots of their problems. Psychiatric hospitals often set up groups to help patients deal with depression, borderline behavior, and other diagnostic issues.

But the differences between these structured, counseling, and psychotherapy groups are not always so clear. A trauma survivor from rape, war, or violence may gain benefit from all three types of groups. Structured stress management may help such group members in getting through the day more comfortably. Group counseling and sharing of experiences and stories may help them feel less alone, and many learn ideas from the group for working with both their internal and external environments. In group therapy, they can examine their conflicts at a deeper level. An effective treatment program may, in truth, offer group work from several perspectives.

Furthermore, it should be obvious that many structured groups are therapeutic in their effects and that effective group psychotherapy may at times involve highly structured programs. When you are participating in a basic encounter or person-centered group, more than personal growth may occur. Often such experiences are highly therapeutic.

If you are going to be an effective, intentional leader, you need skills and strategies to understand group process and make a difference in the groups with which you will work. *Intentional Group Counseling* utilizes a step-by-step introduction to groups that can make a significant difference in your practice.

## THE GROUP MICROSKILLS APPROACH: STEPS TOWARD INTENTIONALITY

The microskills approach to understanding and working with groups breaks down the complex art of leadership into single skills, teaching them one at a time. Thus, in Chapter 2 you will start with attending behavior, a basic and well-established skill of listening, interviewing, counseling, and group work. You will discover how important it is to really listen. You will then have the opportunity to observe listening through process observation and finally to practice listening in small groups and start the process of becoming an intentional group leader.

One advantage of learning microskills is that in doing so you will have a clear sense of growing in your ability to understand and influence group behavior. As you learn one microskill and move to add the next, you will be able to use each new ability with increased competence, gradually learning to lead groups more effectively. Each chapter of this book builds on the preceding set of microskills, and as you progress through the text, you will acquire a growing repertoire of group strategies at increasingly sophisticated levels.

In the early stages of group work, many people find themselves stuck or immobilized when faced with a new or difficult situation in the group. The gradually expanding base of skills and knowledge you will learn here will help you at these times as it leads to increased intentionality. The ability to flex, change direction, and come up with new ideas to facilitate movement is the essence of intentional group leadership. Each chapter of this book is designed to provide alternatives for action—specifics that can make a difference as you encounter multiple issues in group facilitation.

## Moving Through and Up the Group Microskills Pyramid

Equipped with an understanding of attending from process observation and actual practice of the microskill, you will learn in Chapter 3 the central skill of focusing. Here you will note that the specific listening and attending skills of the leader deeply affect what occurs in the group. Chapter 4 extends listening skills to the basic listening sequence (asking open questions, asking closed questions, encouraging, paraphrasing, acknowledging feeling, and summarizing).

You will be asked to lead your own first complete group session when you complete Chapters 5 and 6. There you will encounter the stages or dimensions through which a group typically moves over time. Theme-centered group interaction (Cohn, 1969) will be presented as a specific framework for you to use in testing out your expertise in the group microskills. Chapter 6 presents a transcript of a group interview with detailed analysis of skills and group process. Here you will see the many skills presented in this book integrated into an actual group session. You will also be encouraged to start thinking about your own integration of skills.

The Group Microskills Pyramid (see Box 1.2) provides a visual model of the progression from basic toward more advanced microskills. Note how each new microskill builds on the others as you move in a systematic way toward increased competence and flexibility in managing and leading groups. The Group Microskills Pyramid is based on the Ivey Taxonomy (see page 133). Basic to the pyramid and the taxonomy are the following ideas and assumptions:

▲ *Specific skills of group work can be identified and taught in a clear, sequential manner.* The skills of culturally appropriate attending, observing, and listening form the foundation for all group work. You will move in a step-by-step fashion, increasing your understanding and mastery of group work.

▲ *Each microskill leads to an anticipated result in individual and group verbal and nonverbal behavior.* If you listen to emotions and reflect feelings, your group may be expected to be more attuned and discuss emotions more easily. If you focus on individuals, expect group members to speak about their issues as individuals; on the other hand, if you focus on the group as a whole, expect group members to think about and talk more about what is happening in the group. (See page 133 for examples of predictions based on the Ivey Taxonomy and the Microskills Group Pyramid.)

**Box 1.2**    *The Group Microskills Pyramid*

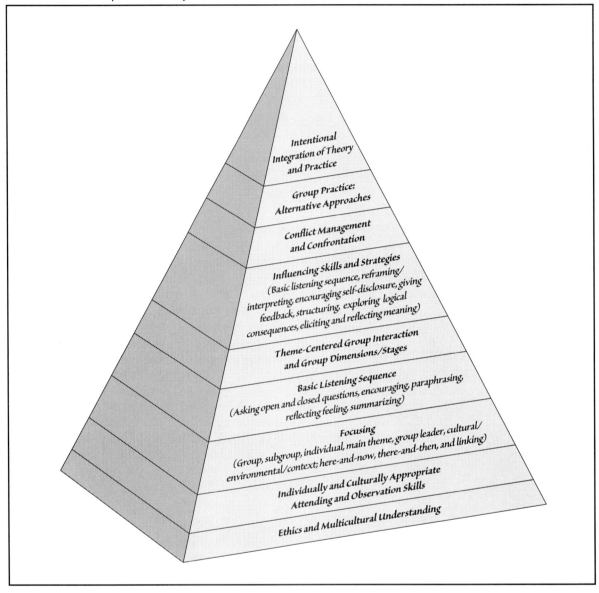

Intentional
Integration of Theory
and Practice

Group Practice:
Alternative Approaches

Conflict Management
and Confrontation

Influencing Skills and Strategies
(Basic listening sequence, reframing/
interpreting, encouraging self-disclosure, giving
feedback, structuring, exploring logical
consequences, eliciting and reflecting meaning)

Theme-Centered Group Interaction
and Group Dimensions/Stages

Basic Listening Sequence
(Asking open and closed questions, encouraging, paraphrasing,
reflecting feeling, summarizing)

Focusing
(Group, subgroup, individual, main theme, group leader, cultural/
environmental/context; here-and-now, there-and-then, and linking)

Individually and Culturally Appropriate
Attending and Observation Skills

Ethics and Multicultural Understanding

▲    *Individuals and groups do not always respond the way leaders expect them to.* Although predictability is an important part of the microskills model, do not expect a perfect correlation between what you say and what your group members do. The ability to be intentional and flexible and have many alternatives for response is an essential skill of any group leader. If one approach doesn't work, have another strategy readily available.

▲  *Different theories and models of group work have varying patterns of microskill usage.* You will see that mastery of the microskills model presented here provides a base for working with many theories and practices of group counseling and therapy. Once you have mastered the skills, you will learn in Chapter 10 how they may be used in many settings and practices.

*Process observation* is critical in each chapter. Process observation may be defined as examining the group from an external perspective. You will be asked to visit groups and note them in action. Specific things to watch for will be suggested. You will find that process observation helps you understand the many complexities of group work. As a prospective group leader, you need to be able to observe what is happening in your group. As a group leader, it is difficult to observe all that is happening, but experience as a process observer will enhance what you see. Most of the ideas for process observations presented here are derived from Bohn [Ivey] (1977) and her personal experience in facilitating many types of groups.

With experience as a process observer, you are ready to begin work as a leader who serves the dual role of participant observer. To be a truly skilled group facilitator, you must have the ability to see what is going on around you.

We are recommending that you gain considerable experience as a process observer. Furthermore, in your early experiences as a group leader, we strongly urge you to find a person to observe your groups and give you and the group feedback on what is observed. If a process observer is not immediately available, various group members can sit out from the group for a period of time and submit their impressions and observations for group discussion.

Each chapter of this book will focus on both the group microskills and specific group process dimensions. Through practice of leadership skills and process feedback, expect to gain considerable knowledge and expertise. The best learning is learning by doing. No book can contain everything you need to know—the awareness, knowledge, and skills you gain from practice and observation will be long-lasting.

## Influencing Skills and Conflict Management

The influencing strategies of group leadership will be explored in Chapters 7 and 8. Important change skills will be emphasized, such as structuring, reframing/interpreting, exploring logical consequences, and reflecting meaning.

Conflict management is the major strategy of Chapter 9. There specific ideas will be presented for working with conflict inside the person, conflict within the group, and conflict with you as leader. Transcript illustrations and practice exercises are presented to help you plan and cope with the challenges and opportunities of disharmony and conflict. An important point of this chapter is that the group can learn the most from conflict. We need to think of conflict as an opportunity rather than a problem.

## Leading Multiple Types of Groups

Chapter 10 turns to the many types of groups you may lead over your career. Each group orientation tends to use different patterns of skills and strategies. Specific ideas for leading different types of groups will be presented; you can use these now or refer to them later as you plan many types of group sessions in the future.

## Determining Your Own Style and Approach

The final chapter of the book, perhaps the most important, asks you to reflect on your present and past experience as a group member and leader. You will have an opportunity to review your level of mastery of the twenty-four major concepts of this book. You'll be asked to start developing your own conception or theory of how groups function and defining your own style of group leadership.

Each chapter of this book is oriented toward taking foundational ideas of group work into practice. Stockton and Toth (1996, 1998) have stressed the importance of helping group leaders learn to *perceive* what is going on in the group, *selecting* skills and strategies for intervention, and *risking*—taking ideas from group work into actual practice. The microskills educational outline for each chapter consists of the following steps:

1. *Chapter Goals*   Specific objectives for action and learning on your part will introduce the concepts within each chapter.
2. *Warm-up Exercise*   There will be a beginning exercise to help you start thinking about the skill as you might have observed it in your own life or in your own classroom or workshop setting. These warm-ups are also designed as exercises you could use in facilitating your own groups.
3. *Defining the Leadership Skill*   The microskills of the chapter will be summarized with an emphasis on their utility in group work. Process observation concepts will be presented with suggestions about what to watch for when you visit and observe groups.
4. *Using the Skill with Children and Adolescent Groups*   This is not a book on youth counseling, but you will find that the skills and strategies emphasized in this book work effectively with younger people. This section will review some highlights of the chapters as they might be applied to children and adolescents.
5. *Moving Toward Your Own Leadership Style*   The central concepts of the chapter will be summarized briefly followed by questions that emphasize the importance of personal reflection. What are *you* going to take away from this chapter?
6. *Practicing Leadership Skills*   A variety of process observation and group leadership practice exercises are presented. It is this active learning that will most likely to be useful to you. There is an old saying:

   Tell me something and I will learn (reading).
   Show me how it is done (process observation).
   Let me do it myself and I will be able to help others do it as well (practice).

7. *Supplemental Chapter Comments*   Each chapter contains several boxes, and these present transcripts of group sessions, suggestions for process observation, and other key points of the chapter.

## INDIVIDUAL, GROUP, AND CULTURAL EMPATHY: CULTURAL INTENTIONALITY

Empathy is most often defined as seeing the world through another person's eyes and as if you were walking in that person's shoes. Carl Rogers (1961), the founder of person-centered therapy, has given both individual and group counseling a major gift through bringing empathy to central attention. In his later career, Rogers (1973) was influenced by early work in encounter groups; from this, he gave us the term *person-centered group.* Some of his basic beliefs are extremely valuable in group leadership:

> I have a great deal of patience with the group and with the individuals within it. If there is one thing I have learned and relearned in recent years, it is that it is ultimately very rewarding to accept the group exactly where it *is.* . . . From my experience I know that if I attempt to push a group to a deeper level, it is not, in the long run, going to work. (pp. 51–53)

Rogers stressed, "Accept the group exactly where it *is.*" Empathy and listening are to be where the group is, not where you want it to be. You are perhaps well versed already in the concepts of individual empathy. The task is to hear the other person or persons as clearly and accurately as possible without mixing in your own ideas. This involves empathy and the ability to be where the individual and group *are* rather than in some place your theoretical idea of leadership may project them. The attending and listening skills presented in the early chapters of this book are centered on hearing your group members accurately and fully. "What is their story?" And in the strategy of reflection of meaning, "What does the story mean to the person?"

## Group Empathy

How does empathy apply in a practical sense to group work? You as a prospective group leader have a challenging task. Ideally, you need to understand how each person in your group is viewing the world and reacting to the moment, but you also need to understand the group mind. The group mind is difficult to define precisely, but it represents the group in action. Some group leaders do individual therapy or counseling in a group. They work first with one individual, then another. The group members and the group mind may be ignored and most of the comments within the group flow through the leader.

Real group work demands that you see the interaction of the group members, that you observe what occurs between two or more members, understanding the variation of worldviews and thoughts among the subgroups, and finally, that you are able to note the group as a whole. In short, group empathy requires that you focus beyond the individual and note what is occurring in the group itself. You will find that process observation is particularly helpful in focusing on the group and not just individuals.

Group empathy might be defined as listening to the group and its process. As you observe the group and comment on what you see the group doing, the group itself will change, move on, and make new discoveries. What is important is pointing out that the group (and subgroups) exist and recognizing them through your comments. Attending behavior and the basic listening sequence (Chapters 2 and 4) are foundations of group empathy. You need to hear what the group is saying. Chapter 3, focusing, will be helpful to you in making the change from individual observation and reaction to group process and action.

## Cultural Empathy

Cultural empathy is also a challenge, but a helpful approach is to start with the idea that all group work is multicultural. Each of us is a multicultural being and we bring that cultural experience directly into any group in which we participate. Sometimes the relevancy of cultural issues will be peripheral, but at other times your ability to understand and be empathic with cultural difference will be the critical issue in the continuation and success of your group. And you will find that multicultural issues are always present in the group.

The Association for Specialists in Group Work (1998) has developed a set of competencies around diversity and multicultural issues that are summarized in Box 1.3. Understanding and mastering these concepts are essential for cultural intentionality and competent professional practice with individuals, groups, and larger cultures.

## STORYTELLING THROUGH GROUP WORK

Group work at times is like listening to a story in which each group member has a role or a contribution to make and the purpose of the group is revealed as the group's total story or narrative is revealed. Narrative theory (White & Epston, 1990), a relatively new model for understanding the helping process, emphasizes generating new meanings based on the experiences or stories contributed by all participants. In individual counseling, we seek to draw out the single client's story. In group work, however, one possible goal is to bring all the clients' stories into a larger or "meta" story.

For instance, in group counseling or therapy with rape survivors, women are often encouraged to tell their individual stories. The members and leader listen carefully in a warm, supportive fashion. Each survivor is provided with an opportunity to share her own story. Then, as the group reflects and reviews the varying stories, common themes tend to appear and the individuals begin to see how their stories are part of a larger narrative of oppression and violence toward women.

Cancer survivors, war veterans, children of alcoholic families, and gay and lesbians who may have suffered violence all have their own individual stories to tell. As they share their thoughts and feelings in a group, again a larger group story begins to appear.

Group stories can be there-and-then stories from the past. Through sharing common experiences around, for example, alcoholism or drugs, substance abusers can develop a new here-and-now narrative of their experience—the restorying of the old into a fresh new meaning. As part of the process of restorying, group members tend to provide empathy and positive support to help people change and grow.

There are, of course, groups that emphasize here-and-now group interaction almost totally. In these the stories focus on what occurs "right now," "in the moment" of immediate group experience. Combining positive feedback and sharing of observed strengths, here-and-now groups, such as person-centered basic encounter, make possible many new life stories and changes in behavior for action in the future.

**Box 1.3**  *Diversity Competencies for Group Workers*

|  |  |
|---|---|
|  | The following is a summary of Diversity Competencies for Group Workers (Association for Specialists in Group Work, 1998). |
| *1. Awareness* | Diversity-competent group workers become aware of their own multicultural heritage—ethnic and racial background, sexual preference, language, spirituality and religion, age (the young, middle-aged, and old), disability, and social class. They are able to recognize their biases and the limits of their competence. In addition, the section "Before You Start" suggested additional dimensions of multicultural difference for your consideration. |
|  | Diversity-competent group workers are aware of stereotyping and varying worldviews held by many different groups. They are aware that skills or strategies they have learned in courses and reading may be biased toward White North American and northern European perspectives and thus limited in their applications in multiculturally sensitive group work. |
| *2. Knowledge* | Diversity-competent group workers possess knowledge or understanding of how oppression in any form such as racism, classism, or ageism affects them personally and in their work. They can anticipate how their own multicultural heritage might be perceived and the impact it might have on group members. |
|  | Diversity-competent group workers possess specific knowledge of multiple cultural groups that they are working with. They are aware of the needs of many types of people they might find among their participants, such as indigenous, African-American, Asian-American, Hispanic, Latino/Latina, gay, lesbian, bisexual, and transgendered group members. They are aware of these and other issues (immigration, poverty, powerlessness) that may affect personality and behavior in groups. |
|  | Diversity-competent group workers are knowledgeable about group work, but they are also aware of how some of these skills and strategies may clash with the beliefs and values of some groups. They constantly seek to develop increased knowledge and skills about the limitations of group work and expand their knowledge through study and participation with multicultural groups. |
| *3. Skills* | Diversity-competent group workers seek out training experiences to improve their competence and skills in working with multiple types of peoples. They also become actively involved with multiple cultural groups in the community outside their group work/counseling setting so that their perspective on minorities is more than academic and abstract. |
|  | Diversity-competent group workers are able to send and receive both verbal and nonverbal messages accurately, appropriately, and across/between the differences represented in the group. They are not tied down to only one method or approach to group facilitation and constantly seek to expand their repertoire of skills. |
|  | Diversity-competent group workers seek to eliminate prejudices, biases, and discrimination in groups. They are also willing and able to exercise institutional intervention skills on behalf of their group members. They can help members determine whether their issues are within themselves or within larger institutional and societal constraints and are willing to act with group members to move toward societal change. |

The concepts of narration, storytelling, and conversation are useful frameworks for the microskills we will develop in future chapters. First we need to hear the stories of all participants about who they are, where they come from, what they need and want. We need to listen for strengths and positive assets that empower the participant. As we understand the participant's context we have a better understanding of each person's behavior and the consequences of changing those behaviors.

## Positive Asset Search

It is not enough to listen actively to stories. Positive strengths and assets need to be discovered within these stories. Otherwise the storytelling becomes a depressing repetition of negative barriers and hopelessness. In working with cancer survivors, for example, we need to focus on resources and positive assets, not just on the negative. People grow from their strengths. Microskills theory talks about the *positive asset search* and it is vital that you facilitate group storytelling and sharing in a positive fashion. All too often, group work can fall into a depressing state of stories about failure. One of your tasks as you hear stories is to listen for strength and accounts of survival. What makes the cancer survivors in your group get through the day and smile? Out of this work, the cancer group can compile a story of success.

## Restory

If group members understand others' stories and strengths, they can then be prepared to help the clients "restory"—generate new and more positive ways to understand themselves in their own cultural context. If we have first listened to the individuals in the group and searched for strengths, we are in a good position to suggest new stories. Effective listening, moreover, may free them to write their own story without external help. This is one place that group counseling can be especially helpful. Working individually with a cancer survivor, a gay individual who has been harassed, or a war veteran, we can help them develop new stories and ways of looking at themselves. We all talk to ourselves—"self-talk"—as we walk through life. Negative self-talk is often the result of negative experience and stories. The restorying process helps us move to more positive internalized self-talk.

It is not just the one individual in the group who restories thoughts and feelings. All who hear the story gain from listening. Each member who participates in a group has the potential to learn from the life experience of others. Listening to others' stories plus their successes enables individuals to start restorying their own lives.

## Action

The narrative framework is also about helping group members move toward new and better ways of thinking, being, and acting. Through the use of action-oriented directives, the skilled use of the interpretation/reframe, or the assertiveness training model you may enable group members to translate their aspirations into reality. The effective group becomes a safe context in which participants can change in positive directions without losing their cultural integrity.

If your work with this book is successful, you will have developed a solid understanding of foundation skills and strategies, an ability to interact in groups, and the skill for helping group members write more positive endings to their own narratives. We hope your personal construction of theory and practice will remain open to constant challenge and growth from your group members and from your colleagues.

## MOVING TOWARD YOUR OWN LEADERSHIP STYLE

Each chapter of the book will end with a section pointing toward your own leadership style. The central purpose is to encourage you to review and think about the ideas presented and develop your own summary of your learning. You may wish to develop a journal summarizing what the experience with the chapter has meant to you. The central ideas of the chapter will be presented briefly and then you are encouraged to start the process of developing your own group leadership style.

This chapter first focused on how groups influence our lives. We are raised in family groups within a community and all exist in a cultural context. The group counseling experience has particular value as it helps the individual begin to see how the self was developed in a broader context. Individual counseling and therapy will always remain important, but we believe that group work provides the most useful way for people to start examining themselves as people in relationship to others.

Three major types of groups were presented—structured groups, group counseling, and group therapy. Although each is distinct, there can be considerable overlap among the types.

A major goal of this book is to introduce intentionality—the increased ability to flex and respond creatively in the often fast-moving pace of group work. The group microskills pyramid was presented as a visual summary of the skills and strategies emphasized in the book, all leading to increased intentionality. Process observation, noting what occurs in a group, was outlined as basic to successful group leadership.

Cultural intentionality, the ability to work with people of many backgrounds, was stressed, and the diversity competencies for group workers were presented. In a sense, all group experience is multicultural and this concept is basic to effective group leadership.

Storytelling and narrative are seen as central to much of group work. The story, positive asset, restory, action model was presented. As you work with groups, it is easy to focus on the negative. A basic approach of this book is that positives need to be emphasized constantly in group situations. Too often, group workers focus on negatives. Those in our groups can only build and grow on their resources. From a basis of strength, we can then look at the negatives.

Think back on this section and the entire chapter. What have you learned here? What points struck you as most important? What stood out for you? What would you like to emphasize as you work through this book to strengthen your intentionality in group work and cultural intentionality as you learn to work with multiple types of people? Make a few notes here to crystallize your thoughts and sharpen your focus.

_____

_____

_____

_____

_____

_____

_____

_____

## PRACTICING GROUP LEADERSHIP SKILLS

As a start, consider how you might initiate your work with groups. Generally speaking, unstructured person-centered groups begin with minimum instructions on how to proceed. Allowing some anxiety and tension to build can be important in helping the group develop. However, in your first work with groups, we recommend a more structured approach, one that focuses first on strengths and positive assets.

If group members are able to talk first about their strengths, good qualities, and positive experiences, they are often better able to work with tension, conflict, and life challenges later. There is a trust-building and safety dimension in sharing positive assets.

The following individual and group exercises are suggested as a route toward building trust on a foundation of strengths within a group. The exercises focus only on drawing out the story and searching for strengths. The early chapters of this book will focus on story and positive assets. Later portions of the book will examine restorying and action in more detail.

The exercises at the end of each chapter are written as if you were the person facilitating them. Thus, as you become expert in group skills, you will have a library of exercises you can use in your own groups at a later time. This textbook is designed as a resource guide for experienced leaders as well as a source for those only starting in groups.

### 1. Process Observation of Positive Assets and Strengths

Observe a group of any type—it could be a family dinner or family meeting, an informal gathering of friends in the dormitory or your home, or a visit to a school board, an open Alcoholics Anonymous meeting, or any formal or informal group that is available.

This first process observation task simply asks you to note the number of positive compared to negative comments you observe in the group. Does the group draw out strengths? Does it focus primarily on problems? What is the balance of strengths versus negatives?

What happens as a result of the focus on negatives or positives? What are your conclusions from your observations?

## 2. The Fish Bowl

The fish bowl is a standard classroom exercise for group interaction and teaching. Four to six class members form a group in front of the larger class. If space permits, the remaining class members form a larger circle around the inner group.

For this first fish bowl, we suggest a ten- to fifteen-minute group. One member of the group is selected as leader. The remainder of the class observes, paying attention to what occurs during a discussion of the positives we all enjoy.

Introduce the exercise with words similar to these:

"I'd like you to tell me a story that is particularly meaningful to you. One major requirement, however, is that I want to hear a positive story of strength that makes you feel good in some way. We all have difficult and problematic stories, but this time I want to hear something exceptional that you feel is really fine. We have (10 minutes); please divide the time equally. The leader's main task is to allow each person to have 'air-time.'

"The story can be about you, a friend or family member, someone you have known, or even a personal hero who is at some distance from you. The only requirement is that we want the story to be personally meaningful to you."

If you are recording, you might say some variation of the following: "May I video or audiorecord our conversation? I might even want to write up a transcript of our interaction so I can understand positive stories more fully and improve my ability to listen to them. But you are in charge of your own story. If you don't want taping, no worries. And if you say yes but change your mind later, we can turn off the tape. I can't offer you legal confidentiality, but I'll only share with others what you permit me to share. What questions do you have about this?"

## 3. Group Practice — Team Building

You are most likely reading this book as a member of a group course or possibly as a participant in a workshop. The following exercise is often very useful to help group members feel more comfortable with each other and develop trust. You may wish to use a variation of this exercise in your own group work.

Before we start, team building involves a central skill of group work—feedback. Feedback is discussed in detail in Chapter 7, but it is a vital part of any group work practice you will encounter. Some of the basics of feedback are presented in Box 1.4. After practice exercises, your small groups will often process and discuss what happened. Accurate and positive feedback is essential to this process.

**Box 1.4** Listening and Feedback: Essential Strategies for Group Work

|  |  |
|---|---|
|  | To see ourselves as others see us<br>To hear how others hear us<br>To be touched as we touch others<br>These are the goals of effective feedback<br>(Ivey & Ivey, 1999, p. 44) |
| Listen | As you practice and discuss varying skills and strategies throughout this book, you will be meeting frequently in small groups. Your first task in group work is to listen carefully to group members. Unless a person feels heard, it is very difficult for that person to hear what others have to say about her or him. |
| Provide Feedback | The process of listening enables you to learn something about the other person in the group, and sharing your observations can be most helpful. In your practice sessions, please consider the following aspects of feedback before you start giving your reactions: |

1. *Is the person ready to hear what you have to say?* Empathy demands not only listening but also being aware of where the other person *is*.
2. *Seek to be nonjudgmental and concrete.* Try to avoid the words *good* and *bad* and their equivalents; also *should* or *must* can be inflammatory. One way to avoid judgments is to be very concrete and specific in your feedback. Instead of saying "You were a good (or bad) listener" or "You *should* listen before you speak," point out observable concrete things that the person can identify and change, if necessary. "As a leader, I noticed you maintained solid eye contact" or "You did maintain eye contact generally, but I noted that you gave the most attention and eye contact to two members and tended not to look at others."
3. *Keep it lean.* You likely have noticed several things going on, but most of us can change only one thing at a time.
4. *Use I/you statements.* Own your feedback and focus on the receiving information. "*You* seem to be avoiding the feelings of the group. *You* need to focus on their emotions more." "*I* saw *you* listening carefully. At the same time, *I* wonder if it might help if *you* reflected feelings a bit more. What do *you* think?"
5. *Search out positive assets.* Catch the leader doing something right. It is always easier to build on one's strengths. Avoid negative feedback as much as possible. Corrections and suggestions are useful but need to be made in a positive context.

The group or class is divided into smaller groups of three or four. As the group is beginning, encourage each small group to share their names and something about themselves for about five minutes. Bring them back together to share something about themselves with the total group. Often it is useful to have different members of the group introduce one another.

Then, assign the following exercise:

"For the next ten minutes, I'd like members of each small group to share a positive story about your backgrounds. This can be any experience at all. You could draw on something you did that makes you proud, a friend or family member who supports you, your multicultural background, just about anything good that occurs to you."

*Multicultural* may need further definition for your group members.

> "We use the term *multicultural* in the following ways: (1) multiculturalism is generic to all groups and speaks to each of us personally—we are all multicultural beings; (2) *culture* is broadly defined to include social factors such as gender, place of residence, economic factors, and many other important characteristics in addition to race, ethnicity, and nationality; (3) all behaviors are learned and displayed in a cultural context; (4) accurate assessment, meaningful understanding, and appropriate intervention require that behaviors be understood in their cultural context." [You may have alternative definitions of multicultural issues yourself (in some cases, you may wish to discuss this issue further with your group).]
>
> "Just be sure that you share a positive story, one that gives you strength and pride. Share the time equally."

Approximately two minutes before time for group reports, break into the discussion and tell the members that you'll be asking them to come together as a larger group shortly. Remind them again of time about one minute before the group is to finish the discussion.

Bring the large group together for small group report-outs. After a brief session, suggest that they return to the small groups for discussion, with these instructions:

> "I'd like you to reflect on the small group experience you just had. How did you feel about talking about positive stories in a small group? What did you learn about the place that multicultural experience has in our lives? What sense do you make of the word *trust,* and is it important in group discussion? Does the telling of positive stories facilitate the building of trust and openness in a group?"

Allow about five minutes for this discussion.

After providing adequate warning, bring the small groups back together to share what they have learned and observed. Use a listening role and encourage the group members to share their experiences.

## REFERENCES

Association for Specialists in Group Work (ASGW). (1991). *Professional standards for the training of group workers.* Washington, DC: Author.

Association for Specialists in Group Work. (1998). *Principles for diversity-competent group workers.* Washington, DC: Author.

Bohn, M. [Ivey, M.] (1977). *Process consultation: A case study of the role of the process consultant in early childhood programs.* Unpublished doctoral dissertation, University of Massachusetts, Amherst.

Cohn, R. (1969). The theme-centered interactional method: Group therapists as group educators. *Journal of Group Psychoanalysis and Process, 2,* 19–36.

Crouch, E., Bloch, S., & Wanlass, J. (1994). Therapeutic factors: Interpersonal and intrapersonal mechanisms. In A. Fuhriman & G. Burlingame (Eds.), *Handbook of group psychotherapy* (pp. 269–318). New York: Wiley.

Daniels, T., & Ivey, A. (In press). *Microcounseling* (3rd ed.). Springfield, IL: Charles C Thomas.

Ivey, A., & Daniels, T. (1999). Microcounseling, brief therapy, and multicultural issues: Developing a database for concrete action. In W. Matthews & J. Edgette (Eds.), *Current thinking and research in brief therapy,* Vol. 3. Philadelphia: Brunner/Mazel.

Ivey, A., & Ivey, M. (1999). *Intentional interviewing and*

counseling: Facilitating development in a multicultural world (4th ed.). Pacific Grove, CA: Brooks/Cole.

Kaul, T., & Bednar, R. (1994). Pretraining and structure: Parallel lines yet to meet. In A. Fuhriman & G. Burlingame (Eds.), *Handbook of group psychotherapy* (pp. 155–191). New York: Wiley.

Rogers, C. (1961). *On becoming a person.* Boston: Houghton Mifflin.

Rogers, C. (1973). *On encounter groups.* New York: Harper & Row.

Sherrard, P. (1973). *Predicting group leader/member interaction: The efficacy of the Ivey Taxonomy.* Unpublished doctoral dissertation, University of Massachusetts, Amherst.

Stockton, R., & Toth, P. (1996). Teaching group counselors: Recommendations for maximizing preservice instruction. *Journal for Specialists in Group Work, 21,* 274–282.

Toth, P., & Stockton, R. (1998). Application of a skill-based training model for group counselors. *Journal for Specialists in Group Work, 23,* 33–49.

White, M., & Epston, D. (1990). *Narrative means to therapeutic ends.* New York: Norton.

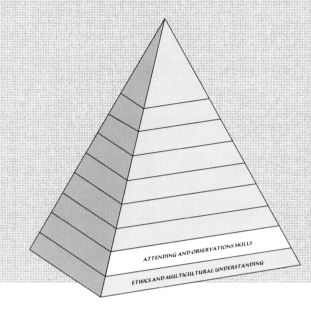

ATTENDING AND OBSERVATIONS SKILLS

ETHICS AND MULTICULTURAL UNDERSTANDING

# CHAPTER 2

# Attending Behavior: The Foundation of Listening and Process Skills

## CHAPTER GOALS

The effective group leader is highly skilled in listening and observing. The skills described in this chapter are basic to your work in groups. Many things happen simultaneously in group work, and you will find that solid understanding of attending behavior will make a difference in your ability to work with many types of groups. Furthermore, no matter how expert you become, you'll find you always want to develop even more competence in listening and observing.

Perhaps the most important skill of all, attending behavior can be overlooked as it is so basic to group facilitation. As a leader becomes more sophisticated, he or she may emphasize theory and many abstract ideas, forgetting this foundation, where group work begins. We all listen and attend to others, but both leader and group members have their own personal ways of selectively "tuning in" and "tuning out." You will find that attending to the many things that occur in a group will give you information you need to plan strategies and skills leading toward more effective outcomes.

Attending behavior is constantly useful in group process. It will help you observe what is going on among group members. It can serve as a foundation for you when you feel lost or confused and wonder how to address the complexities of group work. In short, when in doubt about what to do as a group leader, listen and observe. Attending is basic to bringing out group members' stories—and observing members throughout the group process will be basic to helping them restory and find new ways to think, feel, and behave.

In this chapter, seek to accomplish the following objectives of understanding and mastery:

▲ Understand and master the basic skills of listening:
  *visuals*—individually and culturally appropriate eye contact
  *vocals*—vocal tone, speech rate, verbal emphasis, and speech hesitations
  *verbals*—verbal following, changing the topic, use of key words, and observing what is *not* said
  *body language*—being with the group nonverbally
▲ Utilize attending skills to observe individuals and group process. Group members will have individual styles that vary with their own experience and cultural background. Your ability to employ the subtle aspects of attending will enable you to understand more fully what is going on in the group in the here-and-now.
▲ Apply attending concepts to your own group leadership.

## WARM-UP EXERCISE

Yogi Berra is reported to have said, "You can observe a lot by watching." One of the best ways to understand attending behavior and its importance is to consider what it is not. We have all been in positive, useful groups that accomplish things and make us feel good. And we have all been subjected to groups that simply aren't working. It can be a miserable experience to be in a dysfunctional group. We are suggesting two ways for you to think about groups. Try either one or both.

▲ What was it in that positive group that "worked"? Be as specific as you can. The group may have been meeting at school or work; it might have been a volunteer group at church, synagogue, or mosque. It may have been a community group or perhaps it was even a counseling group. If possible, share your stories of exceptional groups with others. What was done right by the leader and its members?
▲ Think back on a group you personally experienced that was painful. Recall some of the things that did not go well. What was done wrong by the leader and group members?
▲ As an alternative or supplement to this exercise, ask a group of four or more people to demonstrate in an impromptu role-play what they think an ineffective group might look like. While the results of the role-play are often hilarious, it is interesting to note that most of us are already sensitive to many things that make a group helpful or dysfunctional. Then, try a more positive group and compare and contrast the two.

List below what can be done right in a group. Be as specific and concrete as you can.

_____

_____

_____

_____

_____

_____

Now list what can be done less effectively, even wrong.

_____

_____

_____

_____

_____

Compare and contrast the two lists. This exercise is designed to show you that you already know a lot about groups and their functioning. You likely have already noticed that your natural skills of observation can tell you a lot about what is happening in groups. Paraphrasing Yogi Berra, "You have already observed a lot and by continuing to watch further you can learn a lot more."

At the same time, it is important to note that we all make mistakes. Some feel that expert group leaders make about as many errors as beginners. At issue is your ability to acknowledge your slips and recover. A mistake on your part is often an opportunity for the group to see that you are human, just as they are. And your ability to flex and learn from the inevitable mistake can enrich not only your ability as a group leader but also the group process itself.

The remainder of _Intentional Group Counseling_ will focus on honing and sharpening your already considerable listening and observing skills. Throughout this text, we will provide ideas for naming, organizing, and acting on the many skills of group leadership. But despite the obvious complexity of group work, recall that you start with a considerable reservoir of skill. Now let us turn to defining the skills of attending behavior more precisely.

## DEFINING THE LEADERSHIP SKILLS OF ATTENDING BEHAVIOR

Leaders listen and observe. Only through noticing what's going on the group can you truly understand and be facilitative to group functioning. Attending behavior consists of four aspects that are simple, yet profound. When all else fails, we always have attending behavior to rely on as a foundation. In short—listen! (See Ivey & Ivey, 1999, for a detailed examination of these issues from an individual perspective.)

People often fail to listen, even though they think they do. Those who listen _really listen._ And those who pay attention _really pay attention._ Attending behavior is simultaneously a skill and an art. It would be possible for you to demonstrate all the behaviors below and merely "look like" you are listening. However, deliberate practice in these attending skills will deepen your listening abilities and enable you to hear even more completely.

## Goals and Expected Consequence of Knowledge and Use of Attending Behavior.

Each of the major skills and strategies of this book is designed to increase your intentionality and your options for successful leadership in the group.

### Knowledge and skills goals

The leader is able to demonstrate culturally appropriate visuals, vocals, verbals, and body language. The leader is able to observe attending behaviors in group members and to make these observations a foundation for use of listening and observing skills and strategies.

### Anticipated consequences and results

Group members will talk more freely and respond more openly around topics to which attention is given. The leader can observe nonverbal and verbal styles and use these to engage the group members more fully. Sensitivity to individual and cultural differences may be expected to increase.

## The Skills of Attending

What is attending behavior? Most likely you have already identified some or all of the several facets of listening as you thought through your own difficult group experiences or observed a role-play group in operation. If you are to be an effective group leader, consider the following:

### Visuals

In much of world culture, the eyes have it. We communicate with others by looking at them. We hear that the eyes are the "mirror of the soul." In much of the United States, Canada, Australia, New Zealand, and Europe, direct eye contact is stressed. The person who looks at you is often considered more friendly and trustworthy than the person who avoids eye contact, who may appear shy, unfriendly, and avoidant. But before going further, recall the many individual and cultural variations that exist in visual style (see Box 2.1). Some individuals have been taught that it is rude to stare or to look at people too directly. Thus, we must not stereotype individuals and groups, and we must not expect everyone to use "our style" of listening. Nonetheless, in all cultures you communicate, directly or indirectly, with your eyes.

Thus, a most useful leadership skill is using your eyes to see what is going on in the group. You need to make eye contact with all members of the group. An inexperienced or less competent leader may focus primarily on one or two group members and then wonder why the others in the group don't seem to respond. Each of us as leaders may fall into the trap of giving too much attention to one or more individuals. Some of us respond more easily to women, others to men. Most of us tend to give the most eye contact to those whom we particularly like.

**Box 2.1**    *Visual, Vocal, Verbal, and Body Language Attending Behavior: Individual and Cultural Differences*

Stereotyping sometimes occurs around the "correct" style of listening to others. In much of North America, direct eye contact, a medium vocal tone and speech rate, verbal following, and forward trunk lean indicate culturally appropriate attending behavior. However, there are many variations in what is a culturally appropriate way of listening. Some individuals have styles that are vastly different from the one described above.

Consider some of the following issues as you use attending skills:

*Visuals*

Many traditional cultures consider direct eye contact rude and intrusive. In rural Mexico and Puerto Rico, and among many Native American Indian groups, looking down can be a sign of respect. Some children may have been taught not to give direct eye contact. This has been for the child's own protection. Because of their experiences in the family, some children have developed a habit of not looking directly at people. All these individual and cultural differences need to be noted and honored.

*Vocals*

Loudness and speech rate vary. In much of Europe and Asia, people from the United States are often seen as loud. Many cultures and individuals have a quieter style. No style is "right," but it is important to recognize that vocal styles differ. Recognize and expand your awareness of individual and cultural difference. Even a behavior you consider to be right may have negative consequences in certain groups. Rather than evaluating one way of behaving as correct or "better than" another, your time may be better spent learning individual and cultural differences and the consequences of a behavior in the context of different groups or cultures.

*Verbals*

In general, we recommend strongly that you as leader follow the dialogue of your group closely. But it is also important to realize that some cultural groups and individuals use a more indirect style and may want to spend considerable time talking around an issue. This indirect mode of communication needs to be respected. In some Asian countries, for example, being subtle is respected far more than using a strong, direct form of communication.

*Body Language*

Most of the time, a person in a closed body posture with arms crossed seems to be blocking what is going on at the moment. However, for some people, this again may be a sign of respect and a desire to give the person talking more private space, even while talking in the group community. The forward trunk lean with solid eye contact, generally indicative of good listening skills, can get in the way of someone who is hesitant to speak. For some, these active listening skills will come across as intrusive, particularly when the topic is difficult for the speaker to talk about. Thus, in some cases, the best attending posture may be leaning back and looking at the floor, thus respecting the space of the individual who has difficulty expressing his or her thoughts on the current topic. These few examples demonstrate the importance of our being flexible in our use of and understanding of attending behavior.

So, look at all group members in an equitable fashion as you communicate interest in each person. Ask someone to observe your patterns of eye contact in groups from time to time. You will need an external consultant and supervision for this type of awareness. You can't easily do it all by yourself.

### Visual process observation

As you observe your group, start looking for eye contact styles and patterns in your group. You'll note that some members of the group get the most attention and eye contact. You'll also discover that when some members start talking, one or more group participants will look away while perhaps others will give extra attention. The way members use eye contact will provide you with considerable data about patterns of likes and dislikes and support or lack of support within the group.

One technique you can practice is transferring power through eye contact. For example, assume that one of your group members, Juanita, has just said something that you think the group should hear clearly, but after she comments, everyone seems to ignore her. As leader, you want to draw her out more. So, as the other group members talk and you respond, you continue to look at Juanita. You will find that shortly most of the group is looking at Juanita and she can make her comments again.

It is also important, however, to be respectful of individual and cultural differences in attending behavior style. Box 2.1 summarizes examples of cultural and gender differences of which we all need to be aware. Recall that this chart addresses cultural norms and does not take into account the wide range of individual differences. Variations among individuals can override cultural background; we must always be careful to avoid stereotyping any individual or group.

### Visual example

Imagine that you are leading a stress management group in a health maintenance organization (HMO). This is a three-hour session and you have just finished a basic exercise on relaxation training. You know that meditation and relaxation training can be very useful and lead to a healthier lifestyle. Your goal at this moment is to reflect on and think about how relaxation training might be used by each participant in her or his own life.

As a discussion begins, you note that all but two in your group (Perry and Micha) are giving you full attention. Most group members are looking at you with real interest and seem eager to share their feelings about the experience. An enthusiastic discussion ensues for about five minutes, but Perry and Micha seem to be looking down all the time; occasionally they look at each other with raised eyebrows, as if to say "All this is foolish." For the moment, you file this information away and say nothing.

### Vocals

Your tone of voice may communicate your emotions as much as or more than the words you use. For example, say the words "You really know what you are talking about" several times. Change your vocal tone and note the various meanings you can convey. Said in a negative tone of voice, those words can be a major put-down.

Speech hesitations and stumbling over words may indicate an uncomfortable topic. Many people also clear their throats when they have something to say that is difficult for them to get out. Watch for these small indicators of vocal style in yourself and in group members.

Speech rate is another dimension. Some people talk rapidly about a topic they have real enthusiasm for. Some may slow down for important points or when discussing a difficult topic. Different cultural groups have varying natural speech rates.

Sometime in the future, record a group you lead and note your vocal tone and vocal style. You may find yourself rewarding some group members just through your voice while telling others indirectly that they are less important to you.

### Vocal process observation

You will also want to observe vocal tone among group members. Not only do individuals have varying tones of voice, but there is also at times a "group voice." This becomes evident especially during emotional times within the group. The group may at times explode in laughter or anger, or it may be still and quiet as all members listen carefully to a person's difficult story.

Particularly important to observe is the gradual shift of emotion and the building of tension among the group. This may be noted not only in the vocals but also in the other aspects of communication discussed here.

### Vocal example

You next ask your stress management group to share their own plans to use relaxation training during the next week. Perry and Micha are the last ones to respond. Perry says, "I guess it's a good idea; I'll try it." But he says this with a challenging tone of voice, emphasizing the "I guess." Micha chooses a different tack, saying sarcastically, "Sure, I've got a half-hour every day to lie down and relax."

You lean back and ponder what you're going to say. Everything seemed be going fine until these two came along. You have just experienced an "uncomfortable moment" in the group; what you do next will be significant and can influence not only Perry and Micha but also all the group members watching the exchange.

When you are challenged by group members, the most important rule is *don't be defensive.* This means stay calm and maintain steady attending behavior verbally and nonverbally. And when you are challenged directly, it is best to respond directly. Some possible responses you have to Perry and Micha are presented on pages 47–48. Before going further, take a moment and write down how you might respond to the challenge if you were the group leader in this situation.

_____

_____

_____

_____

_____

_____

_____

You will likely want to generate more alternatives for situations such as this. Talk over the challenge with your colleagues or classmates. Over time, you will develop an *action list of things to do* when you face difficult and uncomfortable moments in leadership. This action list can serve as one of the foundations for your developing intentionality as a group leader.

One important concept is "buying in" to the group by the members. A group member "buys in" by making a significant comment or contribution and having it acknowledged by other members and the leader. You will find that positive warm-up exercises that allow and encourage everyone to participate early in the group often prevent the need for dealing with challenges later.

## Verbal following

In general, your task as a group leader is to follow the topic introduced by an individual or by the group as a whole. As a good listener, you need to help the group members bring out their stories and concerns. You also need to model good listening yourself. As a leader, you want to stay with the group as they talk about issues of interest to them.

Verbal following is particularly important when group members are telling their stories. We need to provide solid attending and encourage members to share their stories or issues fully. Similarly, if the group is processing a critical event that happened in the group itself, it is important that you as leader encourage full exploration of the recent narrative. Sometimes groups will avoid examining themselves and their own interactions.

Effective group leadership may also require you to bring a group back to the central topic. For example, you may be working with a cancer or AIDS support group, and members are spending most of their time on negative thinking. Staying with the negative topic for a time may be worthwhile, but the group may need you to lead them in a more positive direction, perhaps the sharing of more optimistic success stories. In this case, what is *not* said in the group needs to be brought out clearly.

## Verbal process observation

You can observe an almost infinite number of things in verbal interactions. Among the most obvious are these:

▲  Who has most of the talk time?
▲  Who doesn't speak? (Or seldom speaks?)
▲  Who speaks after whom? (And is that a support or a challenge to the previous speaker?)
▲  Who provides supportive comments?
▲  Who criticizes?
▲  Who speaks first after you as leader speak and what is the nature of that person's comment? (Challenging? Supportive?)
▲  Who interrupts? And whom do they interrupt?

For the most part, process observation simply means observing what is going on. You may decide to comment on the observations, or you may decide not to mention them at all, or you may wait until later to give the individual or group feedback on what you have seen.

At this point you may have noted that process observation, particularly in the area of attending behavior, will be one of your most valuable skills as a leader. Unless you observe the many details and interactions in your group, the instructions, suggestions, and interventions you supply may be all for naught. The effective leader is always an observing leader.

As you begin the study of group leadership, we strongly urge that you have a process observer outside your group to provide feedback to you and the members periodically. The process observer can be a group member who volunteers to observe for awhile and then returns to the group. At times, an observer external to the group may be brought in to help you understand what is occurring, but always with the knowledge and support of group members.

### Verbal example

This time let us imagine two types of verbal response to the challenge from Perry and Micha:

1. (Leader ignores Perry and Micha.) So we have heard what everybody wants to do with relaxation training. As I said before, it can make a real difference in helping us feel better and move toward a less stressful lifestyle.
2. I think it's important to realize that each of us has different experiences with relaxation training. Perry and Micha have been willing to tell us that the tape and experience was not as meaningful for them as for most of the group. But let us take a moment and listen to them carefully. Unless you personally find the exercise useful, it will do little good.

The first response, of course, represents nonattending. At times, it is appropriate to ignore disruptive comments. But in this case, the subgroup of Perry and Micha appears to represent a challenge to the goals of the entire group experience.

The second possibility, exploring what is going on with Perry and Micha, invites participation and reflection. Perry and Micha can openly share their objections to the relaxation experience. If a group member is resisting what is occurring in the group, it is often helpful to "go with the resistance." Going with the resistance means encouraging sometimes dissident group members to let others know what is going on with them. This acknowledges the importance of diverse opinions and, in an open atmosphere, often results in changing opinions and actions.

We must acknowledge, however, that exploring diverse opinions takes time. If you have a tight group schedule, you may have to simply accept the fact that Perry and Micha can't be reached at this moment. If you have an ongoing group, clearly you will have to deal with this type of potentially disruptive process. If you as leader continually ignore challenges, group tension will gradually build and you may eventually have a very large issue to explore that will be much more difficult to manage effectively than if you had addressed it when it first emerged.

Here are some other possibilities for you to consider for dealing with challenge and potential conflict. The more alternatives for action you have, the more intentional and comfortable you will feel. Any of the following statements could be said in a calm, steady voice with natural body language and appropriate eye contact.

"Perry and Micha, would you mind telling us what is going on for you in this group that makes you want not to participate? (To the group:) How are the rest of you feeling about what they have said and are doing?" (This brings group process to the center and involves the total group as well.)

"We've got some time. Let's stop for moment and hear your thoughts. Not everyone wants to join in at first." (Attending to Perry and Micha's frame of reference.)

"Let's recall our group agreement when we started. Anyone who does not wish to do an exercise is free not to participate or to leave. None of these exercises will be helpful unless they are meaningful to you personally." (Many group problems can be addressed by restating the original group contract.)

"I can understand your hesitation. If you have not done this type of thing before, it does seem strange at times. Just participate as much as you feel comfortable and see how it goes." (This is another standard group rule. All our members should be free to pass when it comes to any exercise or group procedure.)

(If necessary:) "Perry and Micha, I can understand that this exercise doesn't appeal to you. There are others who would like to try it. Perhaps you would like to step out of the room for awhile. After the exercise is finished and we process it, you might want to rejoin us for the feedback discussion." (All leaders at times may need to take a forceful position.)

### Body language

There are those who say that nonverbals represent 85% or more of communication. This may be an overstatement, but clearly body language often overrules what one says with words, the eyes, and vocal tone. Incongruent body language speaks loudly.

Imagine you are leading a group. You maintain balanced eye contact with all members, your vocals are warm and caring, and you listen well, following carefully what is said. But one member troubles you and for some reason you simply don't like her or him. Whenever this individual talks, you find yourself sitting back in the chair, covering your body with wrapped arms while all the time trying to be a "good leader." Your body is giving you away! Often the group members will know how you are feeling even before you yourself do! They already know you have a strong reaction, but they don't know why. If you fail to acknowledge your reactions, over time you are likely to weaken your effectiveness as a leader. If you disclose your reactions carefully and honestly, this may provide the group members with an opportunity to share their own insights and learning and help you—and them—grow.

When your body language overrules what you intend to say, it usually happens unconsciously. You may lean forward with interest as some people speak out on certain topics (e.g., difficulty in making a personal decision, a story about a successful work experience). But when others bring up a topic with which you are less comfortable and sure of yourself (interpersonal conflict, sexism), you may find yourself sitting back and looking away. Some of us are really interested in exploring interpersonal conflict; others avoid it as much as they can. You may find abstract intellectual analysis of problems very interesting or you may prefer to hear concrete stories. Often your preferences will show in your body language and attending behavior. This unconscious body language can be the determiner of your effectiveness as a group leader.

### Nonverbal process observation

All the above behaviors and many more need to be observed in groups. The effective group leader will exhibit appropriate nonverbal behavior and be able to note verbal styles of interaction among group members.

Another vital dimension to consider is the total body language pattern within a group. Careful observation will reveal fascinating patterns of harmony and disharmony. For example, people who tend to be in agreement often assume body postures that are similar to one another. They may even echo each other and move their bodies simultaneously in similar positions. At times, you'll find that whole groups exhibit types of movement harmonics. Generally speaking, harmony in movement means group agreement. You may also find movement complementarity; this may show when one person talks and another moves in a positive fashion, in some way physically echoing what has just been said.

Very often, observation of body language will reveal patterns of disharmony suggesting disagreement and conflict within the group. You may find, for example, that four members of your group are leaning forward with interest listening to another person's story. However, two people are looking out into space and apparently not listening while two others are frowning, also crossing their legs and arms as if to block out words they do not want to hear. In such situations, your leadership skills will be truly taxed. You need to attend and pay attention to the conflicting things happening in your group. At an appropriate point, it may be useful to summarize what you saw happening: "Well, we seemed to have finished that topic. But I noted that everyone was not fully involved. Some of you seemed to be in another space during the conversation. Would you mind sharing what was going on for you?" Such open comments may help the group reach a new level of understanding. If not, such discussion often leads to awareness that different people experience the same event differently.

If you are to manage conflict in a group, you must develop the ability to note varying attending behaviors. You may choose to comment on your observations at an appropriate time, or you may simply note and file this information in your head to help you understand what is occurring in your group.

### Body language example

In dealing with the group resistance issue, it is often helpful to observe what is going on in the body language of the group. In this case, Perry and Micha lean back in surprise and say nothing when you offer them the chance to state their thoughts and feelings. The other members of the group sit back and look at you, the leader, to see how you're going to respond. Kenda, fortunately, breaks in and says, "I can understand how they feel. We are all busy people and taking time out to do relaxation training will be frustrating. However, at the same time, I know if I don't, my body and my personal life will suffer."

The total group appears to relax a bit. Perry and Micha lean forward slightly and seem to be involved for the first time. Other group members also mention having constraints on their time. You then decide to ask Perry and Micha, "What do you think about what the group has been saying?" Micha comments, "I can see that I'm not as alone as I thought I was. It helps to hear that others have the same issues I do." Perry nods in agreement.

At this point, you observe that the entire group is much more in harmony. All group members are sitting with an open posture and seem available to consider how they personally can use the skills you are teaching. There is a natural resistance to change, and Perry and Micha, who originally seemed defiant and resistant, have become important in exploring how relaxation and stress management can truly be transferred to the home environment.

## The Three Vs plus B

The acronym 3Vs + B (visual, vocal, verbal, and body language) provides a useful summary of the main points of this chapter. Box 2.2 provides you with an observation list of the many possibilities within attending behavior. As a first step, we suggest that you take this list with you to a group meeting and use it to help you observe what is going on. As you take on a group leadership role, enlist a friend or colleague to observe you and provide you with written feedback on your own attending style.

Generally, attending skills should help group leaders focus on individual group members rather than on themselves as leaders. As a group leader, you need to know what patterns of attending are most comfortable for the group. At the same time, you need to have alternative patterns of group leadership to fit the requirements of different group members. By attending, you will perceive cues that tell you when a behavior is or is not appropriate.

Finally, it is important not be so distracted by the attending process that you lose track of what is happening in the group itself!

As you begin group practice, learn to relax and realize that wherever you are in your understanding and observing of attending behavior is a good starting point. With time and experience, you will continue to increase your awareness of your own and others' verbal and nonverbal behavior. We have found a simple rule that truly helps the beginning group leader: "When you don't know what to do, attend." By this, we mean sit back for a moment and observe what is going on. Then, use verbal following and respond to some central theme you see the group focusing on. Most likely the group will continue, and then you can use your observation skills to focus more precisely for the future. At the risk of overstating our basic point, when you don't know what to do, attend. The Chinese have a parallel saying, "When you don't know what to do . . . at least don't DO anything."

**Box 2.2**   *Attending Behavior Process Observation Instruments*

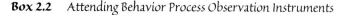

There are many ways to observe attending behavior in a group, and three ideas for observation are presented here. We suggest that you use one or more of these approaches as you observe group exercises in your class or workshop. When you run your own groups, ask a process observer to provide feedback to you and the group on interaction.

*1. Who Talks to Whom?*

It is especially valuable to note the flow of conversation in a group. This will help you understand subgroups, coalitions, and power relations occurring before you. Also, it will help indicate your place as a leader. Are you talking too much? Are you directing your comments to group members unequally?

Draw a circle representing the group. Place the names of the group members on the circle and draw arrows indicating who talks to whom. The reverse arrow near a person indicates that he or she responded. For example, note that the leader spoke to Micha and he answered. If the comments are made to the total group, the arrow is replaced with a "—|," which ends in the middle of the group.

The group portrayed below represents about fifteen minutes of attending behavior. We can see that the leader is directing the conversation and not involving the group. Some group members are left out, particularly women.

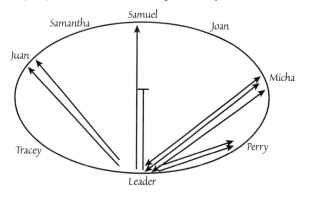

The leader below is using a more balanced approach. Note that most of the comments are directed to the group as a whole. The group members are talking to each other and several are talking to the entire group. Samuel remains silent.

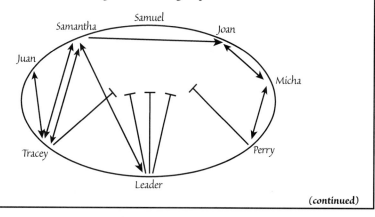

**(continued)**

**Box 2.2 (continued)**

| | |
|---|---|
| *2. Who Interrupts and How Often?* | A major problem in group functioning, whether in a counseling or volunteer group or one in business, is the interruption. Many groups stall and become enmeshed in conflict because no one is able to have his or her say. As you observe the group, give special attention to this dimension. Allen Ivey was participating as a member of a conflicting faculty group. The group was aware of its ineffective process and asked different members to sit outside the group and observe what was happening. During a one-half hour meeting, Allen counted seventy-five interruptions! After giving this feedback to the group, they agreed to listen to each other's comments before moving on. This one process observation made both a short-term and a long-term difference to the group.<br><br>As you engage in process observation of other groups, noting interruptions is particularly important. In your own work as a group leader, note interruptions and who interrupts whom. One of your leading tasks as a group facilitator is to ensure that all are able to make their own comments and tell their own stories. |
| *3. Observation of 3Vs + B (Visuals, Vocals, Verbals, and Body Language)* | The following form summarizes the major verbal and nonverbal behaviors discussed in this chapter. Effective leadership demands the ability to observe what is occurring in your own group. The best route to becoming a skilled observer is constant practice. It will be especially helpful if you observe a videotaped group in which you are a participant or a leader. You may observe leader behavior in any situation, meeting, or group. Over time, your observation skills will improve and you will automatically note much of what is occurring in both verbal and nonverbal behavior. You can also use the form to observe individual members and expand it for observing the entire group.<br><br>**Instructions:** Observe the leader first over a period of ten minutes, then use the following checklist to summarize what you have observed. You will find that you will be able to notice data concerning most of the items in the list. If there is more than one observer, then group members can be observed as well. Consider photocopying this information and use a fresh form for each ten-minute period.<br><br>An alternative to the above is to focus your observation on one or two areas of the checklist. Make checkmarks for the behaviors every minute and draw a circle around the checkmark if the behavior was particularly intense.<br><br>Comments and informal observations can elaborate the behavior. It is useful to write down at least one or two direct quotes capturing the exact words from the interaction; this makes the observation more specific and timely. |

Facilitative Visuals
____ Makes eye contact with all group members
____ Encourages and focuses on individuals or subgroups appropriate to situation
____ Is able to maintain eye contact in difficult situations
____ Breaks eye contact appropriately to respect individual and/or cultural difference

Nonfacilitative Visuals
____ Makes unbalanced eye contact; some individuals appear favored
____ Avoids eye contact on certain topics or with certain people
____ Stares or maintains eye contact in a way that makes others uncomfortable
____ Breaks eye contact awkwardly
____ Gives more eye contact and attention to certain subgroups (e.g., people of status from community, men/women, ethnicity/race)

Facilitative Vocals
*Speech rate*
____ Comfortable
____ Fast
____ Slow
____ Smooth change of pace on certain topics

*Vocal tone*
____ Is expressive
____ Is supportive, encouraging
____ Helps in making appropriate challenge with suitable amount of firmness

*Speech hesitations*
____ Uses hesitations to encourage and help members speak openly
____ Makes effective use of silence

Nonfacilitative Vocals
*Speech rate*
____ Too fast
____ Too slow
____ Awkward change of pace on certain topics

*Vocal tone*
____ Is flat, unexpressive
____ Communicates nervousness, anger, etc.
____ Is too soft
____ Is too loud

*Speech hesitations*
____ Awkward, indicative of tension
____ Clearing of throat
____ Awkward, uncomfortable during silence

Facilitative Verbals
____ Follows or stays on topic discussed by group
____ Allows sufficient time for topics or stories
____ Works with difficult material comfortably
____ Appropriate percentage of talk time for leader
____ Appropriate percentage of talk time for members
____ Encourages all members to talk
____ Does not force reluctant members to participate
____ Is able to interrupt, slow down, or discourage overtalkative members

Nonfacilitative Verbals
____ Jumps from topic inappropriately
____ Does not allow enough time for topic or story to be finished
____ Allows topic or story to continue too long
____ Appears to want to avoid some difficult material
____ Encourages irrelevant off-the-topic discussion
____ Talks too much
____ Talks too little
____ Interrupts inappropriately
____ Encourages only some members to talk while discouraging others
____ Lets discussion wander
____ Allows more verbal attention for certain subgroups (e.g., people of status from community, men/women, ethnicity/race)

*(continued)*

**Box 2.2 (continued)**

Facilitative Body Language
___ Face relaxed
___ Facial tension showing concern and interest
___ Face expressive
___ Smiling at appropriate times
___ Hands and arms relaxed
___ Communication facilitated by gestures
___ Trunk lean (generally forward, but at times appropriately "backing off")
___ Open posture
___ Legs steady and relaxed
___ Body movements shifting appropriately with a change in topic or intensity of group

Nonfacilitative Body Language
___ Face relaxed inappropriately
___ Facial tension that does not fit situation
___ Face inexpressive
___ Inappropriate smiling
___ Hands and arms tense
___ Playing with hands or objects
___ Gestures that are stilted and awkward, getting in the way of communication
___ Trunk lean (leaning back or away from individual or subgroup)
___ Closed posture
___ Crossed arms
___ Leg jiggling
___ Legs crossed away from individual or subgroup indicating a closed attitude
___ Body shifts that seem awkward or unsuitable to the situation
___ Certain subgroups (e.g., people of status from community, men/women, ethnicity/race) receiving inappropriately different patterns of body language

Facilitative Movement Harmonics:
Examples of complementarity (e.g., when one person talks, the other person nods the head, supports and punctuates the conversation in a back and forth fashion):

Examples of movement harmony (e.g., two or more group members move their bodies in a mirroring relationship one to another):

Nonfacilitative Movement Harmonics:
Examples of movement disharmony (e.g., two or more group members move in ways that are dissimilar):

Examples of inappropriate mirroring (e.g., the leader may mirror only some people while being out of synchrony with others. This may happen with some subgroups and include multicultural issues):

Comments, notation of key statements by members or leaders that may help recall of specific situations, and informal observations (include any multicultural observations):

## USING ATTENDING SKILLS WITH CHILD AND ADOLESCENT GROUPS

Attending and observation skills are used essentially the same way with children and adolescents. Children and teens talk most easily to those who are interested in them and listen well and carefully. With younger children, it is often useful to sit on the floor with them or on a low chair so that height differences and your power as an adult are diminished somewhat.

With younger children, you'll find that your talk time may have to increase and that you are running a leader-centered group. This is because younger children especially will tend to speak to the adult rather than to each other. On the other hand, with some teen groups, you may find yourself at times feeling almost invisible. The demand for active leadership varies with the age of the group. Your sense of humor and your willingness to share yourself and self-disclose appropriately will make a large difference in how you are accepted.

Both children and teens respond very well to instruction in listening skills, for the failure to listen is often a problem manifested in poor social skills and difficulty in developing friendships. A communication skills workshop based on attending skills is described in Chapter 10. Peer counseling and mediation training are also very helpful to younger group members and listening skill training is an essential part of this type of group work. Some useful references for peer counseling include Cox (1999), Ivey, Gluckstern, and Ivey (1997), Ivey and Ivey (1999), and Myrick and Sorenson (1997). An excellent summary of the research in the area is found in Dagley, Gazda, Eppinger, and Stewart (1994).

## MOVING TOWARD YOUR OWN LEADERSHIP STYLE

Four group leadership ideas are suggested here for your consideration. The first is that you really need to observe the many verbal and nonverbal interactions in any group. The second is that those who seem to resist leadership often, but not always, represent an important part of the evolving group process. We will talk later in more detail about resistance in the group. We stress that resistance is your friend as a leader *if* you are able to recognize and work with it effectively.

Third, we'd like you to think back on how the leader presented in this chapter responded to challenge and seeming resistance. Rather than answer the questions and issues herself or himself, the leader encouraged the group to discuss the issues. It is important that the leader use the group and encourage members to talk to each other. The group wisdom will often surface if you allow the group to function. This is a major difference between individual and group counseling. In individual counseling, the counselor or therapist usually has to respond. Many times, the group leader can be more effective by attending and encouraging others to speak.

The fourth and perhaps most important issue in this chapter is that individual and cultural styles of behavior in the group vary. It is possible that Perry and Micha's lack of eye contact may reflect their personal and cultural history. When a person doesn't look at you in the way expected in a typical Euro-American/Canadian conversation, this behavior may be either personal style or the result of cultural expectation. *Never stereotype or expect a single meaning around any attending behavior.* We all have unique stories and our own methods of finding new ways of dealing with them. Discovering these differences is one of the great opportunities that exist within group work.

Think back on this section and the entire chapter. What have you learned here? What points struck you as most important? What stood out for you? What would you like to work on in the area of attending behavior to improve your own group facilitation? List the major points below.

_____

_____

_____

_____

_____

_____

_____

_____

## PRACTICING ATTENDING SKILLS

Basic group skills will be learned only through practice and observation. In practice sessions with each of the skills in this book, we provide individual and group suggestions for action on your part. These will include process observation skills as a particularly important part of group leadership.

### 1. Process Observation of Attending Behavior

Box 2.2 provides you with three approaches to observing group process. Photocopy this form and take it with you to a group meeting. This could be a school board meeting, a gathering of the student council, a local meeting of your town planning committee, or any open public meeting. As an alternative, consider observing a smaller group session in which you may be a member. This could be a church committee, an informal discussion group to which you belong, or perhaps even your own family or social group.

It is particularly important, ethically, to share your intentions with the group you observe. Sit back from the group, observe, and make your notes quietly. If the group requests it, share your written observations with them.

Another style of process observation is that of the "participant observer." You may be a member of a group and simultaneously observe what is going on. And of course, group leaders must observe their own groups in action and are always process observers.

### 2. The Fish Bowl

The fish bowl is a standard classroom exercise for group interaction and teaching. Four to six class members form a group in front of the larger class; we suggest a ten- to fifteen-minute interaction. One member of the group is selected as leader. The remainder of the class observes what is going on and uses the concepts in Box 2.2 for process observation and feedback.

The leader's task is to demonstrate good attending skills. The volunteer group members are to engage in a group discussion. The suggested topic for this first fish bowl exercise is: "How I See Myself as a Counselor or Group Leader." This particular topic encourages awareness and reflection on the nature of the way we react in groups. Clearly, different people have different styles of interaction, and that in itself is an important observation skill. Alternative topics include current events, thoughts about life plans, or a discussion about what group each person is going to use for process observation. In short, any topic may be appropriate.

Videotaping can be helpful as it provides objective feedback that can be used to examine verbal and nonverbal attending behaviors. We suggest that you use some part of the alternative methods of process observation presented in Box 2.2.

### 3. Your Own Group Practice

The following exercise can be completed in a class or workshop—or you may elect to develop your own group for practice. If you practice on your own, find a classroom member or friend who will complete the observation form in Box 2.2 with you. If you're working in a classroom or workshop, the following steps are recommended:

1. Divide into groups of five or six. One person is to serve as leader and one as the observer, who uses Box 2.2. The remainder serve as group participants.
2. Select a topic for the small groups. The suggested topic is "something I feel good about from my cultural, racial, or ethnic group," as this topic encourages discussion of positive strengths. It also encourages awareness of multicultural issues. You will find that group members who have the security of saying something positive about themselves may later be able to discuss difficult issues with greater ease. However, any topic of interest to the group may be used.
3. Ten to fifteen minutes should be used for the small groups. Allow five minutes for feedback from the observer. Finally, the entire small group can reflect on and discuss their own group process.

When possible, add video recording and practice to your work with attending skills and observation. Recordings always provide very useful feedback on yourself and the group. Always obtain informed consent from your group members before making any type of recording.

## REFERENCES

Cox, J. (1999). *A guide to peer counseling.* Northvale, NJ: Aronson.

Dagley, J., Gazda, G., Eppinger, S., & Stewart, E. (1994). Group psychotherapy research with children, preadolescents. In A. Fuhriman & G. Burlingame (Eds.), *Handbook of group psychotherapy: An empirical and clinical synthesis* (pp. 340–369). New York: Wiley.

Ivey, A., Gluckstern, N., & Ivey, M. (1997). *Basic attending skills.* North Amherst, MA: Microtraining Associates.

Ivey, A., & Ivey, M. (1999). *Intentional interviewing and counseling: Facilitating client development in a multicultural society.* Pacific Grove, CA: Brooks/Cole.

Myrick, R., & Sorenson, D. (1997). *Peer helping: A practical guide.* Minneapolis: Educational Media.

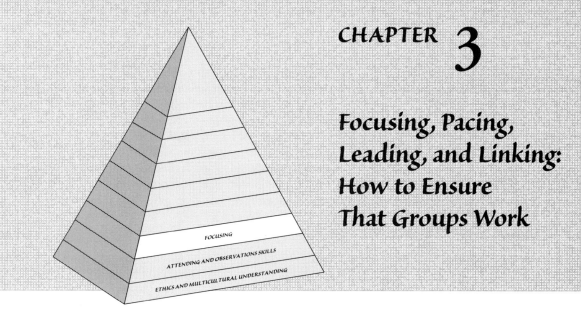

# CHAPTER 3

# Focusing, Pacing, Leading, and Linking: How to Ensure That Groups Work

FOCUSING

ATTENDING AND OBSERVATIONS SKILLS

ETHICS AND MULTICULTURAL UNDERSTANDING

## CHAPTER GOALS

Group leadership involves many of the skills of individual counseling and psychotherapy, but the skills are used in different ways. The three major concepts of this chapter—focusing, pacing, and leading—are particularly important in group work. The focus of individual counseling is to listen and draw out issues and stories from a single client. However, competent group leadership requires you to draw out the individual stories and also focus on the interactions between individuals and among subgroups and facilitate the total group interaction. The ability to balance the relationship of the individual to the group is fundamental; mastering the microskills of this chapter is central to that task.

Focusing is defined as the way leaders and members direct their attending behavior and attention: What are they selectively listening to? At times, the individual counseling tradition carries over into groups and we find the leader doing individual therapy in front of the group. We do not believe this is group therapy; rather, it is *individual counseling with an audience.*

Effective *group* work requires you to *focus* the group conversation not just on individuals, but also on subgroups and the group process itself. *If we are to engage in group work, we need to consider the power of the group.* In addition, focusing and paying attention to the central topic or theme of the group is critical. Two other important dimensions discussed in this chapter include focusing on the group leader and the cultural/environmental context.

*Pacing* and *leading* are closely related to focusing and represent different leadership styles, both important in facilitating a group and in focusing conversation. A pacing style of focusing involves listening to and staying with the group where it is and helping them continue to focus on something that is occurring in the group. Leading, on the other hand, encourages the group to move to another focus or another topic, or perhaps to explore the same topic from another perspective.

*Linking* is another important aspect of leading, also closely related to focusing. Linking may be defined as helping group members see connections, relationships, and linkages among behaviors, thoughts, meanings, or feelings. These connections help members (and leaders) see patterns in their lives, in the group, and the cultural/environmental context that they may not have noticed before.

You will learn that your ability to be intentional and directed in group work will increase markedly through understanding and mastery of the concepts in this chapter. In particular, your cultural intentionality will increase as you gain clarity in how to introduce and attend to broader dimensions of the diversity that you will find in each group experience.

In this chapter, you will have the opportunity to accomplish the following objectives of understanding and mastery:

▲ Understand and master the skills of focusing, pacing, leading, and linking.
▲ Utilize focusing, pacing, leading, and linking concepts to observe group process.
▲ Apply the skills to your own group practice.

## WARM-UP EXERCISE*

In this warm-up exercise and throughout the chapter, we will illustrate focusing-related skills through transcript examples interspersed throughout. Some examples ask you to respond in your own style, while others illustrate possibilities for leader action. Each example is numbered and as a practice exercise at the conclusion of the chapter, you will be asked to classify the focus of the leader and member responses.

Imagine you are leading a group and you're in the fifth session. Recently, there's been some conflict between Robert and Monique. At the present moment, Robert is telling the story of an unhappy childhood. Most of the group is leaning forward with interest, but Monique has a pained look on her face and is leaning back with her arms crossed.

1. *Robert:* . . . So that is how it was—whenever I tried hardest and needed the most help, my dad simply was never there.
2. *Jessica:* Oh, Robert, I feel so sad hearing your story. My dad died when I was five and it just makes me want to cry. I remember the last time I saw him . . .
3. *Brett:* Jessica, you are taking the group off topic. I can really see the need for you to talk now, but can't you wait until Robert finishes?
4. (Jessica sits back and starts to cry.)

*An interesting exercise for classrooms or workshops is to conduct a fish bowl in which volunteers take the role of the group members represented in the brief warm-up script and a role-played leader is added. The volunteers can read the script aloud and take the role of the members, improvising where this situation might go given various leader responses.

---

5. *Monique:* Robert, I think you are full of it. You always want to get everybody's attention. I'm tired of you being so phony. And (more gently), Brett, how could you do that to Jessica?

6. As group leader, what would you say and where would you focus your comments? Write what you think you might say here:

_____

_____

_____

_____

_____

---

Look back at what you wrote. Where did you focus your comments? On Robert, to see where he is after being interrupted? On Jessica, both to support her and to suggest that she might wait until a bit later to talk about her issues? Was Brett's comment appropriate? Should you challenge or support Monique? What about the interaction of the subgroups? At what point do you work on the conflict between Robert and Monique and how can you help Jessica become more sensitive in the timing of her comments? There is a total group as well. What's occurring for them in this discourse? You might want to encourage them to share their observations.

What was the right answer? In truth, all the above issues and more need to be attended to—there is a lot happening right now in this group. But we obviously can't do it all at once. We need to listen to and pace each member of the group, important subgroups, and the group process as a whole. Our decisions around how to listen and how to focus will determine the effectiveness of our group work.

The next step is perhaps the most difficult of all. We need to address the conflict between Robert and Monique. This subgroup conflict can disrupt the group. We might begin by asking Robert how he felt in response to Monique's comment. We also need to listen to Monique and her concerns in some detail. At times, we may need to know what happened in the past to help us understand what is happening now. These stories of the past may relate to present behavior. Having heard the stories and examined the present interaction between the two, we can then focus on the group as a whole and ask them for their feedback and impressions—"How does the group react to Monique and Robert?" Then as Monique and Robert receive feedback from the group, we become involved in a recycling process in which all members learn continuously from one another the impact of what they say and do.

The remainder of this chapter describes in more detail the concepts of focusing, pacing, and leading. We start with the concepts of pacing and leading as they provide a framework for understanding the power of the focusing microskills.

## DEFINING THE LEADERSHIP SKILLS OF PACING AND LEADING

Another term for pacing is *being with.* The caring and effective leader seeks to be with and empathize with each member of the group, pairs and subgroups, and the group itself. In individual counseling, empathy is often defined as walking in another person's moccasins or as seeing the world through another person's eyes. Pacing and empathic understanding in groups place considerable demands on the leader—and group members as well.

Pacing is another way to describe the art of listening and focusing on what is occurring in your group. As group leader, you want to pace by listening to what individuals are saying, hearing the patterns of what subgroups are saying, and "walking with" the group as a whole. There are individual stories, subgroup plots, and holistic group narratives, all occurring at once. The microskills of attending and the basic listening sequence (discussed in the next chapter) are particularly important in the art of pacing.

The difficult exchange among group members presented at the beginning of this chapter suggests that the leader may not have spent enough time building trust. Warm-up exercises and finding something positive in each group member are specific ways that can prevent harsh exchanges in the group. At the same time, these challenging group moments are also the opportunity for significant learning for all members.

Trust building can be the result of effective pacing and listening. Trust building is particularly important in the early stages of a group. As leaders, we all need to remember that each person brings something useful to the group experience. Certain individuals may be especially sensitive to others with a similar life issue as they may have "been there" themselves, and some are very helpful with constructive feedback that leads to change. The effective leader gradually learns the talents of each group and helps the members use them effectively both to learn about themselves and to help others grow. The more you can help members feel that they are a valued part of the group, the less resistance and problems you will find as the group meets rough spots and conflict.

Chapter 4 will review the basic listening sequence, the microskills of pacing. At the most basic level, think of pacing as encouraging the individual, subgroup, or group to develop their own story and their own style. If you use effective listening skills in a warm, caring, and empathic fashion, many of the problems of group work will solve themselves. There is a basic and fundamental axiom of group work that we all need to recall: "When in doubt about what to do, listen."

Some basic pacing statements come to mind and you may want to take special note of them as they can focus on the individual, the subgroup, and the group itself.

---

7. Could you tell us more?
8. What is going on between the two of you?
9. What's happening in the group right now?

---

And for all occasions the next two responses are useful for all types of group focus:

---

10. What else could you say about that?
11. Have we missed something important?

---

For the moment, we would suggest that you simply be aware if you are pacing and listening to the group, subgroup, or individual and appropriately seek to balance listening to all three of these dimensions. For example, subgroups can at times be subversive to the group process. While this needs to be attended to, your major goal may be to change the focus back to groups and a balance between an individual and group focus.

When you pace the group, you seek to minimize your influence on what happens, but even the act of listening has an influence. For example, if you listen to or focus your comments on the individual, the subgroup, or the group, you are already taking an active influencing role. We all need to be aware that even the best listener is in some way leading the group. There is no way for a leader *not* to lead a group.

Nonetheless, leading is a more active dimension of group leadership. You need to decide what you're going to do and when you're going to do it. That decision may involve listening to the group and its members, but it also demands that you have some ideas in mind about where the group is heading and why.

Leading the group focus is best done through first listening and pacing. Then having heard individuals, subgroups, and the group as a whole, you can more easily lead them in new directions. Moreover, most authorities agree that groups require active leadership. One of the roots of leadership is to help the group focus and find a balance of individual, subgroup, and group emphasis. The influencing skills introduced later in the book are all dimensions of effective leading. You will find, however, that the way one listens and focuses attention is a special type of leading skill.

Let us return to our group conflict. Here are some examples of pacing and leading skills that the leader could use with varying results. Note in each of the examples that there is often some leading in pacing while effective leading requires pacing.

---

12. *Leader pacing Robert:* I hear your story and we all hear it. Your dad was such an important person to you. And no matter how hard you tried, it simply did not work. I see and hear your pain and the group does as well. Just look around and see the support you have. What else might you want to say to us?
13. *Pacing Robert and Jessica:* Let's return to Robert and Jessica. Could we hear what's occurring for the two of you right now?
14. *Pacing the group:* I've seen a lot of things going on in the group while Robert told his story. Could some of you share what is going on with us as a total group?

---

Again, while all the above comments are focused on pacing and learning how individuals, subgroups, and the group are taking in and processing information, the decision to focus is itself a leading skill.

Now examine the following leading interventions and think how they are based on pacing and empathic understanding:

---

15. *Leader leading the individual:* Robert, the group has listened to you carefully. Could you share right now some of your thoughts and feelings toward the group?

---

16. *Leading the subgroup:* Robert and Jessica, would the two of you talk directly to each other about your thoughts and feelings as you've experienced each other in the last few minutes? (Each one starts to talk to the leader with their concerns.) . . . No, don't talk to me; tell each other what you want to say directly. And I'd really like you to focus on what you see and hear the other person feeling at this moment. Once we've got the feelings clear, we can move on from there.
17. *Leading the group:* As Robert and Jessica talk, I'd like the group to think about your own reactions to what is happening. What occurs for you at this moment? We can share this later.

Clearly, each comment of the facilitator leads in a specific direction and would tend to make something very different happen in the group. The examination of what goes on with the individual, what goes on between individuals, and what occurs in the larger group is a fascinating and never-ending process. Individual counseling too often locates the problem in the individual and when a counselor is faced with conflict, he or she may miss the deeper complexity that group counseling offers. Group work makes possible both intrapersonal and interpersonal growth.

Chapters 6 and 7 provide many suggestions for leading interventions, but for the moment, we are suggesting that you take the deliberate use of focusing as a way to lead your group to a more evenly balanced discussion. For example:

18. We've been listening to one person's issues for quite awhile now. Let us turn our focus to the group and what has been going on for all of us during this time. (Group)
19. Could we move the focus from the group now to the reactions between Brett and Samantha? Both of you have been very quiet. There seems to be something going on there. What would you like to say? (Subgroup, emphasis on two individuals)
20. Perhaps it is now time to hear from Jessica. You've been very patient. (Individual)

Most likely, Jessica needs the most attention at the moment. Her tearful response to Robert was important to her. The other possibilities likely should wait until her issues are worked through. In the fast-moving world of group work, you can take many directions, and it would easily be possible to miss the importance of Jessica's needs. The effective leader stays alert and paces the member(s) who most need attention at a particular moment in time.

By now, you may be realizing that the leader, even by pacing and listening, exerts a real influence on the group and group process. This is true—we cannot help but influence. Let us hope that we always influence a group with sensitivity, caring, warmth, and empathy.

## DEFINING THE LEADERSHIP SKILLS OF FOCUSING

At this point, the idea of focusing on the group, subgroups, and individuals is likely quite clear. As you know, very different types of group discussion will result from how we focus our interventions and how we listen. There are group leaders who focus only on individuals, giving minimal attention to group interactions. In our opinion this is not group counseling or group therapy, but rather it is therapy or counseling in a group. Experienced group leaders often talk about the "wheel" in which the focus of group discussion will move from one individual to another. There is nothing wrong with this form of therapy, but it can miss the uniqueness and power of the group. Box 3.1 illustrates the wheel. Note how the leader focuses on one individual while other group members also provide comments. After "work" is completed with one person, the wheel turns and another person becomes the focus.

**Box 3.1**    *The Wheel: Focusing on the Individual*

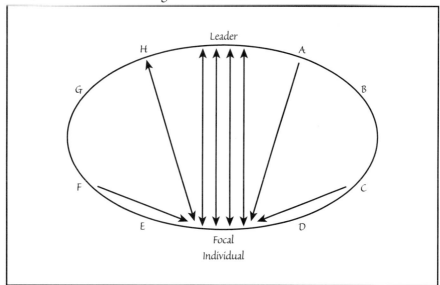

In this section, we would like to expand the focus concept by adding some new dimensions. These may be best illustrated by a concrete example. Let us assume that Robert and Monique have resolved and understood their conflict. Each told her or his story and recognized the other person's feelings, gave each other feedback, and then listened to the group's observations. They resolved their differences and the group moved on.

> 21. *The leader then comments:* Well, we all seem to be feeling somewhat better. We've gone through some difficult and hurtful times, but seem to have come out whole. I appreciate that most of you have been able to share something in this process. Let us stop for moment now and reflect on what just happened.

Here are the three basic focus possibilities:

> 22. *Focus on individual:* Samantha, during this whole discussion, you've seemed to be very tense and concerned. Could you share with us what has been going on for you?
> 23. *Focus on subgroup:* Thalia and Roberta, you seemed to be particularly involved when Monique was talking and at times you seemed to tighten up when Robert told his story. Could the two of you share your thoughts and feelings?
> 24. *Focus on group:* Group, let us think about how we're operating as a group together. How is each of us affecting what happens in our group and how is the group affecting us?

At this point, you may want to return to these three responses and think through which you personally believe might be most appropriate.

Often, people come to groups with particular problems or to work through specific issues that concern them. There's a real need to focus on specific challenges faced by individuals and by the group as a whole. The talking through of problems and difficulties in a group can be particularly helpful.

The multiple dimensions of focus are summarized in Box 3.2. These dimensions are part of the Ivey Taxonomy (IT), a system to facilitate process observation of both member and leader verbal interaction in the group (Ivey, 1973; Ivey & Ivey, 1999). Further classifications using the IT will be provided as we move through this book. Intentional use of the IT provides you with some prediction of what might happen when you use certain types of leads in the group. For example, if you focus on individuals in the there-and-then, your group members can be predicted to talk about things they have experienced outside the group. If you focus on the here-and-now and the group itself, anticipate that group members will follow your focus.

Sherrard (1973) found, for example, that a human relations group responded to fifty-five individually focused leader statements with fifty-four individually focused comments (Carkhuff, 1971). (There was only one group-focused leader comment in the transcript.) In another instance, a group therapy leader focused all his leads on the group and members followed his lead only about 25% of the time (Goldberg, 1970). This may be best explained by the fact that members of groups have not had experience in thinking about themselves as part of a group. The individualistic tradition in the cultures of the Western world leads us all to think of ourselves as individuals and talking about ourselves as *selves-in-relation* is often a new task. Nonetheless, note that the second group examined itself as a group at least some of the time whereas the individually focused group did not do this at all.

**Box 3.2**    *Focusing Observation Form: A Three-Dimensional View*

Note that each focus statement by a leader or by a group member can be classified as to content focus and time focus. Moreover, it is possible in a single statement to have multiple content focus and multiple time dimensions. When classifying group verbal statements, you need to select the predominant content and time focus dimensions, but also include other aspects that are present. Finally, watch constantly for aspects of linking that can be contained in any leader or member comment.

*Content Focus Dimensions*

Group

Subgroup

Individual

Main theme, problem, concern, or issue

Group leader

Cultural/environmental/contextual issues:
   Moral/spiritual/religious context

   Economic/social context

   Family context

   Community context

   Multicultural context

Other contextual issues:
   Health, workplace concerns, leisure time opportunities, issues of aging or youth, experiences with trauma (rape, cancer, violence, war, family death), and many others

*Time Focus Dimensions*

Here-and-now

There-and-then

*Linking*

Note here any instances of linking here-and-now with the there-and-then, linking of individual and group themes and patterns, or other linked focus dimensions.

Focusing is also related to the issue of structuring groups. Dies (1994) reviewed the literature of leader variables in effective groups and found that structured groups tend to be more effective than unstructured ones. Particularly important is providing clarity and structure in the early stages of group process. Once a positive norm is established, most groups will continue as they started. It is also possible to overstructure and overfocus a group. The leader who helps a group focus appropriately in the initial stages has a good start toward a series of positive sessions. Dies (1994, p. 129) comments that leaders "should gradually reduce their level of activity and the focus of their structuring as group members improve in their understanding of the therapeutic (*counseling*) task and their role in helping each other." At times of challenge and crisis in the group, the effective leader will help group members focus appropriately. Chapter 5 on theme-centered groups explores this issue in further detail.

It is a fairly safe prediction that if we focus on individuals in our groups, our members will focus on themselves. We can also predict that they will respond to a theme or topic focus. And we can predict that if leaders don't speak to the group as a whole or to other areas such as the cultural/environmental context, these topics usually will not appear prominently in the group.

Although we can make predictions from our leader behavior, we cannot be sure that members will respond the way we predict (see the group therapy review reported by Dies above). Thus, intentional group leadership requires that we flex and change our style to meet the constantly changing atmosphere and tone in the current group. Intentionality in group leadership asks you to anticipate what will happen in response to your leadership style, but—perhaps even more important—that you be ready with another response when what is predicted doesn't happen.

Now, let us examine four additional focus dimensions.

## Focus on the Main Theme, Problem, Concern, or Issue

This focus theme will be elaborated in more detail in the following section. Many groups are organized around a main theme or central topic. The main theme of a cancer survivor's group is cancer; an Alcoholics Anonymous group focuses on alcohol abuse; a women's or men's group concentrates on gender issues. In these groups, a large percentage of time is focused on joint concerns and issues.

This chapter presents a group oriented to a counseling theme—how our behavior in the group relates to experience outside the group. When here-and-now interaction in the group is identified as related to there-and-then experience in the real world, this is termed linking.* See the example below.

---

25. We have spent considerable time now exploring individual stories, and we've discovered that many of us behave here-and-now in the group in some way similar to the way we have behaved in the past. Where are you all now on the idea that how we behave in the group relates to our past behavior in other situations? And what about the idea that what we learn now in this group can be transferred outside to new behaviors and feelings in the there-and-then of the real world?

---

*This is just one example of linking. The issue will be discussed in more detail later in this chapter.

A comment such as this one helps both individuals and the total group reflect on themselves and the central learning issue of the group. The comment also balances the here-and-now and the there-and-then, facilitating further linking of the two.

## Focus on the Group Leader

A major question faced by beginning group workers is how much they should share of themselves. Leaders can at times focus on themselves, usually in the form of feedback or self-disclosure. Our suggestion is that you be yourself, but it is generally considered best to keep the focus on the leader for only a short time. By engaging in self-disclosure and providing feedback, you as leader model risk taking and may facilitate members to share themselves more openly. At the same time, this needs to be done carefully as group members can be threatened or frightened at times by leader openness.

> 26. May I share some of my own reactions and thoughts about what's going on in our group? I find myself deeply impressed by your openness and willingness to explore some difficult issues and at times have felt tearful myself. I really appreciate the way we've been able to get through this hard spot. How do others feel about what we've been going through? (Feedback with some self-disclosure)

Note that the leader in the example above threw the issue back to the group almost immediately. This self-disclosure is an example of keeping the leader talk-time relatively low. Your own sharing is best if it is brief, positive, and easy to understand. Be particularly careful of negative feedback—the leader is often a very powerful person in the group and a comment from you may be received very differently from that of another group member.

## Focus on Cultural/Environmental/Contextual Issues

The cultural/environmental/contextual focus is one that can greatly enrich the group and bring about increased awareness of how the there-and-then of life outside the group affects the here-and-now of immediate group experience. The cultural/environmental/contextual focus could be illustrated in many ways besides the gender example below.

> 27. One of the things I have noted in this group is that men have been doing most of the talking. Men have interrupted women's conversations a number of times, but the women here have seldom interrupted anyone. Could we talk for a while about the gender roles we're playing out here?

Following are more possibilities for focusing within the cultural/environmental context. All of these will facilitate broader discussion and may become the major theme of the group for a period of time.

28. *Moral/spiritual/religious context:* How do our ethical/spiritual traditions speak to the crisis we are facing? Would you be willing to share some of your experiences in this area?

29. *Economic/social context:* One of the issues in our group has been continued unemployment among some of our members. How does that affect the way a person interacts with others? Social class is a difficult issue, not easy for many North Americans to talk about. Can we really explore this area?

30. *Family context:* Many of us enact the roles that we learned in our family of origin. So would you like to share how your behavior in this group has been similar to what you might be doing in your own family?

31. *Community context:* We learned much of our being in our communities, particularly in the communities where we grew up. Could some of you share some stories from your family, friends, church, school, or other important group that occur to you as they might relate to this group experience?

32. *Multicultural context:* The original comment on gender relations in the group is a multicultural contextual focus. Another one would be this: we are all ethnic/racial beings. This affects our worldview, the way others see us, and the way we interact in this group. As a way to start a discussion of this area, would each of you share in groups of three a story telling when you discovered the importance of your ethnicity or race? Then we can have a report on what you learn. Please share a positive story, one that gives you some sense of pride. Then we can share the stories in a larger group and think about the meaning of them together.

## Focus on Other Contextual Issues

These would be issues about health, the workplace, leisure time opportunities, aging or youth, traumatic experiences (rape, cancer, violence, war), and many others.

As you can see, when we approach the cultural/environmental/contextual area, issues are going to vary widely in the group. Each of us is a multicultural being affected deeply by our experience in social context. If you are gay, lesbian, bisexual, or transgendered, it very much impacts the way you react and are reacted to in the group. If you are a conservative Christian participating in a group, it very much impacts the way you react and are reacted to in the group. If you were raised in a family in which alcoholism was present, it very much impacts the way you react and are reacted to in the group. All these actions and reactions can occur without your awareness or the awareness of the group and leader. But these many multicultural factors are always there in the group.

## DEFINING THE LEADERSHIP SKILLS OF HERE-AND-NOW AND THERE-AND-THEN

An important type of focusing is represented by here-and-now and there-and-then leader comments. The group provides a powerful opportunity for participants to learn how their behavior is received and perceived by others. Thus, focusing is a multiple concept. You can focus on the individual, subgroup, or total group in the here-and-now, or you can focus on experience from the there-and-then, as you see in these examples:

> 33. *Here-and-now subgroup focus:* Let's return to Robert and Jessica. Could we hear what is occurring for you at this moment?
> 34. *There-and-then subgroup focus:* Let's return to Robert and Jessica. Could each of you share what occurs for you when you think of your interaction in this group? Do you get into the same type of situations with other people in your daily life?
> 35. *Here-and-now group focus:* What's occurring inside you right now as you listen to Robert and Jessica?
> 36. *There-and-then individual focus:* Jessica, would you like to tell us more about your family situation and what's going on at home?
> 37. *Here-and-now individual focus:* Brett, you've been quiet quite awhile since you had that conflict with women in this group. What's going on with you right now?

Here-and-now discussion in the group emphasizes what is happening in the immediate moment. Many group leaders, especially those facilitating person-centered personal growth groups, stress the importance of keeping discussion centered on what is occurring here-and-now in the group. In such groups, discussing what is happening "outside in the real world" enables the group members to avoid looking at their own interaction style.

There-and-then discussion in the group occurs when members talk about events outside the group. This often occurs when members tell stories about personal experience, challenges they may have faced, or feelings they had in regard to significant others outside the group. The potential problem with there-and-then discussion is that group members are never able to get feedback about their own immediate behavior in the group session. There-and-then discussion can even be a way to avoid looking at oneself. On the other hand, the there-and-then is where we have learned our ways of thinking, feeling, and behaving. And it is to the real world that we shall return.

## Linking

You and your group members will often note that individual behavior in the here-and-now of the group often relates to an incident that the person may have told us about outside the group. *What is said and done in the group closely parallels life outside the group.* Regardless of the group theory you endorse, the link between the two will appear. At times, you will simply observe it and say nothing. At other times, helping group members find links between the external world and the internal life of the group will be central.

Linking is an important leadership skill that can help members work more as a group and focus less on you as leader. If you find group members looking to you too much for leadership and focusing on leader-member interaction, you can help them move to member-member conversation by linking themes and patterns among group members. Corey (2000, p. 44) comments:

> Encourage members to address others in the group directly rather than looking at the leader and talking about others who are present. Members often have shared concerns, and through talking to others with similar concerns, and

through effective linking they can be helped to work through their problems by talking to others with similar concerns. By being alert for common concerns, the leader can promote interaction and increase the level of group cohesion.

One specific way to facilitate this type of linking is to ask members to speak directly to each other rather than just to you as leader. For example, if the member is talking to you about the group, you might say, "I hear you; could you look at the group and say it directly to them?" To facilitate the sharing of common concerns, "Jessica, you and Robert both seem to share similar thoughts and feelings about loss. Could you just talk to other each now for a few minutes? And, I'd like the group itself to think about themes of loss and how we can support each other. We can talk about that after Jessica and Robert."

Linking also appears frequently as the group thinks more carefully about cultural/environmental/contextual issues. The group member may come to realize that a conflictual aggressive style shown in the group session is closely related to a family history in which the family members resolved conflict with direct argument. The person who tries to please or to mediate to stop interpersonal conflict in the group may discover that this was her or his role in the family of origin. We often tend to repeat what we have learned in our past in the here-and-now of the group—and in our patterns today in our own families and relationships.

As one example of here-and-now and there-and-then linking, think of how your family handled arguments. Now reflect on how you resolve arguments with important people today, perhaps in personal relationships or in business. Particularly, how does it work with your loved one—the person closest to you at present? How are the arguments similar? How are they different? Is there a link between the past and the present? Put your reflections below.* You may want to follow up on this brief exercise by checking with others in your class or group. This exercise helps to clarify the importance of the linking concept.

---

---

---

---

---

---

There is also linking between here-and-now behavior and many cultural/environmental/contextual issues. Vietnam and Gulf war veterans, for example, have often discovered through veterans' groups that personal distress and their daily behavior are related to traumas of war. Women learn that individual behavior is linked to

---

*We have used this exercise on the concept of linking and how the there-and-then relates to the here-and-now extensively in our groups. It is often a useful stimulus to further discussion and understanding.

cultural sexism. Lesbians learn that homophobia and discrimination may lead to internal self-doubt. African Americans may discover that their hypertension and high blood pressure are linked to societal prejudice.

In the following exchange, note that Brett's behavior in the here-and-now of the group consists primarily of analysis and abstract intellectualizing. He learned that behavior as a survival skill in his intellectually demanding but cold family of origin. The process of discovery of the links usually takes longer than the edited and shortened version below. Note that the leader encourages group feedback and a balance of here-and-now and there-and-then statements to encourage self-discovery.

---

37. (This leader comment is repeated from above) *Leader:* Brett, you've been quiet quite awhile since you had that conflict with women in this group. What's going on with you right now? (Here-and-now, individual focus)
38. *Brett:* Yes, I've been quiet, but I've been thinking. (pause) Well, as I think about it, it seems to me that the best way to survive in this world is to observe what is happening and analyze it as carefully as possible. As I look at this group, I wonder if all this emphasis on what you call immediacy and here-and-now isn't just another way to defend and protect yourself. Freud would call what you are doing here merely a defense mechanism, most likely. (There-and-then which specifically avoids here-and-now, focuses on theme and group)
39. *Jessica:* Brett, there you go again, just like yesterday when I saw you in class. Always analyzing and coming on to us as so superior. Small wonder you have difficulty getting along in this group. (Here-and-now reaction, focusing on individual and group)
40. *Brett:* (Looks startled, pauses and slows down) Now, Jessica, I see you wanting to change everyone. You want everyone to be like you. (There-and-then in that he defends himself by generalizing Jessica's behavior, focus on individual)
41. *Leader:* Brett, may we try something? Would you be willing to have the members of the group give feedback of impressions that they have of you so far? It might be helpful. (Here-and-now, focus on Brett as individual and the group as whole)
42. *Brett:* (nervously) Well, OK, but it won't make a difference in what I do. (Here-and-now, individual-focus)
43. *Leader:* I'd like for all of you to share your impressions of Brett in this group, but before each of you does, I want you to share something positive you have noted about Brett. OK? (Here-and-now and there-and-then, focus on group)
44. *Robert:* You're a really bright guy, Brett—and sometimes you have some really helpful insights into what is going on. Yet, somehow you come across as if you are at a distance. I think I'd like to get to know you better. (Here-and-now, focus on individual)
45. *Jessica:* I agree with Robert. You've got a lot of strengths. I feel kind of frightened by all your intelligence, almost as if you are seeing through me sometimes. (Here-and-now, focus on individual)

(The remainder of the group provides similar feedback for about five minutes.)

46. *Leader:* Brett, what's occurring for you right now? (Here-and-now, individual focus)

47. *Brett:* I don't know what to say. I guess I think through things pretty carefully, but it seems to distance me from the group. (Here-and-now, individual focus)

48. *Leader:* Brett, you really haven't told us much about yourself. Could you share a story? (Here-and-now, individual focus also encouraging a there-and-then response)

(Brett shares a story of a conflictual family in which the only way to survive was to observe and analyze.)

49. *Jessica:* So Brett, what I hear you saying is that you learned in your family that it isn't safe to feel, that emotions are dangerous. Small wonder you don't want to open up with us all that much. (Here-and-now and there-and-then linked through individual and family focus)

50. *Leader:* What you are doing in the group is pretty much what you did in the family. (Here-and-now and there-and-then linked through individual and family focus)

Through telling his story and receiving feedback from the group, Brett was able to start the process of learning to live more immediately in the here-and-now. Brett's intellectualizing style was learned as a survival skill in the family of origin and repeated itself in the group.

Linking the past to the present is one useful outcome that can happen in groups. But all this is relatively meaningless unless what is learned is transferred to the future in terms of new ways of thinking, feeling, and behaving. The group experience offers a safe place to test new ways of thinking, feeling, and behaving.

Depending on the type of group you're running, you'll find that at times it is best to focus on here-and-now interaction while other times it is more appropriate to emphasize the there-and-then. The there-and-then becomes important when we really need to hear other people's stories from outside the group. Often we need to learn how what is going on or has gone on outside the group affects what one does inside.

Examples of the above will occur when you are facilitating a women's support group dealing with harassment; a discussion group of bisexual members focusing on their difficulties in a dominantly heterosexual world; a group of Christian, Orthodox Jewish, or Muslim students living on a secular campus. The members in each of these widely varying groups need to tell their stories and how discrimination or lack of understanding in the here-and-now of the group or campus life affects and is affected by there-and-then experience in their home communities.

If you are facilitating a problem-solving or theme-centered group, a part of the discussion may need to focus on the there-and-then and how to transfer ideas learned in the group to the "real world." For example, a theme-centered support group working with those who may have cancer, AIDS, or eating problems is very likely to need discussion of what is going on outside the group as well as examination of immediate group process through the here-and-now.

Balancing there-and-then and here-and-now dimensions is something you'll face throughout your work with groups. Some groups will give more attention to the here-and-now, and others to the there-and-then. Most groups, however, will benefit from emphasizing the here-and-now. What is most important, perhaps, is that you maintain constant awareness of this issue, examine your own group leadership style, and at times discuss the matter with your group.

In this chapter, the leader has chosen predominantly here-and-now comments, although the contextual issues were often related to there-and-then issues. The leader has encouraged participants to share stories from the outside, but you will note that the leader also gave considerable attention to how group members interacted with each other in the here-and-now. For example, Brett's there-and-then story brings about here-and-now immediate feelings in Jessica.

## USING PACING, LEADING, AND FOCUSING SKILLS WITH CHILD AND ADOLESCENT GROUPS

It is important to pace and listen carefully in all groups. Unless you make an effort to hear fully what is said, errors of understanding and distortion can easily occur. In short, even with the youngest children, take time to hear their stories, their concerns, and their problems.

With young children, be especially careful to avoid leading questions or the story they tell may be what they think you want to hear. Often children will turn your overly leading questions into a new view of the situation, and that view may be what you have infused in them, rather than their own. Seek to avoid putting your ideas into children. With adolescents, the natural conflict that many have with authority makes leading questions on your part less of a problem. Nonetheless, the leader remains a powerful figure and pacing carefully before leading remains essential.

With young children, you will find that they often respond best to a focus on individuals and the theme of the group (friendship group, divorce group, social skills). Subgroups of two or three children who have conflict or interests in common is often a useful focus. You will find it difficult for young children to focus on the group as a totality. While children can learn from stories told by other children, they may have difficulty in understanding and/or generalizing from what is happening in the larger group.

Reading relevant stories of how other children have dealt with problems can be helpful. For example, *Dinosaurs Divorce: A Guide for Changing Families* (Brown & Brown, 1986) has become a counseling classic. Clever cartoons of a small dinosaur coupled with real problems that children face provide helpful guidance. The divorce theme then can be individualized with the children in the group as they are encouraged to share their thoughts and feelings more openly.

But you cannot forget to observe group process—children's groups are *groups,* often with as many problems and opportunities as any other group. You may find it necessary to bring out the quiet child or to use constructive discipline to help the acting-out child. You will find that some young people's groups are very similar to larger groups, particularly when you engage in more structured psychoeducational or task group leadership.

Adolescent groups, for the most part, can be expected to function in a fashion parallel to that of adults. They will respond to all focus dimensions, even cultural/environmental/contextual issues. The divorce group is often used in school and community work to help teens share the issues they face.

Here-and-now and there-and-then leadership is less important with children. Your task is to help them feel comfortable in the here-and-now and, where necessary, help them plan for transfer of behavior to the there-and-then of family or classroom. Adolescents, on the other hand, will be able to work in both dimensions and will find it helpful although linking here-and-now behavior to the there-and-then may be difficult for less cognitively complex adolescents to understand.

## MOVING TOWARD YOUR OWN LEADERSHIP STYLE

This chapter has presented focusing as a vital part of effective group leadership. Groups that work realize that indeed they are groups. Perhaps the most important focus is that of the group itself. Group counseling is about what happens to us when we live in groups. We're all members of multiple groups—families, friendship groups, work groups, living groups, and many others.

While many ideas are presented in this chapter, we would like to focus on three concepts as we conclude: (1) if you are working with groups, remember that word *group* and include that focus periodically—or, as we suggested, you may end up doing counseling with an audience; (2) here-and-now focus tends to bring out the power of the group; (3) the cultural/environmental/contextual focus is important in understanding the background in which we all live. It is these dimensions that bring us to an understanding of the self-in-relation within a multicultural context.

Think back on this section and the entire chapter. What have you learned here? What points struck you as most important? What stood out for you? What would you like to work on in the area of focusing, pacing, leading, and linking to improve your own group facilitation?

_____

_____

_____

_____

_____

_____

_____

_____

_____

_____

## PRACTICING FOCUSING, PACING, AND LEADING SKILLS

### 1. Classifying Focus Dimensions

Mastering focus concepts requires you to be able to identify and classify them with some accuracy. Ultimately, you want to be able to observe how your group is focusing its conversation and to act intentionally to help them explore other relevant focuses. Practicing classification through process observation of groups will facilitate your ability later when you actually facilitate a group.

Box 3.2 presents a systematic way to classify focusing. Using this system, go back and classify all the numbered leader and member comments presented in this chapter. It will be easiest if you do your classification on a separate piece of paper. Then compare your classification with ours presented at the end of the practice exercises. Many of the leads are already identified in the text, try to ignore these as you practice classification.

### 2. Process Observation of Focus Dimensions

Observe your own use of the focusing process. We encourage you to take Box 3.2 and observe the multiple dimensions of focusing in action. Specifically, find a group to observe and then record the focus of each member's comments. You might observe such groups as these:

▲ A structured or unstructured group session somehow related to the counseling process
▲ An elementary or secondary school counseling group
▲ A videotape of group interaction—a professional tape or one developed in your own class

If none of the above is available to you, consider observing a town meeting, a faculty meeting, or some other open meeting. You might sit back from a family dinner table and observe how focus works there. You may find that the friendship groups are places where you can observe the process interaction.

Of course, the most valuable of all would be for you to videotape or audiotape your own group and note and classify your own use of the focusing skills.

### 3. The Fish Bowl

Again, four to six class members form a group in front of the larger class and engage in a ten- to fifteen-minute group session. This is to be a leaderless group. The suggested topic is hassles provided by the administrative authority. This could be registration at a college or university, dealing with a government agency, or the complications of dealing with a large company.

Another possible way to approach the fish bowl is to have group members read part of the transcript presented in this chapter as if it were a play and then continue spontaneously role-playing the parts for an extra ten minutes before debriefing.

The group is to start the conversation and talk for about three minutes. Then, someone from the observer group should ask them to change focus in their discussion. For example, start with a focus on an individual, then change focus to the total group's reaction to what that individual has said. Every two minutes, the group will be asked to change to another focus. This may enable increased awareness of the multiple interpretations that can be made of the same event.

## 4. Your Own Group Practice

The following exercise can be done in class or you may elect to find a group outside of class and practice on your own. If you cannot have an observer watch your group work, try to audiotape or videotape the session.

If you're working in a classroom or workshop, the following steps are recommended:

1. Divide into groups of five or six. One person serves as leader and another as observer.
2. Select a topic for the small groups. A suggested topic for the small group is interpersonal conflict. This can be conflict in the past or, if the group is willing, the active discussion of conflict in the here-and-now. If you select a topic from the past, it is important to consider how you can integrate here-and-now thinking into the discussion.
3. Ten to fifteen minutes may be used for the small groups. Allow five minutes for feedback from the observer. Finally, the entire small group can discuss their own group process.

Where possible, add videorecording and practice to your work with attending skills and observation. You will always obtain very useful feedback on yourself and the group. Always obtain informed consent from members.

## CLASSIFICATION OF FOCUS DIMENSIONS

1. Individual, there-and-then
2. Individual, there-and-then, here-and-now
3. Individual, group, here-and-now
4. (Cries, nonspecified) here-and-now
5. Individual, here-and-now
6. How do you classify your own focus in the warm-up exercise?
7. "Could you tell us more?" is an encouraging open question that can be used effectively with individuals, subgroups, and groups in the here-and-now or there-and-then. The pronoun *us* helps relate the individual ("me") to the group.
8. Subgroup, here-and-now
9. Group, here-and-now
10. "What else" types of questions function in a similar fashion to 7 above.
11. "Have we missed something important?" has the same pattern as 7 and 10. Please note this question as a useful one near the end of an important individual, subgroup, or group interaction.
12. Individual and group, here-and-now
13. Subgroup, here-and-now
14. Group, here-and-now
15. Individual, group, here-and-now
16. Subgroup, here-and-now

17. Group, main theme/problem (conflict), here-and-now followed by attention to there-and-then
18. Group, here-and-now
19. Subgroup, here-and-now
20. Individual, here-and-now
21. Group, here-and-now related to there-and-then. The there-and-then in this case refers to past behavior and interaction in the group itself. It is not total here-and-now immediacy; but it is also clearly not there-and-then external world daily life issues. The group leader is asking the group to reflect on what has happened in the group.
22. Individual, here-and-now
23. Subgroup, here-and-now
24. Group, see 21
25. Group, see 21
26. Leader, see 21
27. Cultural/environmental context (CEC), here-and-now, there-and-then. The leader provides a brief, but important summary for the group and encourages reflection once again.
28. CEC/moral, spiritual, religious, there-and-then. Note that this lead and the following several leads tend to focus the group on there-and-then issues with implications for here-and-now behavior.
29. CEC/economic, social status, there-and-then, here-and-now
30. CEC/family, there-and-then, here-and-now
31. CEC/there-and-then, here-and-now
32. CEC/multicultural, there-and-then. This is an exercise that might be used in a structured group. The telling of positive stories from the there-and-then can provide group members with a safe opening to talk later about difficult issues of gender, race, or history of trauma (rape, experience of violence, being raised in an alcoholic or substance-abusing family).
33. Subgroup, here-and-now
34. Subgroup, there-and-then
35. Group, here-and-now
36. Individual, there-and-then
37. Individual, here-and-now
38. Group and theme, there-and-then
39. Individual and group, here-and-now
40. Individual, there-and-then
41. Individual and group, here-and-now
42. Individual, here-and-now
43. Group, here-and-now and there-and-then
44. Individual, here-and-now
45. Individual, here-and-now
46. Individual, here-and-now
47. Individual, here-and-now
48. Individual, here-and-now
49. Individual, cultural/environmental context (family), here-and-now
50. Individual, cultural/environmental context (family), here-and-now

Note that the leader in this chapter focused primarily on the here-and-now with some emphasis on there-and-then. Two types of there-and-then comments were presented. The first encourages reflection on what has happened in the group itself. While the interaction occurred in the visible "here-and-now" of the group, later reflection on the past or recent past is different from immediate experiencing. The second type of there-and-then leader style is more obvious: leader asks or encourages the group to talk about things outside the group from their daily life now to the more distant past.

## REFERENCES

Brown, L., & Brown, M. (1986). *Dinosaurs divorce.* Boston: Little, Brown.

Carkhuff, R. (1971). Demonstration protocol. Cited in G. Gazda, *Group counseling: A developmental approach.* Boston: Allyn & Bacon.

Corey, G. (2000). *Theory & practice of group counseling* (5th ed.). Pacific Grove, CA: Brooks/Cole.

Dies, R. (1994). Therapist variables in group psychotherapy research. In A. Fuhriman & G. Burlingame (Eds.), *Handbook of group psychotherapy* (pp. 114–155). New York: Wiley.

Goldberg, C. (1970). *Encounter: Group sensitivity training experience.* New York: Science House.

Ivey, A. (1973). Demystifying the group process: Adapting microcounseling procedures to counseling in groups. *Educational Technology, 13,* 27–31.

Ivey, A., & Ivey, M. (1999). *Intentional interviewing and counseling: Facilitating client development in a multicultural society* (4th ed.). Pacific Grove, CA: Brooks/Cole.

Sherrard, P. (1973). *Predicting group leader/member interaction: The efficacy of the Ivey Taxonomy.* Unpublished doctoral dissertation, University of Massachusetts, Amherst.

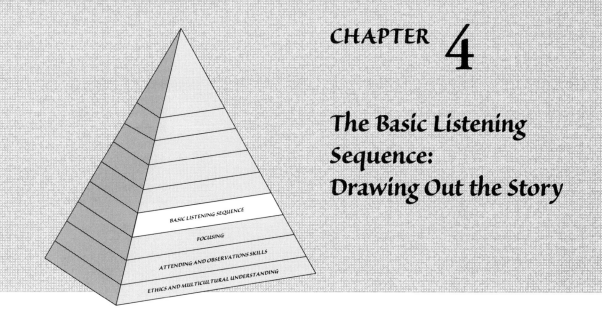

CHAPTER 4

BASIC LISTENING SEQUENCE
FOCUSING
ATTENDING AND OBSERVATIONS SKILLS
ETHICS AND MULTICULTURAL UNDERSTANDING

# The Basic Listening Sequence: Drawing Out the Story

## CHAPTER GOALS

Group members come to you with multiple stories. Each person's life history (the there-and-then) is significantly different from everyone else's, and each individual will also have a unique here-and-now experience in your group. A particular richness of work in groups is the sharing of different perspectives and ways of viewing the world. You will find significant personal gain for yourself and for group members as you all experience diversity.

The basic listening sequence (BLS) is a set of microskills that you will find valuable as you listen to individual stories of your group members. These skills will also help with the group story as it develops. You will find that the story the group members write together as they share their lives will often be a powerful narrative for personal development and change.

In a sense all group work is multicultural as each person brings her or his own background to the group. This is one of the reasons that group work is particularly useful for understanding the multiple issues of diversity. As part of this chapter, we will explore multicultural group counseling as a specific practice within the larger group framework.

> In this chapter, you will have the opportunity to accomplish the following objectives of understanding and mastery:
>
> ▲ Understand and master the basic listening sequence (BLS):
> Ask open and closed questions
> Encourage/restatement
> Paraphrase
> Reflect feelings
> Summarize

> These five microskills together may be used to draw out the key dimensions or facts of the story, the central emotions related to the story, and the manner in which the story is organized.
>
> ▲ Utilize the BLS within the Ivey Taxonomy to observe group process.
> ▲ Utilize the community genogram as a strategy to bring multicultural issues into the group as positive resources.
> ▲ Apply basic listening sequence concepts to your own group leadership.

## WARM-UP EXERCISE

What is multicultural group counseling? The first issue in this warm-up exercise is to define your own view of multicultural group counseling. Three major views or stories about this type of counseling are summarized below. We ask you to decide which of the following frameworks makes the most sense to you. This will be followed by an exercise to encourage exploration of yourself as a multicultural being.

One prominent definition of multicultural counseling argues for a precise definition—counselors and clients are distinguished by their membership in one of five racial-cultural categories: African American/Black, Asian American, Hispanic/Latina/o, Native American Indian/Indigenous, and White/European (Locke, 1990). Proponents of this position argue persuasively that this definition provides greater clarity and permits greater intentionality through its focus on stories of oppression and a legacy of racism. Some biracial or multiracial individuals may have difficulty categorizing themselves, preferring to identify with multiple ethnic/racial backgrounds related to their family history (Wehrly, 1996). This is an issue you may wish to discuss in the group.

Religious prejudice remains an important issue in the world and produces both personal sorrow and intergroup conflict. People of Jewish background have suffered indignities for centuries because of anti-Semitism and oppression. Another group with firsthand knowledge of oppression is women, who experience sexism on a daily basis. Among gay/lesbian/bisexual/transgendered teenagers, suicide is an important issue, a clear indicator of the problems they encounter.

Thus, another view argues for a broader frame of reference and would include multiple categories of race/ethnicity, language, gender, religion/spirituality, sexual orientation, age, physical issues, socioeconomic status, and other delineations (Fukuyama, 1990). In addition, personal experience of trauma (for example, war, rape, experience of abuse or neglect) may represent an additional cultural issue.

The frame of reference this book follows is that "all of the above" have relevance. Matters of race and ethnicity are indeed central issues because of the long history of oppression and neglect that has followed certain groups. Whiteness is clearly an economic and social advantage in many situations, and racism and oppression are background facts in any group with which you work, even if that group is all White. It is also important to recognize that a variety of contextual issues—for example, sexual orientation or spiritual issues—can be vital parts of the group experience. Everyone comes with a distinct cultural history impacted by the multiple cultural encounters he or she has experienced.

Thus, we are suggesting that all group experience is multicultural. But this broad definition can weaken the emphasis and time that may be spent on critical issues. There is real value in groups that focus on culturally specific issues such as race and gender. Our position is that at some times you as group leader will want to take the more specific definition of multicultural counseling while at others you may wish to use the broader definitions. Regardless of what you decide, it is essential that you have clarity in your definition of multicultural group work.

Take some time to summarize your own thoughts on this important issue and write them here. How do you personally see group counseling and multicultural dimensions? Which multicultural issues concern you most? What might be some of your blind spots?

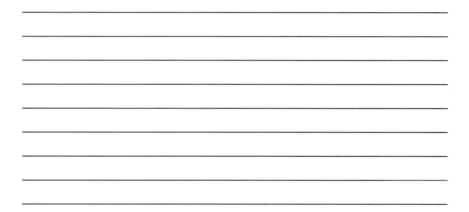

How might all this relate to you personally and how could you introduce these concepts into a group? One route is provided by the community genogram (see Box 4.1). The community genogram (Ivey, 1995; Ivey, Ivey, & Simek-Downing, 1997) is a positive strategy that encourages group members to examine themselves as people in relation to others. An important part of the community genogram is sharing positive stories from the community of origin (or other significant community from the past or present).

The individual exists in a cultural/environmental/contextual framework—the self-in-relation. Okechukwu Ogbonnya (1994) works from an Afrocentric perspective and extends this concept to the *person as community*. In effect, much of who we are is the sum of our past relationships with family, groups, and institutions, particularly as represented by our community of origin.

One of your critical tasks in all group work is to help your group members establish *contact* and learn to trust each other. The *contact hypothesis* (Amir, 1992) states that if you start your group with positive expectations and experiences, you are more likely to have less negativity and resistance and a more positive group result. This attitude becomes even more important with a culturally diverse group. Build early on a positive, cooperative group experience that provides support for all members. The use of positive exercises early in group work will help everyone talk and thus equalize status among your group members. If the group starts on a positive basis, members are more likely to have a foundation of trust; this base can make possible a more fruitful and positive discussion of difficult issues around self-disclosure and/or conflict within the group when they arise.

And how does this tie with the central goals of this chapter around the basic listening sequence? The BLS coupled with attending and focusing is central. We need to listen to others' experience in both the here-and-now *and* the there-and-then. Through contact and support, we can help each other build and grow together. Using the community genogram and storytelling, of course, is only one route toward a positive group session, but we hope you find it interesting and productive.

At this point, please take a break from reading the chapter and involve yourself in an active exercise to create your own personal community genogram. We learn culture in a community and family context—this really is our cultural/environmental/contextual background. Through the community genogram, you may gain an expanded understanding of your own cultural roots. And, as a leader, you can build trust and obtain an understanding of the cultural background of group members by using this exercise.

Note that Box 4.1 begins by asking you to "generate your own style of representing your community." This is an exercise that encourages creativity and individuality of expression. At the same time, it facilitates awareness that we are all members of multiple groups and we have a shared history as persons in a community. This common experience often helps group members bond and build trust.

Before you use this exercise with others, generate your own community genogram. We recommend that you use your community of origin—the main community you think of as the place where you "grew up." After you are finished, think about the images and stories of your community and your family. Then, perhaps, you may want to reflect on yourself as a person in community and how this affects you as a person in the here-and-now. Write your most immediate here-and-now reflections in the space below and then continue your narrative as a person in community on a separate piece of paper.

_____

_____

_____

_____

_____

_____

_____

**Box 4.1**    *The Community Genogram*

It is important that you generate your own style of representing your community. Most often, we suggest you use your community of origin, the place where you "grew up," but it is appropriate to use any location you prefer. Some find it helpful to do a community of origin and their present community, then compare the two. Again, visually represent your community using your personal preference. The map and the star, shown below, are only two examples.* Drawings, photographs, collages, and other symbolic forms are often useful.

1. *The map.* The first genogram is that of Jordan who discusses the meaning of his rural setting in some detail in the transcript presented in this chapter. Note how this view of the client's background reveals a close extended family and a relatively small experiential world. The absence of friends is interesting. Church is the only outside factor noted.

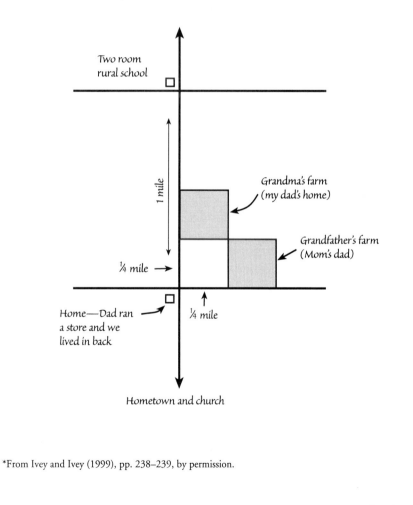

*From Ivey and Ivey (1999), pp. 238–239, by permission.

**(continued)**

**Box 4.1 (continued)**

2. *The star.* This format is more abstract, but still presents a comprehensive picture of Janet's community when she was in elementary school. We see a difficult time in her life. Nonetheless, note the important support systems, which can serve as long-term positive assets and resources.

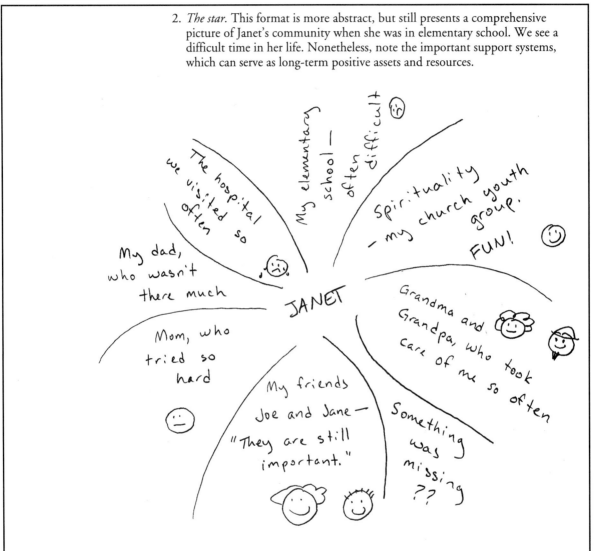

Provide group members with some large newsprint and colorful marking pens. Stress that each person should develop his or her own community genogram in whatever style is meaningful. Once the community genograms are complete, post them on the wall around the room with masking tape.

From this point on, there are several alternatives. One is simply to have all the members talk about their community of origin briefly. First, focus on positive stories from the community. Ask each participant to share one positive story about the community of origin. For some people this is not easy as they have had hurtful experiences in the past. Nonetheless, work hard to find something positive.

The sharing of positive experiences and stories from the community of origin helps group members understand each participant better. We also see varying styles of presentation, both visually and in words. We learn our culture in our communities of origin and very often we obtain sympathetic and powerful stories to begin the process of understanding multiplicity and diversity.

The basic listening sequence, of course, is necessary if both the leader and the participants are to hear the stories accurately. If we start with positive stories, we have established contact and begun the process of building trust. As the group moves on, a certain safety seems to develop. Out of this base of understanding and caring, people are often more willing to share themselves and their deeper concerns. And they are likely to share real issues more quickly. We can always return to the positive stories as a safe base for contact.

## DEFINING THE LEADERSHIP SKILLS OF THE BASIC LISTENING SEQUENCE

The basic listening sequence is a set of five essential microskills: open and closed questions, encourage, paraphrase, reflecting feelings, and summarizing (Box 4.2). These are most often associated with individual counseling and therapy, but they are equally important in group work and are used a little differently here.

As the skills are presented, we will emphasize multiple focus dimensions. We will give some attention to using the skills with individuals but particularly stress the importance of listening to subgroups and the group as a whole. In short, we need to listen to individual stories, but if we are to use groups effectively, we also need to listen to the narratives that unfold in the group itself. As part of that process, we also need to focus on the here-and-now as well as the there-and-then. The story concept is helpful, but focusing on stories alone may lead to an overemphasis on there-and-then experience outside the group.

### Questioning as a Leadership Skill

Question-asking skills increase the group leader's ability to obtain specific information, to discourage some members from consuming too much of the group's time, and to encourage other members to participate more. Questions can help the group leader and members understand specific details about a topic or story in order to make more appropriate decisions based on accurate information.

Questions can control the quantity and also the quality of information in the group. Open questions tend to begin with *what, how, why,* or *could* and encourage members to talk in more detail. Examples include these:

▲ *What* does the group think about what Roberto just said about his community background?
▲ Lisa, *how* do you feel about Roberto's story?
▲ I noted Jordan reacting strongly as Roberto spoke. *Why* was that so?
▲ Roberto, *could* you give us a concrete example of how your spiritual background in your community was important to you?

**Box 4.2**    *The Basic Listening Sequence (BLS)*

|  |  |
|---|---|
| | Effective use of the BLS can lead group members to share their stories more fully. Your objective as a leader is to draw out the facts, feelings, and organization of the story.<br><br>As a leader, note whether you are focusing on here-and-now experience in the group or a there-and-then story from the past. Think of the BLS as a set of micro-skills that facilitate listening to all dimensions of group experience. |
| *Open and Closed Questions* | Open questions provide group members the opportunity to talk at more length whereas closed questions home in on specific data. Expect *what* questions to lead to facts about a situation; *how* to lead to information about feelings or process; *why* to lead to reasons. *Could* is considered "maximally open" as it provides members with the opportunity to say that they do or do not wish to elaborate on the topic while simultaneously giving them room to talk about whatever dimension of their issues they wish to share. |
| *Encourage/Restatement* | Encouraging is a skill that involves nonverbal and verbal ways to motivate members to continue talking. Nonverbal encouraging includes head nods, leaning forward, and smiling. Repeating key words and important ideas in the exact language of the group members can facilitate their elaborating in more detail on their issues. Restatements serve a similar function; pick out important phrases used by group members rather than the briefer key words. |
| *Paraphrase* | In paraphrasing, you capture in your words the essence of what has been said. In this process, longer statements are distilled and made more clear, but important key words are often repeated exactly as the individual or group said them. Paraphrasing can help wordy members who repeat themselves. This technique indicates to group members that they have been heard and it may encourage them to move on. |
| *Reflection of Feeling* | When you reflect feelings you note the emotional tone behind what an individual or group is saying, naming it (if necessary), and reflecting it back (for example, saying "You feel . . . because . . ."). This is a reassuring strategy to group members; it also helps them explore emotional dimensions of their lives and the group more fully. |
| *Summarization* | Related to paraphrasing and reflecting feelings, summarizing covers a longer period of time. Summarizations tend to encompass both facts and feelings while simultaneously helping to organize what has been said. Summarizations may begin or end a group session as a way to integrate and map what the group seeks to do or has been doing. |
| *The Checkout* | While not part of the BLS, the checkout is highly facilitative in encouraging individual and group reaction to the various skills. "Have I heard you correctly?" "Am I close to what you are feeling?" "Is that right?" are three examples. Group participants are encouraged to reflect on and give feedback concerning the leader's accuracy in listening skills. |

Note that "what" questions often focus on facts and encourage people to elaborate and give more specifics. "How" questions are frequently associated with emotions—"How do you feel?" "Why" questions focus on reasons and may tend to put people on the spot; use them sparingly and carefully. "Could" questions tend to be particularly effective as they serve as "double agents." A "could" question, even the most open, can be answered in one word—"yes" or "no." But giving group members permission to say no can be very useful and increase their willingness to be open.

Closed questions tend to be more specific and often result in short answers. *Are, is, do, where,* and *when* are examples of question stems that are usually closed in nature.

▲   Are you finished?
▲   Is that what you meant?
▲   Do you find Roberto's story related to your own?
▲   Where are you from?
▲   When will the group start tomorrow?

Closed questions are particularly useful for filling in information gaps. Some beginning group leaders, perhaps too nervous, find themselves asking primarily closed questions and wonder why their group never seems to talk much. At the same time, effective use of closed questions can encourage an overtalkative member to take less air time.

A skilled group leader will know when and how to use both open and closed questions. However, in some cases a question may be "intended" to be an open question but "received" as a closed question with a one- or two-word response. In other cases a question may be "intended" to be a closed question but "received" as an invitation to make a long presentation to the group.

Some group leaders overuse questions and never give up control. At times, asking questions can become "grilling the witness"; this is generally disruptive to the group. If you question too frequently, the group members then just wait for you to go on to the next topic while they passively follow. Some group leaders try not to use any questions, placing more responsibility for the discussion on the group members. An effective group leader will be selective, purposeful, and intentional in using questioning skills.

Focusing concepts greatly enrich the use of questions. For example, consider the following possible leader responses around Roberto's story:

▲   Roberto, could you tell us a bit more about the meaning of your church experience? (Focus on individual, there-and-then)
▲   Towanda, sounds like your spiritual experience is close to that of Roberto. Could you share that with him? (Focus on subgroup, here-and-now)
▲   What's happening in our group right now as we hear Towanda and Roberto's story? (Focus on group, here-and-now)
▲   Why does the group think spirituality is missing so often in our thinking about these life issues? (Focus on group and cultural/environmental context—spirituality, there-and-then)

Many of us come to group work after being trained as individual counselors. We may be skilled in questioning techniques and run fairly effective groups, but if we fail to focus on subgroups and the group as a whole, we will sacrifice the give and take that is at the heart of group work. Remember always that a major objective of group counseling is to use the power of group interaction.

## Encouraging and Restatement as a Leadership Skill

The encouraging leader is constantly showing the group that he or she is interested in and involved with what they are saying, doing, and experiencing. We show and give encouragement by nonverbal means such as head nods, smiling or being appropriately supportive, leaning forward with interest, and using facilitative and open hand and arm gestures. Verbal encouraging most often involves the well-known minimal verbal utterances "uh-huh" and "ummmm." You are undoubtedly familiar with the concept of active listening. The act of encouraging demonstrates to your group that you are indeed active in listening to them and truly involved. It is not necessary to interrupt; encouraging shows clearly that you are indeed with the individual and the group.

One of the most important things you can do to encourage group members is to repeat key words that you notice in their stories. You'll find that demonstrating your empathic understanding is enhanced when you use the important main words of your group members. Repetition of these key words often helps them elaborate in more depth on what is occurring.

Restatement is another form of encouraging. Here the group leader listens carefully for key ideas and says them back to the group member in the member's exact words. This is not repeating words as if you were a parrot, although jokesters sometimes make fun of this form of active listening. Using the main words and ideas exactly as the group or group members present them can be particularly facilitative. In individual counseling and hearing one group member's story, you will find that nonverbal encouragement and restatement of key words and phrases helps the person get out her or his story and feel heard.

Your style of encouraging for subgroups and the total group is particularly important. Imagine you are dealing with a conflict between two group members. You may unconsciously favor one of the members over another and this preference can show through your nonverbal encouraging behavior despite your best verbal efforts. When working with complex issues such as this, be sure to monitor your own behavior and balance eye contact, head nods, and other nonverbal behavior equally between the pair. This is not always easy. You may find that a process observer outside the group will be useful in giving you feedback as you learn to balance your leadership style and deal with your own natural biases.

Most of us have favorite people, and attending to them is easier than listening to others. When working with a small group, many leaders fall into the trap of giving attention to some people while almost ignoring others. For example, we may be working with a survivor group (cancer, AIDS, rape trauma) and we are encouraging only those who have a positive attitude toward their issues. We may be avoiding eye contact and failing to support those people who really want to deal with the problems in their lives. At the same time, we may be wondering why this group seems somewhat superficial and why some people who started to talk at the beginning no longer speak. What has happened is that we have failed to balance our encouraging and support. Again, the best way to avoid this error is to balance your encouraging among all group members. Periodically, seek external feedback from a process observer to help you assess your encouraging behavior and style in a group.

You may also find that certain words appear consistently in subgroup and total group dialogue. These are important signs of the emerging themes in the group. Keeping attention on these key words through restatement and repetition can help the group focus on common issues. An external process observer can be helpful in noting developing themes within your group.

Let us stop for moment and illustrate the way that questioning and encouraging might be used in helping individual group members tell their stories:

| *Transcript Utilizing the Basic Listening Sequence* | *Process Comment: Microskill, focus, and time orientation* |
|---|---|
| 1. *Leader:* So, we are learning a lot about each other as we think of ourselves as community members. Who'd like to go next? (Jordan leans forward.) Jordan, could you tell us about your community? | Open question, focus on individual, there-and-then—the prediction is that Jordan will respond in the there-and-then with his community story. |
| 2. *Jordan:* I grew up in rural Oregon. My father ran a small grocery store and we lived in back of the store. It was a very small world, for one-quarter mile down one road was my grandfather's farm—on my mother's side—while a quarter-mile the other way was my father's home farm where my grandmother lived. The farms were actually adjoining. One mile from the store was a two-room school. That was essentially my world while I was growing up except for traveling to the town three miles away to attend Sunday school and church. | Self-disclosure, focus on theme of community, self, and cultural/environmental context with special reference to family, there-and-then. Jordan responded as predicted. |
| 3. *Trek:* Wow, that is really different from the city where I lived. | Self-disclosure, focus on theme, there-and-then. |
| 4. *Leader:* We kind of get the picture. Jordan, could you share a story about your background in that community—a positive story and a source of strength, as Roberto did? | Open question, focus on individual, there-and-then—prediction, Jordan will provide a story from the there-and-then. |

*(continued)*

| Transcript Utilizing the Basic Listening Sequence | Process Comment: Microskill, focus, and time orientation |
|---|---|
| 5. *Jordan:* The thing that stands out for me is how cruel the children in the community were to me. The rest of them were all farmers and they seemed to resent the fact that I wasn't. They called me endless names and at one point they called me a number of anti-Semitic, anti-Jewish names—horrible names. It was very hard for me (looks down sadly) and I didn't even know what Jewish was. | Self-disclosure, focus on self and cultural/environmental context, there-and-then. Emphasis on feelings.<br><br>Note that Jordan did not follow the leader's instruction. Many group members have negative experiences that they want to share rather than positive stories. We are suggesting that major exploration of negatives and problems generally needs to wait until a solid base of contact and trust is built within the group. Otherwise, Jordan may be standing outside of the group having shared too much of himself too early in the group process. In this process, the leader was giving full attention to Jordan and encouraging him through supportive body language and eye contact. |
| 6. *Towanda:* I was one of three African Americans in my school. I took a lot of crap too. Our backgrounds are different, but we have more in common than I thought. Oppression is oppression. | Self-disclosure focusing on individual, Jordan, and cultural/environmental context. |
| 7. *Leader:* "Oppression is oppression." One of the things that we want to explore in this group is the working of oppression and how it affects each of us personally. | Encouraging, restatement. *Oppression* and *harassment* are to be themes of this group and repetition of the key word reinforces both Towanda and Jordan. |
| Jordan, I hear your sadness and I appreciate Towanda's support. You are heading in the right direction—we all want to work on these issues. | Reflection of feeling ("I hear your sadness") focused on individual here-and-now followed by feedback with a focus on the subgroup and the group as well. |
| But before we do this in depth, it's important to hear positive group stories and learn a bit about our community and cultural backgrounds. Our goal today is to start with strengths and then keep these positives in mind as we work with some of the difficult issues. | Would you have done this? It is a clear topic jump. Would it have been better to follow up with Jordan and Towanda rather than focus on the community story issue? |
| Jordan, we've heard about your small community and your sad experiences with the cruel children at school. You've indicated how sad it was and how hard it was for you. It really hurt! (Note that the leader emphasizes the key words that Jordan used.) | Brief summary of the key facts and feelings that Jordan expressed from the there-and-then. |
| But before we deal with those issues, it often helps to build on a basis of strength. Could you, Jordan, share a story of positive strength from your past community? | The leader structures and asks Jordan a there-and-then question. |

Group members will often head in their own direction, regardless of what the leader does. The disadvantage of moving Jordan away from his negative story is that some of the immediacy of here-and-now feeling is lost. But this is early in the group, and by discussing an issue in depth in the first session, Jordan may seem threatening to other group members. In this case, the leader decided to hold to the plan of the group in the belief that Jordan could come back to his issues later—and when he does, it will be within a framework of strength rather than one of negativity. We are seeing here a structured theme-centered group. The ideas behind this approach will be outlined in the next chapter.

## Paraphrasing as a Leadership Skill

Paraphrasing restates what group members have said, putting that message in the leader's words, but restating the member's key words or phrases of special importance. The essence of what was said is repeated in shortened form, with the leader providing clarification where necessary to fill in the gaps. If the group leader is accurate, the member or members will validate the paraphrase with a statement such as "That's right!" or some other nonverbal acknowledgment that the paraphrase was on target.

Accurate paraphrasing allows the group member to move on to new material with confidence as it creates consensus among the group about what has already been said. Paraphrasing can facilitate the exploration and clarification of issues in much the same way as questioning. Almost every question can be reframed into a paraphrase just as almost every paraphrase could be reframed into a question, depending on which is the most appropriate vehicle. Paraphrasing the words and concepts of a subgroup or the entire group is a significant challenge to all of us as leaders. Here we have to search for themes, listen for the same key word used by several group members, and then feed back these themes and words accurately.

The checkout is often coupled with paraphrasing, reflecting feeling, and summarizing. It is a short question used by the group leader to determine whether her or his listening is accurate—if indeed the leader heard what the group member or the group itself intended. "Have I heard you correctly?" "Is that right?" "Is that what you said?" These are three examples that encourage members of the group to elaborate if you missed something. The checkout is often seen as a sign of respect.

| Transcript Utilizing the Basic Listening Sequence | Process Comment: Microskill, focus, and time orientation |
| --- | --- |
| 8. *Jordan:* (finishing his positive story) So that's it. My Sunday school teacher at the Baptist Church was also my scoutmaster. He was a wonderful model of tolerance and caring and gave endlessly to me and to others. I don't know how I would have survived the teasing and cruel remarks of the kids without him. | Self-disclosure, focus on self and others and cultural/environmental context. There-and-then. |

(continued)

| Transcript Utilizing the Basic Listening Sequence | Process Comment: Microskill, focus, and time orientation |
|---|---|
| 9. *Leader:* So your Sunday school teacher was truly helpful to you in surviving the oppression you experienced in school. Have I got that right? (Paraphrase, checkout) | Paraphrase followed by checkout ("Have I got that right?"). Focus on individual and theme. |
| 10. *Jordan:* That's right. It was oppression and yet I thought it was my fault. | Self-disclosure, focus on self, there-and-then. We are seeing Jordan begin to reframe his experience from a more positive perspective. |
| 11. *Leader:* Your fault? | Encourage/restatement. The prediction is that Jordan will elaborate on this aspect of his issues and story. |
| 12. *Jordan:* Yes, somehow I thought it was me who needed to be better somehow. | Self-disclosure, focus on self, there-and-then. |
| 13. *Towanda:* Exactly; I sometimes felt the same way when I experienced teasing and harassment as a child. | Self-disclosure, focus on self and other (Jordan), there-and-then. |
| 14. *Trek:* Me too. | Self-disclosure. |
| 15. *Roberto:* Until I came out, I thought there was something wrong about being gay. When you heard my story, you knew I went through a lot of difficult stuff. | Self-disclosure, focus on self and group, there-and-then. |
| 16. *Leader:* I hear the group saying that a lot of us internalize oppression and take it as our fault. Am I close to what you are saying? (Paraphrase, checkout, focus on group, here-and-now) | Summary reframe/interpretation linking member stories together in a larger joint story followed by a checkout inviting the group to participate. The prediction is that the group will work with this summary/interpretation. |
| 17. *Trek:* Yes, living with harassment seems to result in internalization and self-blame. | Reframe/interpretation focus on theme in both the here-and-now and there-and-then. Trek follows up and starts the group process of reframing and restorying their experience. |

In this brief example, we see how one person's story can be related to and linked with the life experiences of others. Given a society focused on individualism, it would have been tempting to focus on each group member's personal concerns and difficulties. While this is valid, a more powerful and potentially more useful approach is to help group members see commonalities and links among their experiences. In this way, an individual story becomes, in the long-term, part of a larger, growing, and changing group story. The paraphrasing of group key words and themes can be critical in moving to new stories for the future.

The narrative model of drawing out stories and defining positive assets and strengths leads to restorying, creating a new narrative for the future. The new story, in turn, provides the potential for both individuals and group members to move toward significant life changes in both attitudes and action.

## Reflecting Feeling as a Leadership Skill

Many argue that significant change rests on an emotional base. If the individuals you work with are to profit from the group experience, special attention needs to be paid to their underlying feelings. This means that you as leader need first to be able to identify emotions as they occur in your group. The four main emotions are often identified as sad, mad, glad, and scared, with an almost infinite array of terms specifying feelings more precisely. Reflecting feelings is, of course, a central counseling and psychotherapy skill. It is also important in group work.

The skill of reflecting feelings most often requires these strategies:

▲ Observing and noting individual feelings expressed verbally and nonverbally in the group.

▲ Feeding back the feelings observed—"You are feeling _____ right now"; or "You felt _____ then."

▲ Adding context in the form of a paraphrase—"You are feeling *relieved and more at peace* right now as the group has given you a lot of support"; or "You were *scared and a bit afraid* of sharing your story, but *glad* that you did as it has worked out well."

▲ Adding a checkout so the individual can react. If you have missed the feeling, this provides an opportunity for the member to share a better name for what has been experienced—"Have I heard you correctly?" or "Is that right?" or "Am I close?"

In dealing with positive or negative experiences in groups, we might find individuals saying things like the following. Possible leader reflections of feelings are also presented.

*Jordan:*    (in a sad tone of voice) I really am angry at what happened to me in school.

*Leader:*    Jordan, you feel both sad and angry at what happened.

*Roberto:*    (with a smile) Being gay has become a positive experience at long last.

*Leader:*    Roberto, sounds like you really feel good after all this time.

*Towanda:*    (hesitantly) I suppose this group has been good for me.

*Leader:*    Towanda, you sound a bit doubtful about your feelings about the group so far. Am I hearing you accurately?

Each response focuses on the individual and her or his feelings. You will also find that there is a general feeling in the group as a whole, and each member contains a part of that generalized emotion. Groups at varying times can be joyful, playful, tense, or anxious. In short, the general tone of a group can reflect all the emotions that any individual can experience, as shown in these examples:

*Leader:*    As I look back on the positive stories of the communities from which each of you came, I get a general sense that the group feels more relaxed and trusting. Have I heard correctly? (Reflection of group here-and-now feeling followed by checkout for accuracy)

*Leader:*    As we heard Towanda's story about experiencing discrimination in her school setting, I saw a lot of tension in the group. What are some of you experiencing right now? (Reflection of there-and-then feeling followed by here-and-now open question)

*Leader:*    I sense a lot of anxiety in the group right now. (Reflection of feeling, here-and-now)

*Leader:*    The group seems to be heading in different directions. I sense some feel quite *comfortable* with where we are now while others may be a bit *tense* talking about this.

Some group leaders find their members spending much of the time intellectualizing and talking about things rather than really allowing themselves to experience. Often this is because the leader fails to acknowledge and reflect both individual and group emotions. Unless you listen for feelings and attend to them, do not expect your group to share emotion.

You may also find it helpful if you establish contact and trust in your group through sharing positive stories that then lead to the discussion of positive emotions and strength. Once they are on a solid basis, individuals and groups are better able to explore negative emotions, complex concerns, and problems. In addition, they can deal with interpersonal conflict and issues within the group itself more effectively. It is our belief that we can best deal with the negative if we start with positive assets.

**Box 4.3**    *Helping Group Members Increase or Decrease Emotional Expressiveness**

| | |
|---|---|
| *Observing Nonverbals* | Keeping a constant eye on your group members is essential for understanding how emotion is being played out. Which members are involved and interested and which seem distant from the group? Does a group member cross her or his legs at a critical moment and sit back in the chair? <br><br> Note patterns of eye contact, fidgeting, speech hesitations, and changes in vocal tone—in short, all the process dimensions stressed in the chapter on attending behavior. Breathing patterns often reflect emotion, and more rapid breathing may indicate real tension. |
| *Pacing Emotion* | You can pace group members and help them express more emotion in several ways: <br><br> ▲  By providing a safe atmosphere for personal contact and sharing of positive stories. <br> ▲  By matching and mirroring their body language. |

*This box is adapted from the work of Leslie Brain as summarized in Ivey and Ivey (1999), pp. 140–141.

▲ By encouraging group members to share what they are feeling in both the there-and-then and the here-and-now. Many people find it safer to share past emotions first and then move to exploring here-and-now emotions. However, there-and-then emotional discussion can be a way to avoid real exploration of what is going on in the moment.

▲ By encouraging immediate expression of emotion with the direct question—"What are you feeling right now?" Ask individual members or the group as a whole. At this point, that question is so well known that it seems stereotyped. However, if used authentically, it is usually helpful.

On the other hand, some group members may start emotional expression and then stop. This is often a wise choice on their part. We need to respect their desire to back off. As they develop greater trust in you and the group, they will often return to the place where they turned off their emotion and continue again in more depth.

*Managing When Fear, Rage, Despair, Joy, or Exhilaration Come Up*

Your comfort level with your own emotional expression will affect how your group faces emotion. If you are uncomfortable with a particular emotion, your group will likely avoid it. What is required is a balance between being very aware of your own internal thoughts and feelings and showing culturally appropriate and supportive nonverbals. Acknowledging and reflecting the feeling that is there is, of course, necessary.

Consider using such phrases as these:

▲ We are all here for you.
▲ Those feelings are OK to have.
▲ I (We've) been there too.
▲ Let it out . . . that's OK.
▲ I (We) hear you.

Generally speaking, keep emotional expression that is deeper and intense to only a minute or so. Five minutes is a long time when a group member is crying. To help group members reorient themselves after intense emotional expression, consider the following:

▲ Encourage slowed, rhythmic breathing and awareness of the here-and-now; standing, walking, or centering the body firmly on the chair can help a group member to come out of an overly deep discussion.
▲ Discuss positive strengths inherent in the group member and the situation.
▲ Discuss positive steps the member can take in response to the feelings generated.
▲ Use positive reframing of the emotional experience.
▲ Encourage positive feedback from group members (often around the positives of allowing one to express and feel emotion).
▲ Note that the story needs to be told many times and each time helps.

*A Caution*

As you work with the emotion, there is always the possibility of reawakening issues in a member who has a history of painful trauma. This is an area in which the beginning group worker often needs support from a more experienced professional. In such situations, seek supervision and assistance. There is also the possibility that one member's deep emotional experience will trigger parallel experiences in other group members. In the early stages of group leadership, you will want to keep emotional expression brief until you have developed sufficient skill to handle it.

## Summarizing as a Leadership Skill

Many, many things are happening in a group all the time. Often you feel like you are managing chaos or perhaps not managing at all. The effective leader is somewhat like a traffic cop, making sense of and organizing multiple things that are happening.

The skill of summarizing is a particularly essential group skill. In individual counseling, you use summarization to help clients organize their thinking—the facts and feelings of their situation. You will want to do this with individual group members as they tell their stories.

You will hear many stories, themes, and issues in a group. For these, the skill of summarizing is particularly helpful—at times, the most important skill you can have. You will find summarizing especially beneficial in the following situations:

▲ Starting a group. Here you can summarize what the group is about and what members can expect.

▲ Starting a group session. Transitioning into a weekly group meeting can be slow. The leader can often move the group along by summarizing the last meeting or session and talking a bit about what the members might expect in the present session.

▲ Ending a group session. A useful way to end the group is to summarize the main points of what has been said.

▲ Encouraging group participation. For both beginning or ending a session, try to involve the whole group; for example, "As we begin today, could the group share what we learned last time and what we hope for today?" "Time is just about up. Could you all help me summarize what happened today?"

Another way that summarizing is helpful is when the leader brings together and links various strands and ideas of what the group has expressed over a period of time, as in this example:

*Leader:*  A lot has been happening in the last ten minutes. We heard Jordan's story and that seemed to bring out parallel thoughts in Towanda and Roberto of their own experiences of oppression. We saw a lot of anger in the group. Trek didn't say much, and Lisa didn't say anything, but they certainly looked involved. Right now, we seem to be catching our breath as a group. What is going on for us right now?

Another type of summary might appear in this group at the end:

*Leader:*  We've each summarized what we've learned today. I hear a general feeling of support and caring for one another, but at the same time I hear a sense of incompleteness—almost as if we have defined the problem but aren't quite sure where to go next. Have I heard it correctly? Is this something we all want to think about individually and then we can share what we have discovered at our next meeting?

In these examples, the leader has encouraged each group member to summarize his or her experiences from the session but has brought out a new dimension—incompleteness. The leader has used this as both a marker for the concluding session and a place to go during the next meeting. This group seems to have started the process of restorying, but it also needs to consider action on the new group perspectives.

You will also find it helpful to summarize issues from past sessions and link them to present here-and-now concerns in the group. This lets you discover underlying patterns of behavior and language in the group that reappear over time, and your ability to observe, map, and interpret this information can reveal significant connections to group members.

## THE IVEY TAXONOMY: PROCESS OBSERVATION

The skills and behaviors that leaders use will vary widely both within and across groups, often depending on the circumstances of the moment. Those who work with structured groups may use one set of microskills; leaders of counseling and therapy groups may use other skill patterns. You can gain valuable insights by observing different leaders—and yourself—as you interact with groups. You can, of course, observe other leaders directly as they work; to examine your own behavior, you can watch videotapes or listen to audiotapes of yourself as you lead your group. Merely observing, however, will not allow you to comprehend the richness and significance of the many things that are happening at once. By classifying leadership behavior using microskills analysis, you can more fully understand what you and other leaders are doing.

As you attempt to analyze and classify a leader's use of microskills, a valuable aid can be a process observation instrument. This is a tool used by an observer to capture with great specificity a group leader's words, to whom the words are directed, their intent, and many other nuances that are occurring simultaneously at one moment in the group interaction. We encourage you to sample several different approaches to process observation, as each has a contribution to make to group work. One such instrument that has wide applicability in many situations is the Ivey Taxonomy (IT).

The Ivey Taxonomy (IT) consists of three domains—microskills, focus, and time orientation. *Microskills* are leader actions such as those of the basic listening sequence—asking open questions, paraphrasing, and so on. *Focus* indicates where the skill is directed: at the group, subgroup, individual, leader, main theme or topic, or the cultural/environmental context. *Time orientation* indicates whether the skill elicits a response about the present (here-and-now) or something in the past (there-and-then). Each leader or member comment is classified on all three dimensions. To make accurate and consistent classifications will take practice on your part, and in the early stages, you will want to concentrate on only one or two dimensions.

At least once during your work with this book, we recommend that you audio-record yourself as a group leader and, ideally, make a transcript of a group session. In this way, you can obtain a very precise picture of what you are doing in a group. Box 4.4 illustrates the IT in action.

## USING THE BASIC LISTENING SEQUENCE WITH CHILD AND ADOLESCENT GROUPS

All the skills of this chapter can be used successfully with younger groups. Children and adolescents need to tell their stories; get out their problems and concerns; and organize their thoughts, feelings, and behaviors. The community genogram is especially effective with both children and adolescents.

**Box 4.4**    *The Ivey Taxonomy: Process Observation*

The Ivey Taxonomy (IT) for process observation will be expanded as we move through the chapters of this book. A brief transcript below illustrates the IT in action. Again, note that while predictions of member response can be made, intentional group leaders realize that groups and individuals do not always react as expected and the leaders should always be ready with an alternative response.

Reviewing your use of microskills through this type of analysis allows you to determine whether you are indeed doing what you want to be doing as a group leader. You may find, for example, that you are using relatively few reflections of feelings or working primarily in the there-and-then—and that your group leadership skills could be more effective through attention to these areas.

| Leader Comment | Microskill | Anticipated Result of Skill | Focus | Time Orientation |
|---|---|---|---|---|
| 1. What is happening in the group right now? | Open question | Group members will respond to the question at some length, focusing on the here-and-now. | Group | Here-and-now |
| 2. Is the group ready to go on? | Closed question | Responses are expected to be generally shorter than with open questions and specific information will be obtained. | Group | Here-and-now |
| 3. Uh-huh (with a smile) | Encourage | Members are supported and will continue. | Not classifiable | Not classifiable |
| 4. Roberto, you say "gay pride." | Restatement | Members feel heard when their own words are repeated. May encourage them to say more and enable them to move to a new topic. | Individual | Here-and-now |
| 5. So, the group is saying that it wants to examine and reflect on gender issues as they have experienced them outside the group. | Paraphrase | Similar to restatement. Accurate paraphrases tend to help members feel heard and this enables them to move on further with their issues. | Group, cultural/ environmental/ contextual | There-and-then |

| | | | | |
|---|---|---|---|---|
| 6. Sue, I hear you saying that societal sexism in your work setting has really become intolerable to you and makes you very angry. | Paraphrase, reflection of feeling | Expect group members to respond with more discussion of their emotions. | Individual, cultural/environmental/contextual | There-and-then with undertone of here-and-now anger |
| 7. So, to summarize what we've been doing so far—we have shared our stories around oppression and shared our common feelings of anger. Have I heard the group accurately? | Summarize | Helps members to organize their thinking to feel heard. The noting of similarities and differences facilitates connections in the group. Serves as a transition to the next topic. | Group, cultural/environmental/contextual | There-and-then and here-and-now |

Once the community genogram is drawn, both children and adolescents are good at telling stories about their experiences. In the early, trust-building phases of groups, it is important to focus on positives. As you work with positive stories in the community picture, you build a reservoir of strengths that can be drawn on throughout the group.

Training children or teens to use peer counseling or mediation is an effective route toward personal growth and building community in the schools. When children are helping other children or teens are helping their peers, they can use the basic listening sequence very successfully.

If open questions are difficult for younger or less verbal children, they may respond in short sentences or with just a few words. You will often find it necessary to be very active, sharing your own self in a humorous way. You may need to read stories to the children. If you simply listen and use only the skills of the basic listening sequence, children may fall silent. Accurately paraphrasing children's comments helps you track what they are saying and helps them understand what they have just said. Visit an elementary school and note that the most effective teachers are continuously paraphrasing what children say. The most competent teachers, counselors, and group workers use active listening with children constantly to show clearly that they are there and are fully involved.

Artwork, games, and activities can be helpful. Children often find "just talking" not sufficiently involving, but they can draw pictures in the group while discussing their issues. The child may be encouraged to draw pictures of the family.

Adolescents need to learn to listen to each other and can benefit from social skills training that stresses the importance of listening. Carrell's (1993) *Group Exercises for Adolescents* provides a wide array of exercises that are suitable for teens. One exercise, "Breaking the Ice," offers a series of open questions and leading statements to get teens started talking. They include such topics as "What is the best movie you've ever seen?" "What was the best day of your life?" and "One of the things I like most about me is . . ." (p. 35).

The highly recommended *American Indian Life Skills Development Curriculum* (LaFromboise, 1996) has demonstrated effectiveness with adolescents through extensive research. Designed for Native American Indian youth, it nonetheless has important implications for teens of all ethnic and racial backgrounds. This book, which we consider an essential source for anyone working with adolescents, includes topics such as community building, listening skills, learning about one's family history and cultural background, and building self-esteem. Anger and stress management, suicide prevention, and life planning are some of the issues included.

## MOVING TOWARD YOUR OWN LEADERSHIP STYLE

The basic listening sequence (BLS) is designed to remind all of us that attending to and being with individuals and groups is one of the most significant gifts we can give. The idea of listening as a set of skills that we must learn can be challenging, as most of us think of ourselves as "good listeners." However, we can all improve our listening skills, particularly in groups where we need to listen intentionally. We need to listen to what is happening not only in individuals but also between and among them—and, in addition, what is going on in the group as a whole.

Many different things happen in groups. Just like us, you will sometimes feel lost and wonder what is happening. When in doubt—listen! Nothing can be more useful in bringing you back to the present. Listening helps us understand what is going on here-and-now and leads to better understanding of the there-and-then.

Long term, we hope you will audiotape or videorecord a group session. Ideally, consider making a written transcript of the entire session. This would give you the opportunity to study your leadership and your group interaction in extensive detail. If time does not permit this effort, then listening to or observing your tapes several times and making classifications as you watch can be quite beneficial.

Think back on this section and the entire chapter. What have you learned? What points struck you as most important? What stood out for you? What would you like to work on in the area of basic listening skills to improve your own group facilitation? Write your notes here.

_____

_____

_____

_____

_____

_____

_____

_____

_____

_____

## PRACTICING BASIC LISTENING SEQUENCE SKILLS

### 1. Process Observation of Basic Listening Skills

Box 4.5 provides a form for using the Ivey Taxonomy to observe the microskills of listening as they occur in group work. You may wish to photocopy this form and use it as you observe a group session or a meeting. An excellent way to practice process observation is to observe a group interaction in your classroom or, better yet, your own group work. The session can be audiotaped or videotaped and then you can review the session and classify leader behavior, comparing your classifications with others who may observe the same session.

As you use this form for the first time, it is best to note and classify only leader comments. If the leader comment is not a listening skill, simply note that an "other" skill was used. As you gain experience with this type of observation, you will find it possible to classify group members' behavior using the same system. In later chapters, more skills are added to the Ivey Taxonomy.

This system will be useful as you observe other groups in schools, agencies, and the community. As in other observation situations, share your intentions to observe with the group and provide them with feedback, if they request it.

### 2. The Fish Bowl

For this fish bowl, we recommend sharing positive stories from the community genogram. By constructing the genogram, the group members should already have developed a visual picture of their communities.

Four to six class members form a group from the larger class. One member is selected as leader. The remainder of the class observes the group, doing process observation using the form in Box 4.5. This practice exercise will take a minimum of fifteen minutes and perhaps as long as thirty or more. Even more time will be required if all members share their experience in community.

The leader's task is to draw out two stories, positive in nature, from two members of the group. Using the BLS, the leader will attempt to draw out key facts and feelings around the story by asking open and closed questions, encouraging, paraphrasing, and reflecting feelings. After the story has been brought out, the leader summarizes what has been heard. Once the two stories have been presented, we suggest that the leader turn the focus to the group as a whole and invite participation from members—for example, "What did the group observe during the presentations? How did this sharing affect us as a group?"

**Box 4.5**    The Ivey Taxonomy: Process Observation of the Basic Listening Sequence

| Leader Comment | Microskill | Anticipated Result of Skill | Focus | Time Orientation |
|---|---|---|---|---|
| | | | | |

### 3. Your Own Group Practice

The following may be completed in the class or workshop—or you may elect to organize your own group for practice. If you develop your own group, try to find a classroom member or friend to observe, using the observation form in Box 4.5. We suggest that you consider two alternatives for this exercise, ideally doing both. The first is to use the community genogram exercise with your own group. This allows you to experience a structured situation for using the basic listening sequence. As you work with the BLS, make some effort to note commonalities and patterns that appear in the group as they present their backgrounds.

The second alternative is less structured and can be done with virtually any topic. We suggest focusing on what is occurring in the group as a whole while giving less attention to individual stories. As you begin, inform the group members that you are going to focus on what is happening in the group as a totality and that you are asking them to note what is going on in the here-and-now. Some sample dimensions of the basic listening sequence might include the following:

▲ What do you see going on in the *group* right now as we begin? What is happening right now in the *group*?
▲ The *group* so far seems to have a little trouble focusing on the here-and-now experience.
▲ There seems to be some anxiety in the *group*.
▲ The *group* seems to be beginning to focus on itself as a *group*.

Avoid using personal names or focusing on individual comments. All this will seem at first unusual to both you and your group members. It can be a source of anxiety for some, perhaps including you. Keep this practice session relatively brief. You'll find that fifteen minutes of focusing on the group for the first time is a real challenge for you and the members. Allow another fifteen minutes at least for the debriefing of the experience.

1. Divide into groups of five or six. One person is to serve as leader and one is observer, who uses the form in Box 4.5. The remainder serve as group participants.
2. Define the topic for the small groups. The suggested topic is the community genogram; an alternative is an unstructured focus on the group as a whole. However, feel free to select topics of interest to you and the group.
3. Fifteen minutes should be used for the small groups. Allow five minutes for feedback from the observer. Finally, the entire small group can reflect on their own group process.

Where possible, add videorecording and practice to your work with attending skills and observation. You will always obtain very useful feedback on yourself and the group. Be sure to obtain informed consent from your participants.

## REFERENCES

Amir, Y. (1992). Social assimilation or cultural mosaic. In J. Lynch, C. Modgil, & S. Modgil (Eds.), *Cultural diversity and the schools* (Vol. I). Washington, DC: Falmer.

Carrell, S. (1993). *Group exercises for adolescents.* Newbury Park, CA: Sage.

Fukuyama, M. (1990). Taking a universal approach to multicultural counseling. *Counselor Education and Supervision, 30,* 6–17.

Ivey, A. (1995). *The community genogram: A strategy to assess culture and community resources.* Paper presented at the American Counseling Association, Denver.

Ivey, A., & Ivey, M. (1999). *Intentional interviewing and counseling: Facilitating multicultural development.* Pacific Grove, CA: Brooks/Cole.

Ivey, A., Ivey, M., & Simek-Downing, L. (1997). *Counseling and psychotherapy: A multicultural perspective* (4th ed.). Boston: Allyn & Bacon.

LaFromboise, T. (1996). *American Indian life skills development curriculum.* Madison, WI: University of Wisconsin Press.

Locke, D. (1990). A not so provincial view of multicultural counseling. *Counselor Education and Supervision, 30,* 18–25.

Ogbonnya, O. (1994). Person as community: An African understanding of the person as an intrapsychic community. *Journal of Black Psychology, 20,* 75–87.

Wehrly, B. (1996). *Counseling interracial individuals and families.* Washington, DC: American Counseling Association.

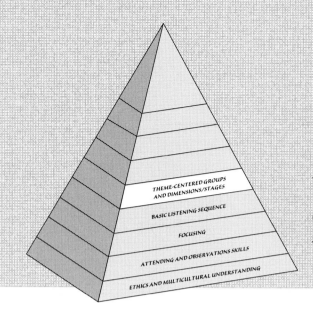

## CHAPTER 5

THEME-CENTERED GROUPS
AND DIMENSIONS/STAGES

BASIC LISTENING SEQUENCE

FOCUSING

ATTENDING AND OBSERVATIONS SKILLS

ETHICS AND MULTICULTURAL UNDERSTANDING

# Integrating Microskills in a Full Group Session, Part I: Theme-Centered Group Interaction and Dimensions/Stages

## CHAPTER GOALS

The microskills have thus far been presented as individual units. It is time to bring the pieces together into a more coherent whole. This chapter, based on a theory that can be taken directly into practice, presents theme-centered group interaction as a basic system for skill integration.

Chapter 6 is best read in conjunction with this chapter as there you will see a transcript showing extensive process analysis of a group in operation. If you master the theme-centered approach of these two chapters, you will have a solid foundation for learning many alternative types of group leadership.

In this chapter, you will learn some basics of theme-centered group interaction developed by Ruth Cohn (1969a, 1969b), as adapted to the microskills framework. Theme is another word for topic. For example, you may some day facilitate theme- or topic-centered groups on subjects such as cancer survival, weight loss, gender relations, multicultural understanding, or community-police relations. If you work with children or adolescents, expect to run groups with themes such as divorce, friendship, social skills, study skills, and time management. As you will discover, individual and group subthemes arise out of the central theme or topic of the group.

Theme-centered groups as conceptualized by Ruth Cohn have a simple but important basic premise: one-third of the time is to be spent listening to individual stories, one-third focused on the topic itself, and one-third focused on the interaction within the group itself—the process. In particular, theme-centered groups help individuals see how their stories are similar to and different from others in the group. As a conductor leads an orchestra through the many themes and variations of a symphony, you as group leader will enable the group to move to multiple individual and group focal points within a major group theme.

In this chapter and in Chapter 6, seek to accomplish the following objectives of understanding and mastery:

▲ Integrate observing, attending, and basic listening and focusing skills in a full group session.
▲ Understand the basis of theme-centered groups and how you can balance discussion of individual, group, and thematic issues.
▲ Conceptualize group process as a series of sequential *stages* of movement in a group or recycling of *dimensions*.
▲ Apply theme-centered group methods to facilitating your own groups.

## WARM-UP EXERCISE

Theme-centered groups build on a theme or topic around which the group interaction is focused. All groups are defined by central themes. Go to any college or university bulletin board and you will see advertisements about forthcoming and ongoing groups with a wide array of topics. On one recent campus visit we noted listings of groups including "Men's Consciousness Raising," "Take Back the Night Planning Session," "Anger Management," "Moving Against Racism," "Encounter for Personal Growth," "Stop Smoking and Start Living," and "Advanced Yoga." Also, you will find less formally structured groups in which people get together to share ideas, and eventually themes will emerge there as well. For example, an interpersonally oriented person-centered or therapy group does not always have an announced beginning theme, but the theme or themes develop out of the immediate group experience.

For this warm-up exercise, we suggest that you work on your own through Box 5.1, which emphasizes the theme or topic of *gender connections and sex roles*. After you have completed this exercise, return and either write or think through the questions explored below.

In theme-centered group work, the members focus on the individual (the "I"), the group (the "we"), and the theme (the "it" or topic). In the exercise of Box 5.1, you have experienced, in a beginning way, the three aspects of theme-centered group work. You have looked at yourself, you have looked at connections with others, and you have considered the theme of gender.

### The "I"

*Fact: All of human behavior includes both female and male characteristics.* What do you observe or think about yourself as a gendered human being?

_____ _____

_____

_____

_____

**Box 5.1**     *Gender Bender: Sex Roles in Our Society*

Much of who we are as individuals comes from our sex roles prescribed by society. Both men and women learn these roles through their relations with significant others in their developmental history. We have strengths that we can draw on, we have challenges that limit us—and we all can profit from learning better how to cope with both the men and the women who are a part of our lives.

The practical goal of this exercise is to examine our past connections with self and others around gender. Like the community genogram of Chapter 4, this exercise emphasizes that we are persons-in-relation and shows us how we can use our connections to build a stronger sense of self and community. We would argue that the best place to find one's connections with others and self-in-relation is through group work. Nonetheless, individual reflection can be a useful place to start. Later you can share your observations with others.

The following steps are suggested:

1. *Positive gender connections:* Sit quietly and meditate specifically about the concept *gender connections as they have had a positive impact on me.* Some of you will draw a blank at first and find the idea of connections a bit too abstract. Others will think of specific people who have helped them as models of effective men or women. As part of this exercise, note that men can learn from women models and women from male models. Read the key statement again—*gender connections as they have had a positive impact on me*—and sit quietly (perhaps with your eyes closed). Allow yourself to experience the positive associations. Enjoy them and then write down your reactions briefly.

   _____

   _____

   _____

2. *Gender challenges:* Sex roles, so basic in our lives, present innumerable challenges and difficulties. Sexuality and male/female relations often dominate our thoughts and lives. Whether one's sexual orientation is heterosexual, gay, lesbian, bisexual, or transgendered, gender often becomes a basic theme. Developmentally, sex roles influence our behavior, thoughts, and feelings throughout our lives. Write briefly about what occurs for you.

   _____

   _____

   _____

3. *A repertoire of connections:* As time permits, either stop here or continue to develop a repertoire of connections consisting of images, stories, and reflections. You may want to recall connections with key nuclear and extended family members, friends, or strangers. You may want to elaborate on connections revealed in your community genogram. Allow each recollection

   *(continued)*

**Box 5.1 (continued)**

to build and note the feelings in your body. Some recollections may bring about feelings of warmth and unity near the heart or in the chest while others may suggest feelings of strength and power, perhaps in the arms or legs. Still others may contain holistic feelings and thoughts covering your whole body. Each connected resource can be called on to help you understand yourself and your strengths—and, furthermore, to enable you to draw on those strengths during times of trial and problems. Write briefly here your experiences of this exercise.

_____

_____

_____

_____

A theme-centered group on "Connections: Building Resources" would be expected to begin with the leader outlining the purpose of the group briefly. For example, "We are here to examine our connections, both from the past and in the here-and-now. I'd like to begin with an exercise that all of you are asked to complete and then each of us can share what we have observed and learned. Later, we can jointly reflect on our discoveries." The group is given five to fifteen minutes to spend personal time on the exercise.

The leader then brings the group together asking members to share personal stories around the theme. One-third of the time in the group focuses on individual stories and one-third of the time on the more general concept of each of us as people-in-connection and how we can use our connective experience as resources in the group and in the future. The final one-third of the time focuses on connections here-and-now within the group itself.

## The "WE"

*Fact: Gender shapes our relationships with others.* What occurs for you as a human being connected with others as a person of gender?

_____

_____

_____

_____

_____

Integrating Microskills in a Full Group Session, Part I **111**## The "IT"

*Fact: Gender is a controversial topic.* What does the theme say that strikes you as relevant or important. What does this brief exercise tell you about the importance of gender relations? How does all this relate to sexual orientation?

_____

_____

_____

_____

_____

Now, imagine that you are participating in a theme-centered group on the concept of gender connections. There is a need to hear other people's stories, images, and reflections around the topic (their "I-stories"). It is also important to look at the group process and members' interactions around gender (the "we"), and for the group to discuss the meaning and importance of the theme (the "it").

In a theme-centered group, expect the leader to use the microskill of focus to balance individual, topic, and group. The balancing of time equally among these dimensions will enable you as leader to make sure that you do not end up with an unbalanced group that is either too focused on individual stories or that ignores the central topic. In this way, individuals and group process are considered in turn and balanced with an emphasis on the specific theme or topic.

## DEFINING THE LEADERSHIP SKILLS FOR FACILITATING A THEME-CENTERED GROUP

First, let us consider some basic aspects of theme-centered work that have special implications for practice. This will be followed by an illustrative group transcript in which these ideas as well as some other important theoretical/practical issues will be demonstrated.

Theme-centered group work is often presented visually as a triangle within a globe (see Box 5.2). The individual or "I" interacts with the group ("we") around a central theme ("it") within the globe or context. In the examples in this chapter, the focus will be on a gender socialization group with both men and women. The theme or "it" is gender socialization patterns, the "I" represents each individual's relation to the theme, and the "we" the interactions among and between group members as well as emerging commonalities and differences among group members.

The focusing skill is particularly useful in theme-centered work in that it helps leaders remember to balance individual, group, and topic emphasis. Other dimensions of focus (subgroups, leader, and cultural/environmental/contextual issues) need to be considered, but in early work in theme-centered practice, focus on Cohn's basic triad. In addition, helping your group members link their patterns and similarities throughout the group will be useful.

Groups are dynamic not static. Each group is different and presents a microculture of its own. Do not expect it always to be easy to balance discussion between and

**Box 5.2**    *Theme-Centered Globe and Leader Role*

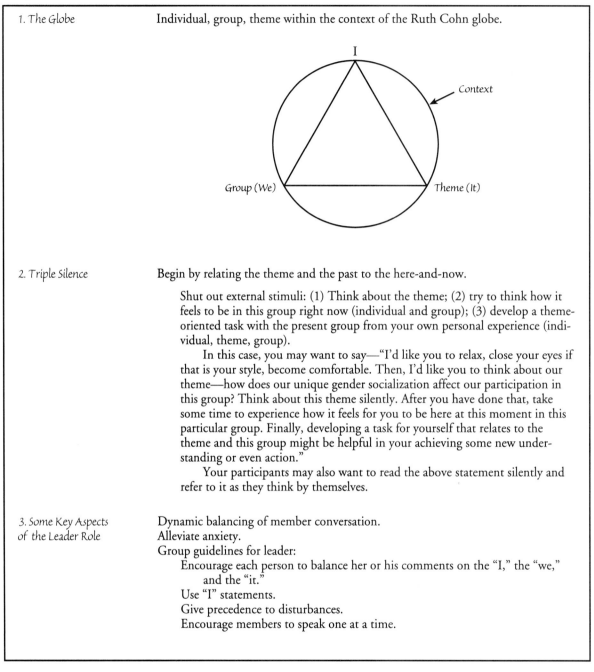

| | |
|---|---|
| *1. The Globe* | Individual, group, theme within the context of the Ruth Cohn globe. |

*2. Triple Silence*    Begin by relating the theme and the past to the here-and-now.

Shut out external stimuli: (1) Think about the theme; (2) try to think how it feels to be in this group right now (individual and group); (3) develop a theme-oriented task with the present group from your own personal experience (individual, theme, group).

In this case, you may want to say—"I'd like you to relax, close your eyes if that is your style, become comfortable. Then, I'd like you to think about our theme—how does our unique gender socialization affect our participation in this group? Think about this theme silently. After you have done that, take some time to experience how it feels for you to be here at this moment in this particular group. Finally, developing a task for yourself that relates to the theme and this group might be helpful in your achieving some new understanding or even action."

Your participants may also want to read the above statement silently and refer to it as they think by themselves.

*3. Some Key Aspects*    Dynamic balancing of member conversation.
*of the Leader Role*    Alleviate anxiety.
Group guidelines for leader:
    Encourage each person to balance her or his comments on the "I," the "we," and the "it."
    Use "I" statements.
    Give precedence to disturbances.
    Encourage members to speak one at a time.

among the three dimensions, even though they provide a useful model and outline for group process. A more dynamic picture is shown in Box 5.3 in which the major focal point of discussion changes from time to time. You as leader will seek to balance this discussion so that all issues receive attention during the life of your group.

**Box 5.3**    *Multiple Globes and Change in Emphasis Over Time*

While the overall goal of theme-centered groups is dynamic balancing of focus on the individual, the group, and the theme, expect varying emphasis on each point at varying times in the group.

The four circles below represent the changing emphasis that can occur in groups over a single session. The arrows between all circles indicate that the change could occur in any direction.

▲   Upper left circle—emphasis is on balancing individual, group, and the theme focus
▲   Upper right circle—discussion emphasis is on individuals and the theme with minimal attention to the group
▲   Lower left circle—discussion emphasis is primarily on the group with some attention to individuals and minimal attention to the theme.
▲   Lower right circle—discussion balances group and theme dimensions with minimal attention on the individual

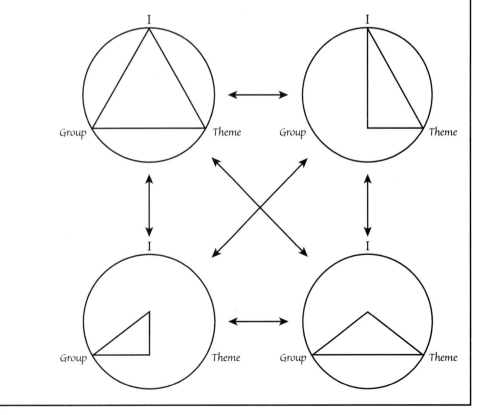

Notice that the globes in Box 5.3 place primary differential emphasis on the individual, on the group, and on the theme. Imagine you have observed a group for fifteen minutes in a strict theme-centered framework. The first five-minute block represents the leader and the group focusing on individual stories, the second on internal group process, and the last on the theme itself. When running a theme-centered group, your task is to balance the time the group spends among the I, the we, and the it. In addition, you may wisely give some time in group discussion to focus on broader contextual issues (for example, family, culture). To monitor your adherence to this time division, you may wish to have a process observer outside your group giving you and the group feedback on the balance of discussion maintained in this particular group session. (See Box 5.4 for a suggested process observation form.)

Pacing and leading ideas from Chapter 3 become important here. For example, you as leader need to pace and walk with the group as they tell their individual stories, but you also need to lead them so that a balance is possible between and among the multiple dimensions. Ruth Cohn talked of *dynamic balancing,* which means the strategic timing of leading the movement from individual to group to theme discussion. Obviously, if an individual is distressed, he or she needs to be given time to work things through. However, the leader must also encourage other people to share their issues around related concerns and, finally, enable reflection by the entire group on how individual and group issues relate to the central theme.

The process observation form in Box 5.4 reemphasizes the importance of your noting here-and-now and there-and-then statements. A theme-centered group can easily end with a total focus on issues outside the immediate group interaction. Ensure that you encourage group members to share their here-and-now immediate feelings and thoughts as well as stories from outside the group. Without the immediacy of here-and-now conversation, the impact and insights of the group will be less powerful.

As each individual tells her or his story, attend to body language, vocal tone, and nonverbal behavior as they will help you in noting, acknowledging, and reflecting feelings and bringing the here-and-now to awareness. Equally important, use your attending and observation skills to grasp what is happening among group members. For example, as one client tells a painful story, five members are leaning forward with interest and support while two members are not in synchrony with the total group. One is looking down and seems almost tearful while another is looking stonily ahead as if to ignore what is going on. As the individual finishes the story, you can then either focus on the group as a whole, commenting on the varying patterns of attention, or move to a focus on a single individual who now seems to need attention. In this case, it might be wise to summarize the general group condition, but then turn to the individual who seems to be hurting and especially in need of talking. If the "stony" individual continues this behavior over time, you may wish to return individual focus to her or him.

Awareness of and discussion of the context surrounding the theme-centered triangle is also a significant leadership issue. For example, you might be leading a "captive" group that participants are required to attend (prison population, spousal abusers, drunk drivers, students who are on probation, teachers needing inservice

**Box 5.4**     *Process Observation of Theme-Related Leader and Member Comments*

This form introduces a new style of process observation and requires some speed and agility. You are asked to write down the name of each person who speaks in the group and a few key words from her or his statement. You will obtain a surprisingly accurate summary of the group using this method. Thus recorded, the sequence of the group discussion becomes a useful way for the group to reflect on what occurred through the session or meeting.

Consider using this form for any session or meeting you observe. Each statement by a leader or by a group member can be classified as to I, We (group), and It (theme). A single statement may include more than one dimension or focus. You may notice that some members prefer to talk about the theme (and thus avoid self-disclosure) while others emphasize their own stories to the neglect of the theme or group. Also record here-and-now and there-and-then with "H" and "T."

If you are observing a group that is deliberately using the theme-centered model, you will want to give special attention to balance. The leader may ask you to inform the group if they are failing to balance time among the three dimensions.

| *Who spoke and key words from her or his comment* | *I, We, It* *(or other focus)* | *Here-and-Now,* *There-and-Then* |
|---|---|---|
| 1. | | |
| 2. | | |
| 3. | | |
| 4. | | |
| 5. | | |
| 6. | | |
| 7. | | |
| 8. | | |
| 9. | | |
| 10. | | |
| 11. | | |
| 12. | | |
| 13. | | |
| 14. | | |
| 15. | | |
| 16. | | |
| 17. | | |
| 18. | | |
| 19. | | |
| 20. | | |
| 21. | | |
| 22. | | |

(Note: Continue numbering on a separate piece of paper.)

credits). Dealing directly and honestly with these critical contextual issues will often be necessary if you are to succeed with your group. Contextual issues of race, gender, and other multicultural issues often need to be discussed as part of the background for the group sessions.

In short, be prepared to bend and change the triangle of discussion as the group progresses. Again, think of the orchestra conductor. The conductor finds a dynamic balance by pacing and leading both individuals and the total ensemble. Listening to each player is central, but awareness of the totality of the orchestra or group is essential for the conductor to merge instruments and musical ideas into a unity of harmonious sound.

Just like the orchestra conductor, you will find that the microskills of attending, the basic listening sequence, and focusing are most useful in your conducting an effective theme-centered group.

## DEFINING THE LEADERSHIP SKILLS FOR UNDERSTANDING AND WORKING WITH VARYING STAGES AND DIMENSIONS OF GROUP PROCESS

The microskills presented thus far provide you with the ability to attend and observe, to listen, and to focus. Theme-centered ideas provide all of us with a basic time-centered framework for utilizing the skills. However, we still need to think about the *process* of groups. How do we start? What do we do to integrate these microskills in practice?

Theorists have offered many ideas about what occurs in groups. Particularly influential have been those who emphasize stage theory, a time-focused, expected, logical sequence of events that usually occur in any group—structured or unstructured. Examples of theorists who present varying theories of stages are shown in Box 5.5

The history of stage theory was first carefully reviewed by Gazda in 1971; he cites Bach (1954) as the first theorist who attempted to organize group process into seven sequential stages. Gazda himself has been highly influential in stage theory as it was he who originated the language and ideas of four time-centered sequential stages: exploration, transition, action, and termination; these still dominate the field. In addition, Gazda should be particularly noted as perhaps the first major theorist promoting group work as development. His educational emphasis remains important for psychoeducational and theme-centered work today (Gazda, 1989).

### Theme-Centered Theory

Ruth Cohn (1961, 1969 a, 1969b) is not generally cited by texts and researchers in group work even though her theme-centered ideas have become generic and central to group counseling and therapy. Many authorities suggest that women pioneers in the field tend to be ignored by predominantly White male writers (see, for example, Jordan, Kaplan, Miller, Stiver, & Surrey, 1991). Cohn suggests beginning the group by providing structure and information about the theme followed by a second stage in which dynamic balancing of focus (individual, group, theme) brings the group together. In the third stage, the theme is the connecting link for discussion in depth. Finally, the group experience is related to daily life in the "real world."

**Box 5.5**   *Stages in Group Process as Viewed by Varying Theorists*

| Theorist | Stage 1 | Stage 2 | Stage 3 | Stage 4 |
|---|---|---|---|---|
| **Cohn** (1961, 1969a, 1969b) | Structuring the theme | Dynamic balancing of individual, group, and theme | Theme as connecting link to which individual and group relate | Relating group experience to the "real world" |
| **Tuckman** (1965) Five stages | Forming | Storming Norming | Performing | Adjourning |
| **Yalom** (1970, 1995) | Orientation and hesitant participation | Conflict, dominance, and rebellion | Intimacy, closeness, and cohesiveness | Termination |
| **Rogers** (1970) Fifteen issues expected to appear in roughly sequential order | 1. Milling around | 2. Resistance to personal exploration<br>3. Description of past feelings<br>4. Expression of negative feelings | 5. Exploration of personally meaningful material<br>6. Expression of immediate personal feelings<br>7. Development of healing capacity in the group<br>8. Self-acceptance and the beginning of change<br>9. The cracking of facades<br>10. The individual receiving feedback<br>11. Confrontation<br>13. The basic encounter<br>14. The expression of positive feelings and closeness<br>15. Behavior changes in the group | 12. The helping relationship outside the group sessions<br><br>Behavior change outside the group (not part of list, but stressed in a later chapter) |
| **Gazda** (1971) | Exploration | Transition | Action | Termination |
| **Corey** (2000) | Initial | Transition | Working | Ending |

*(continued)*

**Box 5.5 (continued)**

| Theorist | Stage 1 | Stage 2 | Stage 3 | Stage 4 |
|---|---|---|---|---|
| **Pack-Brown, Whittington-Clark, & Parker** (1998) Five stages | *Umoja*—unity, developing group cohesiveness | | *Kujichagulia*—authenticity and self-esteem *Ujima*—collective work responsibility *Imani*—faith | *Kuumba*—self-determination and empowerment |
| **Ivey Taxonomy** (Ivey, 1973; Ivey & Ivey, 1999) Five stages and dimensions. The third dimension—the positive asset search—appears in all stages and dimensions | Initiating the group—rapport and structuring, establishing goals | Gathering data—stories, dynamic balancing of focus | Working—examining goals, sharing, confronting, restorying | Ending—generalizing and acting on new stories |

## Forming, Storming, Norming, Performing, Adjourning

This catchy, rhyming approach to stage theory (Tuckman, 1965) has been highly influential in the way the field thinks about groups. There is an expectation that tensions will inevitably arise before a group settles down (norming) and gets to work. This expectation for problems in the group is reiterated in the work of such prominent theorists as Yalom (1970, 1995) and Rogers (1970).

In contrast with these views, we, the authors of this text, believe that you will find potential for conflict at all stages of the group. The idea that conflict occurs only in the second stage is an oversimplification. You will have resistant group members just as the group forms, some will have difficulty in Stage 2, but many others will save their contentious issues for the working and termination stages of the group. This is one reason we prefer the word *dimensions* to stages; groups often have "everything happening at once." Chapter 9 on managing conflict emphasizes the point that conflict can occur at any time in the group process. Furthermore, along with Ruth Cohn, we suggest that adequate rapport building and structuring can greatly reduce the time spent on harmful conflictual issues and ease resolution when such difficulties occur.

## Descriptive View of Process

Carl Rogers's description of what occurs in his person-centered groups is highly insightful and clear. He accurately describes fifteen issues that tend to occur sequentially in most groups, both structured and unstructured. Although fifteen issues are more than many of us can remember, most group leaders can benefit from reviewing his classic small paperback *Carl Rogers on Encounter Groups* (1970). His specific and humane style of group leadership will be helpful to you throughout your career as a group leader.

### Initial, Transition, Working, Termination

The neutral and brief description of group stages by Corey (2000) is currently one of the most influential, along with that of Gazda (1971) cited earlier. Corey suggests specific actions for each group stage and is particularly strong in discussing major ethical issues. The titles and view of the stages/dimensions used in this book have been influenced primarily by Cohn, Corey, and Gazda.

### An Afrocentric View

A culture-centered view of group work is presented in *Images of Me: A Guide to Group Work with African-American Women* (Pack-Brown, Whittington-Clark, & Parker, 1998). Although the discussions are women's issues within a specific cultural context, this book has major implications for group work in general and for men as well.

*Images of Me* is built around African values of unity (*umoja*) and collective responsibility *(ujima)*. The goal of group work is to facilitate both individual self-esteem and group pride. Issues of race and ethnicity become central themes around which groups develop. In this sense, this work is similar to that of Ruth Cohn in its dynamic balancing of the individual, the group, and the theme. Significantly, however, *Images of Me* builds on a very different cultural base. Whereas most group theory focuses on helping individuals find their place in a Euro-American view of the world, the book demonstrates how group theory is culturally based.

Box 5.6 illustrates critical gender and racial worldview factors among different perceptions of group process. The authors of this Afrocentric theory and practice suggest that all group workers would do well to examine the underlying worldview exhibited in our group practice. Individual and group goals in this approach are very much in harmony. This chart is helpful in raising some critical issues of similarity and difference, but be aware that individuals in your groups will vary widely on these issues. For example, competition can be valued by both men and women and, at times, some males may be more emotionally expressive than some women.

## A HOLISTIC PERSPECTIVE: THE IVEY TAXONOMY

There are many useful theoretical stage theory models. It is important that, over time, you become familiar with each as they all provide useful ways to think about what is happening in your group. However, groups don't always follow a linear stage model. Conflict can occur at any time from beginning to end. Rogers himself indicates this point and recognizes, for example, that confrontation may occur early, or that even late in the group some members may discuss negative feelings or stories from their past.

Issues and concerns in group process can arise at any time—their appearance is not predictably sequential. The holistic orientation to groups endorsed here suggests the importance of a *both/and* approach. Sequences such as those described by

**Box 5.6**    *Selected Gender and Racial Worldview Factors**

| *Worldview Factors* | *African-American Females* | *European-American Females* | *European-American Males* |
|---|---|---|---|
| Axiology (What is valued) | Cooperation<br>Emotional vitality<br>Community<br>Self-in-relation<br>Direct/Open<br>Nonverbal and verbal expression | Cooperation<br>Open emotions<br>Community<br>Self-in-relation<br>Direct/Controlled<br>Verbal and nonverbal expression | Competition<br>Controlled emotions<br>Individualism<br>Self as individual<br>Direct/Open<br>Verbal expression |
| Ethos (Guiding beliefs) | Interdependence<br>Collective behavior<br>Harmony | Interdependence<br>Collective behavior<br>Harmony | Independence<br>Separateness<br>Mastery/Control |
| Epistemology (How one knows) | Feelings<br>Experience (African-Americans and women) | Feelings<br>Experience (other women) | Thoughts<br>Count/Measure |
| Logic (Reasoning process) | Diunital (both/and)<br>Employment (survival/fulfillment)<br>Relational<br>Connectedness | Dichotomous (if/then, either/or)<br>Employment (fulfillment/survival)<br>Relational connectedness | Dichotomous (if/then, either/or)<br>Employment (survival/fulfillment)<br>Self as individual |
| Concept of time | Event-focused<br>Present/Future–focused<br>Cyclical | Precise<br>Future/Present–focused<br>Cyclical | Precise<br>Future-focused<br>Measurable |
| Concept of self | Extended self (I am because we are. Racial and gender factors are significant.) | Extended self (I think, therefore I am. I am because we are. Female factors are significant.) | Individual (I think, therefore I am.) |
| Critical needs in relationships | "We" care (relate)<br>"We" understand (connect)<br>"We" appreciate each other | "We" care (relate)<br>"We" understand (connect)<br>"We" appreciate each other | "I" can do/am trusted<br>"I" am accepted<br>"I" am appreciated |

*From Sherlon P. Pack-Brown, Linda E. Whittington-Clark, and Woodrow M. Parker. *Images of Me: A Guide to Group Work with African-American Women*, p 5. Copyright © 1998 by Allyn & Bacon. Reprinted by permission.

stage theory do occur, but issues constantly surface and resurface in a *cyclical* fashion. Expect termination issues to appear sometimes just as you are starting a group; conflict and negative verbal encounters can occur any time; and just as you are thinking the group is about to end, a member may start telling a new story from the past or provide a new view of what has occurred in the group.

**Box 5.7**    *A Cyclical View of Stages and Dimensions in Group Process*

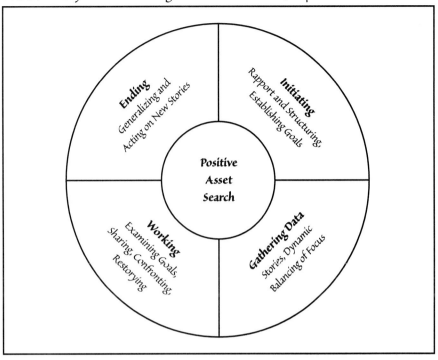

Box 5.6 on gender and racial worldviews talks about the cyclical orientation of African-American and European-American females. In truth, we believe, the cyclical dimension occurs for males of both races, but perhaps with less awareness on their part. Moreover, those of other ethnic/racial backgrounds experience the repeating dimensions of cycles again and again. *Recycling* has been identified by Parham (1989) as central to both individual and group change processes. While sequential stage theory is important, it may not describe the full picture of what occurs in the group.

The Ivey Taxonomy and the microskills group work model (Ivey, 1973; Ivey & Ivey, 1999) endorses linear stage theory *and* simultaneously emphasizes the importance of a recycling circular model (see Box 5.7). The words *stage* and *dimension* are used interchangeably to emphasize sequence and holistic recycling.

Note that positive asset search—the fifth dimension or stage—serves as the central hub of the Ivey Taxonomy. This is in the belief that a positive approach to groups will provide a base for growth and understanding. Conflict management and confrontation of difficult issues become more possible when positive resources and strengths are identified.

The figure in Box 5.7 is another challenge to your ability to orchestrate a dynamic balance between pacing and leading. With experience, you will gradually learn when to hold to a sequence from beginning to end and when to deviate with the immediate emerging needs of the group. We suggest that your observational skills will be important in this process. As you note an individual or the total group with emergent emotional or cognitive needs, allow that subtheme to come out in detail, even though at the moment it seems disruptive. A good rule is to tell your group ahead of time "Disturbances take precedence." In her theme-centered work, Ruth Cohn recognized that individuals and groups as a whole have new needs that they discover in the group process. This can result in the necessity of hearing new stories and perhaps even negotiating new themes and goals for your group.

The next question is an important one: How can we integrate all this theory directly into practice? How might these ideas be relevant to your personal work in leading groups?

## INTEGRATING THEME-CENTERED GROUP WORK AND THE IVEY TAXONOMY

This section provides a foundation for implementing a theme-centered group within the holistic stage/dimension constructs of the Ivey Taxonomy. Following you will find specific descriptions of activities you can use as you develop your own theme-centered group, and Chapter 6 provides a transcript illustrating the concepts in action.

Box 5.8 summarizes this section with a practical checklist of the most critical items for generating your own approach to holistic theme-centered group interaction. You may wish to refer to this box as you think through your reactions to this approach.

**Box 5.8**   *Integration of Skills Group Checklist: Theme-Centered Group Interaction and the Ivey Taxonomy*

|  |  |
|---|---|
|  | The following list is not complete, but it represents a general summary of points made in this chapter that you may wish to think about as you facilitate your own group experience. |
| *Preplanning* | ▲ Co-leader? Meet to plan collaboratively.<br>▲ Theme? What topic will you select?<br>▲ Obtaining volunteers? Who? When?<br>▲ Prescreening? Meet with each volunteer and go over the group and share basic rules and plans with them. Share the group contract.<br>▲ Location? Include time to straighten up the room before you start and make it as attractive as possible.<br>▲ Recycling: *Be prepared to move to any stage or dimension at any time.* While sequential views are helpful, each group represents its own microculture and members may be expected to recycle issues in their own unique manner. |
| *Facilitating the Group* | *1: Initiating the Group—Rapport and Structuring, Establishing Goals*<br>▲ Share names and expectations and wishes for the group experience.<br>▲ Structure the group and establish goals. We recommend that you use a wall-board or newsprint to outline the sequence for the session. Then, with the group, establish individual and group goals.<br>▲ Discuss rules for conversation, including confidentiality, and invite group members to share their ideas. It is often useful to talk about theme-centered group interaction and your plan to divide time equally among individual, group, and theme discussion. |

*2: Gathering Data—Stories and Dynamic Balancing of Focus*

▲ Using observation, attending, basic listening skills, and focusing, draw out individual comments and stories and theme.

▲ Move to commenting on the group process and encourage group members to do the same.

▲ Encourage group members to offer each other feedback.

▲ Balance focus among the "I," "we," and "it."

▲ Summarize what has occurred in the group before moving to the next phase or stage.

*3: The Positive Asset Search—The Third Dimension*

▲ This can be a special section before or after gathering data or you may wish to include it as part of all phases of your group.

▲ Use the BLS to draw out data. Draw on information here periodically as needed when group members need support.

*4: Working—Examining Goals, Sharing, Confronting, Restorying*

▲ Continue dynamic balancing by establishing both individual and group goals around the theme.

▲ Use listening skills to encourage further stories, but expect participants to share in ways that may lead to confrontation, challenge, and angry, troubled feelings. Do not be afraid of conflict, but reframe it as an opportunity to learn diverse views and perspectives.

▲ Through listening and summarizing, start looking for new stories and new perspectives from group members.

▲ During the working phase, focus on the here-and-now and on the group as a totality or on subgroups.

*5: Ending—Generalizing and Acting on New Stories*

▲ Summarize what has occurred in the group, but also encourage members to take on the task of summarization, thus encouraging more ownership of the process and perhaps better generalization of learning.

▲ Encourage members to share what they have learned about themselves, the topic, and the group.

▲ Encourage plans for transfer to learning to outside the group.

## Dimension 1: Initiating the Group—Rapport and Structuring, Establishing Goals

Following are typical activities that would occur during the initial phases of the group with emphasis on rapport and structuring:

▲ After greeting the group, it is usually wise to go over administrative details and ground rules for discussion briefly as the first group activity. *Keep this short and indicate to your group clearly that you are open to talking with them further about these issues at any point.*

▲ A next step is often to ask people to tell their names and why they decided to come to this particular group. Each person would have an opportunity to disclose what he or she chooses. Goals can be discussed at this point.

▲ Many leaders also include a structured exercise at the beginning. For example, you could divide the group into pairs, trios, or groups of four and jointly work through a structured exercise such as the one on gender connections in Box 5.1. Then each pair or small subgroup could share their experience and learning with the total group.

The goals of Dimension/Stage 1 include informing participants of the process, alleviating anxiety and building comfort and trust, and enabling each person to say something in a safe way. This is particularly important and is sometimes called informally "buying in" to the group. We "buy in" or join a group by saying something meaningful and/or self-disclosing. Structured exercises are particularly helpful with anxious or shy participants and those who may be mistrustful of the group process. On the other hand, unstructured activities are favored by some leaders, who believe they bring a certain reality that forces the person to look at his or her personal style of communication more closely. Some unstructured interpersonal person-centered counseling and therapy groups might have the early building of anxiety as a goal.

## Dimension 2: Gathering Data—Stories and Dynamic Balancing of Focus

Having started group formation in Stage 1, it is now appropriate to encourage more group talk. As much as possible, you as leader move to a backup but very active role of observing, listening, and helping the group move in its own direction. Note that in the initiation process discussed earlier, the leader took charge in a formal way to initiate the group. Now he or she has the challenge of turning participation over to the group. This redirection to group participation is less prominent in unstructured groups as the lack of structure has already demonstrated that the group is for the participants present.

The theme of the group is by now well known and the leader usually sits back quietly while the group begins to explore the topic and tell their stories. If members are hesitant to begin, you may need to open the topic and ask members to share their stories. In the early stages, you may find yourself using the basic listening sequence to help individuals talk about themselves and the theme.

▲ After several individuals have told their stories, the leader may say something like "Several of us have shared so far. What has the *group* noticed about what is happening?" This focus on group process enables the participants to stop, slow down, and examine the group as a totality rather than just individual story tellers. Through this type of discussion, members can start learning commonalities and differences between themselves and others.

▲ As part of this process, the leader likely would introduce the original group theme more clearly—"Together we will share our thoughts and feelings around connections. The group seems to be able share rather openly. What understandings, or perhaps even new understandings have you discovered about the theme of connections and its importance or relevance to you and the group?" This focus on the theme would be repeated periodically throughout the group. Note that as members talk about the theme, their conversations change to a topic focus as compared to an "I" focus.

▲ Theme-centered group interaction throughout would continue with a balance of individual focus, group focus, and theme focus. In addition, you could anticipate appropriate emphasis on other focus dimensions such as cultural/environmental/contextual, family, significant others, and so on. The leader might ask, "How has the context and theme changed as we have viewed this issue from varying perspectives?" At this point, it may be appropriate to specify other cultural/environmental/contextual factors such as the family, spiritual/moral issues, or community issues.

Assuming a time-limited one-session three-hour group, the leader can lead to another dimension by summarizing what has occurred in the group thus far or by asking members to say what has occurred for them in the group to this point. It is not necessary for the leader to do all the summarizing and listening. With the leader balancing the focus between the group and individuals, groups will often be able to provide key observations themselves.

## Dimension 3: Conducting the Positive Asset Search

The positive identification of strengths can be a third stage of group development or it can be integrated throughout all stages. For example, drawing out stories of strengths could be part of a warm-up exercise in the initiation process. This third aspect could be completed as the second activity or topic within the group. When ending a group, leaders often close with positive stories and encouraging feedback to members. In short, the positive asset search should recur during all portions of the group work; the leader can use it as part of the pacing and leading functions of dynamic balancing.

As leader, you should not forget to encourage the group as a whole to examine its own strengths: "What are some positive things that this group does for us?" Similarly, the theme-centered talk can help group members learn practical strengths to deal with daily life issues. The influencing skills of feedback and positive reframing of stories (see Chapter 7) will be especially helpful here.

## Dimension 4: Working—Examining Goals, Sharing, Confronting, Restorying

The implicit goal for group members when they joined the group was to explore the theme and what it meant to them personally. It is often helpful in the working phase to explore personal and group goals more specifically and openly in the group. Individual and group goals may have changed from the initial stages of the group.

One obvious option is for the group to continue general exploration as they have done in earlier parts of the group experience. People and groups are constantly dealing with goals at a conscious or unconscious level. The more unstructured the group, the less specific attention will be given to goals and goal setting.

However, for your early work in theme-centered group interaction, we suggest that you give explicit attention to both individual and group goals. This could be done by making some variation of the following statement:

> We have been talking for quite a while; now I'd like us to stop and think by ourselves what the group has meant for us so far. Also what might we personally have as a goal for ourselves and for the group as a whole for the rest of the time we have together? Just sit quietly for a moment and think about goal setting and our group theme.

Out of this process will come several possibilities. Some members will be happy just to explore the issue further; others may want to set up individual objectives for themselves. At this stage it is important for people to think through why they are in the group; your task is to help them begin exploring how something learned in this group might be transferred later to real life.

Some theme-centered group leaders at this point might ask the members to sit quietly and think carefully about themselves and their goals as these relate to the theme. It may be useful to have members share their goals. Then they can review how the group, the theme, and individual goals are related. This is an ideal place for the leader to practice dynamic balancing of focus.

The theme-centered group may also work at this point to develop joint goals, perhaps leading to a communal project. If the group has joint goals, then a working session might follow in which action plans for individuals and the group could be worked out.

In this stage, participants may confront one another, discussing differences and similarities, perhaps giving advice and direction (both desired and undesired). For the moment, we suggest that you as leader continue to emphasize listening and focusing skills. It is easy to lose focus on the theme and the group at this point. Thus you as leader need to pay particular attention to the dynamic balance occurring in your group. If you hold true to a listening style, you will find that your group will function quite well.

Restorying and thinking in new ways about personal and group issues is an important part of this dimension. You can encourage restorying in several ways by helping the group with linking. As leader, you will note similarities and parallels as well as marked differences among group members' verbalizations and stories. You can direct your members' attention to the similarities and differences in individual statements by summarizing what is happening in the group and by linking discussion points on the major theme.

There is also a group story with its own special relationship to the theme. If you focus on the group and listen carefully to what the members are saying, you'll find yourself increasingly able to make more and more of your leads focus on the group itself. Focusing on individuals and stories is, of course, vital; but group work is about focusing on groups and their processes.

### Dimension 5: Ending—Generalizing and Acting on New Stories

Each group will be evaluated in terms of the products that result from the group interaction. Theme-centered group sessions generally end with a summary of what individuals have said, observations of what occurred for the group as a whole, and new insights and points made about the theme itself. The leader can provide this summarization, but a more useful tactic is encouraging group members to share their own summaries of what has happened in the group. As appropriate, the leader might add "a summary of summaries" linking various themes commented on by the members.

It is important to realize that endings or concludings are continuous throughout the life of the group. Every time the topic was changed or something significant happened in the group, there was an ending and a new beginning. The final stages of a group are simply a continuation of this process rehearsed throughout the life of the group.

The group leader typically has the responsibility of defining the products or outcomes of the group as they relate to the goals generated and the working alternatives discovered in Phase 4. The meaningfulness of the group will be judged according to the process- or content-related products that have emerged from the group activity.

In summarizing, the group leader might articulate the history of the group as it moved through the previous four stages of development and recycled stages as necessary. Each group writes its own history with pleasant and challenging stories about itself that will give meaning to the group experience.

The group members may want to articulate action plans about how this group experience will lead to changes in their back-home activities. While the members may need some time to think about what, if any, changes they will make as a result of participation, it will still be appropriate for the group leader to challenge them to apply what they have learned.

Sometimes it is useful to ask each member to state what he or she has learned so far in the group. Other alternatives are to ask the members, "What has stood out for you in this group thus far?" "What might you take home from today's group?" If the members do not articulate what they have learned, they may be left with only a warm feeling that will evaporate quickly and be lost forever. If the members express what they have learned in their own words, however, group learning may be more lasting.

In many cultures, any group of importance will end with the members eating together. Serving food becomes a symbolic act that can provide meaningful closure for a group, expressing feelings and belonging that might be more difficult to articulate in words.

## USING THEME-CENTERED GROUP INTERACTION AND STAGES/DIMENSIONS WITH CHILD AND ADOLESCENT GROUPS

Most groups for young people are theme centered. For both children and adolescents, groups that are focused on divorce, social skills, bereavement, and friendship are especially useful and widespread. Children whose parents are moving to a new location often profit from attending moving or transition groups. Children's theme-centered groups tend to be shorter and more structured in nature, with more active direction by the leader.

Special topic groups on sexuality, family issues, dating concerns, and drug and alcohol abuse are important for teens. At the more structured level, topics such as stress management, study skills, and college choice are frequently offered.

One area of increasing importance is work with trauma and violence, helping children or teens who have suffered severe distress meet together and discuss their issues. The linear stage model may be a good beginning point with this type of work, but the more serious the emotional impact, the greater will be the likelihood that the planned structure will be changed by what occurs in the group. For example, the holistic orientation of this chapter may be useful in that some youth may be very hesitant to discuss their issues at the beginning while others will want to share their deep emotional scars. You may find yourself discussing a serious concern one moment, then examining individual and group strengths through the positive asset search immediately afterward. Then, an individual may want to tell a story from the past while another person seeks to work on behavior outside the group. Many things can be happening at once.

In such groups, the stage model remains useful, but perhaps it is better thought of as dimensions one must be sure to include as part of each group. Nonetheless, a planned sequential structure may be needed so that the group does not lack direction and purpose. We suggest that you take time for each stage/dimension but remain flexible so as to meet the emerging needs of the group. Remember that children and teens are naturally less structured than adults and can generally benefit from a solid underlying framework.

## MOVING TOWARD YOUR OWN LEADERSHIP STYLE

Three major ideas are presented in this chapter that you will likely find useful in generating your own approach to group leadership. First, the basic ideas of theme-centered group interaction were presented as they relate to microskills concepts.

What are your own thoughts and feelings about theme-centered groups? What stands out for you as something you would particularly like to emphasize in your own development as a group leader? Write your notes here.

_____

_____

_____

_____

Second, stage theories of group development were presented. This linear model of group process progression over time can be highly useful in helping you understand how to manage a group. But, as emphasized throughout this chapter, individuals and groups don't always fit easily into a theory. Thus, as the third idea, a circular, holistic circle was drawn integrating stage theory with the microskills framework of story–positive asset–restory–action. You have been presented several alternatives for constructing the group over time. What sense do you make of this presentation? What stands out for you and what type of model do you prefer?

_____

_____

_____

_____

_____

_____

# PRACTICING THEME-CENTERED GROUP INTERACTION: STAGES AND DIMENSIONS, SKILLS, AND STRATEGIES

## 1. Process Observation of Themes in a Group

Box 5.4 provides you with a process observation form for considering the balance of "I," "we," and "it" in a group. Photocopy this form and take it to a group session or a business meeting; use it to record your observations of the balance of attention to individuals, the group, and the theme.

In addition, consider the five-stage/phase/dimension model:

1. Initiating the Group—Rapport and Structuring, Establishing Goals
2. Gathering Data—Stories and Dynamic Balancing of Focus
3. Conducting the Positive Asset Search
4. Working—Examining Goals, Sharing, Confronting, Restorying
5. Ending—Generalizing and Acting on New Stories

Note how the group progresses through time. Is the positive asset search part of the group that you observe? Do they take time to build rapport and structure what is to happen? Does each individual have a chance to provide data and her or his own story? What happens during the work phase? Does the group allow for generalization and follow-up of their discussion?

## 2. The Fish Bowl

As you might anticipate, at this point we'd like your class to conduct a full group session using the ideas presented here. Two major possibilities exist. The first is for two volunteer leaders and six to eight volunteer members to conduct a group while the class observes. The second possibility is to divide the class into groups of six to eight, assembling in various parts of the room in which the class is held. Anticipate at least a half-hour, but more likely an hour, for this exercise.

One or two members serve as leader.

A minimum of four members participate within the group (we suggest six as the ideal number, but adjust your group size to number of participants and leaders available).

One person serves as external observer and provides concrete feedback through the use of observation techniques such as those in the exercise above.

Multiple themes or topics are possible. We suggest you select your own and expand from the suggestions given below:

▲ Sexism and sex-role stereotyping
▲ Racism, heterosexism, language discrimination, ethnic bias, prejudice against a non-English speaker, prejudice against people with handicaps, and social-class intolerance
▲ Ways to handle conflict. (Members discuss past and present conflicts and their styles in "working things out." Sometimes group members are willing to take on immediate conflict they have with their classmates, thus bringing here-and-now immediacy to the situation.)

▲ Alcoholism, drug addiction, smoking, food addiction, and eating difficulties

▲ Family stories (both positive and negative—what do we learn from our families? How do we carry on family stories in our own lives?)

▲ Strengths I gained from my community, family, or friends

▲ No topic (This becomes a modified encounter group in which participants go through a structure very similar to that presented in the transcript in the next chapter, but no topic is presented.)

### 3. Your Own Group Practice

Complete this exercise in conjunction with reading Chapter 6. There are also other group practice exercises in that chapter.

It is appropriate that you by yourself or with a co-leader find a set of volunteers and conduct a group session for a minimum of two hours. If possible, audiotape or videotape your session and ensure that you have an external observer, ideally someone from the class or workshop who will observe you.

Box 5.8 presents a checklist of items that you (and your co-leader) can use in planning. If your session is audiotaped or videotaped, use Box 5.4 to classify the comments of your group members. Did this group balance the "I," "we," and "it"? What proportion of comments were here-and-now and there-and-then? What type of stage/dimension model best characterizes the progress of your group?

## REFERENCES

Bach, G. (1954). *Intensive group psychotherapy.* New York: Ronald Press.

Cohn, R. (1961). A group-therapeutic workshop on counter-transference. *International Journal of Group Psychotherapy, 11.*

Cohn, R. (1969a). From couch to circle to community. In H. Ruitenbeck (Ed.), *Group therapy.* New York: Atherton Press.

Cohn, R. (1969b). The theme-centered interactional method: Group therapists as group educators. *Journal of Group Process, 2,* 19–36.

Corey, G. (2000). *Theory & practice of group counseling* (5th ed.). Pacific Grove, CA: Brooks/Cole.

Gazda, G. (1971). *Group counseling: A developmental approach.* Boston: Allyn & Bacon.

Gazda, G. (1989). *Group counseling: A developmental approach* (4th ed.). Boston: Allyn & Bacon

Ivey, A. (1973). Demystifying the group process: Adapting microcounseling procedures to counseling in groups. *Educational Technology, 13,* 27–31.

Ivey, A., & Ivey, M. (1999). *Intentional interviewing and counseling: Facilitating development in a multicultural world.* Pacific Grove, CA: Brooks/Cole.

Jordan, J., Kaplan, S., Miller, J., Stiver, I., & Surrey, J. (Eds.). (1991). *Women's growth in connection.* New York: Guilford.

Pack-Brown, S., Whittington-Clark, L., & Parker, W. (1998). *Images of me: A guide to group work with African-American women.* Boston: Allyn & Bacon

Parham, T. (1989). Cycles of psychological Nigrescence. *The Counseling Psychologist, 17,* 187–226.

Rogers, C. (1970). *Carl Rogers on encounter groups.* New York: Harper & Row.

Tuckman, B. (1965). Development sequence in small groups. *Psychological Bulletin, 63,* 384–399.

Yalom, I. (1970). *The theory and practice of group psychotherapy.* New York: Basic Books.

Yalom, I. (1995). *The theory and practice of group psychotherapy* (4th ed.). New York: Basic Books.

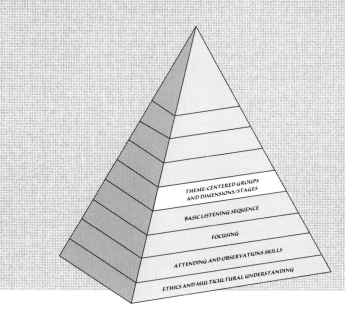

THEME-CENTERED GROUPS AND DIMENSIONS/STAGES

BASIC LISTENING SEQUENCE

FOCUSING

ATTENDING AND OBSERVATIONS SKILLS

ETHICS AND MULTICULTURAL UNDERSTANDING

# CHAPTER 6

# Integrating Microskills in a Full Group Session, Part II: Transcript of a Complete Theme-Centered Group Session

## CHAPTER GOALS

One of the major premises of this book is that group leaders can intentionally plan interventions with some expectation that their actions will often result in predictable results in group behavior. But as we have often said throughout, groups are ultimately unpredictable and the effective, flexible leader is constantly ready for change.

This chapter continues exploring skill integration by presenting a process analysis of a theme-centered group session utilizing the full Ivey Taxonomy (IT). The IT summarizes the major ideas of this book and provides a statement of expectations one can associate with each skill, strategy, or concept. The multiple skills and strategies of the IT offer actions for versatility. *When the first skill or strategy is not effective, be ready with another; and when in doubt, listen and observe!*

The chapter has the same objectives for understanding and mastery as Chapter 5, with one additional objective emphasizing process analysis:

▲ Integrate observing, attending, basic listening, and focusing skills in a full group session.
▲ Understand the basis of theme-centered groups and how you can balance discussion of individual, group, and thematic issues.
▲ Conceptualize group process as a series of sequential *stages* of movement, including recycling of *dimensions*.
▲ Apply theme-centered group methods to facilitating your own groups.
▲ Utilize the Ivey Taxonomy for process analysis of groups.

# THE IVEY TAXONOMY: INTENTIONAL PLANNING FOR CHANGE

The microskills and strategies of this book are organized into five major groupings:

▲ Attending and observing skills (Chapter 2)
▲ Focusing skills (Chapter 3)
▲ The skills of the basic listening sequence (Chapter 4)
▲ Stages and dimensions (Chapters 5 and 6)
▲ Influencing skills and strategies and confrontation (Chapters 7, 8, and 9)

Together these concepts represent the Ivey Taxonomy (IT), which is summarized in Box 6.1. The IT is a system for organizing group leader *and member* verbal and nonverbal behavior. It is a method you can use to observe what is going on in a group; it is a way you can examine your own behavior as a leader; and it provides a modus operandi for intentional action and flexibility.

Intentionality implies that the group leader can anticipate and predict the consequences of her or his actions in the group. Extensive research on the microskills approach reveals that counselors and leaders can expect certain actions to lead to certain results (cf Daniels & Ivey, in press; Ivey & Daniels, 1999; Ivey & Ivey, 1999).

As we have learned from Ruth Cohn's theme-centered concepts (1961, 1969a, 1969b), however, *expect the unexpected.* Intentional predictions don't always have the consequences we anticipate. It is here that intentional thought and action become all the more important. Expect each group to be somewhat the same as other groups, but always anticipate something you did not predict in the interaction and microculture of any group you lead.

Your level of intentionality will be tested when you meet surprises, new challenges, and disturbances in your groups. Being equipped with multiple skills and strategies, several theories of group process and stages, and experience over time will enable you to meet challenges—and, as we cannot say too many times, when the going gets complex and difficult, listen and observe carefully before acting.

The summary of the Ivey Taxonomy in Box 6.1 includes several skills and strategies that you have not yet encountered. Likely you are already familiar with several of them and they will be discussed in detail in ensuing chapters. You may find Chapter 9 on conflict management and confrontation particularly reassuring and relevant. Chapter 10 will show you how to use the IT as a basis for understanding and working with multiple approaches to groups—structured, unstructured, and therapeutic. The final chapter will review the book and ask you to sort out and rate your level of understanding and mastery of each skill, strategy, and concept.

The IT will be used in the following example transcript as a process analysis system. One of our major recommendations as you work with this book is that you transcribe one or more sessions in which you serve as group leader. This is a challenging process, but we have found that both beginning students and long-term professionals come to view self-analysis of their own work through process analysis and review as the highlight of their work with this book and its concepts.

As mentioned, the transcript in the following section includes a few strategies that will be new to you. And we are asking you to consider conducting a full group session using the theme-centered framework. In this session, we don't expect you to

**Box 6.1**    *The Ivey Taxonomy: Intentional Planning for Change*

| | |
|---|---|
| *1. Attending Behavior* | Culturally Appropriate Listening (by the leader)<br>Observing group members with awareness of individual and cultural differences |
| | Expected consequence: The leader is able to demonstrate culturally appropriate visuals, vocals, verbals, and body language. The leader is able to observe attending behaviors in group members and use the observations as a foundation for applying listening and observing skills and strategies. Group members will talk freely and respond openly, particularly around topics to which attention is given. The leader can observe nonverbal and verbal styles and use these to engage the group members more fully. |
| *2. Focusing* | 2.1. Focusing (Pacing and Leading)<br>Pacing<br>Leading |
| | Expected consequence: The leader is able to "walk with" the group and its members listening to them where they "are" and is also able to lead them toward other focuses and emphases as appropriate. Group members will talk more freely and respond openly, but they will also follow the leader interventions in other appropriate directions. Focusing provides structure and structure provides safety to discuss topics that would otherwise be difficult or dangerous. |
| | 2.2. Focusing (Topic Aspects)<br>Individual<br>Subgroup<br>Group<br>Main theme (problem or issue)<br>Group leader (yourself)<br>Cultural/environmental/contextual issues (moral, spiritual, or religious, economic or social, family, community, multicultural context) |
| | Expected consequence: The leader is able to focus on specific dimensions in the group, both pacing and leading in all areas. Group members and the leader are able to focus their discussion on multiple issues. |
| | 2.3. Focusing (Time Dimensions and Linking)<br>Here-and-now<br>There-and-then<br>Linking here-and-now to there-and-then thoughts, feelings, and behaviors and helping members find patterns and similarities among their lives. |
| | Expected consequence: Participants will discuss their issues in the here-and-now or the there-and-then in ways that correspond to the focus of the leader. If links (relationships, parallels, patterns, or similarities) are suggested by the leader, these links will be discussed—and may lead to new insights in thoughts, feelings, and behavior. |
| *3. Basic Listening Sequence* | 3.1. Open Questions<br>Expected consequence: Participants will answer open questions in some detail. |
| | 3.2. Closed Questions<br>Expected consequence: Participants will give short answers. |

(continued)

**Box 6.1 (continued)**

|  |  |
|---|---|
|  | **3.3. Encourage/Restatement**<br>Expected consequence: Participants will be encouraged to keep talking about the same subject, particularly when encouraged by the leader in a questioning tone of voice.<br><br>**3.4. Paraphrase**<br>Expected consequence: Participants will feel heard. They will tend to move on and not repeat the same story again. If a paraphrase is inaccurate, it provides the participant with an opportunity to correct the leader. If a questioning tone of voice is used, the participant may elaborate further.<br><br>**3.5. Reflect Feelings**<br>Expected consequence: Participants will go more deeply into their emotional experience. They may correct the reflection with another word. A focus on group general tone and feeling can be useful.<br><br>**3.6. Summarize**<br>Expected consequence: Participants will feel heard and often learn how their stories are integrated. Particularly useful is summarizing the group's stories so that varying thoughts, emotions, and behaviors of the group to that point can be integrated, thus facilitating a more centered discussion that builds on past work in the group. The summary provides a more coherent transition from one session or topic to the next. |
| *4. Dimensions/Stages* | **4.1. Initiating the Group—Rapport and Structuring, Establishing Goals**<br>Expected consequence: The group members will feel at ease with each other, know what to expect, and have goals for everyone's participation.<br><br>**4.2. Gathering Data—Stories and Dynamic Balancing of Focus**<br>Expected consequence: The group will share their stories, concerns, and issues and eventually be able to focus on multiple perspectives on these data. The group is also writing a combined story even as the members are telling or listening to each other's stories.<br><br>**4.3. The Positive Asset Search**<br>Expected consequence: Each group member will feel identified as a valuable contributing member with positive strengths. This dimension can be treated as a separate phase or integrated throughout the group process. When the work of the group begins with the positive resources already available and builds on them, the accomplishments of every group member are validated, giving each one hope for the future. In the absence of a positive attitude and hope, change becomes extremely difficult and slow.<br><br>**4.4. Working—Examining Goals, Sharing, Confronting, Restorying**<br>Expected consequence: Through group experience, goals may change. "If you don't know where you are going, you are likely to end up somewhere else." Members work through their issues, experience both conflict and trust as the group moves toward more depth, and may restory their issues. Members may move in positive directions on the Observation of Change Scale. Movement toward action begins. |

|  |  |
|---|---|
|  | **4.5. Ending—Generalizing and Acting on New Stories**<br>Expected consequence: If all stages are completed successfully, expect movement toward change in behavior, thought, and feelings outside the group. |
| *5. Influencing Skills* | Expected consequence: Special note—all the influencing skills may lead to reframes, new ways of thinking, and behavior changes. |
|  | **5.1. Basic Listening Sequence and Focusing**<br>Expected consequence: Effective listening can lead to restorying on the part of group members. |
|  | **5.2. Reframing/Interpreting**<br>Expected consequence: The group or group member discovers another perspective on a story, issue, or problem. The perspective can be generated by a theory or simply by looking at the situation from a new viewpoint. |
|  | **5.3. Self-Disclosure**<br>Expected consequence: Brief self-disclosure by the leader may encourage group members to self-disclose in more depth. |
|  | **5.4. Feedback**<br>Expected consequence: Group members obtain the perspectives of the leader or group members on thoughts, feeling, and behaviors and this may lead them to make changes in their own behavior. |
|  | **5.5. Structuring**<br>Expected consequence: Group members will listen to and follow the directives, opinions, and structures suggested by the leader. |
|  | **5.6. Exploring Logical Consequences**<br>Expected consequence: Participants will discuss their issues in the here-and-now or the there-and-then in ways that correspond to the focus of the leader. If links (relationships, parallels, patterns, or similarities) are suggested by the leader, these links will be discussed—and may lead to new insights in thoughts, feelings, and behavior. |
|  | **5.7. Eliciting and Reflecting Meaning**<br>Expected consequence: Group members will discuss their stories, issues, and concerns in more depth with a special emphasis on deeper meanings and understandings. |
|  | **5.8. Confronting**<br>Expected consequence: Group members will confront discrepancies and conflict with new ideas, thoughts, feelings, and behaviors and these will be manifested in observable change. |

attempt these new strategies; we suggest that you work primarily from the skills and concepts presented thus far. If you focus on listening to your group and work through the stages/dimensions step by step, you have the foundation for successful group work.

## THEME-CENTERED GROUP WORK IN ACTION: TRANSCRIPT

The following transcript has been selected and edited to illustrate several points. The first, and perhaps most important, is that you have the basic preparation so you can facilitate your own theme-centered groups. By now you should have a good command of attending and observation plus skills with the basic listening sequence and focusing; combining these with the ideas in this chapter, you should have a solid foundation and sufficient understanding for reasonable success in facilitating your own groups. However, this is the mid-point in the microskills approach to group work. There is still much to learn about both microskills and theories and practices.

Theme-centered groups are partially structured groups. They have an overall plan and an expected set of events, but the content of each group session is unpredictable. Thus, expect considerable overlap with counseling groups and, occasionally, even therapy groups as compared to other kinds of groups. Issues that emerge from a discussion often change the stage, phase, or dimension of the group instantly.

The five group stages/dimensions provide a structure and checklist for working with the group over time. You may plan to move through the stages/dimensions in a linear order, but very likely you will move back and forth as suggested in the preceding chapter. Notwithstanding, these stages can serve as a checklist for planning and action. In this transcript, the third dimension, the positive asset search, was integrated throughout all the group activities.

The transcript presented below focuses on gender socialization in a group with men and women members. Working with an all-male or all-female group would, of course, change considerably the nature of the group and how issues are discussed. However, the same points of facilitating the group remain: planning the group; considering the structure with stages, phases, and dimensions; and using microskills appropriately.

Jennifer and Ted are co-leading a group of three men and three women. They are students taking a group counseling course similar to the one you are now experiencing. They recruited their group from friends on campus. They chose the topic of gender socialization and male/female sex roles as one they felt would challenge them and, equally important, one that might enable them to recruit volunteers as they practiced their group leadership skills. Prescreening and a group contract were used.

### Initiating the Group—Rapport and Structuring, Establishing Goals

A structured group begins with the leader establishing rapport and letting participants know what is going to happen. The intent is to alleviate anxiety and promote comfort and openness. Usually you'll find some opening activities to help the group get started. However, as a group moves further into the process, specific structure provided by the leader becomes less evident and the group begins to find its own direction. Note that preparation before the meeting begins is an important part of developing rapport and establishing structure or ground rules.

In the example below, Jennifer and Ted decided not to recruit a process observer. By failing to do so, new group leaders miss valuable feedback on their work. The process comments on this session were generated by the authors.

**Edited Transcript**

**Process Comments**

Jennifer and Ted had reserved a room at the campus counseling center for their three-hour session. They had been in the room before and knew it would be a good setting for the group meeting. Nonetheless, they arrived a half-hour early to check out arrangements and organize themselves. To their distress, they found the room in a mess—coffee cups and papers were all over the floor. They quickly picked up and straightened the room. They also arranged the chairs comfortably in a circle. As the volunteer group members arrived, Jennifer and Ted greeted each one and offered them something to drink. They were lucky that all the members arrived on time and were ready to start. These activities were all essential to creating the favorable conditions that would result in positive outcomes.

1. *Ted:* Welcome. As we get started, I'd like make sure we all know one another. Let's start by moving into pairs—select someone you don't know or someone you'd like to know better. (Stops for a moment as the group divides into pairs.) Now, I'd like you to talk to each other for five minutes. Learn the person's name, where he or she is from, and then introduce that person. (Pause as he checks to see that everyone understands what he has said.) And, as part of that introduction, we want to hear a positive asset, strength, or experience representing that person. It is OK to write down a few points for your introduction if you wish.

1. This group spends considerable time in getting to know one another. Ted wisely gives only *one* instruction at a time. Too many leaders give all the instructions at one time, thus confusing a group. Then instructions may have to be repeated several times. Note the emphasis on finding positive assets even in Ted's first set of comments to the group. Each person has a chance to say something and have an early opportunity to "buy into" the group. If we feel good about ourselves, we are more likely to explore issues about which we are less certain. Ted knows that some people are a bit shy in front of groups and gives permission to write down basic information. A few participants get nervous when introducing someone else and forget the name—not a good way for either of the pair to "buy into" the group. This is the strategy of structuring discussed in Chapter 8.

2. Names and introductions omitted in this transcript.

2. Allow sufficient time for getting acquainted, but also recall that some unstructured groups will begin with complete silence. Do you want to build comfort or anxiety? If you use introductions, don't fail to participate yourself in the beginning exercise.

3. *Jennifer:* So, we all have something to contribute to this group. It's good to see familiar faces and to hear the good stories. I also noted that this group already seems to have some strong feelings about gender issues. And I see pride in being male and female.

3. Jennifer uses the microskills to summarize what has been occurring in the group. She gives some focus to individuals but emphasizes the group as a whole, and also emphasizes the theme.

*(continued)*

**Edited Transcript**                                    **Process Comments**

4. *Jennifer* (beginning the session): Well, we're all here and Ted and I thank you for coming. We have three hours to explore issues of gender socialization and sex roles. As we begin, we would like to share a few things with you. It's important that we have some ground rules for our discussion. First, it is important that you only share what you wish to. Feel free to pass and not comment on anything that happens. This is not a therapy group nor are we professional leaders; but we suspect that all of us can learn a good deal from each other. While we can't offer legal protections of total confidentiality, we also think it is important to stress that whatever is said within our group remains private and protected.

    An important general rule of theme-centered groups is "Disturbances take precedence." If you become angry, troubled, or feel something welling up, bring it to the group if you can. If you hold back when something important is occurring for you, then the group as a whole will miss an opportunity. Do the points I've just made serve as a reasonable group contract?

    All of this might be summarized as "Be your own person with an awareness of other group members' needs." As we mentioned when we talked with you before you came here, we'd like to audiotape the group. This tape will be kept confidential between us and our professor, but if anyone has an objection at any time, let me know and we will turn off the recorder.

    What else might you like to add to our contract?

5. *Candace:* I don't really see it as a problem. I think I'm ready. (Other group members nod in agreement.)

6. *Ted:* In this group, we're going to explore the theme of general socialization and sex roles. What does it mean to be male or female in this culture and on this campus? As we explore this, we'd like to look at our own personal stories, the way we interact as men and women in our group, and how the general theme relates to us and our lives. I'd like to begin with a little meditation on

4. Virtually all groups need to begin with some variation of this statement including the invitation to participate in developing unique rules for each group. The invitation to involvement begins the process of giving power to group members. Again we see the skills of structuring. The focus here is on the group with a brief mention of the thematic topic.

    Saying that disturbances take precedence invites participants to speak out freely. It is also one reason that we cannot count on any group following a preset plan. If we ignore disturbances, we may find ourselves in trouble later on.

Note the closed question at the end that serves as a checkout and encourages group members to respond.

    Another invitation to participate. Obviously, you must obtain permission from the group members to audiotape or videotape your session. When the members allow you to make such a tape, you will find it invaluable as a way to examine your own style of group leadership.

    Open question inviting participation.

5. Often participants will want to ask questions at this point. Be ready with answers and also encourage the total group to generate a group response to a member's question.

6. It is sometimes wise at this point to ask group members to share their expectations and needs around the group experience. If expectations are shared, the group can move forward with both individual and group goals. In this warm-up exercise of the triple silence, Ted approaches the issue of expectations and early goal setting through personal self-exploration.

**Edited Transcript**

**Process Comments**

our topic in silence. It will help us all get started and put us on the same wavelength. Our first exercise is called the triple silence. We'll focus on our group theme, on ourselves as individuals, and on our total group.

Often it is important to make goal setting more explicit. It is useful simply to ask, "What needs/expectations/goals do you have for our time together?" This starts the goal-setting process early.

7. *Jennifer:* Could we just sit quietly now for a few moments—perhaps you may even want to close your eyes. I'd like you to think about the group theme—gender socialization and sex roles. What do these words mean for you? Could you think about this just for a moment by yourself?

7. This is a structuring directive followed by an open question with a focus on the theme.

Note the flow between the two group leaders. Working out a complementary style is not always easy. Nonetheless, having someone work with you in the early stages of group work can be valuable and reassuring. Allow yourself time to plan and communicate freely. Follow-up discussion after the group is essential.

8. (one minute of silence)

8. How comfortable are you with silence? Using silent times allows you to observe nonverbal communication in your group.

9. *Ted:* Now, please turn the focus to you as an individual. How are you feeling right now—comfortable? anxious? excited? What is going on with you at this moment? What led you to join this group?

9. With the open questions, Ted moves the focus from the theme to the individual. Note the emphasis on here-and-now rather than there-and-then. Ultimately, this shift is useful in helping the group move to a more open, emotional level.

10. (one minute of silence)

11. *Jennifer:* Now, please open your eyes and look at the people about the room. How does it feel for you to be here with these people at this time? Finally, think of this group with whom you'll share the next few hours. What would you like to tell them and what would you like members of the group to tell you?

11. Open question, focus on group. Members are encouraged to look at themselves as a group and people-in-relation one to another. Again note the focus on the here-and-now.

12. (one minute of silence)

12. How comfortable will you be with periods of silence?

13. *Ted:* What occurs for you right now as we start this group?

13. Open question, focus on individual and group with here-and-now emphasis.

14. (long silence from the group, the tension is clearly rising)

14. Should the leaders wait and see what happens? Often, this is wise and helps the group learn that they need to speak up.

## Gathering Data—Stories and Dynamic Balancing of Focus

This second group stage or dimension builds on the rapport developed earlier and allows participants to introduce themselves individually as to how they relate to the theme. This sharing moves toward the end goal of developing a group identity. The leader will not take as active a role as in the initiation stage, allowing members to present themselves and their individual stories.

As each individual tells her or his story, the focus is primarily on the "I" as it relates to the theme. The basic listening sequence is modeled by the leaders, thus helping the group participants also to learn how to hear others. It is the leader's task to use attending and observation skills to note individual and group nonverbal and verbal behaviors, remain aware of multicultural and gender differences, and help the group members become aware of themselves as a *group*.

As the stories can go on for some length, certain of the following members' comments have been shortened for instructional clarity.

| **Edited Transcript** | **Process Comments** |
| --- | --- |
| 15. *Jennifer:* Ted and I would like to hear from each of you so that everybody can come to know everyone else in this group. Each of you comes to the group with your own resources, ideas, and stories, and each of you has something to teach the rest of us about yourself and about how you see the theme or topic of sex-role stereotyping and gender relations. We would also like to hear how you are feeling in the immediate present as you tell us your story. | 15. Jennifer is providing structure for the second stage of the group by specifying more precisely what she and Ted want from the group. She is also including elements of the positive asset search. Her focus is on individuals and theme with both a there-and-then and here-and-now emphasis. Her last comment begins to help the group members link the here-and-now to the there-and-then. |
| 16. *Cheryl* (after a short pause): As a woman in this group I am concerned that I will be perceived as a radical feminist. I'm not angry at anybody and I just want to be accepted for myself. Let me tell you about an incident when I was stereotyped as a radical feminist just because I was a woman . . . (she goes on to tell her story). It still bothers me even as I talk about it now. | 16. Cheryl's story discusses herself as related to the theme. She started with the there-and-then past, but did say at the end that she still experiences the feelings in the here-and-now of the group. She appears congruent in her verbal and nonverbal behavior. She looks at everyone in the group during her story. As people share their stories, concerns, and problems, we see the microskill of self-disclosure (see Chapter 7). |
| 17. *Jose:* I'm glad to hear that you are not angry at me for being a man. Sometimes I get nervous talking in a group about gender issues because I feel like I'm being set up as the bad guy. One particular incident comes to mind . . . | 17. Jose starts with a here-and-now self-disclosure focusing on the theme and the group. He moves on to tell a there-and-then individual story. As Jose talks, the leaders observe physical tension and speech hesitation in him, suggesting nervousness. He seems to focus his eye contact on Ted, perhaps looking for understanding and support. |

| Edited Transcript | Process Comments |
|---|---|
| 18. *Nadia:* Well, I'm a feminist and I'm proud of it. I don't have to be angry at anybody just because I am proud of being a woman. I think that the whole topic of sex-role stereotyping contributes to these stereotypes that make everybody seem radicalized, like we are choosing up sides for a game of some sort. Yet, I've had lots of experiences with men that make me very angry . . . for example . . . (she shares her story). | 18. Nadia's self-disclosure focuses on herself and the theme with primarily a there-and-then focus. As she talks. she looks mainly at the women in the group. |
| 19. *Michael:* I've been embarrassed too many times opening doors for a woman out of politeness and being scolded for being sexist. My parents brought me up to be polite and I value what my parents taught me. Talking about these issues makes me feel nervous, but I guess that is why I am here. | 19. Michael seems hesitant to talk but also seems to want to say something. He needs encouragement to open up a bit more. He looks down at the floor throughout his comments. |
| 20. *Jennifer:* Michael, could you tell us how it feels right now to be here in this group? | 20. Open question focuses on individual's relation to the group with a here-and-now emphasis. If Michael is really nervous, this may be pushing him a bit too much. |
| 21. *Michael:* Well (pause), OK. I think what bothers me is that I don't know what to do. I was raised with fairly strict rules in my family and the rules seem to be changing. (He goes on to tell of an example from the past.) | 21. Jennifer's question helps Michael talk, but note that he is answering in the there-and-then. And during the telling of the story, he pauses several times. During that time, Jennifer encourages him to continue through use of the microskills of encouraging, paraphrasing, and at one point, reflecting his feelings. Her use of basic listening skills helps Michael get through his story. He is able to look up and give the group eye contact, but his eyes are mainly on Jennifer.<br><br>At critical points, the leader should use listening skills to help quiet or resistant members speak out from their own framework and beliefs. |
| 22. *Nadia* (after Michael finishes his story with the help of Jennifer): You see, that's an example of why things are going to be so hard to change. Michael, you have to take a stronger stand. | 22. Nadia gives Michael feedback on his comment. Feedback on behavior is, of course, an important goal in groups. Her feedback combines elements of the here-and-now and the there-and-then. Her nonverbals are calm and nonthreatening. This participant also helps Michael with linking the past to the present. Note that not only leaders can be helpful; group members also contribute. |

*(continued)*

| **Edited Transcript** | **Process Comments** |
|---|---|
| 23. *Mark:* We all seem to be nervous about this topic as though we are afraid of one another. I think we can make our own rules here and agree not to hurt one another even though the topic of sex-role stereotypes is controversial. I was part of a group in which we talked about sex-role stereotypes and I learned a lot of valuable information . . . (he continues his example). | 23. Mark's comment is helpful as it focuses first on the group. He then continues to share some of his own there-and-then experience. He appears confident and sure of himself. But is he the "expert" among the group members and will that build resentment over time? He moved the focus of the group from Michael to himself, perhaps before Michael was ready for the group to move away from him. |
| 24. *Candace:* I'm kind of like Michael. All this stuff puzzles me. I see some people getting angry and frustrated over what at times to me seems like no big deal. Things are going OK for me. Sure, guys are a pain at times, but that's the way it is. I can tell one time though that did bother me . . . (she shares her story). | 24. Candace is open about the issues, but note that she gives mixed messages. She says it is "no big deal," but follows with a story of sexist behavior that was rather "difficult to take." She gives mixed verbal and nonverbal messages as well. |
| 25. *Ted:* Well, may I summarize what I have heard so far? I hear each of you willing to share a story openly with the group and I see that as a strength we can draw on. Each of you has a different viewpoint about sex-role stereotyping. As group members, you are willing to hear each other out. How would you describe what has just happened in the group to an outsider? How do you feel right now about this group and what people have said? How are we doing as a group? | 25. A summary of what has happened in the group can be useful in maintaining flow of discussion and keeping things to the point. This summary also serves as a transition point for later work in the group. Ted focuses on the group as a whole. This should encourage group members to let one another know where they are in the group at this moment. His multiple open questions can be confusing, but at the same time they provide options for group members to share whatever reaction they have in their own way. There are also some aspects of linkage shown here as Ted is helping the group see their commonalities. |
| 26. *Mark* (speaks immediately, almost breaking in): Yes, I think we are moving pretty well. Everyone told a story. It reminds me of when I was in the last group . . . (he continues on with an old story that basically repeats what has happened in this group). | 26. The "expert" may ultimately want to challenge the leader. The first part of Mark's comment is helpful, but during the repetitious story, the leaders note that the group starts to tune out and fidget. There-and-then behavior not directly related to the group's immediate experience can slow down movement in a group. Mark's tone of voice seems superior and condescending to other members. |
| 27. *Nadia* (somewhat impatiently): I do appreciate what the group has said so far. Let us hope we can continue to discuss things openly. | 27. Nadia's impatience also shows through her foot jiggling, but she has made an effort to keep the group moving. Will she and Mark conflict later? |
| 28. (brief silence) The rest of the group sits silently. No one else seems to want to say anything. | 28. A critical point in group development. Should Jennifer and Ted follow up on the apparent conflict or move on and see what happens? They decide to move on, somewhat at their peril. |

## The Positive Asset Search

We recommend that the positive asset search dimension be integrated throughout the group process. This does not mean that we seek to avoid conflict. Rather, it is simply a way to help groups retain attention on their strengths and thus avoid moving to a deficit model. We believe that we can deal best with difficulties if we are aware of strengths. Talking of one's personal power, healthy capabilities, and positive experiences and supports provides a foundation that centers both the individual and the group. This recommendation holds whether you are conducting a structured group, a counseling group, or a therapy group.

It would also be possible at this point to stop and spend time discussing positive assets further. This would be especially important if you were team building. The exercise could include a listing of the strengths of individual members and the story of their past histories. In addition, external supports (family, friends), resources (spiritual, community groups such as Alcoholics Anonymous, specific information sources), and group strengths (what this group can offer as support) can be noted. Strategic planning, for example, is oriented to developing systematic ways to solve organizational problems. But this planning can be more effective if the multiple strengths of individuals, groups, and organizations can be noted and incorporated where they fit best.

Similarly, imagine you are facilitating a group that is highly conflictual but must work together toward an important action. The conflicts need to be worked out, but if you start on a basis of strength and positive assets, the chances for success are greatly strengthened.

Any time a group seems to face real challenges, it can be useful to take "time out" and focus on positives. We build on our strengths! At the same time, this does not mean that we avoid difficulties, problems, and challenges. Do not use the positive asset search as a way to avoid dealing with problematic or complex issues.

Let us review how the positive asset search has been used by Jennifer and Ted so far in this group. (The numbers refer to numbered passages in the transcript.)

1. Ted begins by asking members to describe strengths noted in the introductory pairing exercise. This helps participants buy into the group and feel safe.
3. Jennifer summarizes the positive stories and gives the group positive feedback.
15.–23. Due to the positive start, the group individual stories related to the theme came out fairly easily. You will find that the same is true even if you are working with groups who face difficult problems (abuse, neglect) or complex life issues (divorce, serving a sentence in prison, or making financial ends meet). Nonetheless, we note that Nadia (22 and 27) and Mark (23 and 26) indicate some negativity. This is not to be discouraged. It is a normal and healthy part of group process—but it does challenge the leader! Handled well by the leaders, Mark's experience and Nadia's keen insights can be developed into positive assets for the group over time. Handled ineffectively, they could destroy the potential of the group.
25. Ted summarizes the group's comments with an emphasis on strengths. Leaders hope for positive comments from the group at this point and often get them, but Mark (26) and Nadia (27) did not provide the desired support.

As the group continues, be alert to the use of the positive asset search. This particular group came out relatively well. In several places the group could have fallen apart or become highly conflictual without any resolution. The positive asset search coupled with a clear structure helped the group leaders make it through the rough spots. Chapter 9 provides ideas for dealing with challenges in group process.

## Working—Examining Goals, Sharing, Confronting, Restorying

The fourth dimension or stage depends on members' having developed good rapport and having come to know one another in the group. However, you should not be surprised if the discussion here tends to become "hot"; if this happens, you may direct the group back to rapport building, identifying positive assets, and gathering more data about individual members. Goal setting occurs when the group moves from an individual "I" focus to a group "we" focus. At the same time, it is important that individual goals be in agreement with group goals. This is the point at which the group sets its agenda and helps identify possible outcomes from the group experience that will benefit individual members.

Some leaders skip over goal setting and move directly to sharing, confronting, and restorying in this work phase of the group. A therapy group, for example, has the explicit and implicit goal of helping members look at themselves and work toward greater mental health. A person-centered encounter group has the implicit goal of helping members understand their behavior in the here-and-now of groups. Specifying goals more precisely in these situations is potentially counterproductive. However, even in these situations, the authors would argue that general goals need to be articulated to serve as a measure the group can use to verify that it is moving in the right direction.

The next example discusses goal setting in depth. See passage 6 (page 138) for Ted's introduction to goal setting via storytelling.

| Edited Transcript | Process Comments |
|---|---|
| 29. *Jennifer:* Ted and I would like the group to make a list of what you want to know about sex-role stereotyping so that we can address your individual concerns in the group and work together to find answers to your questions. | 29. Jennifer and Ted had previously chosen to set up a more structured approach to theme-centered work. An alternative leadership style would be to simply continue and "let it happen," and throughout the process the major leadership task would be to balance the I, we, and it—the individual, the group, and the theme. |
| 30. *Ted:* I am impressed by how every group member contributes a different perspective on the topic of sex-role stereotyping. By looking at the theme from all these different perspectives, we have the opportunity to come up with a comprehensive understanding of sex-role stereotyping. I see the differences of opinion as a very strong positive contribution to the success of this group. | 30. Ted's feedback to the group is once again positive (see Chapter 7 on positive reframing and feedback). Most people like others to agree with their frame of reference and this can lead them to maintain that their viewpoint is the only "correct" one. Ted sets up the implicit standard that difference in viewpoints or ideas is something to be valued rather than to be seen as a difficulty. |

| **Edited Transcript** | **Process Comments** |
|---|---|
| 31. *Jose:* You mean we have the responsibility to keep one another honest so nobody gets to blow smoke? | 31. Focus on group with a here-and-now emphasis. |
| 32. *Cheryl:* OK, so one goal for this group is for each individual to say what he or she is really thinking rather than go along and pretend to agree because that would be safe. | 32. Cheryl paraphrases Jose and elaborates further. |
| 33. *Jennifer:* That's a valuable goal for our group. Another possible goal might be to identify ways we could deal with sex-role stereotypes when we encounter them. | 33. Summary, structuring. Is Jennifer coming in too soon? When a leader provides a goal too early, even though it is a useful goal, it takes a bit of power away from the group. Perhaps she should have waited a bit to see whether the group would identify that goal for themselves. |
| 34. *Nadia:* I like that. I want this group to be practical and useful for helping me get along. | 34. The positive tone to the group established earlier enables Jennifer to come in and Nadia appreciates what she sees as support for her need for action. Nadia focuses on herself and what she hopes to gain from the group. |
| 35. *Mark:* I am especially concerned about how a man can avoid getting nailed just for being a man when I'm around a group of women who are angry about stereotypes. | 35. Nadia, who was leaning forward and showing considerable enthusiasm, draws back and looks down as Mark speaks. |
| 36. (An awkward silence descends on the group.) | 36. A critical choice point. Should the leaders draw out the building conflict between Nadia and Mark? At this point, it may be best to "wait and see." Jennifer notes that Cheryl is uncomfortable with what has just occurred. Ted seems not to notice. This illustrates one major advantage of co-leading groups. What one leader may miss, the other will catch. |
| 37. *Ted* (who has been writing down the goals on a large piece of newsprint): Well, for the moment, let's look at these goals and maybe we will generate others along the way. | 37. The goals set the direction for the group, even though that direction can change many times as group members get to know one another. This tentative agenda helps show the members that they are not wasting their time but that there is a promise of some product or outcome that will be useful to everyone in the group. |
| 38. *Jennifer:* Cheryl, you seem upset by something. Can you tell us what's happening for you right now? | 38. Reflection of feeling, open question, focus on individual, here-and-now. |

*(continued)*

| **Edited Transcript** | **Process Comments** |
|---|---|
| 39. *Cheryl* (somewhat angrily): I just think that everybody is buying into these stereotypes even as we discuss how to minimize them. I feel as though Mike and Mark in particular think I owe them an apology for the times they were embarrassed by feminists. I don't want to apologize for being a woman. | 39. Here-and-now focus with an emphasis on herself (the I), the gender theme (the it), and Michael and Mark, a subgroup—men—within the group (the group). Michael leans forward as if trying to hear better while Mark sits back with his arms crossed. |
| 40. (The group sits in silence.) | 40. The rest of the group sits in anticipation, watching as if they were spectators. Mark seems deep in thought. Michael looks puzzled. |
| 41. *Jennifer:* I sense some tension in the group right now. It's OK to have differences. This is our chance to get things out and learn from one another. What are you all thinking and feeling? | 41. Reflection of feeling and open question, focus on group. The issue of gender roles has moved from the there-and-then of past stories and theories to the here-and-now. This was partially activated by both Jennifer and Ted as they emphasized the group and what is happening in the moment. Jennifer reflects the general emotional or feeling tone of the group, offers some structuring, and then asks an open question of the total group. Note also that she reframed the tension as an opportunity rather than as a problem. This is the type of language that helps to defuse conflict but keep the door open for discussion of serious differences of opinion. |
| 42. *Michael* (after a brief pause): Maybe you're right. I've been burned so often on this sex-role issue that I tend to get defensive too easily. | 42. Note that Michael tends to take a pacifying role. Is he playing the "polite child" or saying what he really feels? He appears sincere and anxious to learn, however. |
| 43. *Mark:* Look. If we dance around this subject being soooo careful about one another's feelings nobody is going to learn anything. How about we make a pledge to trust one another even when something the other person says seems like a personal attack—like we decided in our goals? | 43. A positive comment from Mark and maybe the sign of his finally joining the group in a sincere fashion. Later discussion with him after the group finished revealed that he had been feeling frustrated because the group was moving slowly. He was ready to "get into it" in depth. |
| 44. *Nadia:* I like that. Maybe this can be a safe place to argue about what we believe without the danger of anyone being hurt. | 44. Nadia discloses some of her fears and concerns in the here-and-now that likely have background in her experience in the there-and-then "real world." |
| 45. *Jose:* I think I'm going to just listen for awhile longer. I've been quiet for a long time and only a few people have talked. But I'll come in later with my two cents' worth. | 45. There have been two silent members observing what is going on. The leaders were aware of their participation style and wondering if they would start talking on their own. It is usually wise to |

| **Edited Transcript** | **Process Comments** |
|---|---|
| | wait until people want to talk, but note their nonverbals and search for opportunities to include less talkative members. There is always the danger in groups that certain people will monopolize the discussion. |
| 46. *Candace:* Thanks, Jose. I've been quiet too. I guess it is time for me to have my say. I've been holding back because Michael is so polite that he almost seems scared. And Mark struck me as a typical male "pain in the ass." But I can see this is an open group and perhaps I can really tell you how I feel. (She starts telling the group of her past experience with a devastating incident on a date and becomes teary. She comments frequently in her story that it was at least partially "her fault" because she didn't notice what was happening.) | 46. A safe group with a trusting atmosphere allows members to share what they really feel and think. Candace gave Michael and Mark challenging feedback, but her focus is mainly on her own pain and frustration. Notice how she moves from here-and-now to there-and-then experiencing and then returns to the present. As group members can relate past life to present group experience, the possibility of generalization to the real world increases. The leaders have built trust and a valuable set of joint rules so that the group can move to deeper levels. |
| 47.–83. The group explores issues at a deeper level. Candace is able to tell her story and receive positive support from both men and women. | 47.–83. We see here that the group has developed enough trust that participants will let their real issues come out. The theme-centered principle of "disturbances take precedence" must be honored. Through effective listening skills, the leaders helped Candace tell her story and she provided a dramatic view of what sexism and gender discrimination do to women. The focus of the discussion was primarily there-and-then as the story was outside the group's immediate experience.<br><br>At the same time, Jennifer and Ted recalled that this group is concerned with gender relationships, not counseling or therapy. How will they balance the discussion while honoring emerging needs of individuals? How can they maintain a focus on the group and the theme? How can they encourage restorying, not only for Candace but also for the group itself? Time is running short. |
| 84. *Jennifer:* Candace, thank you for sharing. I see you thinking in new ways about that difficult story. I'm delighted that you no longer see the issue as "your fault." All too often, women think that they have done something to bring on abuse. Let us pause for a moment and find out where the group is at this moment. (Pause) What happened here, right now? | 84. As a group member tells a powerful story, people in your group will vary in their reactions from empathy and sensitive listening to avoidance. Note the nonverbal and verbal behaviors of the entire group when the focus shifts to an individual's pain. |

*(continued)*

| **Edited Transcript** | **Process Comments** |
|---|---|
| 85. *Michael:* I feel like crying myself, Candace. You were brave to share that story. Thank you. | 85. Michael offers feedback to Candace and support. This is another positive asset that occurs in the here-and-now of group experience. |
| 86. *Nadia:* I was crying. I like to think that I was there with you and I know all of us in this group were. I was deeply touched by your honesty and we all thank you for sharing. It will help us all. | 86. More feedback and Nadia brings in the total group. If she hadn't, it would have been appropriate for the leaders to bring back the focus to the group as well as just individual feedback. |
| 87.–95. All the group members were supportive, especially Mark, who perhaps had even more group experience than the leaders. But when Candace said to Mark, "Mark, I'm sorry I called you a 'pain in the ass.' I wonder how you felt at that time and how you feel now. . . . I'm sorry," Mark's response was supportive to Candace the person, but he clearly did not want to explore personal issues of sexism and gender relations. | 87.–95. It is important to note that group members' participation and enthusiasm will vary. In this case, Mark had joined the group almost as a co-leader, but when it came time for him to examine himself, he opted out. Given sufficient time, his reasons for doing so probably need to be explored. |
| 96. *Ted:* After all that positive feedback and support, where are you now Candace? | 96. Open question, focus on individual, here-and-now. Ted offers Candace an opportunity to review and restory the difficult issues she shared with the group. |
| 97. *Candace:* Actually, Ted, I am beginning to see the situation in a different way. It was comforting to share what I have never talked about before. The group made me feel safe and comfortable. As I think about it, I had always blamed myself for the problem. I thought it was "my fault." Now I realize that it was not me, but the guy who is responsible. I should not take on the problem. It was a clear example of sexism and oppression. | 97. Candace has restoried her issues in a new way. This new perspective, developed in the safety of the group, will enable her to act more positively and forcefully in the future. The act of restorying is closely allied to the strategies of reframing/ interpretation of Chapter 7. |
| 98.–110. The leaders and group support Candace's new story. Michael feels safe enough then to open up and tell a story of a restricted family background. The group supports him in his effort to become liberated. For a time, the group moves from focus on gender to Michael's issues. When Michael comes to a beginning resolution, the leaders turn the focus back to gender issues, realizing that the individual focus on Michael was almost turning the group into therapy. | 98.–110. At this point, the theme of gender relations becomes a bit tenuous, but Michael's issues and response are also that of a man dealing with a complex matter. The leaders help the group return the focus to gender issues and show how the concerns expressed by both Candace and Michael are related to societal sexism and demands on men and women. |

### Ending: Generalizing and Acting on New Stories

The conclusion of a group can be difficult, especially if the group has been a positive experience (or a really negative one). There is a temptation to let the group go on and on and postpone the ending. Conclusion provides a reality check for the group about how beginnings and endings are part of life. The group has rehearsed ending every time they have changed the subject or moved from one level to another. The final breakup of the group is really a continuation of what has already happened.

Some groups would simply end shortly after the events described in 110 above, particularly in a nonstructured group that will continue to meet in the future. However, this group is ending, so a clear termination is important. Most structured groups with a fixed ending time will benefit from a planned ending such as the following. (Note that Jennifer and Ted return to the goals established by the group as part of their conclusion.)

| Edited Transcript | Process Comments |
|---|---|
| 111. *Ted:* Our time is near a close and I'll try to summarize what has happened just now for all of us. We started with a general theme of gender relations. We established some important joint goals (points to the goal sheet hanging on the wall) of being honest, sharing what we are really feeling, and learning from one another. Mark commented that he wanted to avoid "getting nailed" as a man. Seems that we have been able to accomplish these aims, although I'm not sure where Mark is at this moment on that last issue. Everyone has not had time to tell his or her story in depth, but it seems clear from what you have all said that we have Candace and Michael to thank for sharing. I am sure our discussion with them helps us all rethink the story of gender relations. | 111. Ted summarizes key points from the group experience, relating them to the original goals of the group. He introduces the concept of developing a new story that might lead to action in terms of gender relations. |
| 112. *Jennifer:* And we appreciate your honesty. We have shared a lot in a short time. Let's go around the group and give every member a chance to tell us what he or she learned or relearned from participating in this group. What will we all do to take what we learned in this group back home? How does this all apply in the "real world"? In many ways this group is going to continue in our heads as we encounter sex-role stereotypes and sexism. Perhaps it can continue in our actions as well. | 112. Generalization and take-home change is all too often neglected in group work. Members and leaders can get caught up in the here-and-now power of the group and fail to think about how learnings can generalize back home. Generalization can be thought of in two ways: first, individuals can do something different; second, group action may be useful. |

*(continued)*

| Edited Transcript | Process Comments |
|---|---|
| 113. *Cheryl:* I hate to end. My head is buzzing with ideas right now and it will take me a long time to sort out what I have really learned. I know it was a good experience but I would have a hard time saying exactly what I have learned. | 113. A common response from members. Processing what has occurred often takes time. Note that Cheryl has said nothing about generalization and action. |
| 114. *Nadia:* I've used a lot of the ideas we talked about in our group already when I've seen sex-role stereotypes in my workplace. I was able to help some colleagues understand that they were stereotyping even though they didn't intend to. But now I am more determined than ever. Hearing Michael's issues has given me a better understanding of some of the difficulties men face. I plan to listen to men a bit more, but I will perhaps even challenge them more directly in the future. | 114. It is easier for someone who has already dealt with an issue to generalize. However, note that Nadia is rewriting her story about gender relationships with a bit more understanding of the male frame of reference. She intends to take this understanding into practice outside the group. This ideal outcome of positive restorying coupled with action can happen in groups but is more likely to occur with planning and follow-up. |
| 115. *Jose:* I feel a lot more comfortable with talking about sex-role stereotypes now than I did before. It's like this group provided a chance for me to hear others. I wish I had been able to share more of myself. I was too quiet. But I sure will give it thought. I wonder if we could meet again? Perhaps we could all work together toward a common goal? | 115. Jose raises the possibility of continuing. Many members will want this if the group is effective. |
| 116. *Michael:* It seems as though we accomplished the goals we identified awhile ago and probably a lot of additional goals as well. I feel as though our group has started something for me that I want to continue on my own. I'd like to get together again too. | 116. Note the joint focus on individual and group. Members have moved from an individual focus to a constant reference to themselves in relation to the group. The theme of gender remains prominent. |
| 117. *Mark:* This was a great group and I really appreciate Candace sharing and hearing about Michael's family history. It gives me a lot of things to think about. But my schedule is so tight, I can't come back. Thanks for letting me be with you, however. You did a great job, Jennifer and Ted. Thank you Candace and Michael. | 117. Reality intrudes. Groups take time! Even though he has participated actively, it is interesting to see that once again Mark is reacting somewhat differently from others in the group. No group is ever complete nor does each person open fully. Perhaps he will do so in some group in the future. |
| 118. *Candace* (brief pause): I really see things differently. I've been quiet the last few minutes and not really listening to what you've all been saying—so much is going on in my head. First, | 118. Candace has clearly restoried her situation and is constructing issues differently, thanks to the group. She is, however, focusing on herself as an individual in her verbalizations. This is appro- |

| **Edited Transcript** | **Process Comments** |
|---|---|
| thanks so much for listening. I'd really like to get together for a follow-up. I know I want to do things differently in the future, but I'll need someone to work with. | priate and illustrative of how personal change can come from group experience. The theme and the group has been especially meaningful to her. |
| 119. *Jennifer:* Well, Ted and I weren't expecting that. It makes us feel good to realize that this time has been helpful. Perhaps we can continue. What about you, Ted? | 119. Jennifer might have been wise to summarize the various viewpoints and experiences as the group closes. But she and Ted were surprised at their success and the desire to continue. Her ending comments are fine, however, as it appears the group will continue. |
| 120. *Ted:* It has been a powerful experience for me. Perhaps we can. Let us all look at our schedules and see what works? Then we can break for coffee in the Campus Center and continue more informally. | 120. Ted self-discloses, something that the leaders have not done much of in this group. This is a useful leadership skill if used sparingly, as discussed in Chapter 7. Meeting members informally after the group session ends is not appropriate in therapy groups but may at times be suitable with theme-centered or psycho-educational groups. What are your thoughts and feelings on this issue? |

## MOVING TOWARD YOUR OWN LEADERSHIP STYLE

Examining your own group leadership style through transcript analysis and/or observing yourself on videotape is an important part of becoming a group leader. The detailed analysis you read in this chapter is not something you want to do for every session, but you will find that reviewing your performance carefully at least once or twice a year can be extremely beneficial. The vocabulary and concepts of the Ivey Taxonomy plus the ideas of the multiple theories available for group work (see Chapter 10) will provide ideas for your personal and professional growth.

This group is also representative of what might happen in many other groups, both structured and unstructured. Even with highly structured groups, such as one exploring assertiveness training, you can predict that some emerging disturbance will often arise similar to the one presented by Candace. When this happens, even though your goal is teaching skills of assertiveness or working on some other topic, you will have to take time out and work with the immediate needs of members in your groups. If you don't, you may lose the group. Facilitating a group requires flexibility. Once the emerging issues and disturbances are attended to, you can use them as a cognitive and emotional base to make assertiveness training (or another topic) more meaningful to all members.

Leaders of therapy and counseling groups can be expected to operate in much the same way Jennifer and Ted did with Candace, but these student leaders are *not* therapists or counselors and were conducting an introductory theme-centered group. It is important to lead all groups with discretion and ethics. Jennifer and Ted had the support of a supervising practicum instructor in their class. If issues become complex, contact your supervisor and seek consultation. Remain available to your group members until a satisfactory referral has been arranged.

The dialogues in this chapter have been highly edited, but the words here are representative of what indeed happens in a theme-centered group. The dynamic balance of individual, group, and theme has been maintained and we see that individuals become much more aware of themselves in relation to others through the group process.

Think back on this chapter and the material presented in Chapter 5. What have you learned here? What points struck you as most important? What would you like to emphasize most as you conduct your own theme-centered group?

_____

_____

_____

_____

_____

_____

_____

_____

_____

_____

## PRACTICING THEME-CENTERED GROUP INTERACTION: STAGES AND DIMENSIONS, SKILLS, AND STRATEGIES

No additional practical exercises are presented here as Chapters 5 and 6 are designed to be complementary. It is particularly important for you to examine your own group leadership style through transcript analysis.

## REFERENCES

Cohn, R. (1961). A group-therapeutic workshop on counter-transference. *International Journal of Group Psychotherapy, 11.*

Cohn, R. (1969a). From couch to circle to community. In H. Ruitenbeck (Ed.), *Group therapy.* New York: Atherton Press.

Cohn, R. (1969b). The theme-centered interactional method: Group therapists as group educators. *Journal of Group Process, 2,* 19–36.

Daniels, T., & Ivey, A. (In press). *Microcounseling* (3rd ed.). Springfield, IL: Charles C Thomas.

Ivey, A., & Daniels, T. (1999). Microcounseling, brief therapy, and multicultural issues: Developing a database for concrete action. In W. Matthews & J. Edgette (Eds.), *Current thinking and research in brief therapy* (Vol. 3). Philadelphia: Brunner/Mazel.

Ivey, A., & Ivey. M. (1999). *Intentional interviewing and counseling: Facilitating development in a multicultural world.* Pacific Grove, CA: Brooks/Cole.

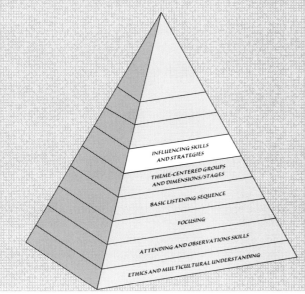

INFLUENCING SKILLS
AND STRATEGIES

THEME-CENTERED GROUPS
AND DIMENSIONS/STAGES

BASIC LISTENING SEQUENCE

FOCUSING

ATTENDING AND OBSERVATIONS SKILLS

ETHICS AND MULTICULTURAL UNDERSTANDING

# CHAPTER 7

# Skills and Strategies for Interpersonal Influence, Part I: Listening, Reframing/Interpreting, Using Self-Disclosure, and Giving Feedback

## CHAPTER GOALS

People come to groups—whether task, psychoeducational, counseling, or therapy—seeking to meet personal goals. Becoming a member of a group and staying in that group is a purposive activity. An individual's intent may be to solve a problem, learn a new skill, obtain feedback from others, or receive therapy; alternatively, the purpose may be to maintain the status quo and avoid change. Whether a person's goal is transformation or avoiding change; interpersonal influence is central in the group process.

*You cannot not influence.* Each action you take as a group leader will influence members of your group and each member's response will influence others. Whether you engage in direct structuring of a group or simply sit in silence, you impact what is happening; and you can expect all the members to respond to what happens in the group in different ways. Some will move in the directions that you expect and desire while others will move either deliberately or unconsciously on opposite routes.

For all these reasons, mastering the interpersonal influencing skills and strategies will be essential if you are to succeed as a leader. Whatever you do will have a positive and/or negative effect on the group and the individual members.

In this chapter, work toward accomplishing the following objectives:

▲ Understand and master skills and strategies of interpersonal influence. Skills are defined as specific microskills in their own right. Strategies are broader areas that often involve combinations of skills:
The basic listening sequence (BLS) and focusing as influencing strategies
Reframing/interpreting

Self-disclosure

Feedback

▲ Utilize interpersonal influencing skills and strategies as a framework for observing group process. You will find that observing groups in action from an influencing frame of reference helps you understand power dynamics and change processes.

▲ Assess the change process among group members through the Observation of Change Scale.

▲ Apply interpersonal influencing skills and strategies to your own group leadership.

## WARM-UP EXERCISE

We are people in relation; we have learned about ourselves and our ways of being through contact with others. Their examples, stories, and feedback have been important in what we have become. Our history of interpersonal influence has much to say about who we are and where we want to go. Thus, from a personal perspective, we have extensive experience with interpersonal influence.

From a microskills perspective, we can learn to distinguish specific skills that have been influencing us over the years. You already have a considerable amount of information about the nature of interpersonal influence, and the goal of this warm-up exercise is to remind you of your already considerable expertise in this area.

Think of a recent change in your life that was important to you. What was your part in that event? For example, perhaps you were admitted to graduate school or did something very well that made you proud. Perhaps you broke up a significant relationship or your parents or an important friend divorced. You may have experienced an oppressive event such as racism, sexism, or classism.

These changes are there-and-then events and stories external to the group. You may prefer to talk about your own here-and-now experience in a group in which you are currently participating. What is your particular personal experience in this group? What story would you tell about the group that has special meaning for you?

Briefly define or give a name to the story or experience you select. Include your central emotions related to what you select:

Change/group experience

_____

_____

Associated emotions

_____

_____

Write down your story in journal form on a separate piece of paper and/or use the following lines to provide an outline of your story. It may be helpful to use the newspaper sequence of questions to describe your experience: Who? What? When? Where? How? Why?

_____

_____

_____

_____

_____

_____

Your life experience is filled with interpersonal influence. What we would like to do now is to draw on your intuitive understanding of microskills and how they can influence the way you can use them to think about your story.

First, let us imagine that someone has used the basic listening sequence and focusing to hear your story fully and accurately. The person has just summarized your story and your feelings in a very complete way. How does being listened to influence you and your thoughts about your own story? What are the specific behavioral cues that let you know you have truly been heard as you tell your story?

_____

_____

Generally, if we are heard fully and accurately, we are influenced to feel better about ourselves and more certain about what happened. Listening skills influence other people in powerful ways. Remember that listening remains at the core as you learn other influencing skills and strategies.

Reframing/interpreting could be described as viewing the event or story from a different perspective. How could your story be reframed, how could you think about this story differently? How could this story be reinterpreted, particularly from a theoretical framework (psychodynamic, cognitive-behavioral, existential-humanistic, multicultural)?

_____

_____

Giving feedback is a central skill of group work. Imagine that a sympathetic friend gives you positive feedback on your story. Then imagine that a less supportive individual gives you negative feedback.

Positive feedback

_____

_____

Negative feedback

_____

_____

Corrective feedback is often useful later in the group process and is more effective than negative feedback. Corrective feedback builds on positives and encourages people to change as they learn how they might be better received by others if they altered some of their behaviors. Identify below some instances when you have been encouraged to change or grow through corrective feedback.

_____

_____

We suspect that you have been able to come up with reasonably accurate approximations of the skills and strategies to be discussed in this chapter. The more formal definitions of the skills and strategies presented here are designed to build on your present expertise and add further depth to your existing skills.

## DEFINING THE LEADERSHIP SKILLS AND STRATEGIES OF INTERPERSONAL INFLUENCE

Groups are about change, expansion, and possibility. They provide us all with a sense of wonder as we discover the complexities and mysteries of what it means to be in relation to one another. As beings-in-relation, people-in-community, and selves-in-context, we can have no better place than group work to discover our full humanness and the influence we share with each other.

A basic premise of this book is that we cannot avoid influencing others and being influenced by them. Sitting back and doing nothing can be fully as active as telling every member in the group what to do. Every action or inaction somehow reverberates through the whole system. At the same time, what occurs around us influences us as well. We have termed this reciprocal influencing procedure the _dialectics of change_. The word _dialectics_ is used to describe the mutual interchange that is human interaction. Box 7.1 depicts in a two-person interaction the way a counselor influences a client and how the client, in turn, influences the counselor. In group work, this dialectic change process is much more complex, as your leadership style influences multiple members of your group (and group members each receive and appreciate your leadership style differently from the people sitting beside them). The circle of interpersonal influence in Box 7.2 illustrates the multiple dynamics that are possible within a group. (See Ivey, 2000, pp. 48, 112–116, on dialetics.)

Recognizing the richness of group work for understanding who we are and how we are seen, and for contributing to our mutual growth, let us turn to a review of specific microskills and strategies building for change.

**Box 7.1**   The Dialectics of Interpersonal Influence

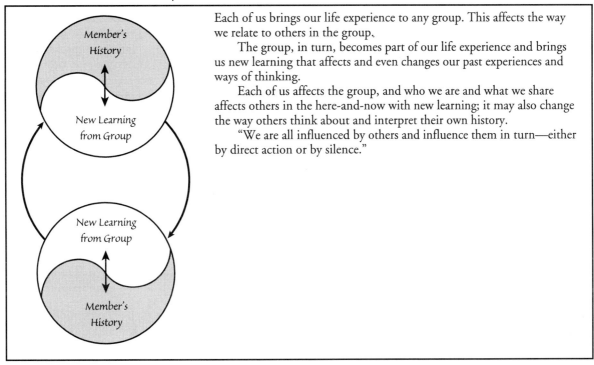

Each of us brings our life experience to any group. This affects the way we relate to others in the group.

The group, in turn, becomes part of our life experience and brings us new learning that affects and even changes our past experiences and ways of thinking.

Each of us affects the group, and who we are and what we share affects others in the here-and-now with new learning; it may also change the way others think about and interpret their own history.

"We are all influenced by others and influence them in turn—either by direct action or by silence."

**Box 7.2**   The Group and Dialectics of Interpersonal Influence

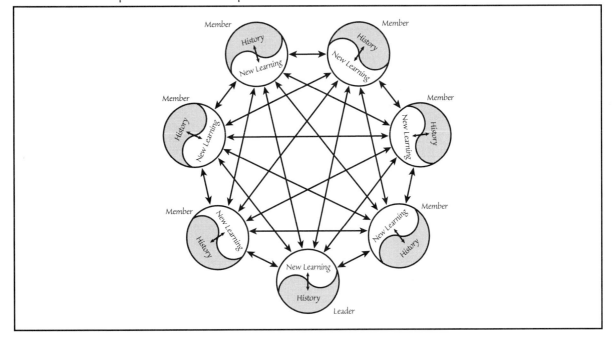

### The Basic Listening Sequence and Focusing

As leaders or members, when we listen to someone's story, problem, or description of an important life event, the very act of hearing that person talk changes her or him in important ways. First among these is a *sense of being heard and being recognized as a person.* Think about the times you have spoken and no one truly listened to you. Most likely you felt diminished, frustrated, unappreciated, or perhaps even angry. Being heard tends to make us feel stronger and more confident. Being listened to centers us and frees us to hear others. Many people who don't listen have not enjoyed being truly listened to themselves.

Effective listening also opens us up for the dialectics of change. If our story has been heard fully, the person who has listened carefully to us has already been changed and your regard for the listener has likely been enhanced. If that listener provides us with a good summarization of what we have said, or an influencing microskill of feedback, we are more open to looking at our story in new ways, modifying the way we think and talk about that story, and even changing our behavior should we face that problematic event again in the future.

In sum, active listening and using the basic listening sequence is a foundation for change. If you as leader model effective listening, your group members will also learn to listen more effectively. Your ability to listen to one member of the group not only influences that one person but the whole group as well.

The basic listening sequence could be called a minimally intrusive way to help members of your group grow. Start by working with the group member's perspective—what is he or she actually saying? Build trust by listening; as people feel heard, they are often more able to take on a new way of thinking on their own.

The focusing microskill moves toward more interpersonal influence; when you focus on the individual and the individual's topic, you have influenced that person to continue the story from her or his own frame of reference. But as you use your leadership skills of focusing on that member's story from other perspectives—for example, how do other group members, family, or cultural and contextual issues affect how the story is told?—you are directly influencing the client in reframing or thinking about what has occurred in new ways.

Each chapter in this book contains transcript examples from varying types of groups. Conflict and problems in the workplace are common, particularly as employees face the demands of increased productivity, often with few supportive colleagues and a difficult boss. Planning to explore the issue of the workplace, a leader advertised the group as follows:

*Workplace Challenges?*
Hassled on the job? Overworked? Promotions passing you by? Is your boss hard to live with? Your colleagues nearly impossible? All of us have concerns in the workplace. Come together to share your concerns in a group discussion and see what we can do together. (Information on location, time, cost, and place.) Contact Melanie Klein at 962–7948 for an interview and information.

Melanie met with each member of the group for prescreening and told them the purposes and goals of the group. The first session went well as people got to know each other and began developing trust. They discussed their goals, which almost all focused on working through a specific issue in the work setting. One person mentioned her concern about a difficult and demanding boss and received supportive feedback from the group. Following this good start, the group agreed to meet for five more two-hour sessions after work. In the second session, a group member brings up the following concern. As you read the transcript, note that this is an active group in which the leader does not have to do all the work. The group members here can use positive active listening skills. This often happens as groups mature when they work with a positive, supportive leader.

| Transcript | Process Comments |
|---|---|
| 1. *Imani:* I've been at the insurance company now for seven years. I got promoted early on right on schedule, but now for the last three years, I've been in the same position. I've seen three White people that I've trained move on to higher positions while I just sit with minimal raises. | 1. Self-disclosure, focus on self, problem, and cultural/environmental context, there-and-then. |
| 2. *Melanie* (the leader): So, Imani, you sound like you're frustrated with this. You've been training White people and they move on, but the company just lets you sit there without a promotion. If you are the one doing the training, you must be the expert. | 2. Reflection of feeling, paraphrase, focus on individual, problem, and cultural/environmental context. The reflection of feeling helps move Imani from a there-and-then orientation more to the here-and-now. |
| 3. *Imani:* Yeah, I think I'm doing a good job and my performance reviews are fine, but I get really frustrated just doing the same thing all the time. (She pauses.) | 3. Self-disclosure, individual and job context. Imani acknowledges her own feelings. The focus is primarily on self and problem. |
| 4. *Hal:* You're doing the same thing all the time. | 4. This group member's minimal encouragement in the form of a restatement helps Imani continue her story. At the same time, note that he left out feelings. If group members are to talk about emotions, reflecting feelings needs to be a frequently used skill. |
| 5. *Imani:* Yes, the same thing. I want more challenge and I think I'm capable of more. But maybe I'm doing something wrong. Maybe it's my fault. | 5. Self-focus with a here-and-now emphasis. Imani starts to take the blame for the problem on herself, a common issue in work situations among people who are not necessarily at fault. Self-blame in this case indicates openness to talk about the issues, but also if reinforced by the group, it could end up in denial of what is really happening. (See Observation of Change Scale, Box 7.3.) |

*(continued)*

| Transcript | Process Comments |
|---|---|
| 6. *Cherlynne:* You are capable. . . . What has your boss said to you about this? Could this be a racial issue? | 6. Encouragement, restating the positive asset of capability and competence, open question, focus on other person—the boss—including cultural/environmental/contextual issues. There is an emphasis at this point on the there-and-then as the story is brought out. Here-and-now discussion can occur once the story is told. This is an example of positive active listening. It would have been possible to focus on "Maybe it's my fault" and lead Imani to take a more negative view of herself. At the same time, the boss is not here to explain his point of view. Be careful in making conclusions about people who are not present in the group. |
| 7. *Imani:* Well, he hasn't said anything. He's pleasant enough, but he keeps his distance. Well, I don't know if it's discrimination or not, but sometimes I wonder. I haven't said anything to anyone. I'm the only African American in the office. The more I think about it, the more angry I get. | 7. In this self-disclosure, Imani is starting to reframe her story—talking about the story in a group often leads to a change in the way the group member thinks about the story. As she speaks of anger, she is moving toward more here-and-now expression of feelings. The cultural/environmental/contextual issues become clearer, most likely as Imani feels listened to. Her anger is moving to the here-and-now. She is moving to Level 2 of the Observation of Change Scale (see Box 7.3). |
| 8. *Melanie:* What I've heard so far is that you, Imani, have been doing a great job. I see the group as being very supportive right now, but the more we hear your story, the more angry and frustrated you seem to be. I also see some others in the group getting angry at the way you have been treated. Could we pause for a moment and see where all of us are at this time and perhaps give Imani some feedback? | 8. The leader summarizes what has occurred to this point including both feelings and thoughts. She focuses on the individual and the group starting to link the there-and-then to the here-and-now. She finishes her summary and asks an open question focusing on the group. Some leaders might have focused their discussion only on Imani, failing to bring in the group. |

In this exchange of strengths, Imani is influenced by the leader and the group members to evaluate and examine herself in a situation of group safety and trust. The group has listened for positive strengths while also listening to her very real concerns about possible discrimination. Through respectful listening in this group setting, we can anticipate that Imani will gain the strength to deal with her problematic situation in a more assured fashion.

Note that this example is both there-and-then and here-and-now. Many times, the sharing of concerns from outside the group in the supportive here-and-now atmosphere of the group can lead to new ways of thinking and behaving. At the same time, a group that focuses exclusively on external events can lose power over time.

The exploration of emotions in individuals and the group as a whole is important in this process.

We stop the example transcript at this point but will take it up again for the final microskill of this chapter—feedback. Melanie, the leader, needs to encourage more here-and-now interaction and feedback to Imani. This group session transcript will be continued later to demonstrate use of feedback.

The basic listening sequence has been used by Melanie and the group to bring out the facts, thoughts, and feelings Imani experiences. Not just the leader but the whole group is responsible for listening. Melanie uses her observation skills to note body tension and support for Imani. At Number 8 above, she links what is occurring for Imani with what group members are showing in the here-and-now—"I see the group as being very supportive right now, but the more we hear your story, the more angry and frustrated you seem to be. I also see some others in the group getting angry at the way you have been treated."

We next examine reframing/interpretation and a scale to assess change among group members. This is followed by discussion of the skills of self-disclosure and feedback. Again, in the feedback section, we will explore this example transcript in more detail.

## Reframing/Interpreting

A central goal of much group work is to help members look at themselves, events, life challenges and concerns, and problematic situations in new ways. Reframing—viewing the situation from a new perspective—can occur in many ways. Imani, helped by being listened to by the group, gradually reframed "her problem" as not so much "her problem" as a dilemma of coping with a prejudiced boss who was supported by an insensitive and discriminatory system. If Imani role-played the situation with her boss in front of the group, more specifics would emerge and possibly new insights into his perspectives might appear as well.

> *The microskill of reframing/interpreting may be formally defined as providing a new frame of reference from which the group member or group itself can look at a story, situation, or event from a new perspective. Reframing/interpreting often provides a fresh explanation or a new meaning for what has occurred.*
>
> *Reframing/interpreting can appear in a positive fashion, but it can also be deeply challenging. A new way of interpreting the world is not necessarily "sunny." It can be painful, even though ultimately revealing and helpful.*

Reframing occurs when members of your group can engage in one or more of the following:

▲ Tell their story from a new, usually more positive, perspective.
▲ Move from seeing themselves as the "fault" to finding a balance between internal and external issues. (For example, Imani begins to see that her lack of promotion is more likely a result of external prejudice and discovers that she can take new internal responsibility for action.)
▲ Find a new meaning in the situation. (A group member may redefine a difficult, seemingly impossible problem as a spiritual challenge or as an opportunity to grow or learn.)

▲ See a problem accurately from someone else's perspective. (A person may be blaming her parents or colleagues for difficulties, but then is able to describe the situation from the other person's frame of reference.)

▲ Label or name their story, concern, or problem in a new way (A gay group member may feel bad about difficulties on the job and the group can help him rename the problem as heterosexist harassment and gay bashing.)

▲ Learn to think and behave in new ways about old issues. (A college student has difficulty with an insensitive professor and thinks it is a personal fault; the group helps the student think in new ways about the professor's failure and suggests ways the student can take action.)

The skilled leader can help group members reframe and think in new ways through using a variety of microskills and strategies. As we saw in the transcript focusing on Imani, active listening can lead Imani (and the group) to think in new ways about her story. Focusing skills, feedback, self-disclosure by others of their experience and stories—in short, all microskills and strategies—can result in reframing and reinterpreting the world in new ways.

All the above approaches indirectly help the individual or group think about the situation or themselves in new ways. The actual skill of reframing/interpreting *directly* addresses this issue by providing a new frame of reference, a new way to think about the issue, concern, or problem. The responsibility for providing the reframe/interpretation rests with the leader or member who provides the new frame of reference.

Some leaders avoid reframing/interpreting as they prefer their group members to find their own direction. Those who do use the skill actively and frequently point out that the gradual approach is just as much an influencing and directive skill as the more overt interpretation.

Regardless of your position on reframing/interpretation, the test of whether a new perspective is successful and useful occurs when individuals or groups do something new and different in their thinking, feeling, and behaving—either in the here-and-now of the group or the there-and-then of daily life. This same criterion for measuring the value of new perspectives and change occurs in all leader and member behavior regardless of the skill used.

Box 7.3 presents the Observation of Change Scale. This scale will be useful to you as you observe group members respond to input and experiences in the group. Are members of your group in denial about a new way of thinking, feeling, or behaving? Are they starting to change? Are they able to incorporate a new way of thinking and change their way of being in the group? Can they accept a reframed interpretation and incorporate it into their thinking, feeling, and behavior? Finally, and most important, are group members able to take learning from the group and generalize this to their daily life?

The Observation of Change Scale can also be related to the story, positive asset, restory, action model. If the group member does not deal with or change problematic behavior or stories, this is an example of Level 1—denial. When the group member tells a new story, he or she is moving toward Level 2 of the scale—full consideration and some change in the group. When the group member acts on the story in daily life, he or she has achieved Level 3 of the Observation of Change Scale.

**Box 7.3**    *Observation of Change Scale: Assessing Group Member Perspective and Behavior Change*

Group members receive a constant flow of new information. Some absorb the data readily and incorporate it into their daily lives; others may be resistant. You will find that people change (and remain the same) in front of your eyes.

Leaders (and members) can use the following *Observation of Change Scale* to assess the degree of influence that new information has on member thinking, feeling, and behavior. (This scale is adapted from the five-point Confrontation Impact Scale; Ivey, 2000; Ivey & Ivey, 1999.)

A group member may respond to reframing/interpretation, feedback, self-disclosure, being listened to, or other microskills or strategy in several ways:

1. *Denial or partial examination.* The person may actively dispute information from the group or may passively ignore it. Despite extensive feedback from the group, no change occurs in the person's attitude or behavior. At a slightly higher level ("1+"), the individual attends to the new information and may even incorporate part of it, but she or he deals with important aspects only superficially, or denies them.
2. *Full consideration and some change IN the group.* The individual attends to new information, listens carefully to group members. No major change in thought, feeling, or behavior is observed. At a slightly higher level ("2+"), the individual assimilates feedback and data from the group and changes thought, feeling, or behavior in the here-and-now of the group.
3. *Generalization OUTSIDE the group.* The individual assimilates feedback and data from the group and changes thought, feeling, or behavior in the there-and-then of daily life. The group member may report change to the group in the next session, or another group member, the leader, or a designated person may observe the change.

The Observation of Change Scale is not just for assessing reaction to reframing/interpretation strategies. It is also a way to examine group members' response to all the microskills and strategies of this book. If group members are standing still or are in denial, the Observation of Change Scale may indicate that you, as group leader, need to change your style and use of skills and strategies. If the members are moving and growing, the Observation of Change Scale provides a way for you to assess their growth and development.

At the same time, it is helpful to think of reframing/interpretation as a specific microskill of group leadership. While we believe that generally it is best for group members to reframe their own stories or situations, many times, you as leader will have to supply the reframe/interpretation yourself; sometimes the indirect approach is ineffective or you believe that the insight you provide will be timely and appropriate. Timely reframes/interpretations by the leader (or group members) can make a significant difference.

Reframing/interpreting then is the skill of providing group members with new ways of thinking about old situations. In group work, the reframing process is most often experiential, in that leaders and members can—from their own life experience and observations in the here-and-now of the group—provide new ways to think about old situations.

In certain counseling and therapy groups, the reframing/interpreting can come from a theoretical system such as existential-humanistic, cognitive-behavioral, psychodynamic, or other frame of reference. While these types of reframing/interpreting are not stressed here, keep in mind that their major effect is also to help group members see their situations from new perspectives derived from the theory.

A useful leadership strategy is to encourage your group members to make reframes and new interpretations rather than making them all yourself. The leader can be a "superstar" and make brilliant reframes/interpretations, but it is often wiser to encourage your group members to provide the new perspective. As an example, examine the reframing/interpretation process in the following transcript of our group.

| **Transcript** | **Process Comments** |
|---|---|
| 1. *Cherlynne* (after some hesitation and a one-minute group silence): Well, I've got something I'd like to share. My boss assigned me this major advertising project and I'm stuck. (hesitates again) | 1. Self-disclosure of facts and thoughts, but emotion shows underneath. Unless we deal with emotion as well as the content of the story, change may be unlikely. One senses the emotion in the here-and-now while the conversation is primarily there-and-then.<br>    Observation of Change Scale: Level 1 with openness to start examination of the issue. |
| 2. *Melanie:* You're stuck. Would you like to share more? | 2. Encouragement, open question, there-and-then focus on individual and problem. |
| 3. *Cherlynne:* Yes, I've been sitting at my desk for three days now and nothing seems to show up on the computer screen. It's a new account—a large hardware firm—and they want a new ad series. John, who works in the new office, was unhappy he didn't get the assignment and he keeps barging in and making suggestions. He's making me so nervous that I can't do anything. | 3. Self-disclosure of thoughts and feelings with primarily a there-and-then focus on the problem, herself, and John, who makes her nervous.<br>    Observation of Change Scale: Level 1+ moving toward 2 as Cherlynne is obviously anxious to deal with this problem. |
| 4. *Imani:* I understand; I hate monitoring. I simply can't get anything done when someone is hanging over my shoulder. I even see that you are nervous now as you talk about John. | 4. Self-disclosure, Imani uses observation skills to bring Cherlynne's talk to the here-and-now. |
| 5. *Cherlynne:* Yes, I'm terrified. It's the biggest assignment I've had in the agency. (She goes on to describe the assignment, but as she talks with the listening and supportive group, her voice becomes calmer and more relaxed.) | 5. The here-and-now and there-and-then are linked in this self-disclosure of feeling. Talking about issues in the safety of the group often helps members later deal more calmly with stressors.<br>    Observation of Change Scale: Level 2. |
| 6. *Melanie:* Could the group share ideas for Cherlynne that could help her think about her situation differently? | 6. Open question with a multiple focus—the group member, the group as a whole, and the problem that Cherlynne is presenting. Melanie could play |

| Transcript | Process Comments |
|---|---|
| | "superstar" leader and help Cherlynne find new ways of coping, but she prefers to use the group process. |
| 7. *Ralph:* Cherlynne, I've heard you in this group. You come across as a very competent person generally, but sometimes you seem anxious to please us rather than say what you really feel. Could it be that you are doing that on the job and not standing up sufficiently for yourself? How does that sound to you? | 7. Ralph starts with positive feedback, then provides a new name by reframing/interpreting Cherlynne's behavior in a new way—*anxious to please*. We also note that her behavior seems to appear both in the there-and-then of the workplace and the here-and-now of the group—anxious to please. |
| 8. (Cherlynne sits back listening with her hand to her mouth.) | 8. This would be a sign of Level 2, full consideration of the data, and again illustrates the importance of observing nonverbal behavior. |
| 9. *Joanne:* Ralph makes sense, Cherlynne. You are competent and able, but I wonder if sometimes your desire to please doesn't get in your way. I've seen this in the group as well. | 9. Another group member picks up the language of the reframe and follows this with feedback on Cherlynne's behavior in the group. |
| 10. *Cherlynne* (close to tears): I do try to do my best. I really appreciate what you are saying. You are really helpful. Why only yesterday . . . | 10. Self-disclosure and feedback to the group. Note that Cherlynne is once again trying to please the group. She does this by agreeing too quickly with what has been said. <br><br> Observation of Change Scale: Assessing this statement is a bit more difficult as she is indeed engaging with the group (Level 2), but she is also repeating the pleasing behavior (Level 1). |
| 11. *Ralph* (breaks in gently): Cherlynne, you are doing it again—being kind to us. The message we are giving is that you are competent and can do it. Your desire to please is fine, just as long as it doesn't get in your own way. | 11. Here-and-now feedback followed by positive asset emphasis. |
| 12. *Melanie:* Cherlynne, could you respond to Ralph and Joanne with what you are feeling now? | 12. Open question, focus on individual, here-and-now. |
| 13. *Cherlynne:* You are right. (A small tear falls.) I'm always trying to please. And it worries me so. It's hard to hear that message of competence. I know I can put the ad campaign together. I guess I just need to tell John to get out of my office and get on with it. | 13. Linking of there-and-then and here-and-now as the reframe has been incorporated more fully into Cherlynne's thinking. <br><br> Level 2, full consideration, but the test will be whether she generalizes her new information outside the group to behavior change in the office. |

*(continued)*

| Transcript | Process Comments |
|---|---|
| 14. (Cherlynne tells the group of other situations in which she tries to please people too much and thus hasn't done as good a job as she might have. The group listens, but also asks Cherlynne for examples of success from the past. They work with her, providing suggestions for dealing with the intrusive colleague and pointing out to her once again how her behavior in the group is similar to what she describes in the workplace.) | 14. It is easier to generalize behavior to the real world if one has a positive base of support in the group. Practicing the new behavior in the group through role-play prior to applying it outside in the real world can also be invaluable. (See the discussion of assertiveness training in Chapter 10.) |

Learning to view a situation in a new way—the reframing and reinterpretation of reality—is a vital part of all group work. The leader could have provided the new way of thinking but encouraged the group to participate. Note that the combination of movement from here-and-now to there-and-then plus the skill of feedback were important in Cherlynne's movement.

*Linking* is a way to describe an important aspect of reframing/interpretation. The group member learns through the group that he or she may be repeating patterns of behavior from the there-and-then past in the here-and-now action of the immediate group. Once a person becomes aware of links such as this he or she can accelerate the process of personal change. When group members see behavior in the immediacy of the group, they can provide more accurate feedback and frames of reference for personal growth and change. Furthermore, this type of discussion often leads other group members to see how their own lives link with the lives of members in the group.

Interpretations and reframes can also be linked to a theoretical base. A theory-oriented behavioral group leader might have interpreted Cherlynne's behavior as lacking assertiveness and could have emphasized the role-play alternative. A psychoanalytical leader might see the problem as one of insufficient ego strength. A feminist multicultural group leader might interpret the whole situation as cultural sexism. Theory provides a set of glasses with which we can examine the situation. The existential/humanistic group leader would tend to avoid direct interpretation but might think of Cherlynne's thoughts and actions as representative of a self that is not yet actualized.

All theoretical orientations can provide a new way to examine the situation. The utility of theory-based reframes/interpretations will vary with the needs and interests of the individual and group. Theme-centered, person-centered, and existential-humanistic group orientations tend to emphasize and work with what each unique individual and group provide. Behavioral, psychoanalytic, and multicultural orientations generally come to group work with more specific expectations and understandings of what is happening. None of the styles (person-centered or other theories) is right or wrong. All can offer benefit for the right group at the right time. The effective group leader over time will become equipped to work with groups from multiple theoretical orientations.

Again, note the leader's behavior in this group. Rather than responding to Cherlynne directly, Melanie asked members to respond, thus sharing leadership with the group. The effective leader can provide reframes and interpretations, but whenever possible he or she encourages the full group to participate.

## Self-Disclosure

*Self-disclosure may be defined as the sharing of stories, information, thoughts, and feelings about oneself in the group. Self-disclosures can be from the there-and-then, such as telling stories from the past, or they can be immediate as to feelings and thoughts in the here-and-now of the group.*

Group experiences become more powerful if self-disclosures are based in the here-and-now. The immediacy of what one is feeling or experiencing in the moment through a self-disclosure is a major characteristic of most effective counseling and therapy groups. It can be important in structured tasks and psychoeducational groups as well.

Yet, storytelling and bringing out problems and concerns from the there-and-then are essential in most groups. The effective leader encourages both there-and-then and here-and-now disclosure. Linking information from the past (there-and-then) to the immediacy of the group (here-and-now) is often a central task and experience in successful groups.

For members of a group, self-disclosure is the microskill classification you will see most frequently. The reason is obvious; the major content of group process revolves around group members' sharing themselves, their experiences and stories, and their feelings and thoughts in the here-and-now or there-and-then. Effective working groups have extensive self-disclosure at the center.

Leaders, on the other hand, need to monitor their own self-disclosures carefully. With too much self-disclosure by the leader, the group's attention turns to the leader and group members may withdraw. Whatever the leader discloses will be noticed and can serve as a model for the group. If you are working with a group that is skirting or edging around an issue, you can be helpful by disclosing your own experience. But the self-disclosure needs to be brief, returning the focus to the group—"I feel tension in my work setting too. My boss tends to think she is God and wants to be worshipped and she demands a lot. What are some of your experiences with your boss?"

When a member is receiving support or encouragement from the group, the leader usually needs to participate with appropriate self-disclosure, feedback, or reframing/interpretation. When you use self-disclosure as a leader, you are becoming a member, but it is always important to recall that you are a member with a *difference;* you are the leader and what you say has different impact from what is said by other members.

Some group members will self-disclose "touchy" and difficult stories and issues early in the group and that can be threatening to other group members. Group members who share too much may decide not to return because of embarrassment and fear. The level of self-disclosure is an important dimension of the helping process that you as leader will seek to monitor. Shallow and superficial group self-disclosure often represents failure—but equally, be guarded against disclosure that is too much, too deep, and too fast.

The microskill of self-disclosure can be identified through the following:

1. *"I" statements.* Self-disclosures focus on the person speaking.
2. *Description of thoughts, feelings, or facts and behaviors.* Note how your group members self-disclose. Some will tell concrete, detailed fact-filled stories about themselves and their behaviors; others will share internal experiences of thoughts and feelings. What is desired, of course, is a sharing appropriate to the situation and to the moment.
3. *Here-and-now versus there-and-then.* Making "I" statements in the immediacy of the group is very different from telling stories external to the group. Both are relevant, depending on the nature of your group. Again, the linking of here-and-now experience with past behavior can be particularly helpful.
4. *Appropriateness of depth.* Self-disclosures ideally are paced to the group process stage and to the needs of the individual. A group member who discloses a serious personal problem in the initial stages may frighten off other members.
5. *Parallel self-disclosures and linking.* If one group member is self-disclosing, it is often helpful for her or him to hear other members share similar experiences and how they dealt with them. Parallel self-disclosures often help the group member sharing an issue of concern feel safer and more included in the group. This sharing of related experience is an important part of the linking process.

As a group leader, you will want to watch for these varying aspects of self-disclosure and encourage members of your group to share both here-and-now and there-and-then experiences with appropriate depth and similarity.

You will also find that some self-disclosures, particularly those that parallel the here-and-now experience of the group members, are very similar to and sometimes indistinguishable from feedback. In a sense, all honest feedback is a self-disclosure of how the group member comes across to you.

In our workplace group, Jerzy shares the following:

| Transcript | Process Comments |
|---|---|
| 1. *Jerzy:* This last week I got into it with Jack again. He thinks he is so superior and knows it all. I tend to focus on getting things done and Jack thinks he's the greatest humanist that ever was. He just "feels" all the time. I don't know why the boss stands him. | 1. Self-disclosure, there-and-then, fact and thought centered, although Jerzy's feelings of anger show clearly. Jerzy appears willing to deal with this issue at Level 2 of the Observation of Change Scale, but is his level of anger really more Level 1? |
| 2. *Melanie:* You seem pretty angry right now, Jerzy. Could you be just a little more specific? Perhaps an example? | 2. Reflection of feeling, here-and-now open question asking for concreteness from the there-and-then. |
| 3. *Jerzy:* Well, I supervise three mail handlers as part of my job. By the end of the route, one of them, George, has recently been an hour late getting | 3. Self-disclosure, there-and-then, but here-and-now in terms of nonverbals. |

| **Transcript** | **Process Comments** |
|---|---|

information out to the plant. I brought it up with my boss and I wanted George fired. (The nonverbals of anger increase as he talks.) Before I could even get the story out, Jack overheard me and climbed all over me telling me that I should listen more and that I am always jumping the gun. My boss just sat there.

Despite the anger, this appears to be engagement of the issue at Level 2 of the Observation of Change Scale.

4. *Cherlynne:* I guess I'm like your boss. I always give attention to the other person first and too often I just sit. But right now, I am hurting for you, Jerzy. I sense you are really trying, but it isn't working for you.

4. Self-disclosure emphasizing feelings, there-and-then followed by here-and-now. This self-disclosure is almost indistinguishable from feedback.

5. *Imani:* Jerzy, right now, you make me angry. I've seen you in this group lay back, then at the last minute use a subtle attack. I really think you are into control.

(The entire group leans forward in full attention. Cherlynne looks even more surprised than Jerzy, but all sit in silence.)

5. Self-disclosure, here-and-now feelings, feedback followed by a reframe/interpretation—"into control."

While difficult for the group member, receiving conflicting self-disclosures and feedback from others in the group is usually ultimately helpful. A major learning in group work is that people experience us differently. Thus, hearing positive, negative, and corrective feedback and self-disclosures in a group can help a group member realize that people see the same person or event differently—and that it is a "part of life" we all need to recognize and live with.

6. *Melanie:* So, Jerzy has shared what's going on in his job. Cherlynne and Imani have shared their feelings and thoughts. I wonder what others of you are experiencing right now?

6. Summary, open question—focus on group here-and-now. This is likely a wise intervention on Melanie's part. When things get heated or moving fast in a group, some members sit back and let a few people do all the talking.

7. *Ralph:* I'm startled. What's happening? I was listening to Jerzy and then something happened. Conflict scares me.

7. Self-disclosure—here-and-now and Ralph links his feelings to the there-and-then.

8. *Jeannie:* I was drifting off. I've heard Jerzy trying to gain attention again, so I was thinking about something else. I think Imani is onto something.

8. Self-disclosure, here-and-now coupled with a reframe ("trying to gain attention").

9. *Melanie:* You look pretty quiet, Jerzy. What's happening for you right now?

9. Feedback based on observation skills. Open question, here-and-now focus on Jerzy.

10. *Jerzy:* Whew! I didn't expect that. I thought everyone was on my side. Makes me wonder if I shouldn't look at it a bit more. Imani, I particularly thought you would understand. What happened? What did I say?

10. Self-disclosure, here-and-now. Open question, there-and-then.

Observation of Change Scale: Jerzy gets even more "into" the here-and-now of exploring issues at Level 2; before, it was a bit questionable whether he was honestly participating.

The varying types of self-disclosure coupled with here-and-now feedback enabled Jerzy to look at his behavior. In this example, the leader wisely did not self-disclose as plenty of action was occurring in the group. Melanie might have felt very similar to Imani, but if she had made the challenging comment, it likely would have stopped the whole group from sharing as they did. As you spot issues of difference in the group, allow your group members to air them. Through your observation and listening skills, you can often identity group members who might possibly say what you think needs to be said at a particular moment. And—even if Jerzy does need the corrective feedback on how some people see his behavior, it is likely better to say nothing than to take on the monitoring role in most group situations. With a strong leader-based therapy group, however, it might be appropriate for the leader to make some of the more challenging comments here; even then, it has to be done with extreme care. A strong comment such as that made by Imani and later by Jeannie—you are "into control"—if made by a powerful leader could be emotionally damaging to Jerzy.

As you can see, self-disclosure varies widely from lengthy storytelling to short comments that are very difficult to distinguish from here-and-now feedback. In fact, recall that much of the best feedback is made from an "I" statement framework.

## Feedback

> To see ourselves as others see us
> To hear how others hear us
> To be touched as we touch others
> These are the goals of effective feedback.
> (Ivey & Ivey, 1999, p. 44)

The microskill of feedback was introduced in Chapter 1 as it is so central to group experience. Through your chapter practice exercises, you are already aware of how helpful it is to obtain information on how others react to your thoughts, respond to your emotions, and think about your behavior. We are interdependent beings, and learning specifically how others look on us is one of the great gifts of group work.

You saw how closely feedback and self-disclosure are related in the above encounter with Jerzy. Before we start elaborating on the skill of feedback, think about what you have already learned about the skill and its value in groups. Take a moment and outline your present conceptions of the microskill of feedback. It is important to recall that you have important life experience with feedback that can be valuable to you as a group leader.

_____

_____

_____

_____

_____

As a group leader, your main task is to facilitate members of your group in providing feedback to each other. Periodically you will want to provide feedback yourself, and at times, you may need to teach skills of feedback to your group directly.

*Feedback may formally be defined as verbal and nonverbal information from others concerning their impressions of one's thoughts, actions, and behaviors.*

While we tend to think of feedback as consisting of words, an important underlying part of all feedback is how it is presented nonverbally. For example, our vocal tone, the look in our eyes, and our body language modify and often become more powerful than our actual words. "To be touched as we touch others" implies that feedback is inclusive.

Basic principles of effective feedback include these:

1. *Give feedback when the person is ready.* Feedback is heard most clearly when the individual is willing to hear it. It does little good to bombard the group member with how others see him or her if that person is in denial or is extremely vulnerable. Feedback needs to be timely. If the group member is not ready, it can still be useful to provide limited feedback and then follow up later. Another way to say the same thing is that the person receiving feedback should be in charge as much as possible.

2. *Be relatively nonjudgmental.* Seek to avoid evaluative "good/bad" feedback. "You're great, but . . ." or "That was a terrible thing to say." Central to this is acceptance and caring for the person receiving feedback. People can deal with troublesome feedback more easily if they sense that the group is ultimately supportive of them, and this support is often communicated nonverbally. Corrective feedback can be given in a way that is not evaluative and is useful to the person receiving it.

3. *Be concrete and specific.* Vagueness is usually not helpful. Provide feedback that is clear, concise, and understandable. Compare the following: "You've been helpful in the group" to "Today I saw you as really involved. I really liked the way you listened to Cherlynne and gave her useful suggestions." "You goofed again" versus "Ralph, you are interrupting the speaker again."

4. *Focus on strengths and positive assets whenever possible.* Individuals grow best and change most easily when they have a positive regard for themselves and a sense of self-efficacy. Pointing out people's skills and abilities often enables them to cope more effectively with corrective feedback and personal weaknesses.

5. *Use "I/you" statements.* You are the person giving feedback and it is important to own what you're saying. Different people in the group will usually offer different feedback to the same person. Hearing how several others see you can be extremely helpful. Thus, rather than saying, "*You* are a person of many strengths, but *you* need to listen to others more carefully," try "*I* see *you* as a person of many strengths. At the same time, *I'd* feel safer with *you* if *you* listened to others more carefully."

A comprehensive, research-oriented view of feedback (Morran, Stockton, Cline, & Teed, 1998) supports the above points and adds the following:

▲ Early positive feedback facilitates group process. Corrective feedback is better received by members after trust is developed.

▲ Group leaders can help teach feedback skills to their members by modeling feedback style. At times, brief instruction to group members on how to provide feedback can be useful, but avoid lecturing.

▲ Sometimes group members have difficulty hearing feedback. The leader may suggest that the recipient of feedback paraphrase what has just been said.

In the following transcript example, we continue the discussion with Imani, who has presented us with her concerns in her workplace.*

| Transcript | Process Comments |
|---|---|
| 1. *Melanie:* Imani, let me summarize where we are so far. We've heard you say that you have been in the same job for the last three years. You've seen Whites, whom you have trained, promoted beyond you. You come across frustrated . . . and getting angry about it. The group really seems to want to support you and so do I. | 1. Summarization focusing both on Imani and the group process around the issue. Melanie self-discloses her own desire to be supportive. Effective groups and effective leaders themselves become positive assets. |
| 2. *Imani: Am I crazy or is this what's going on? I am angry, confused, determined not to give in to any negative consequences that might emerge from my thinking. Once I am in meetings, for example, I find that I am often being discounted or, at the very least, ignored. It feels like I am invisible, but I'm talking and sharing my thoughts and ideas and those in my presence simply do not hear or even see me. I try again to make my point, but it takes a lot of energy to continue. I know I am strong and intelligent and often, when I continue to make myself heard, I'd do so in a professional way, but then I am perceived as aggressive or something negative. Then I find myself asking myself again, "Am I crazy or is this what's going on?"* | 2. Self-disclosure, there-and-then linked to here-and-now. The focus is on the problem and on Imani herself. In the supportive group, she is able to talk openly about her strengths and positive assets. The cultural/environmental context begins to come in when she talks about herself as being "perceived as aggressive or something negative." A lot of people, particularly women, minorities, and other oppressed groups often have an internal struggle in which they try to decide whether their issues are "their problem" or they are actually suffering something from the external world—thus, the comment "Am I crazy or is this what's going on?" Observation of Change Scale: Imani is clearly Level 2 and this continues throughout the exchange discussion here. |
| 3. *Binta: Yeah, I know what you mean. I share my thoughts with my boss who is a White woman. She acts like she doesn't even hear what I say.* | 3. Here-and-now feedback, there-and-then self-disclosure. The focus is on the cultural/environmental context, Imani, Binta, and the problem all in this one short integrative statement. |
| 4. *Jerzy:* Wow! As I listen to you, it reminds me of what might be going on my office. We have this | 4. Self-disclosure, cultural/environmental context, there-and-then. |

*The early part of the dialogue around feedback is adapted by permission from Sherlon P. Pack-Brown, Linda E. Whittington-Clark, and Woodrow M. Parker, *Images of Me: A Guide to Group Work with African-American Women.* Copyright © 1998 by Allyn & Bacon, pages 121ff. Specific words or paraphrased dialogue are indicated in italics.

| Transcript | Process Comments |
|---|---|
| terrific African-American woman, Callie, who shared almost the same thing with me. She said that sometimes she was *perceived as too direct and aggressive.* From my perspective, however, she had *done her homework and invested a lot of time and energy.* | |
| 5. *Imani:* Yes, no matter what I'd do, it isn't quite right. (self-disclosure) *Am I crazy or is this really happening?* | 5. Self-disclosure, there-and-then. |
| 6. *Melanie:* Imani, *take a moment to ask someone in this group how they view you.* (Imani looks about the room. There is a brief pause.) | 6. Structuring directive calling for feedback from the group. |
| 7. *Binta: No!* You are not crazy. I see you as just fine. *You become a part of the woodwork in your boss's mind because he cannot handle what you're saying.* | 7. Feedback, here-and-now linking to the there-and-then. |
| 8. *Cherlynne:* Imani, when you shared how you also got upset when someone watches you too closely, it really helped me to think about things in new ways. I see you as really on top of things and being treated very unfairly. Thank you for helping all of us. | 8. This feedback focuses on an I/you framework. Cherlynne shares something about herself in a form of self-disclosure.<br><br>Important here is the positive support from all members of the group. This group support will enable Imani to reframe/reinterpret her situation more positively and hopefully to act in new ways in the future. |
| 9. *Ralph:* Imani, you are one of the most capable people I know of. You've been so aware in this group and so helpful to so many people. I really appreciate what you have done here. You need the same appreciation outside. | 9. Feedback, here-and-now linking to the there-and-then. |
| 10. *Binta:* You're special. I feel close to you right now. | 10. "I/you" here-and-now feedback and self-disclosure. |
| 11. *Joanne:* I think we all feel close right now. This group makes me feel safe and protected. | 11. Here-and-now self-disclosure with focus on group and self. |
| 12. *Melanie:* Imani, I hear a lot of positive feedback and support for you. I want to add my own feelings to the group. You've been very clear and upfront with us and you are getting a lot of support from this group. It does seem that prejudice and racism may be involved here. Could we explore how we might help you cope with them? I really appreciate your sharing. How has all this been for you? | 12. The leader summarizes the positive feedback and provides further data on how Imani has participated in the group. By saying "How has all this been for you?" Melanie passes the focus of the group to the members once again. The cultural/environmental context has been related to the problem clearly.<br><br>At this point, it might be appropriate for the leader to introduce a role-play in which Imani could test out new behaviors with the support of the group. |

"Am I crazy or is this what's going on?" is a rhetorical question central to understanding what is happening in difficult situations (see Pack-Brown, Whittington-Clark, & Parker, 1998). Timely, clear, and accurate feedback that we can obtain in a group helps us understand whether the "problem" is indeed "our" problem or whether the issue is external to our experience and not our fault. In the example here with Imani, Imani learns that she is "not crazy," that what is really occurring is discrimination in the workplace. Feedback from group members helps her see herself in an appropriate perspective.

Many of us find ourselves in situations that are confusing. We may be unable to decide whether what is occurring is "our fault" or whether the problem rests in what others are doing to us. Such situations, indeed, are "crazy making." The group situation can be extremely helpful in sorting out what happened and how to interpret and make sense of complex, confusing experiences.

There is also the possibility that group feedback itself can be oppressive. If group members had perceived that Imani was responsible for the problem and it was Imani's "fault," group feedback could have "helped" her to come to a false and oppressive belief about what had happened. When multicultural issues of oppression are discussed, there are some people who might seek to "help" members adjust to society as it is. A gay or lesbian group member could, for example, be encouraged to remain hidden in the "closet." A woman or Imani as an African American might be told by a group "that's just the way it is. You'll have to adjust."

The authors would agree with Pack-Brown, Whittington-Clark, and Parker (1998) that adjustment to oppressive environments is inappropriate. One great opportunity for individual and group growth is developing the awareness that positive change can be made. A positive role-play may support group members in taking specific action on this awareness.

Note the leader's role in the feedback process. She encouraged feedback from the group and involved herself briefly with some sharing and feedback, then turned the central focus back to the group. An especially important part of effective use of microskills in group leadership is helping group members to do the work and use the microskills themselves. In this way, group members are more likely to transfer their learning back home. If Melanie, the leader, did all the work, behavioral generalization might be more difficult. Certainly, the learning for members would be less.

This general pattern of learning how others see us can be extremely helpful in personal growth and change in groups. In the example here, Imani uniformly received positive feedback from group members. Often, individuals will receive a mixture of positive and less supportive feedback from those in the group, particularly when their behavior has been uncomfortable to some group members. This mixed feedback can be useful to change, for part of our important learning in groups is that our thoughts, feelings, and behaviors are viewed differently by diverse people.

Positive or corrective feedback from group members can be helpful in our growth. The position of the authors is that negative feedback is to be avoided wherever possible. If we start with strengths and positives, it then becomes possible to help those in the group to change. What would have once been negative feedback becomes challenging, facilitative, and corrective. This issue will be explored in more detail in the following chapter under the microstrategy of confrontation.

## USING THE INFLUENCING SKILLS OF LISTENING, REFRAMING/INTERPRETING, USING SELF-DISCLOSURE, AND PROVIDING FEEDBACK WITH CHILD AND ADOLESCENT GROUPS

Peer counselors and mediators have been an important part of elementary, middle school, and high school experience. For example, at the Fort River School in Amherst, Massachusetts, Mary Bradford Ivey taught systematic listening and helping skills through the microskills framework to sixth-grade classes. These children in turn worked with young children in kindergarten and the first two grades as peer helpers. Out of such programs come increased self-esteem and self-efficacy for both peer helpers and the young children with whom they work.

More recently, the Fort River program extended peer helping to the mediation process. A cadre of eight students was chosen to learn problem-solving and conflict-resolution skills (see Chapter 9). When children conflict and get into arguments, peer mediators can step in and help resolve differences before they become serious.

Similar programs for middle and high schools exist throughout the country. The concepts of advice listening, honest self-disclosure, and accurate, timely feedback are usually part of the training these students receive. In addition, the student mediators and peer counselors meet frequently with their adviser and trainer for discussion and support. When peer educators work with these students, all the skills of this and following chapters on influencing skills are usually found as part of the training.

The concepts are important; they can all be adapted. At the same time, children's groups must be short; for sixth-graders, a half-hour can be handled, but if you are working with first- and second-graders, some groups will be as brief as twenty minutes. As adolescents work with complex programs, the nature of skill and strategy usage on the part of leaders and the length of groups will appear very similar to that of adults (microskills training is often a part of adult peer and volunteer helper programs).

## MOVING TOWARD YOUR OWN LEADERSHIP STYLE

Four areas of microskills and strategies for interpersonal influence have been presented in this chapter—listening, reframing/interpreting, self-disclosure, and providing feedback. Basic to all of these is the leader's modeling these skills and encouraging group members to engage in them. It will do little good over the long run if you are a "superstar" leader, for such behavior takes the opportunity to learn away from your group members. The effective leader is there at appropriate times but knows when to step back.

The Observation of Change Scale can be useful to you as you think about how various members of your group are allowing themselves to participate. You will often find a pattern of early denial and partial examination of issues before your participants fully engage the issue. With an ongoing group that meets over several sessions, you will have the opportunity to see whether members have generalized learning in the group to their home settings.

Once again, think back on this chapter. What have you learned here? What points struck you as most important? What stood out for you? What would you like to work on in the four skill areas of interpersonal influence presented here?

_____

_____

_____

_____

_____

_____

_____

_____

_____

_____

## PRACTICING INTERPERSONAL INFLUENCING SKILLS: LISTENING, REFRAMING/INTERPRETING, USING SELF-DISCLOSURE, AND PROVIDING FEEDBACK

### 1. Process Observation of Interpersonal Influence

The Observation of Change form in Box 7.3 provides you with still another way to observe group process. Most often you will use it informally to assess where a particular group member is and how that person is progressing as he or she discusses a particular topic. You can also use the scale at the end of a group session to classify each member's openness to discussion. With an ongoing group, you can measure how much people actually learn skills, taking learning from the group to their home settings.

A second process observation activity would be to observe a group and notice the occurrence of listening skills, reframing/interpretation, self-disclosure, and feedback. It would be especially useful to examine the nature of self-disclosures in the groups you observe using the following questions:

1. Are group members making "*I statements*" as they share ideas and experiences or are they generalizing and failing to take responsibility for their own verbal behavior?
2. Are group members describing facts, thoughts, feelings, or behaviors? Is their sharing appropriate for the group within which they are working.
3. Is the sharing here-and-now or there-and-then?
4. Are the self-disclosures appropriate in their depth?
5. Are the self-disclosures parallel (on the same or a related topic) or are they off in a different direction?

## 2. The Fish Bowl

This fish bowl can be used to cover the four skills and strategies of this chapter. Five class members form a group in front of the larger class. There is no leader and class members observe the process and then discuss what they have seen after various phases of the fish bowl. This leaderless fish bowl is designed to remind us that skills of interpersonal influence can be contributed by members, not just by the leader.

As there is no leader, it is important to follow the specific steps below fairly carefully.

▲ A topic for discussion needs to be selected. Possibilities include a past interpersonal conflict; difficulties in the workplace; self-evaluation of oneself as a prospective group leader; a positive experience with friends, work, or family; or no topic at all in which case the speaker is asked to share whatever occurs to her or him in the here-and-now.

▲ One member speaks for one to two minutes on a selected topic. The member stops and waits for response from the group.

▲ Another group member uses active listening skills to summarize what the member has said. (The speaker may continue the story or react if he or she wishes, or may wait for further group response.)

▲ The next group member responds with a reframe/interpretation providing the speaker with a new frame of reference. (The speaker may continue the story or react if he or she wishes, or may wait for further group response.)

▲ The next group member makes a self-disclosure on an issue relating to something the speaker said. (The speaker may continue the story or react if he or she wishes, or may wait for further group response.)

▲ Several group members provide the speaker with feedback about her or his story and participation in the group. (The speaker may continue the story or react if he or she wishes, or may wait for further group response.)

At any point in the above steps, the entire group may stop and discuss the specific skills of interpersonal influence. This exercise can generate a fair amount of interest and involvement as each skill area is examined in detail.

## 3. Your Own Group Practice

The following exercise can be completed in class or you may elect to find a group outside of class and practice on your own. If you cannot have an observer watch your group work, try to audiotape or videotape the session.

If you're working in a classroom or workshop, the following steps are recommended:

1. Divide into groups of five or six. One person serves as leader and another as observer.
2. Select a topic for the small groups. The suggested topic for the small groups is interpersonal conflict. Alternatively, the groups may select a current topic of interest to them.
3. As group leader, follow the general design of the fish bowl exercise above, but allow yourself as well as the group members to provide listening skills, feedback,

and reframing/interpretation. It may be particularly useful to engage in a self-disclosure as a leader and to observe and learn how others react to the leader's sharing information.

4. Ten to fifteen minutes may be used for the small groups. Allow five minutes for feedback from the observer. Finally, each small group can discuss its own group process.

Where possible, add videorecording and practice to your work with attending skills and observation. You will always obtain very useful feedback on yourself and the group. Always obtain informed consent from members before recording a session.

## REFERENCES

Ivey, A. (2000/1986). *Developmental therapy: Theory into practice.* North Amherst, MA: Microtraining.

Ivey, A., & Ivey, M. (1999). *Intentional interviewing and counseling: Facilitating client development in a multicultural society* (4th ed.). Pacific Grove, CA: Brooks/Cole.

Morran, K., Stockton, R., Cline, R., & Teed, C. (1998). *Journal for Specialists in Group Work 23,* 257–268

Pack-Brown, S., Whittington-Clark, L., & Parker, W. (1998). *Images of me: A guide to group work with African-American women.* Boston: Allyn & Bacon.

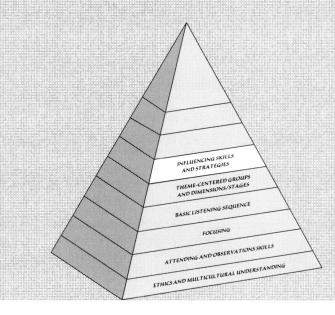

INFLUENCING SKILLS
AND STRATEGIES

THEME-CENTERED GROUPS
AND DIMENSIONS/STAGES

BASIC LISTENING SEQUENCE

FOCUSING

ATTENDING AND OBSERVATIONS SKILLS

ETHICS AND MULTICULTURAL UNDERSTANDING

CHAPTER **8**

# Skills and Strategies for Interpersonal Influence, Part II: Using Structuring Strategies, Exploring Logical Consequences, and Eliciting and Reflecting Meaning

## CHAPTER GOALS

All leaders guide their groups, in varying ways, through the sequence of stages or dimensions over time. In highly structured groups, the leader will actively explain what is to happen and you will see structuring and directive skills clearly in operation. Less structured groups still require the use of these skills, but they will appear less explicitly.

Exploring logical consequences helps group members look at themselves and the resulting outcomes of their thoughts, feelings, and behaviors. We can learn significant information about ourselves and our relations through work with this strategy.

What underlies our thoughts, feelings, and behaviors? Many would argue that personal issues of meaning, purpose, and values are central issues. Eliciting and reflecting meaning can become an important skill in the later stages of a group.

These three strategies will be considered in this chapter in the context of a psychoeducational group on anger management. This group and its members will also appear again in Chapter 9 in which issues of conflict management and confrontation are explored.

In this chapter, you will have the opportunity to accomplish the following objectives of understanding and mastery:

▲ Understand and master three additional skills and strategies of interpersonal influence:

Structuring strategies—directives, suggestions, and instruction

Logical consequences with special attention to behavioral functional analysis and rational emotive behavior therapy

Eliciting and reflecting meaning

▲ Continue the process of assessing change among group members using the Observation of Change Scale

▲ Apply interpersonal influencing skills and strategies to your own group leadership

## WARM-UP EXERCISE

The transcript examples in this chapter will center on a structured psychoeducational group working with issues of anger management. Most of the examples from previous chapters have come from less structured counseling groups, often built around a theme with topics such as gender roles, community experiences, and workplace issues.

While it is appropriate to conduct a theme-centered group on issues of anger, you'll be expected at times to conduct psychoeducational groups. Psychoeducational groups are also typically theme-centered but they include particular information that the leader wishes to share, a specific sequence of exercises and activities, and a planned time schedule. The goal is educational—to impart information—although theme-centered discussion will also be prominent as the participants process the exercises. Thus, psychoeducational groups have counseling and therapeutic functions as well as instructional purposes. For example, the transcript selections from the anger management sessions presented here and in the next chapter move between highly structured exercises, in which the leader clearly structures and directs what is happening, to theme-centered discussion around topics of anger that at times verge on therapeutic discussion. However, the major focus is on learning anger management skills and strategies.

For the warm-up exercise in this chapter, you are asked to complete the exercises in Box 8.1. You can use these same exercises in your own anger management workshop. They are most likely to be used in the first two dimensions of a group—initiating and gathering data. Note that the third dimension, the positive asset search, is integrated throughout this entire workshop and appears prominently in the exercises. At this point, take time out and complete the exercises in Box 8.1.

What stands out for you from these exercises? How could you use them yourself in an anger management session?

_____

_____

_____

_____

_____

_____

**Box 8.1**    *Two Handouts for an Anger Management Workshop*

There are many varieties of anger management workshops and the microskill session presented in this chapter is just one of them. As such, it cannot cover everything and you will want to expand your expertise in this critical area. Nonetheless, you will find that the exercises give a fairly effective outline of some vital dimensions for understanding and working with anger. Note that Dimension 3—the positive asset search—is integrated with Dimension 1 in the belief that people who work with a difficult issue such as anger may be more comfortable if they start by identifying personal strengths and not just problems.

You may wish to photocopy the following form and pass it out to your group members—or you may wish to use the same ideas informally.

Handout 1

*Dimension 1: Initiating the Group—Rapport and Structuring—Goals*

Please stop for moment and think of a time you became angry, perhaps even appropriately, and managed to maintain calm and work through the situation to your satisfaction. Share that story as fully as you can.

_____

_____

What did you do in this situation specifically that enabled you to resolve the issue? Be as concrete and clear as you can. What feelings do you have about yourself *at this moment* as you think about yourself as competent to handle a difficult situation?

Concrete actions:

_____

_____

Feelings about self at this moment:

_____

_____

Imagine that you are participating in a workshop on anger management. If each member of your group shares similar stories and information, you'll have a rather solid background of positive rapport and specific actions that all members can draw on, and you will have set the stage for establishing goals.

What goals do you have for yourself as you start thinking about anger management?

_____

_____

*(continued)*

**Box 8.1 (continued)**

| Handout 2 | *Dimension 2: Gathering Data—Stories and Dynamic Balancing of Focus* |
|---|---|

Share a story or tell about a time when you were not able to control your anger so effectively. Consider the following questions as you think about your story; again, be as concrete and specific as you can. The following framework—behavioral functional analysis—can be used to help you and group members clarify the specifics of the story (questions adapted from Ivey, Ivey, & Simek-Morgan, 1998, pp. 282–283).

A = Antecedents: What happened just before the incident around which anger arose? What was the situation? What were you doing/saying? What was the other person doing/saying? What feelings were there? (and as appropriate) Who else was there and how did they participate?"

_____

_____

B = Behavior/thoughts: What is the story of the angry incident itself? What happened first? What happened next? What did you say and do? What did the other person(s) say and do? How did you feel? The other person(s)?

_____

_____

C = Consequence: What happened afterward for you? Other(s)? What emotions were felt?

_____

_____

R = Reflection on meaning of event: What sense do you make of all this? What is the underlying meaning or reason? What one thing stands out for you from this exercise?

_____

_____

_____

The ABCs of behavioral functional analysis are presented in Box 8.1. You may wish to duplicate them for your group members as they examine their stories. In the ABC analysis here the story focuses on an issue of anger, but it could just as easily be used to help group members enlarge brief statements to full stories, including underlying emotional issues. For example, functional analysis could be used to flesh out member discussion of positive assets and strengths, stories of argument or conflict, difficulties with daily life (counseling and therapy groups), workplace and career issues, problems with roommates or partners, and many others—including multicultural stories and topics such as racism, sexism, homophobia, or lack of sensitivity to the handicapped.

In short, the ABC analysis of behavior is a basic sequence of questioning skills that can clarify many situations. You will find it valuable in your own leadership of groups. Furthermore, it will be helpful in working with members as they learn to listen more carefully—and recall that one of the great learnings of group membership is how to *really* listen to others. You as leader can help group members learn to listen through your own modeling and also through structuring skills.

## Structuring Skills

Structuring skills, which include directives, suggestions, and instruction, are explicitly designed to make things happen in the group and they influence what occurs directly, often immediately. You can see very clearly if your group members follow your directives and suggestions and if they understand your instructions. A brief definition would be as follows:

> *Structuring skills influence the group to follow strategies and actions suggested by the leader. They help the group take action, develop new skills, move in new directions, restory and reframe old issues, and take concrete action and follow-up on what is learned in the group. Structuring skills make things happen.*

"The issue is not *whether* a group leader should provide structure, but rather *what degree* of structure" (Corey & Corey, 1997, p. 164).

In the early days of group work, many believed that ambiguity was basic to effective groups. It was thought that anxiety and tension helped people express themselves more honestly. Kaul and Bednar (1994) have challenged this idea, and over the years, their point of view has become central to most group thought. In 1974, they "postulated that if group leaders thoughtfully structured at least the early group sessions, clients would be able to take greater interpersonal risks and engage in less stereotyped, exaggerated, and ineffective behavior" (1994, p. 176). Research and practice in many types of groups now support this point of view.

How you structure your group will be determined by your theory of group work and by the purpose of each particular new group with which you work. If you are managing a psychoeducational anger management group, you could structure the group in this way:

▲ Provide them with an overview of what to expect early in the session.
▲ Ask them to share their names and why they are in the group. Explain each activity and provide them with handouts such as the one in Box 8.1.
▲ Direct them to work in subgroups and ask them to report on their observations.
▲ Inform them that it is time to move on to a new activity.
▲ Instruct them in skills and strategies of anger management.
▲ Encourage them to think in new ways about old stories of anger.
▲ Work with them to transfer new ideas from the group to real life.

Structuring skills are important in all groups. The theme-centered group leader also shares what the group is about and asks the group to tell their stories. While not as defined as psychoeducational groups, the theme-centered group needs to be moved through the stages or dimensions of the group—initiation, gathering data, the positive asset search, working, and ending. Similarly, relatively unstructured person-centered encounter groups, counseling groups, and therapy groups need structuring skills from the group leader as they work through the group process.

The principles of effective structuring are defined as follows (Ivey & Ivey, 1999, p. 298):

1. *Involve your group as much as possible.* While you often will simply tell the group what to do, be sure that they are ready for the information or change in activity. Allow them to provide feedback and ask questions to you about the structure you provide.

2. *Use appropriate visuals, vocal tone, verbal following, and body language.* Even though you are talking, your attending skills remain important, but you need to be more assertive and stronger than when you are listening. In short you need to be more authoritative or the group may not follow your directions. But each group and individual is different. Modify your behavior to meet the developing group culture.

3. *Be clear and concrete in your verbal expression.* Know what you are going to say so that it is said explicitly and clearly. Compare the following examples:

   ▲ Vague: (In a tentative voice looking at no one in particular) Would everyone mind if we start now? (pause) Why are you here?

   ▲ Concrete: (Looks at each member of the group with a slight forward trunk lean) Let's start now, if that is OK. I'm Shomari and we are going to work on anger management now for about two hours. Could you get together in pairs right now? It is best if you work with someone you don't know well. (She looks at the group and pauses while the members pair up and shift chairs.) Now, I'd like you to share your names, where you are from, and what brought you to this workshop on anger management. Then, in about five minutes, we will get back together and learn who we are and why we are here. OK? Any questions?

   ▲ Vague: I wonder if we could look at our stories now. What do you think?

   ▲ Concrete: We've had the chance to hear everyone's story about anger now. Each of us has had a chance to share. What, specifically, do we share in common? And, how are we different? (Some group leaders would make this even more explicit by writing down commonalities and differences on a flip chart or wallboard.)

4. *Do one thing at a time.* Notice that Shomari, the leader, paused after each part of her instructions above before moving on. If you give your group multiple instructions (e.g., three things to do at once), expect that you will spend a lot of time saying what you said again (and perhaps again and again with resulting hostility from confused group members).

5. *Check out whether your directive, instruction, or suggestion was heard and understood.* Just because you are clear doesn't mean the group understands what you

have said. Sometimes, just observing the group will be sufficient. At other times you may need to ask "Could you repeat back to me the three things I'd like you to do while you work together in pairs?"

A variety of activities and strategies fall within the purview of structuring. Box 8.2 presents five examples. Note that directives such as the ABC analysis, relaxation training, thought-stopping, role-plays, and skills training are often drawn from the cognitive-behavioral theoretical tradition. Psychodynamic directives include free association and sharing of dreams and focused analysis of how the past affects the present. Example directives from existential-humanistic theory include imagery, Gestalt strategies, and here-and-now focusing. Multicultural counseling and therapy (MCT) and family theory offer us meditation, the community genogram, the family chart, circular questions, and self-in-context directives.

**Box 8.2**    *Five Example Structuring Activities Using Directives*

| | |
|---|---|
| | Directives, while highly important in group leadership, are most effective if used sparingly and with caution. Following are five example directives that might be used by Shomari, the group leader discussed in this chapter. Further reading and study are required to master each of these, and these five are only a brief sample of many possibilities. There are many more useful structuring strategies that you will want to learn. |
| *Specific Suggestions/ Instruction for Action* | "As our first activity, let us look at our strengths and the ways we have been able to manage anger reasonably effectively in the past. When we start this activity, I'd like you to close your eyes, but feel free to leave them open if you prefer." (She pauses as all members but one close their eyes and relax in their chairs.) <br><br> "Now, think of a time when you were angry and somehow managed to maintain your cool. If possible, get the image in your mind." (She pauses and watches the nonverbals among her group members. She then continues the next phase of the activity. She has chosen not to give handouts for this activity but will provide them for the next one.) |
| *Relaxation Training and Body Awareness* | Learning how to relax on the spot is a vital part of most anger management programs. You as trainer will want to know this strategy well so that you can teach relaxation skills to your participants. <br><br> "Relaxation and body awareness is an important aspect of anger management." (Pause for questions and discussion.) "As a first step toward relaxation we will start with an awareness exercise. I'd like you to close your eyes and notice your breathing right now. (pause) Now, imagine an angry situation from the past or the relatively immediate present. Note your breathing patterns now." (Later, more body awareness and systematic relaxation can be taught.) |
| *Thought-Stopping* | "I'm passing out some rubber bands now and I'd like each of you to put one on your wrist. We all have internal speech that we use to talk silently to ourselves. For some of us, negative self-talk, internal speech or things we say to ourselves, leads us to negativity—and then, later, to anger. I'd like you now to think about something negative that often occurs to you; when you get it in your mind, SNAP the rubber |

*(continued)*

**Box 8.2 (continued)**

|  | band (Shomari demonstrates) and say 'STOP.' Then I'd like you to think about something good about yourself." (pause) "If you learn to substitute something positive about yourself for negative self-talk, eventually the negative self-statements will diminish." |
|---|---|
| *Imagery* | "Several of you have shared in the group and with me that spirituality is important in your life." (Pause for discussion.)<br>    "I'd like you to sit quietly and meditate in your own way. (pause and observation of group nonverbal behavior) Now allow a positive spiritual or religious symbol to come into your mind. Make sure that it is a positive, supportive one. If a negative one comes to you, just notice it and then let it go. Focus on the positive image and what you are feeling in your body as you experience it. (pause) When you have finished, open your eyes, and when your partner is ready, share your experiences." (She pauses again for questions and discussion, then repeats the directive.) |
| *Role-Play Enactment* | Talking about events is helpful, but at times they need to be made really explicit through role-plays. When the group sees the actual action happening, they often develop new perceptions of them. Even more important, the individual who is the focus of the role-play may learn new ways of thinking and behaving. Role-plays such as the following are often used in assertiveness training groups.<br>    "Ramon, I've heard your frustration in dealing with the co-worker who laughed at your accent. And it appears that there is more than that. Could we role-play step-by-step what happened? Michael, would you take the oppressive role? You're a good actor. As we start, Ramon, could you tell Michael just a bit more so he knows how your co-worker behaved? . . . (continues instruction)." |

Another important form of structuring is the teaching function that involves instructions and information giving, especially in psychoeducational groups. As part of group practice, you will be giving brief presentations ("mini-lectures") on a variety of topics. With anger management, for example, you provide information for your group members on the physical dangers to the heart and immune system that come with hostility. You may summarize key research findings. You may decide to teach your participants how to engage in meditation and relaxation.

## Exploring Logical Consequences

Allied to the skill of feedback is the strategy of pointing out logical consequences, which enables group members to see themselves in relation to their environment. Whereas feedback lets us know how others see and hear us, considering the logical consequences of an action allows us to think ahead to the reaction someone will probably have to a certain behavior on our part.

    "*IF* you do this, *THEN* this is likely to happen." Dreikurs and Grey (1968) have observed that our learning is often based on consequences of our actions. For example, if the member receives feedback about her or his disruptive behavior in the group, that person has learned something valuable. Moreover, if feedback is coupled with a discussion of the logical consequences, the group member is likely to know what will happen if he or she continues the behavior.

The exercise in the second handout of Box 8.1 presents the ABCs of behavioral functional analysis. Here we see how behavior may be viewed in context and what may be expected to happen if the behavior continues. The ABC analysis can be extended to thoughts and feelings as well.

While using the microskill of exploring logical consequences in the group, consider the following:

1. Use listening skills carefully to draw out the situation fully. This is particularly important in understanding antecedents and specifics of what happened in the situation.
2. Although you can use an "if–then" statement—"If you continue this behavior/ thought/feeling, then . . ."—the preferable strategy is to encourage group members to do the thinking themselves. For example, you might ask them to think about the positive and negative results of their behavior/thinking/feeling. It is best if members can generate their own "if . . . then . . ." statements.
3. You and/or the group members can provide corrective feedback about the positive and negative aspects of continuing or changing the behavior. This feedback helps the group member reflect on her or his behavior and personal style. People learn more from examining their own situations and drawing their own conclusions than from being told about possible consequences. In short, encourage group members to anticipate their own consequences.
4. As appropriate to the situation, provide a summary of positive and negative consequences in a *nonjudgmental* manner.
5. Encourage group members to make their own decisions and live with the consequences of those decisions.

The Observation of Change Scale can be useful here. As you work to help a group member understand the logical consequences of behavior, the person may deny the consequence or only partially work on the issue in a Level 1 response. Noting this response, the intentional leader observes what is happening with the member and either clarifies the logical consequences strategy or moves to another strategy that might be more effective. Again, intentional leadership asks you to select your skill or strategy after anticipating what the outcomes might be. If the outcome is not as expected, change the strategy or skill.

Albert Ellis's rational emotive behavior therapy (REBT) is closely allied to behavioral functional analysis, but with some important differences (1994, 1995). Most specifically, REBT emphasizes *internal cognitions and emotions* whereas behavioral functional analysis emphasizes *observable behavior*. Ellis talks of the ABCDEF while the behavioral approach uses ABC (antecedent, behavior, consequence).

Needless to say, using the same first three letters can be confusing to those introduced to the systems for the first time. While there is some overlap between the two, you will find it helpful to think of ABC as emphasizing primarily observable behavior and ABCDEF as focused primarily on internal thoughts and feelings. Both systems are valuable to the group leader.

Particularly important in Ellis's REBT is noting and observing irrational thoughts and challenging group members to rethink ineffective cognitions. Ivey, Ivey, and Simek-Morgan (1998, p. 319) summarize Ellis's ABCDEF system as follows:

A—the "objective" facts, events, behaviors that an individual encounters. (Similar to antecedents in functional analysis, this is the story that our group members share in the here-and-now or the there-and-then.)

B—the person's beliefs about A. (REBT emphasizes thoughts whereas functional analysis focuses on behaviors with a secondary emphasis on thoughts and feelings.)

C—the emotional consequences, or how a person feels and acts about A.

Important in Ellis's REBT is disputing and challenging the ineffective *irrational* thought patterns that are discovered. Many times in group work, members will bring up situations about which little or nothing can be done except to reframe the situation differently. For example, a woman in a group may share a story of (A) how she was mistreated in the past. She may believe (B) that the mistreatment was her "fault," and (C) she may feel guilty about the situation.

This is clearly a time for the leader and members to dispute her views of the situation and help her reframe reality in more positive ways. This inappropriate placing of responsibility is a variation of "Am I crazy or did this really happen?" discussed in the preceding chapter. Feedback from the group and active disputation can help a person taking too much (or too little) responsibility for what happens to find a more appropriate balance.

At the start of the women's movement, women got together in consciousness-raising groups and shared their stories (A). They discussed (B) faulty cognitions ("Women's place is only in the home") and (C) irrational emotions such as guilt and fear. Through sharing stories and disputing old cognitions, they evolved new ways of thinking and feeling about women's lives.

Ellis adds D, E, and F to the above pattern. D represents disputing members' irrational thinking patterns, and direct, honest feedback from members of the group can be invaluable in helping the individual move to a change in cognition and emotion ("Joanne, my impression is that you are a skilled individual. I see you as capable of maintaining a solid home front AND allowing yourself more room for YOU.") E is the effect of the disputation and would mean that the member has changed thought patterns (Level 2 of the Observation of Change Scale). F represents the actual new feelings and behaviors. If group members take home the new thought and feeling patterns and do something different, they will move to Level 3 on the Observation of Change Scale.

Patterns similar to those that occurred in the women's movement were seen among People of Color, Vietnam veterans, the disabled, the gay/lesbian/bisexual/transgendered, and other groups. Consciousness-raising groups are, in terms of microskills, deeply involved in story (the basic listening sequence), functional and REBT analysis of the common stories, and reframing/reinterpreting reality. Then, they often band together to promote individual, group, and societal change.

## Application of Microskills and Strategy—Considering Logical Consequences

| Transcript | Process Comments |
|---|---|
| 1. *Shomari:* We've all shared stories of anger. We've had a lot of pain but also a lot of success. Each of us has many strengths and we've identified them clearly. Let us take a moment and look at what we've got in common as a group and what we've learned so far. Let's continue the exercise by using the ABC analysis. (She explains the behavioral system to the group.) What do you see as the common antecedents of anger in our stories? | 1. Shomari is structuring a change in activity. She summarizes the sharing of stories and reflects the group's general feeling of pain. She notes the positive assets and strengths and then moves the group in a new direction. Note that she is focusing on the group as a whole at this point rather than on individual stories. |
| 2. *Anne Marie:* Well, the first thing that stands out to me is Ramon's story about coming back from Vietnam. It makes me cry. First, he told the story of coming home and finding that no one wanted to hear his stories. Worse, neighbors called him a killer even though he'd only done what he was ordered to do. I guess the next thing is "B"—behavior. | 2. Anne Marie is showing good listening skills and has self-disclosed her feelings. She has learned the ABC analysis as part of the instructions and practice of this psychoeducational group. Here she is demonstrating her understanding of the behavioral logical consequences strategy. Shomari is seeing the effectiveness of her teaching and exercises here in the group members' behavior. |
| 3. *Michael:* (interrupts) . . . Yeah, small wonder he blew and hit the guy. I would have done the same. | 3. Feedback and self-disclosure. |
| 4. *Anne Marie:* And that's the "B." | 4. Logical consequences analysis. |
| 5. *Anthony:* But the consequence wasn't so great. Going to jail overnight isn't fun and only seemed to alienate him further from the neighbors, even though they were wrong. | 5. Logical consequences analysis plus feedback. |
| 6. *Shomari:* And is that a pattern for the group? Is there a general thing that happens when we "lose it"? | 6. Returns focus to group with open question oriented to helping group members think about how one person's issues and discussion can help those who are listening and observing. |
| 7. *Camille:* Yes, that seemed to happen in different ways for us all. As we shared our stories, they all made sense. I don't really blame any of us for getting angry. But the consequence of what we did with our anger seemed to hurt us almost as much as those we lashed out at. | 7. Focus on group pattern using the logical consequence strategy. |
| 8. *Shomari:* Could you put that in an ABC pattern? | 8. Open question oriented to considering logical consequences. Note how Shomari is involving the group rather than doing all the analysis on her own. |

*(continued)*

| Transcript | Process Comments |
|---|---|
| 9. *Camille:* "A," all of us faced challenging situations; "B" we blew; and "C" the consequences weren't so good for us or for others. | 9. Logical consequences summary with focus on entire group. |
| 10. *Shomari:* Thanks, Camille. What would others like to add? | 10. Positive feedback, open question oriented to group focus. The group continues for a short time and then Shomari leads them to the next phase of the workshop in which they will reflect on the meaning of anger. Later they will work on strategies to manage anger more effectively (Chapter 9). |
| 11.–18. Other members share their understanding of the ABC pattern and the group "R" reflects on the fact that we all face these issues in different ways. Individual stories start to emerge. | 11.–18. During the more reflective discussion, Camille withdraws from the group, apparently thinking something to herself. Her body language communicates worry and anxiety. The group notices her tension. |
| 19. *Anne Marie:* Camille, you look upset. What's going on for you?<br><br>*Note: The following illustration of Ellis's ABCDEF pattern is greatly abbreviated in this editing.* The logical consequences ABC is related to but different from the Ellis framework. The Ellis ABCDEF model can be especially valuable in helping a group member work through an issue whereas the logical consequences behavioral analysis of ABC provides an underlying structure for observing what is happening. | 19. Feedback, open question focused on individual. Group members can take leadership functions.<br><br>*Expect the analysis, disputation feedback, and group discussion leading toward change as shown here to take a minimum of fifteen minutes and more likely a half hour.* |
| 20. *Camille:* I see that blowing and anger don't do much good, but I'm different. I tend to hold anger in. Listening to all this makes me upset. | 20. Self-disclosure. Camille has been affected by the group discussion in a personal way. |
| 21. *Anne Marie:* You hold anger in . . . you look really upset. | 21. Encourage, restatement with observable feedback. |
| 22. *Camille:* Last night my boyfriend got angry with me and threatened me. I didn't clean the apartment as well as he wanted and the meal wasn't ready on time. He does that a lot. I try hard. I guess I'm the reason he blows. (Starts to cry.)<br><br>(Anne Marie reaches over and holds Camille's hand.) | 22. Self-disclosure. Here we see the beginning of an irrational story. In the Ellis ABCDEF framework, the objective facts (A) can be identified as Camille's efforts to handle routine housework and her lover becoming angry. Camille's beliefs about the facts (B) are that the situation is her fault and as a consequence (C), she feels bad about herself and is tense and anxious and tries harder to please. |

| Transcript | Process Comments |
|---|---|
| 23. *Michael:* (gently) Camille, you're a really good person and I hate to see you hurting. You really try hard to be supportive to everyone. I've sensed that in the group. | 23. Feedback which (D) disputes Camille's beliefs. |
| 24. *Anne Marie:* Yes, I feel that too. You come across as a very caring person who wants to help everyone. | 24. Feedback which (D) disputes Camille's beliefs. |
| 25. *Camille:* It feels good to hear that. Perhaps it isn't just me. | 25. Camille starts to restory and we begin to see (E) the effect of feedback and disputation. Recall that this account is highly edited and abbreviated. Change does not occur this fast. On the Observation of Change Scale, we are seeing movement toward Level 2. |
| 26.–30. Other group members provide feedback and support the process of reframing the story in a different perspective. | 26.–30. Sometimes it is tempting to stop with feedback from just one person, but various comments from members provide alternative perspectives and a more solid foundation for personal growth and change. |
| 31. *Shomari:* Camille, you've been getting lots of support from the group. I hear their caring and respect for you. They seem to feel that you are in the right. (gently) Has Jonathon been physically hurting you in any way? | 31. Summary with focus on group and the individual with an interpretive reframe supporting Camille's position. The direct question concerning physical abuse is important. Group members may sometimes avoid the most critical issues and leaders need to be concerned with personal safety. |
| 32. *Camille:* No, it is more the threat that scares me. Most of the time he is wonderful, but he does get so angry when things don't go right. I should try harder. | 32. Self-disclosure; note that Camille returns to the same self-defeating thinking. In this case we have an example of emotional abuse and domination. Members will often bounce between Levels 1 and 2 on the Observation of Change Scale. |
| 33. *Shomari:* We are glad that Jonathon has not physically hurt you, but it does at least sound like emotional abuse. Camille, could you paraphrase what the group has been telling you? | 33. Self-disclosure ("We are glad . . .") coupled with the reframe of emotional abuse. Camille's story has been that she needs to try harder and Shomari, with the group's help, is encouraging her to restory the situation. This is an example seeking "E" in Ellis's framework—the effect of disputation leading to change in cognitions and emotions. Asking Camille to paraphrase what the group has been saying is a way to facilitate Camille's internalization of the feedback. |

*(continued)*

| Transcript | Process Comments |
|---|---|
| 34. *Camille:* (hesitates) Well, I guess they are saying that I'm not the problem. They seem to be saying that it is Jonathon, but if only I did a better job . . . (starts to cry). | 34. Paraphrase with a focus on group rather than herself. Camille obviously has not internalized the feedback and returns to her original thoughts and feelings, but they are now more amenable to change. |
| 35.–42. Several participants provide more feedback and directly challenge Camille's self-blame. | 35.–42. As the group is moving in an appropriate supportive direction, Shomari remains silent, but she also notes that Michael seems increasingly distressed by the discussion. She holds that observation and eventually plans to ask Michael to share what is going on for him. |
| 43. *Camille:* So, what you all are saying is that I'm OK. I guess I am and perhaps I've been too naïve. I care deeply for Jonathon, but perhaps he isn't good for me. I hate to accept it, but it is emotional abuse he dishes out to me. | 43. Camille starts to reframe her own experience from a new perspective. We are seeing (E), the effect of the disputation, and the start of (F), the movement toward new feelings and behaviors. We are also seeing the effect of the positive support from the group as Camille starts to restory her life. Restorying and action are important components of F, the development of new feelings and moving toward change. Camille has reached a solid Level 2 on the Observation of Change Scale. Real change, however, depends on her taking learning from the group home to the real world. |

## Eliciting and Reflecting Meaning

The second handout of Box 8.1 has a final set of questions around meaning:

R = Reflection on meaning of event: What sense do you make of all this? What is the underlying meaning or reason? What one thing stands out for you from this exercise?

Eliciting and reflecting meaning helps your group explore deeper issues underlying their stories. After one tells a story, describes an event or situation, or tells of an interpersonal conflict, it is often helpful to step back and *reflect* on what happened or what has been said. In a group, several people may have shared stories or perhaps you have just worked through a difficult issue of conflict in the here-and-now. Step back, think about what has occurred, and reflect on the underlying issues. What did the conflict mean? What sense do the participants make of it?

Meanings are often thought of as the central dimension underlying behaviors, thoughts, and feelings (see Box 8.3). They are obviously deeply interconnected. A change in one changes the entire system. For example, if Ramon, the Vietnam veteran, starts to think or feel differently about his war experience, his behavior is likely to change, particularly if the underlying meaning of the war changes for him.

**Box 8.3**    *Relationship of Meaning to Behaviors, Thoughts, and Feelings*

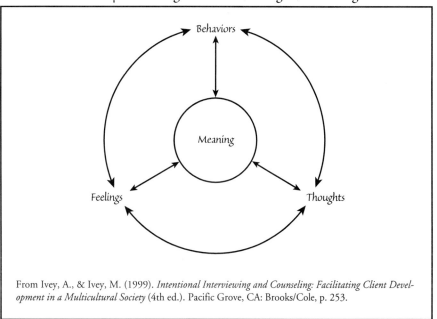

From Ivey, A., & Ivey, M. (1999). *Intentional Interviewing and Counseling: Facilitating Client Development in a Multicultural Society* (4th ed.). Pacific Grove, CA: Brooks/Cole, p. 253.

Similarly, a woman may have found meaning in a traditional role. But on examining her thoughts and feelings about that role, the meaning can change in radical ways—and thus, her behavior changes significantly.

The strategy of eliciting and reflecting meaning may be defined as follows:

1. Use listening skills carefully to draw out the story or situation fully, with attention to eliciting behaviors, thoughts, and feelings.
2. Use questions to draw out meaning. Some useful ones include these:
   ▲ "What does this *mean* to you?"
   ▲ "What *sense* do you make of it?"
   ▲ "What *values* underlie your actions?"
   ▲ "*Why* is that important (or unimportant) to you?"
   ▲ "Could you give me examples of some *values* that are important in your life decisions? How have those *values* been implemented in your life?"
   ▲ "What are some of the *reasons* you think that happens?"
   ▲ "Which of your *personal values* support/oppose that behavior/thought/feeling?"
   ▲ "What *one thing has stood out* for you from the discussion?"
   ▲ "*Why*?" (by itself, used carefully)
   ▲ "What *purpose* do you have in life? How do you *want to be* remembered?" (Adapted from Ivey & Ivey, 1999, p. 259)
3. Reflect the meaning, much as you might reflect feeling. Rather than "You feel . . .," use one of the following: "You mean/value/care/desire . . ." or "Your reason is . . ." and "Your underlying intention was . . ."

Note that reflection of meaning is closely related to reframing and interpretation in that group members are learning to think about themselves in situations from new perspectives and vantage points. A major distinction, however, is that the goal is to draw out new meanings from the individual or from the group as a whole. Meaning is very personal; we all need to avoid imposing our meaning on somebody else's life experience. If we do, we need to acknowledge that we are sharing our own meaning or reframing of the world and that this interpretation is not necessarily the underlying meaning that individuals or the group will find. Let us consider how Shomari might reflect meaning with her anger management group.

## Application of Microskills and Strategy—Eliciting and Reflecting Meaning

| Transcript | Process Comments |
|---|---|
| 1. *Shomari:* Well, we seem to be fairly clear about the ABCs of behavior, thought, and feeling around our experience of anger. It was good to work through those issues with Camille. Thank you again for sharing. I think we'll return to the more structured part of our workshop session. It's time for us to examine what all this means. As a start, would you divide into pairs. (pause as the group moves into two's) I'm going to ask you to examine two questions. "What one thing has stood out for you from the discussion so far?" "What does our discussion mean to you?" | 1. Shomari is structuring the group by giving directives. It would have been possible simply to have asked the group as a whole to consider these questions. In that way, the entire group would be included in the discussion. The pairing, on the other hand, permits everyone more time to talk about the issue. Which of these two options (or other approach) would you select as a leader? |
| 2. The pairs discuss the questions for five minutes. When one minute is left, Shomari says "Less than a minute left—start winding up and summarizing your discussion." | 2. It is important to inform your group shortly before you are going to call them together again; this provides time for them to complete discussions and transfer their thinking to the full group. |
| 3. *Shomari:* Let's get together and share our observations. (pause as group assembles) Let's start by going around the circle and each person sharing what has stood out for him or her so far. | 3. Eliciting meaning by having all members respond. Another possibility would be to have each pair report their discussions in more detail. Going around the group circle in this fashion gives everyone a chance to participate and increases feelings of personal membership and inclusion. It also provides extensive feedback for both the leader and group members on where the group is on a particular topic. |
| 4. *Camille:* The way all of us have lost control really impresses me. I hear us all trying to do the right thing, but we need help. | 4. Sharing meaning, focus on group. |
| 5. *Lynn:* I hear everyone trying so hard. | 5. Sharing meaning, focus on group. |

| Transcript | Process Comments |
|---|---|
| 6. *Michael:* Discovering how angry I still am about what happened to me in my divorce. I feel anger all over me right now. | 6. Sharing meaning, but perhaps more of an emphasis on self-disclosing feelings in the here-and-now and how they relate to the there-and-then. The focus is on self. Shomari notes here in the group what she observed in Michael during Camille's sharing. It is an issue that needs further work at a later point. |
| 7. *Anne Marie:* Reexperiencing my pain. | 7. Sharing feelings, but again a focus on self, similar to that of Michael. Note that both Michael and Anne Marie are not working so deeply on meaning issues at the moment. When one is overwhelmed by emotion, thinking about meaning can be too abstract and distant from the here-and-now. |
| 8. *Ramon:* The willingness of everyone to share and how similar we are in so many ways. I don't feel so alone now. I guess it means to me that there is hope. | 8. Ramon focuses on the group and how it helps him personally. He draws a meaning of hope from the group. |
| 9. *Anthony:* Many of us have a right to be angry, but all of us seem to need to learn how to control it better—for our own good! I've got more hope too, Ramon.<br><br>(Brief report-outs such as this given periodically are useful for the leader and members to get a here-and-now sense of what is going on in the group and for everyone to learn that each member of the group has a different opinion and experience of the same event. That later point, of course, is one of the main learning objectives of group work—becoming aware of and appreciating vast individual differences. In this case, Shomari was lucky as the group as a whole is moving toward engaging the issues of meaning—Level 2 of the Observation of Change Scale. However, Michael and Anne Marie are caught in the moment experiencing the past.) | 9. Focus on both self and group, picks up and supports Ramon's hope factor—note that the group itself is becoming a positive asset for security and personal growth. |
| 10. *Shomari:* What sense does the group make of all this? What meaning does it have for us as a group? | 10. Eliciting meaning, focus on group. |
| 11. *Michael:* I'm not sure I get it. | 11. Self-disclosure—Observation of Change Scale (OCS) 1. |

*(continued)*

| Transcript | Process Comments |
|---|---|
| 12. *Ramon:* It gets me in touch with the fact that all of us are caring people. We are trying to do the right thing, but we can't always succeed. | 12. Developing a new meaning, focus on group—note how similar this is to what might occur if you interpret or reframe an individual or group effectively. OCS 2+. The meaning Ramon selects is caring. |
| 13. *Anthony:* Oh, I see; we are talking about the group together. Yes, I think we are caring people; perhaps we all care too much. We all need to look at how we can care more effectively and stay out of trouble. I'm not alone. | 13. Self-disclosure, focus on group as he shares his personal meaning—OCS 2. Anthony picks up on the caring. |
| 14. *Anne Marie:* I think we all need to think about spiritual foundations more. Blowing up is not what I want to do. I need to be more patient and understanding and I suspect that is true for many of us.<br><br>(Other members share their meanings as well. Camille focuses on society pushing us all too hard and Ramon picks that up, talking a bit more about how opinions concerning the war in Vietnam were so divided. Lynn doesn't say anything, but seems interested in the group discussion. As they talk further, the group seems to focus on multiple meanings around anger—the expression of anger as the result of caring and not knowing what else to do, the pressures of society, and the need for new ways of handling issues. Anne Marie again stresses the potential value of spirituality.) | 14. Self-disclosure, focus primarily on self—OCS 2. Her meaning focuses on spiritual values and patience and understanding. |
| 30. *Shomari:* I hear several underlying meanings here from the group—caring, perhaps too caring. I hear several of you seeing society's values and behavior as an issue. I hear you all trying very hard. And for Anne Marie at least, spirituality is useful. Have I heard you correctly? What would others add? | 30. Summaries of the several meanings shared by the group with an individual reflection for Anne Marie, followed by a checkout inviting the group to continue to respond. The total group appears to be ready to explore issues in more depth and has achieved a Level 2 on the Observation of Change Scale. However, Michael and Lynn as observers and relative nonparticipants at this point may have other issues. |

Groups that explore meaning gradually come to examine the foundations of their commonalities and differences. They can, over time, reach basic values. Values such as caring, spirituality, and the very meaning of life can become central to the group. At another level, demonstrated in this session, elicitation and reflection of meaning is used to help group members realize that anger management is more than technique. It is also an expression of one's core values and life desires.

If your group tends to be too superficial, a helpful tactic is to stop for a moment and explore underlying issues of meaning and values. Consciousness-raising groups, in particular, are amenable to meaning issues. A male or female consciousness-raising group, for example, is ultimately exploring the meaning of gender. A Native American Indian consciousness-raising group may seek to return to basic meanings of tradition and connection, a gay liberation group may want to turn fear and hesitation into gay pride, and Vietnam and Persian Gulf veterans have profited from working together and developing new meanings of their war experience.

Anger management groups and all the groups discussed above need to find new, more positive meanings in their life experience. Then, armed with new ways of understanding the world, they can address change within and outside the group through thinking and feeling in new ways and adopting different behaviors. Nowhere does taking new thoughts into action both here-and-now and there-and-then appear more important than in the strategy of managing conflict, which we will address in the following chapter.

## USING THE INFLUENCING SKILLS WITH CHILD AND ADOLESCENT GROUPS

Structuring strategies are perhaps even more important with child and adolescent groups than with adults. Clarity and direction help the group move and maintain organization. The skill of exploring logical consequences cannot be taught to young children using the ABC analysis as presented here, but helping them see the consequences of their actions can be very useful. The mode of instruction and use of the skill becomes more concrete and specific and *briefly* helps youngsters examine the consequences of their action. The word briefly is stressed, as logical consequences can degenerate into discipline and lecturing if overdone.

Issues of meaning are sometimes important for adolescents engaging in discussion of complex issues such as morality, sexuality, and life goals. If the topic is of deep interest, adolescents will enjoy and work with meaning issues. The ideas behind underlying meaning structures are too cognitively complex for most younger children, but they too can explore meaning through discussing what is important to them and what they value in their lives.

Anger management, of course, is an important topic for both children and adolescents. Many of the activities presented here can be highly useful if adapted appropriately. Two useful resources for young people's groups on these issues are *The Child and Adolescent Psychotherapy Treatment Planner* (Jongsma, Peterson, & McInnis, 1996) and *Group Exercises for Adolescents* (Carrell, 1993). LaFromboise's (1996) *American Indian Life Skills Curriculum* is also particularly strong and brings multicultural issues to a more central place in group work. Although designed for Native American Indian youth, the book has wide implications for youth of all ethnicities and races.

## MOVING TOWARD YOUR OWN LEADERSHIP STYLE

This chapter has presented three interpersonal influence microskills and strategies for change: structuring, exploring logical consequences, and eliciting/reflecting meaning. All have emphasized the importance of first listening to the individual before engaging in these targeted interventions. In addition, we have strongly recommended identifying positive assets and using positive reframing as an important part of effective interpersonal influence. Following are several questions for you to consider about each skill and strategy area:

*Structuring:* Where do you stand? No matter what you do, you will structure what happens in your group work, but what kinds of structure do you favor?

*Exploring logical consequences:* Are you comfortable with the highly structured suggestions of this chapter presented in Box 8.2? Would you rather work with this microstrategy more informally? Recall that simply helping a person or group look at the likely consequences of their behavior, thoughts, or feelings can be very useful.

*Eliciting and reflecting meaning:* Is this something you want to continue? What is the appropriate place and time for exploration of meaning? Not all groups will examine meaning issues.

Think back on this section and the entire chapter. What have you learned here? What points struck you as most important? What stood out for you? What would you like to work on in the area of interpersonal influencing microskills and strategies to improve your own group facilitation?

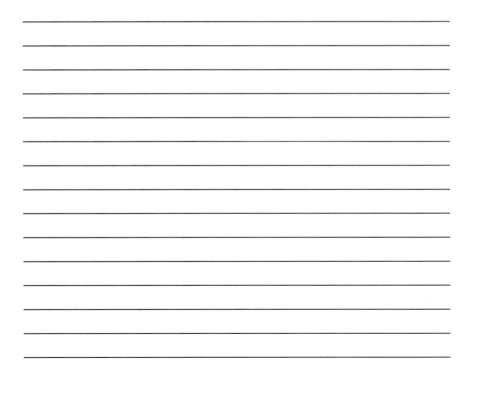

_____

_____

_____

_____

_____

_____

_____

_____

_____

_____

_____

_____

_____

_____

# PRACTICING STRUCTURING, EXPLORING LOGICAL CONSEQUENCES, AND ELICITING AND REFLECTING MEANING

### 1.    Process Observation

Structuring will be relatively easy to observe in groups, but the other two strategic skills are used far less frequently. We suggest you watch for the use of exploring logical consequences and eliciting and reflecting meaning in this observation exercise, but realistically give your primary attention to how the leader structures the group. Box 8.4 provides a process observation form for observing a leader's ability to structure a group. The evaluation questions are organized around the five dimensions introduced in Chapter 5.

Visit a group session or meeting. How does the leader guide the group through the various stages or dimensions? Does the leader seem to let the group evolve in its own style? In either approach, note formal and informal ways of structuring provided by the leader. Watch the group for the flow as they move from initiation through ending. Some groups will have a definite identifiable structure; others will seem to have everything "happening at once."

Summarize your observations here or in more detail in a formal report and analysis of the group you observe.

---------------------------------------------

---------------------------------------------

---------------------------------------------

---------------------------------------------

---------------------------------------------

---------------------------------------------

---------------------------------------------

### 2. The Fish Bowl

For this fish bowl, we are recommending the use of Handout 2 from Box 8.1. Individuals who volunteer to work in the fish bowl are asked to share a story of when they were angry; however, in a brief fish bowl, only one participant will have time to share.

It should be possible to use all three microskill strategies from this chapter in this exercise: (1) the group will require some structuring and the use of directives; (2) there will be an opportunity to work through ABC analysis and thus examine the strategy of exploring logical consequences; (3) the final portion of Handout 2 asks for R = reflection; you should be able to engage in eliciting and reflecting meaning.

Four to six class members form a group from the larger class. One member is selected as leader and helps one individual work through the ABC analysis and

**Box 8.4**    *Process Observation of Structuring in Groups*

All group leaders use structuring skills, even the most nondirective. In observing a group, search for ways the group leader used structuring to cover the five dimensions or stages. As the skills of exploring logical consequences and eliciting/reflecting meaning are important in this chapter, do you see them utilized in the group you observe? They are skills that tend to be used specifically in working groups as a way to explore issues, and you may not observe them very often.

*Dimension 1: Initiating the Group—Rapport and Structuring—Goals*

▲ Did the group leader involve group members?
▲ How were the issues of rapport handled?
▲ Were group goals outlined? Concrete or vague?
▲ As the group began, were specific directives utilized? Were they clear and concrete or vague?
▲ What did you observe nonverbally and verbally about the leader and group members?
▲ What is your personal evaluation of Dimension 1?

*Dimension 2: Gathering Data—Stories and Dynamic Balancing of Focus*

You will find some task group leaders almost seem to skip this stage or dimension and move immediately to working. They may interweave aspects of this dimension with Dimension 4.

▲ How was gathering data handled in the group you observed?
▲ Did the leader draw out data or stories from the group?
▲ How many members participated in the process?
▲ Were specific directives utilized? Clear and concrete or vague?
▲ What did you observe nonverbally and verbally about the leader and group members?
▲ What is your personal evaluation of Dimension 2?

*Dimension 3: The Positive Asset Search*

▲ Was this dimension included? During what portions of the group process?
▲ Were certain members favored over others?
▲ Were specific directives utilized? Clear or vague?
▲ What did you observe nonverbally and verbally about the leader and group members?
▲ What is your personal evaluation of Dimension 3?

*Dimension 4: Working—Examining Goals, Sharing, Confronting, Restorying*

▲ What was the nature of leader behavior during the work stage?
▲ Were goals addressed?
▲ Were specific directives utilized? Clear or vague?
▲ What did you observe nonverbally and verbally about the leader and group members?
▲ What is your personal evaluation of Dimension 4?

*Dimension 5: Ending—Generalizing and Acting on New Stories*

▲ Was there an organized termination?
▲ Were goals addressed in terms of follow-up?
▲ Were specific directives utilized? Clear or vague?
▲ What did you observe nonverbally and verbally about the leader and group members?
▲ What is your personal evaluation of Dimension 5?

involves other members of the volunteer group as much as possible. The remainder of the class observes what is occurring using the process observation questions of Box 8.4, giving special attention to the structuring skills of the volunteer leader.

### 3. Your Own Group Practice

The above exercise is repeated for your own practice in small groups.

1. Divide into groups of five or six. One person is to serve as leader and one is observer, who uses Box 8.4. The remainder serve as group participants.
2. Define the topic for the small groups. The suggested topic is anger management as you work through Handout 2 from Box 8.1. However, feel free to select topics of interest to you and the group.
3. Fifteen minutes should be used for the small groups. Allow five minutes for feedback from the observer. Finally, each small group can reflect on its own group process.

Where possible, add videorecording and practice to your work with attending skills and observation. You will always obtain very useful feedback on yourself and the group.

## REFERENCES

Carrell, S. (1993). *Group exercises for adolescents.* Newbury Park, CA: Sage.

Corey, G., & Corey, M. (1997). *Groups: Process and practice.* Pacific Grove, CA: Brooks/Cole.

Dreikurs, R., & Grey, L. (1968). *Logical consequences: A new approach to discipline.* New York: Dutton.

Ellis, A. (1994). *Reason and emotion in psychotherapy.* New York: Birch Lane.

Ellis, A. (1995). Changing rational-emotive therapy to rational-emotive-behavior therapy. *Journal of Rational-Emotive and Cognitive-Behavior Therapy, 13,* 85–90.

Ivey, A., & Ivey, M. (1999*). Intentional interviewing and counseling: Facilitating client development in a multicultural society* (4th ed.). Pacific Grove, CA: Brooks/Cole.

Ivey, A., Ivey, M., & Simek-Morgan, L. (1998). *Counseling and psychotherapy: A multicultural perspective* (4th ed.). Boston: Allyn & Bacon.

Jongsma, A., Peterson, L., & McInnis, W. (1996). *The child and adolescent psychotherapy treatment planner.* New York: Wiley.

Kaul, T., & Bednar, R. (1994). Pretraining and structure: Parallel lines yet to meet. In A. Fuhriman & G. Burlingame, *Handbook of group psychotherapy* (pp. 155–190). New York: Wiley.

LaFromboise, T. (1996). *American Indian life skills curriculum.* Madison: University of Wisconsin Press.

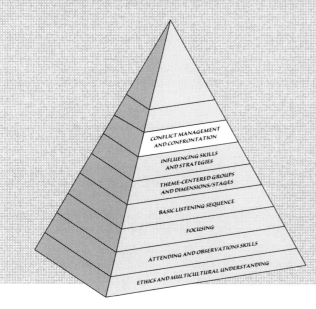

CHAPTER 9

CONFLICT MANAGEMENT
AND CONFRONTATION

INFLUENCING SKILLS
AND STRATEGIES

THEME-CENTERED GROUPS
AND DIMENSIONS/STAGES

BASIC LISTENING SEQUENCE

FOCUSING

ATTENDING AND OBSERVATIONS SKILLS

ETHICS AND MULTICULTURAL UNDERSTANDING

# Skills and Strategies for Interpersonal Influence, Part III: Managing Conflict via Confrontation

## CHAPTER GOALS

It seems that a natural condition of humankind is to engage in conflict. The complexity of the world we live in is such that we will constantly encounter people who think, feel, and behave differently from us. Thus, one of the central challenges for you as a leader is to learn how to work with, manage, and even enjoy the inevitable conflict that will appear in all groups.

It is important to recall that creative human growth often occurs in conflict situations. As you start this chapter, you will find it helpful to reframe and reinterpret conflict as an opportunity for movement rather than as a static problem to be solved. Individuals who face internal contradictions in their thoughts, feelings, and behaviors have the opportunity to move, change, and enhance their lives.

Confrontation involves a group of microskills oriented toward a "win-win" approach to individual and group conflict. Ivey and Ivey (1999, p. 196) define the philosophy of confrontation this way:

> Confrontation is *not* a direct, harsh challenge. Think of it, rather, as a more gentle skill that involves listening to the client carefully and respectfully and then seeking to help the client examine self and situation more fully. Confrontation is not "going against" the client; it is "going with" the client, seeking clarification and the possibility of a new resolution of difficulties. Think of confrontation as a supportive challenge, even when it requires firmness and assertiveness on your part.

Fundamental to conflict management is noting and observing discrepancies, incongruities, and contradictions. These can be within a single individual or between individuals in your group, and they may include conflict with you as the leader.

This chapter will continue the anger management issues from Chapter 8. The same cast of characters from the Chapter 8 group will appear again. Anger is obviously related closely to conflict management and thus the transcript examples presented here apply to group process in general.

---

In this chapter, seek to accomplish the following objectives of understanding and mastery:

▲ Understand and master positive skills of confrontation, the supportive challenge. Confrontation involves multiple microskills and intentional flexibility on your part.

▲ Utilize the constructs of conflict management as a framework to observe group process; in particular, it is important to observe individual and group conflict. In addition, conflict and challenges directed toward you the leader need to be observed and anticipated. Particularly helpful in this process is noting discrepancies, incongruities, and contradictions.

▲ Assess the change process among group members through the Observation of Change Scale.

▲ Apply conflict management skills and strategies to your own group leadership.

---

## WARM-UP EXERCISE

Group work is seldom dull. There's always something happening, more than you can always be aware of and anticipate. Avoiding all conflict would be to deny one of the great learning opportunities. Therefore, it is important to search out the positives underlying conflict. When you start thinking about handling conflict in your groups, we suggest that you think about the positive asset search and how you can help your group members feel more included in the process. Generally, the more included your group members feel as individuals, the more likelihood there will be for resolving conflict in a positive direction.

Conflict is not always a negative. It provides an opportunity for learning. As you start thinking about this topic, consider the question, "What are some times in your own past when you have learned a valuable lesson through conflict?"

_____

_____

_____

_____

_____

_____

Many of us do not particularly enjoy dealing with conflict. As an important part of group leadership, this is an area in which you will want to increase your skills. Following are some ideas to help you think about ways to understand and cope with conflict, disruption, challenge, and disturbances that can occur in groups.

What are some of the things you already know that can help members of your group to feel included and to know that they are valued members? Write below your ideas and then compare them to ours, which we summarize in the footnote at the bottom of this page.*

_____

_____

_____

_____

_____

_____

_____

_____

_____

_____

Given that we want to start conflict management in a positive manner, what types of individuals are we likely to find bringing challenges in the group? Box 9.1 describes several types of group members and their behaviors that might cause conflict in the group. Also presented are specific suggestions for effectively coping and responding to members (some styles adapted from Carroll & Wiggins, 1997, pp. 55–74). Note especially that it is important to search for strengths and positives in the behavior of these more difficult group members. Finally, recall that the issues they present are opportunities for growth, not only for them, but also for the group and you personally.

---

*There are many things that can help group members feel included. Most of the warm-up exercises in this book are oriented to having all group members talk in a positive way. We suggest almost any exercise in which all members are encouraged to share something in the group. The community genogram and the sharing of stories about the ability to handle anger are just two of these. We believe that warm-up exercises help to open a group to discuss things freely. Openness builds trust.

Beyond this, your ability as a leader to constantly find positive assets and strengths in each individual is important. Inevitably, you will like some group members more than others. If this becomes a problem, you may need consultation with an external observer or supervisor. Seek to find things you like in each member.

The circle of discussion in which each person is invited to share perceptions and ideas is helpful in promoting inclusion. You will find at certain difficult points that stopping and asking each member to share what she or he is experiencing at the moment can be helpful. Seek to reward members' participation and positive reframe and reinterpret what they say. Having different perspectives helps.

If you sense a specific member having difficulty in feeling included, consider the possibility of bringing out the member in a positive way through an exercise or through storytelling. If you can help the group offer positive feedback and strengths through a circle of discussion, this can sometimes be highly useful.

What else did you come up with?

**Box 9.1**   *Some Personal Styles and Behaviors That May Lead to Conflict in the Group*

| Example Group Members and Potential Positive Contributions They Can Make | Possible Microskills and Confrontation Strategies That Might Be Employed |
|---|---|
| *The participant experiencing a life crisis*—may be experiencing a major crisis that dominates life (divorce, illness, loss of job). This crisis can appear directly as the topic of conversation or can be played out through difficult behavioral patterns in the group. (Positive—may model openness and willingness to share real issues.) | Prescreening can be helpful as this member may not belong in the group unless it is therapy oriented. If a major personal crisis comes up that is not appropriate to the group, listen, stress positive feedback, and structure by seeking referral. Mention to the member that you will talk to her or him after this session is completed. |
| *The silent member*—not usually thought of as presenting conflict, but silence is an issue that often needs to be challenged and confronted. (Positive—may be very good at listening and observing. If drawn out, often provides useful new perspectives on what is happening.) | Provide opportunity for inclusion early through safe exercises that permit all to speak. Group members may all be asked to speak on an issue and when the silent member remains silent, the group members themselves will often encourage participation. Consider the direct approach—"Ramon, we haven't heard from you today. What do you think about this?" |
| *The member who seeks to please*—very good at accommodating to the group, but may give little attention to personal needs. Closely allied with being dependent, the person who tries too hard to please others often tries to smooth conflict in the group, even to the point of interfering with change and movement among members who need to work through conflict. (Positive—often makes the group and leader happy because of a positive style.) | Often a useful member to have in the group but may be paying a personal price. Observe behavior over time and if problematic, feedback from you and the group is often helpful. This style can be closely related to dependency. The pleaser may smooth over conflict too quickly, and this behavior may need to be confronted. *Humor is potentially helpful with all challenging group members if used sensitively.* |
| *The participant who dominates or monopolizes conversation*—tends to be the first person to talk time after time with an opinion on each issue. May seek to draw focus to her or his own issues. (Positive—always has something to say, often insightful and valuable.) | Feedback on behavior from group may be useful. Logical consequences analysis and an attempt to elicit meaning underlying the behavior are possibilities. May require you to give direct structuring suggesting that the individual hold back and give others a chance to speak. In addition, one who dominates may be internally insecure and need positive feedback. |
| *The member who may be hostile or aggressive*—uses anger as the major way to cope in the group. This may be direct or more subtle, passive-aggressive behavior. (Positive—may serve as a catalyst; many of us have trouble getting in touch with our anger and this person may help spark useful group encounters.) | Listen carefully and try to find underlying meaning and desires. May require direct structuring and active confrontation. It may be especially important to allow this person to tell her or his story fully. Afterward, feedback from the group as a whole can be useful. Logical consequences analysis can be beneficial. |

| Example Group Members and Potential Positive Contributions They Can Make | Possible Microskills and Confrontation Strategies That Might Be Employed |
|---|---|
| *The would-be leader*—both directly and indirectly tries to take over leadership of the group. (Positive—often has real leadership skills that need to be recognized.) | Direct challenges to your leadership are best met face on with structuring and brief self-disclosure with opportunity for group to provide feedback. Try to determine the underlying meaning of this person's behavior—consider reflection of meaning. Some leaders mistakenly accept the individual as an informal co-leader. |
| *The member who is dependent*—may find the group a great place for support; constantly seeks attention and advice from the group. (Positive—similar to pleaser, tends to be open and active participant. Often very supportive of other group members.) | At first, support and encourage with a strong emphasis on the positive asset search followed by feedback and the opportunity to explore dependency in other situations as well as the here-and-now. Consider reframing the dependent behavior as sensitive to others, but with an underlying desire to receive attention and closeness. |
| *The person who intellectualizes*—very good at abstract discussions and analysis, but often limited in feeling. (Positive—may be particularly good at reframing issues from new perspectives. At times, a more distant abstract approach can be useful.) | "How are you feeling? What's going on in your gut?" Feedback from group members on behavior more likely to be successful than from the leader. Reframing and interpretations by the leader and members can be helpful. Expect individual to divert attention by further abstract intellectualizing. |
| *The member too deeply in touch with emotion*—the opposite of the intellectualizer. Constantly in touch with feelings, but unable to distance self appropriately. May become the major "feeler" of the group and enable others to avoid emotional disclosure. (Positive—can model emotion and help others to get in touch with feelings.) | Allow cathartic expression, then emphasize concrete storytelling. Feedback and logical consequences skills may be useful. Acknowledge feelings briefly and then seek to place emphasis on content aspects of the comment via paraphrasing and/or questioning. |
| *The member who blocks*—also known as "yes . . . but . . ." Just as the group seems to be making positive movement, this person comes in with an objection. Over time, this individual can be one of the most difficult for leaders to manage. (Positive—at least they see the situation differently from others!) | Search for positives and build a feeling of inclusion, although the true blocker may use inclusion as a way to block the group more effectively. Note pattern of blocking and ask group members to provide feedback, particularly when the blocking obviously frustrates the group as a whole. A positive reframe for this member can focus on her or his ability to bring alternative perspectives to the group. |
| *The member with low-impulse control*—acts without thinking, even if intentions are good. Little sense as to appropriate timing of comments. (Positive—very good at here-and-now behavior.) | Feedback from group most useful, particularly a short time after the individual has interfered with group progress. Specific structured directions may be necessary—"Wait a moment, let Joan speak first." |

Review the beginning list and constructs of Box 9.1. What would you add and change as you examine this list? What types of individuals might be more difficult for you to work with than others? Where might you be most effective? How do you react to the initial positive contributions difficult members can make to the group?

_____

_____

_____

_____

_____

_____

To this list you may want to add other types of individuals that occur to you and your own ideas for helping cope with the kinds of conflict they might present. And—as you review this list—take a moment to think about how you yourself at times may have caused or triggered conflict.

_____

_____

_____

_____

_____

_____

All the types of group members described earlier can potentially benefit from being actively included in the group, as many of their thoughts, feelings, and behaviors come from a history of exclusion and the failure of others to truly listen to them. Thus, the positive asset search and an opportunity to share one's self in a positive way are vital as part of the group process in resolving personal and group conflict.

## DEFINING THE LEADERSHIP SKILLS AND STRATEGIES OF MANAGING CONFLICT

This chapter begins with the idea that conflict often is a stimulus to growth and change. As part of structuring, the leader can point out that conflict and differences are often the windows to learning. Then, when conflict does appear, the group will be more likely to work with it directly as they anticipate that something positive can come from it for all of them. A four-step model for managing conflict is presented here.

## Step 1: Maintain Positive Intentional Leadership

Your intentionality, that ability to generate multiple responses on the spot, will be useful. The challenging group member may need to share thoughts and feelings or may have an irrational idea that needs to be worked with. Feedback on the member's behavior from both you and the group may be helpful or a reframe/interpretation may be useful. At other times, the group member may be so disruptive that you need to take firmer steps, perhaps even referring the person to help outside the group. Managing conflict provides space for you as leader to utilize the multiple possibilities of interpersonal influence presented in Chapters 7, 8, and 9. If the first idea doesn't work, you've got another!

Intentionality also means selecting your influencing strategy in anticipation of specific results. If you listen to someone's story fully, the individual often will feel more comfortable and included and may even start down the path of looking at the issue from a new perspective. If you help the pair having conflict express their here-and-now feelings, anticipate that they will indeed talk about their feelings and provide you with further opportunities for other interventions. Each microskill and strategy can be used with expectation of results.

However, these results clearly do not always happen. You may provide a very useful reframe or interpretation and it will be rejected. The intellectualizer who receives feedback may continue to intellectualize. It is here that your intentionality is most important. Move to another skill, another strategy, another focus and things may well start moving again in a more positive direction.

*You are not necessarily the target!* The issues around conflict management can certainly be anxiety provoking. It is important to be aware that conflict in the group, even though seemingly directed at you, is generally not "your problem." The leader is often a symbol of authority, and group members may be responding to their history with leadership figures rather than to you personally. In short, you are not necessarily the target of even the most difficult challenge.

General guidelines for dealing with challenging leadership situations start first with you, the leader. Relax; never be defensive; see the encounter as a learning opportunity for you, the challenger(s), and the group. Having allowed yourself to breathe, use your observation and listening skills to understand what is going on. Those who seek to provoke you usually have a story to tell and you as leader need to hear it. Ask yourself why this group member is doing this. Try to understand the person's viewpoint and how she or he came to think and act that way. Search for the positives underlying the behavior.

Both individual and multicultural awareness and sensitivity are particularly important when using confrontation. A classic research study of encounter groups found that insensitive and highly confrontational leaders can produce casualties—individuals who actually are harmed by group experience. However, groups that have first developed trust and cohesion can deal with confrontation more effectively (Lieberman, Yalom, & Miles, 1973). The general rule is that confrontation should be used gently and generally not until the later stages of the group experience.

Perhaps it is *you* who are the problem. Some leaders have a natural tendency to please, block, or dominate. We have all experienced difficult leaders in our lives. Consider the possibility that the difficulty in the group is your personal style, not that of the group member(s). Open yourself to change, seek supervision and consultation, and invite others to observe your behavior in groups. Audiorecord and videorecord your sessions so that you can obtain necessary feedback around your observable work as a group leader.

If you have clearly made an error, admit it nondefensively. None of us is perfect. It is not the errors we make but our ability to correct them that is most important. You as leader are human and all of us are prone to make mistakes. The mistakes are not as important as your ability to recover, which is central in moving on.

Take just a moment and think how you deal with errors and the mistakes you make. Expect to find this past style appearing in your work as a group leader. Will it be helpful or harmful? What are some times that you demonstrated the ability to work effectively with your mistakes?

_____

_____

_____

_____

_____

## Step 2: Listen and Observe

Let us begin with what you already know: *if we are to confront and challenge and work with conflict, we need to begin with listening.* It does little good to seek to resolve struggles and disharmony in your group if you have not heard the members' individual issues, thoughts, and feelings thoroughly. The group itself cannot help a person provoked by a racist or sexist incident unless that individual's story has been told—and heard. Two people in your group suddenly erupt in an argument and lock horns; the first step is to understand the antecedents of their discord and where they are "coming from." When you are dealing with angry feelings and friction, what are the underlying narratives in both the here-and-now and the there-and-then?

Group leaders learn over time to anticipate conflict and often can set the stage for resolution and growth even before the conflict is shown openly. You will find that managing conflict requires less effort if the group has developed trust and each member in some way feels included and a part of the group. If a foundation of basic trust is established, then conflict is often seen by the group as an opportunity for all to learn rather than as a problem to be solved. The goal is "win-win" rather than "win-lose."

Use your process observation skills to note developing discrepancies, incongruities, and mixed messages within and among group members. Three major types of conflict within groups are (1) conflict internal to a group member, (2) conflict among group members, and (3) conflict with the leader. Box 9.2 summarizes these three types with specifics for observation. Conflict possibilities, of course, are infinite and the list here should be considered preliminary for your years of work as a group leader.

**Box 9.2**   *Conflict Process Observation Summary:* Identifying Incongruities, Discrepancies, and Mixed Messages

|  |  |
|---|---|
| | Following is a partial list of incongruities, discrepancies, and mixed messages that you may observe in any group. You will want to add to this list through your own experience over time. |
| *Incongruity/ Mixed Messages in Nonverbal Behaviors* | Internal to a single group member: |

Internal to a single group member:

▲ Leans forward in interest, but suddenly starts jiggling foot or leg rapidly.
▲ Avoids eye contact on certain topics.
▲ When talking about a difficult topic, shows speech hesitations.
▲ Raises vocal tone when speaking of an issue of concern.

Between or among group members:

▲ The group moves to a new topic and most members seem interested, but two sit back with arms folded.
▲ One member avoids looking at certain other group members or always seems to direct attention to one person.
▲ Two members stare at each other angrily.

Between leader and group member(s):

▲ All of the above apply, both individual and group examples, and the leader becomes the focus of the encounter.
▲ Note particularly the visuals, vocals, and body language of each participant in relation to you.
▲ It will be useful to have someone observe your own nonverbal styles.

*Discrepancies/ Mixed Messages in Verbal Behavior*

Internal to a group member:

▲ Mixed feelings toward people, decisions, or issues ("I love my job, but . . ." "Mother always treated me well," followed five minutes later by "She favored my brother all the time").
▲ Meaning and value conflicts ("My spiritual life has always been so important to me, but now in college I am beginning to wonder." "My family is vital to me, but am I really meeting their expectations?").
▲ Problems and concerns outside the group ("I have this problem on the job with sexual harassment." "I'm wondering if I am drinking too much." "How can I tell my parents that I am gay?")

Between or among group members:

▲ All of the above apply, but will be manifested between members of the immediate group—for example, expect group members to have mixed feelings toward one another and conflicts on meanings and values.
▲ Problems of relationship inside the group—"Inez, you really annoy me." "Gene, why are you always so quiet?" "Hal, that was a lousy thing to say." "George, I've watched you for three weeks in this group; now let me tell you what I really think of you."
▲ Disagreement—"I see it differently." "I think you are wrong and here's why."
▲ Interruptions—some members may interrupt rudely and frequently, particularly certain people.

*(continued)*

**Box 9.2 (continued)**

| | |
|---|---|
| | Between leader and group member(s): |
| | ▲ All of the above can occur, both individual and group examples, and the leader becomes the focus of the encounter. The conflict with the leader may come from one or several members and even the entire group at times. |
| | ▲ Challenges to the leader can be both direct and indirect—"Shomari, you have not given us enough direction." "You're a good leader, but . . ." A popular sport in groups can be "Get the leader." |
| | ▲ Leaders, too, can give mixed messages—for example, faint praise such as "That was a good little comment you made" or "Some people in the group appreciate your contributions." |
| *Discrepancies or Mixed Messages Between Verbal and Nonverbal Behavior (What is said does not agree with the speaker's body language)* | Internal to a group member: |
| | ▲ Smiles inappropriately while talking about a difficult and/or negative experience. |
| | ▲ Makes a positive and supportive comment while simultaneously jiggling the foot or presenting a tightly close fist. |
| | ▲ Hesitates when saying that he or she has "no problems." |
| | Between or among group members: |
| | ▲ All of the above can occur, but the mixed messages are directed from one group member to another. |
| | ▲ A member says "I like this group" or "I agree" while sitting back in the chair with arms folded. |
| | Between leader and group member(s): |
| | ▲ All of the above apply, but the focus turns to group members' interaction with the leader. Is the leader sending mixed messages and discrepancies? |
| | ▲ The challenging styles of the would-be leader, the blocker, and the dominator/ monopolist are often oriented toward the leader, either directly or indirectly. Other styles may be reacting to the leader as well. Leaders can engage in the same behaviors. |
| | ▲ Members may come to the group late or not come at all; the leader may consistently start late. |
| | ▲ Members may be unwilling to follow structured suggestions, or the leader may give confusing directions. |
| | ▲ Members may not participate verbally, or the leader may ignore some members while attending to others. |

The ability to observe conflict through incongruity, discrepancies, and mixed messages is something you will want to develop over your life span as a group leader. Box 9.2 provides an outline of things to watch for, but it is you who will supply the important content and context. Consider photocopying this list and using it as a basis for observation of conflict in groups. Especially helpful, of course, will be videorecording groups in which you participate, both as a member and as a leader.

### Conflict internal to a group member

Each person in your group exhibits a massive amount of verbal and nonverbal behavior through the group session. Each of us has a general style; some of us show ourselves as generally tense and anxious while others are more reserved and hard to read. It is wise to observe each person's general style so that you can note *changes* in that style as they appear. Sudden changes in verbal or nonverbal style may indicate that something immediate is going on with a person. Groups oriented to therapy especially require a leader who observes members carefully and sensitively.

You can also sharpen your observation of internal conflict simply by watching those around you. This, of course, has its problems and dangers. It is usually not wise to become the family or dormitory "shrink," so when you are watching people you know, make your observations brief and keep them to yourself. Grocery stores, playgrounds, and long lines at movies are just a few places to observe potential conflict.

### Conflict between or among group members

When you are working with conflict within the group, you need to observe discrepancies in the interactions between individuals. Start observing conflict in groups that you attend. Even in a college class, look around at the patterns of verbal and nonverbal attention. To whom does the instructor give eye contact? Attend a school board session or a management decision-making group, especially when a conflictual issue is to be discussed.

As you observe the conflicting individuals or small groups, also observe the observers. What are the nonparticipants doing verbally and nonverbally? Is the conflict affecting them?

### Conflict between members and the leader

Observing leader behavior in conflictual situations is helpful. Don't be surprised when you find leaders displaying blocking, pleasing, hostile, or other behaviors described in Box 9.1. You will also note that some leaders are hostile to certain members while being very supportive of others. Whom does the leader listen to? Ignore?

Most helpful of all, search out and note effective leader behaviors. What specifically did the leader do that was right? What can you learn from this observation?

## Step 3: Confront and Challenge Conflict and Discrepancies

You have already listened to and observed conflict. At times, simply listening carefully, reflecting, and summarizing are all that is needed to resolve problems. In addition, the following specific actions can be used by a leader to confront conflict.

3.1. *Summarize the conflicting behaviors/thoughts/feelings and perhaps meaning differences clearly.* When you are working with an individual, model confrontation/challenge statements are often helpful. "On one hand . . . but on the other hand . . ." is often effective, and many group leaders will summarize the conflict nonverbally as well, using appropriate hand movements. Follow the confrontation/challenge statement with a checkout. "How does that sound to you?" "Variations include 'You say . . . , but you do . . . ,' 'I see . . . at one time, and at another time I see . . .' and

'Your words say . . . but your actions say . . . ' " (Ivey & Ivey, 1999, p. 199). Pointing out the inconsistencies often leads individuals to see ways to resolve the differences.

Note that the model confrontation statement is essentially the microskill of summarization coupled with aspects of the feedback skill. The individual (or individuals) are confronted with observable things that they said or did in the group. Their discrepancies, incongruities, and mixed messages are fed back to them.

Being nonjudgmental and not attacking are critical in this type of statement. If group members feel pinned down, the confrontation is moving toward failure. Thus, being supportive while providing major challenges is critical.

With group members in conflict, the model sentence becomes, "Camille, you feel/think . . . and Anthony, you feel/think . . . Have I heard you each fully? What might you add?" The task focuses on clarifying differences. This clarity itself can lead to problem resolution. In some cases, take time to summarize the two differing stories in detail.

When the challenge is directly focused on you, the leader, the model sentence changes to this: "Ramon, you feel/think . . . about me. My reaction to that is . . . How does that come across to you?" It may be tempting to defer the direct challenge so that group members answer for you, and occasionally that may be wise; but at times you need to stand strong and respond directly, openly, honestly, and most of all—nondefensively.

*3.2. Consistently bring in the positive asset search and positive reframe.* We can best resolve our discrepancies from our strengths. Part of listening and observing needs to be focused on identifying member strengths. As you summarize or react with the confrontation strategy, ensure that you emphasize positives as part of the process.

*3.3. Observe reactions to the confrontation and move intentionally to other microskills and strategies.* As appropriate to the situation, utilize reframing/interpretation, self-disclosure, more feedback, eliciting and reflecting meaning, and any of a variety of structuring strategies and directives. All are designed to further clarify thoughts, feelings, and behavior and can lead to new ways of thinking. It is important to avoid "right-wrong" thinking. Encourage the groups members to provide these clarifications. The leader who takes over in difficult conflict situations may be a superstar, but he or she takes away from the power of group work and individual growth.

Most situations can be viewed from multiple perspectives, and learning to live with difference, incongruity, and difficult conflicts will often be a central result of effective conflict management in the group. As an example, imagine that a group member is about to visit the hospital for a prostate or breast biopsy for possible cancer. The conflict cannot be denied, but the group can help the member live with the situation more effectively. All issues do not have immediate and positive resolutions—losing a job, death, serious interpersonal conflict, divorce, living with an alcoholic or substance abuser often require us to learn to live with "what is."

### Step 4. Evaluate the Change Process with the Observation of Change Scale

The Observation of Change Scale (OCS) can be especially useful to you as you work with conflict and resolve discrepancies. It can help you (and often group members as well) understand where we are in the process of change and movement. You may observe significant Level 2 change in members of your group in the here-

and-now of the group experience as they change behavior, thoughts, feelings, and meanings in front of your eyes. When working in the there-and-then, as members discuss external issues, you will need follow-up to determine whether change has indeed occurred and been generalized to real life. If the confrontation effort is only partially successful, use your intentional leadership style to change interventions and focus as you continue to seek results. Box 9.3 presents a summary of some key individual and multicultural issues in confrontation.

**Box 9.3**    *Individual and Multicultural Issues in Confrontation*

People differ in their response to challenge and confrontation in the group. Following are some issues for your consideration.

1. Individuals differ. For some group members, simply quietly and gently pointing out incongruities in their thoughts and behaviors will be sufficient. They may be ready and anxious for change. For some others, perhaps less secure in themselves and the group, the same gentle confrontation may be highly disrupting. Help both (and all other) types by establishing trust and inclusion in your group early and respecting individual differences.

    Those who seem to require a more forceful confrontation may have difficulty in even hearing the discrepancy. They may be defensive or exhibit one or more styles described in Box 9.1. These likely will require the full treatment suggested in the four-step confrontation model.

2. Multicultural groups differ. For some traditional Asian and Native American members, the direct confrontational style of middle-class America may be considered rude and offensive. Most, not all, African-American and European-American members will be open to supportive and direct confrontation and some will even enjoy it. A prison population or a drug or alcohol group may thrive on sharp confrontation. Latina/o members may also be expected to be open to confrontation, but the words *respect* and *dignity* become especially important with them. All cultural groups need to be treated with respect and dignity.

    Zhang, for example, comments on the need not to hurt a traditional Asian person's feelings, reminding us that politeness is of the utmost importance. It may be helpful to "use ambiguity extensively and 'beat around the bush' at times." It is important to respect age and gender differences, particularly if the leader is younger than the group member (see Zhang's comments in Ivey & Ivey, 1999, pp. 200–201).

    Women likely will respond to men differently. Gay and lesbian group members may distrust heterosexual leaders. The handicapped may anticipate a lack of understanding. Those from a fundamentalist spiritual tradition may distrust the group process. All these and other group differences can modify how one uses confrontation.

3. Consider the potential *strength and power* of your confrontation. If the leader, rather than the group members, confronts the person, often the same words will have different meanings. The general rule is to support while providing gentle confrontations. But some members will need more assertive and direct challenges. Be ready to offer stronger confrontations as the situation indicates, but always within an attitude of support.

# SUMMARY

The many points about managing conflict that we have discussed are summarized here:

1. *Maintain positive intentional leadership.* Be flexible and open. Have multiple responses ready and prepare for conflict by making your group as trusting and positive an experience as possible.
2. *Listen and observe.* Do this *before* the conflict appears, not just in the moment. A conflict anticipated is one halfway understood and perhaps even halfway worked through. Learn to look for the multiple discrepancies, incongruities, and mixed messages.
3. *Confront and challenge conflict and discrepancies.* Do this calmly, nonjudgmentally, and with deliberation. You have a lifetime of observation and experience before you. We need to be able to work with an immense variety of conflict situations. The methods of confrontation presented here, even though detailed and specific, are at best a beginning.
4. *Evaluate the change process.* If what you have attempted does not work, return to the first point above: Maintain positive intentional leadership.

Direct, mutual communication (DMC), a microskill strategy helpful in conflict resolution, is presented in Box 9.4.

**Box 9.4**    *Direct, Mutual Communication: A Here-and-Now Conflict Resolution Strategy*

|   |   |
|---|---|
|  | This microskill strategy—direct, mutual communication—has been used to expand understanding of deeper conflicts (Higgins, Ivey, & Uhlemann, 1970; Ivey, 1971; Ivey & Gluckstern, 1976). It requires structuring skills on the part of the leader and focuses on deeper listening to thoughts and feelings on the part of participants. The procedure can be used for an entire group, but it is most often used for two- or three-person problem resolution. You may wish to photocopy the summary here, use it as is or adapt it for your own language, and share it with participants the first time you try it. For people who are willing to work through this process, it is often helpful in getting them to the basics of conflict and moving them toward a resolution. |
| *1. Outline of the Direct, Mutual Communication Strategy* | Introduce the strategy and summarize it for the participants. In the early stages, you may even wish to read the following summary.<br>"I'm going to introduce a strategy that I'd really like you to try. It's called direct, mutual communication (DMC) and is a systematic listening and problem-solving method that helps us understand conflict and differences in a safe and mutual manner.<br>"Essentially, what I'll do is ask you to listen to each other's story and opinions until the other person is ready to stop. And remember, even if you strongly disagree, your role is first to listen. You are not to speak until the other person has finished.<br>"Now comes the hard part. Before you can respond to what the other person has just said, you are to repeat what he or she has just said to you as completely as |

possible. You may have to say it back until he or she feels that you have heard adequately. Let that person indicate that he or she feels heard.

"And when you respond, note and reflect the other person's feelings as well as his or her thoughts. Recognizing emotions honestly is important in this process. I'll likely help you with this along the way.

"Once the first person's thoughts and feelings have been heard, then the second person gets to respond. You are simply to respond in your own way, saying whatever you wish. Include both your thoughts and feelings.

"Then, of course, it's the first person's chance again. BUT, before anything is said, you are to repeat back to the second person her or his thoughts and feelings until that person is satisfied. Then you can respond in any way you wish. Again, include both thoughts and feelings.

"The rotation continues until you are both satisfied—most likely several times. I'll interrupt if you get off target as it is important to listen carefully to the other before you comment. One thing that is valuable in the long run is that we include dimensions of here-and-now thoughts and feelings as well as running through your older there-and-then experiences.

"What we often find at the end is that you are not as far apart as you thought. I think you'll discover direct, mutual communication is well worth the effort."

*2. Leader Role*

As leader, your primary task is to ensure that the objectives above are accomplished. You will find it necessary in the early stages to interrupt and remind participants of the specific steps. Once the pair or group is working well with turn-taking, then shift your emphasis to ensuring that both thoughts and feelings are presented and encouraging members to focus increasingly on the here-and-now.

After each pair of exchanges, it is sometimes helpful to take a time-out and obtain feedback on the process from the participants in the exchange. You, as leader, can give them support and positive feedback and explain the process a bit more. This process works, but it takes time.

*3. The Result and Important Process Dimensions*

Those who commit themselves to the process often find their disagreements disappearing as they really hear what the other person is trying to say. Both emotional and cognitive understanding seems to be required, and instruction in emotional expression and recognition may be necessary for some people.

Finally, helping the pair or group move to discussion of the here-and-now rather than just the there-and-then is important. Linking the present to the past may help generalize conflict resolution out of this controlled and safe practice setting.

The system, incidentally, is particularly effective in couples and marriage counseling.

## MANAGING CONFLICT IN THE GROUP: SPECIFIC TRANSCRIPT EXAMPLES

Theories and procedures for dealing with difficult situations may be useful, but how do they look in actual practice? The transcript from our anger management group, briefly presented in the preceding chapter, will continue, with specific examples of how Shomari, the leader, directed and guided the management of complex situations. In this section, we will present possibilities for managing conflict internal to the individual, conflict among group members, and conflict with the leader.

To provide more context, the background of the anger management group is presented. As one of the first exercises in session one, group members told their stories—their reasons for attending the group. Each group member is briefly defined here and the nature of his or her participation in the group so far is summarized. This is what we know about each individual as we begin session 3:

Shomari, age 25, African American, completed her master's degree in counseling with a social work minor. She is employed by a health maintenance organization. As part of a preventive mental health program, an anger management psycho-educational group, designed for four sessions was announced through a mailing list, with Shomari as leader. Eight area residents signed up, but only seven appeared for the first session.

Anne Marie, 21, third-generation Irish American and Roman Catholic, has just started her master's degree in counseling. She is an active participant but is somewhat anxious and covers this with intellectualizing about her issues. Her reason for attending was to understand more about group work. She only briefly talked about her own story concerning anger, preferring to focus on others.

Anthony, 35, second-generation Italian American, manages a local restaurant. His stories of anger focused on handling difficult employees and the increasing frustration he feels in dealing with customers. While generally cooperative and helpful in the group, he seems to be the "yes, but . . ." member potentially blocking group progress at times.

Camille, 42, is an African American managing her own small business. She is going through a divorce and is currently working through financial challenges with her spouse. She has considerable anger around this issue, which is at times disrupting to her children.

Lynn, 28, identifies herself as "American" and states that her family has been here forever and from whence they came she does not know. She is one of the most popular group members, always supportive and anxious to please. Her own story of anger was somewhat limited and she focused on her own difficulty in getting in touch with her anger.

Michael, 19, third-generation Catholic Polish American, is a sophomore at the local junior college. He is gay and has just told his parents, who are not understanding. His story of anger contains much hurt. He has been an active and supportive member of the group.

Ramon, 51, is a second-generation Mexican American who teaches at the local high school. He is a Vietnam veteran who was referred to the group by an HMO social worker who mentioned that he is showing signs of posttraumatic stress. His story of anger focused on his inability at times to contain his rage and his lashing out at students, friends, and family.

Rosalind, 25, is a New England Yankee who is newly married. Her comments in the group have been minimal. Her story about anger focused on a difficult relationship with her sister but was only sketchily presented.

By the time this third session begins, the group has gone through the early stages of tension and storytelling. Shomari has worked hard on inclusion issues and has ensured that each member has received some positive feedback. She has used a combination of structured exercises and theme-centered discussion around issues of anger. Each session has included relaxation training and some elementary meditation. The participants have worked closely with the handouts on ABC behavioral analysis of anger. At appropriate times, Shomari has brought there-and-then situations to the here-and-now of the group through role-play enactment.

Even though the group is moving well, Shomari is concerned that Lynn continues her superficial pattern of sharing, Rosalind still seems at the fringes of the group, and Ramon, who speaks frequently, still seems to have deeper issues to explore. She wonders what this third session will bring.

In the third session, the group has clearly moved to center on the fourth dimension (or stage) of working—examining goals, sharing, confronting, restorying. Nonetheless, all five dimensions or stages of group process remain active through constant recycling. For example, rapport and trust gained from the first two sessions remain important and are constantly revisited through all group meetings. Dimension 2, data gathering, continues although now new information builds on original stories and experience in the group. The third dimension, the positive asset search, is a constant. While we see group stages operating in a natural flow over time, each of the five dimensions remains continually present. Stage theory is useful for seeing group progression over time, but the stages are also dimensions that recycle themselves again and again.

The following transcript illustrates how a group can help a member deal with problems outside the group. In the following example, Michael had shared some of his anger toward his father and had received considerable group support. He found the ABC analysis of anger useful and decided to tell his parents he was gay. It did not go as well as he had hoped. Although we are in the working stage of group process, note that all dimensions of the group are present and that especially relevant in this example is Dimension (or Stage) 5 in which Michael has made an effort to generalize learning from the group to his home setting.

| Transcript—Conflict Internal to an Individual | Group Process Comments—Working with Family Concerns External to the Group |
|---|---|
| 1. *Michael* (anxiously): Now that we've started, could I share what's happened since our last session? It's been tough. | 1. Michael brings the there-and-then to here-and-now immediacy within the group through a question and a self-disclosure of feeling. |
| 2. *Shomari:* You're feeling really tense right now—could you share what's happening for you? | 2. Reflection of feeling and open question, focus on here-and-now |

*(continued)*

| **Transcript** | **Process Comments** |
|---|---|
| 3. *Michael:* Yes, I sat down and finally told my parents that I'm gay. My mom seemed to take it OK, but my dad just blew up. Being gay just isn't all that acceptable among Polish people. . . . (Michael continues the details of the story.) | 3. Self-disclosure, focus on self and others in the there-and-then, but Michael also shows considerable bodily tension in the here-and-now and the cultural/environmental context. On the Observation of Change Scale, we should note that Michael made an effort to generalize learning from the group to the real world outside. This is where we see Level 3 operating, but the impact of the change was not as positive as he had hoped it would be. |
| 4. *Shomari:* So, Michael, you felt supported by us last week as you discussed coming out as gay. This prompted you to open up to your parents—that was very gutsy of you considering what you said about your dad in the last session. On one hand, you really began to feel it was OK to share yourself as gay with group members who are heterosexual, but when you opened up to your folks, particularly your dad, it didn't work out so well. Have I heard you correctly? | 4. Summarization including confrontation of the discrepancy between Michael's experience with the group and with his father. Note the positive statement when Michael is called "gutsy" by the leader, even though his timing of disclosure to his parents may have been a little too early. In the previous session, the group had suggested he "hold off" until he had discussed the issue further with them, particularly as Michael seemed very angry with his father. |
| 5. *Michael:* Yes, perhaps I moved too fast. I thought I was able to understand all the anger in our family, but I guess not. It just felt so good to be with the group here and I felt so safe to be me for a change. I can sense even now the support of you people here even though you haven't said anything yet. | 5. Michael starts the process of resolving the discrepancy and begins reframing the negative experience with his parents and differentiating what occurs in the here-and-now of the group from what might happen when similar behavior is tried in daily life. |
| 6. *Ramon:* You're on the right track, man. Being open takes risks. | 6. Positive feedback. Sharing of information on the difficulty of risk-taking. |
| 7. *Lynn:* I hurt for you Michael, but I really like you as a person and admire your courage and honesty in coming out to your family. | 7. Self-disclosure here-and-now with positive feedback. |
| 8.–15. (Other members share their support for Michael) | |
| 16. *Michael:* I feel better already, but I still have my parents to cope with. | 16. Michael defines the contradiction between himself and his parents. |
| 17. *Shomari:* So, we see you have a lot of support here, Michael, but it is a little bit more challenging with your parents, particularly your dad. Michael, last week, several people suggested that you might hold off on sharing with them just a | 17. Shomari summarizes the incongruity between the group's supportive attitude and the more angry relationship with Michael's father. She also confronts Michael with the fact that he missed seeing the differences between the group and his father. |

| Transcript | Process Comments |
|---|---|
| little bit more, perhaps because of the anger you feel toward your dad. Does that make sense? | One problem of generalization from new learning in the group occurs when members expect newly learned behavior that works well in the group to work equally well on the outside with others. Not always so! "Does that make sense?" operates as a checkout and allows Michael to evaluate what has been said in his own way. |
| 18. *Ramon:* Yeah, you were really sailing last week with our support. I wonder if you moved too fast because you are really angry with your dad and somehow wanted to get him? What do you think? | 18. Ramon provides a new perspective on the situation by suggesting Michael might have been seeking to punish his father. He is learning the importance of the checkout and asks Michael to evaluate the situation in his own way. The discussion moves easily between there-and-then behavior and the here-and-now of the group. |
| 19. *Michael:* Uh-huh . . . I guess you are both right. I've been upset since I told my folks, but just getting this feedback helps me to see that perhaps they (and I) weren't quite ready yet. Could we talk about it a bit more? | 19. Michael draws on here-and-now group interaction to examine his own behavior. His self-reflective attitude suggests further growth on the Observation of Change Scale. If he is to generalize his new learning and rapport with the group to his parents and others, further discussion in the group should be helpful. |
| 20.–30. (Further discussion of Michael's issues) | |

In this segment, we have seen how Michael has gained from and grown in the positive atmosphere of the group. He has been able to address the conflict he has with his father in the context of a supportive group. An advantage of group work over individual therapy is the strength of multiple perspectives through feedback from the group. We should note that Michael responded positively and openly to the confrontations provided by the leader. One reason for this was the positive support he felt from the leader and the group. On the Observation of Change Scale, he clearly operated at a functional Level 2 and will continue to make efforts toward Level 3, appropriate generalization of learning from the group to the external world.

Conflict internal to an individual often plays itself out group process. Group members may be expected to exhibit behaviors in the group that represent their basic style of interacting outside the group. Lynn, in the following example transcript, has been a popular group member as she is so supportive and encouraging of others. At the same time, however, Lynn is so anxious to please that she gives little attention to herself. At this moment in the group, it has become clear that Lynn is not in touch with her own feelings and at times uses her desire to please as a way to cover up underlying angry feelings.

| Transcript—Conflict Internal to an Individual (Internal Conflict That Might Appear in the Group) | Group Process Comments—Working with the Group Member Who Seeks to Please |
|---|---|
| 31. *Lynn* (smiling): I'm really glad that Michael was able to share what's going on with his family. I just know, Michael, that you'll work things out much better next week. And Ramon, I think you were really helpful. | 31. Self-disclosure and feedback with an emphasis on positive assets. |
| 32. *Ramon:* Thanks. | |
| 33. *Michael:* I appreciate your being there for me Lynn . . . and the rest of you too! | 33. Feedback, focus on an individual and group as a whole, here-and-now. |
| 34. *Camille:* Lynn, you have been a wonderfully supportive person as I've gotten to know you, but I wonder if you aren't paying a price. Somehow, something seems missing for me. | 34. Feedback, interpretation, focus on individual. Often in groups, the "group wheel" turns and individuals suddenly find themselves the focus of the group discussion. Camille begins the process of confronting Lynn on the discrepancy between her consistent pleasing and supportive behavior and the price she might pay for failing to consider herself. |
| 35. *Anne Marie:* Yes, you really listen to others, but I wonder where you are? | 35. Feedback, open question. |
| 36. (Lynn sits in surprised silence.) | 36. Observation of Change Scale, Level 1, failure to deal with question and feedback. |
| 37. *Shomari:* What's happening for you right now, Lynn? | 37. Open question, focus on individual, here-and-now. Shomari has been observing the group, but now turns her attention to Lynn and she notes her verbal and nonverbal discrepancies. |
| 38. *Lynn:* Wow, I really feel like I'm on the spot. All I want to do is to be helpful. | 38. Self-disclosure, here-and-now. |
| 39. *Michael:* I think, Lynn, that what people are saying to you is that you make such an effort to be helpful and please others that you really don't give enough attention to your own needs. I can't even imagine you being angry. | 39. Confrontation of possible discrepancies within Lynn through feedback. Note how the here-and-now of the group has blended with Lynn's pattern of behavior over the three sessions thus far. |
| 40. *Camille:* Michael's very much on target. You seem to give so much attention to others that there may not be enough room for you. | 40. Confrontation in the form of feedback. |

| Transcript | Process Comments |
|---|---|
| 41. *Lynn* (appears tense and a little frightened): You don't like the way I am? What am I doing wrong? | 41. Open question, Lynn provides her interpretation of what the group is saying. The interpretation is incorrect and so we again see Lynn operating at Level 1 on the Observation of Change Scale. |
| 42. *Shomari:* Lynn, what the group is saying is that they like you, they appreciate your consistent support, but on the other hand, they are concerned that you don't give enough attention to yourself and your own needs. What do you want, Lynn? | 42. Confrontation in the form of a summary with a focus on the group as a whole and on Lynn. Note the emphasis on Lynn's strengths. The open question asks Lynn to respond to group feedback. Shomari is demonstrating that all-important leadership skill of summarizing. This helps the group look at where it is and where it might be going. |
| 43. *Lynn* (starts to cry): I just want everyone to get along. I can't stand conflict and anger. My parents argue all the time and I'll do anything to stop tension and problems. (Lynn goes on to present some example stories from her family and how she works to prevent conflict in many situations.) | 43. In this self-disclosure, Lynn's response to the confrontation is at a Level 2 on the Observation of Change Scale. She is now encountering the feedback from the group. |
| 44.–56. (Following Lynn's self-disclosure and story, several group members provide positive feedback and support, while simultaneously challenging her to stand up for herself and take stronger positions.) | 44.–56. Group feedback can help many members examine themselves and test out new behavior in the safety of the group. |
| 57. *Shomari:* The group seems to be saying they see you as a strong and capable person and they really like you, but they also wish you could take your own positions more frequently and allow yourself to think more about your own needs. Part of anger management is assertiveness training, being able to state what you need in an appropriate fashion, neither aggressively nor in a submissive fashion. If it is OK with you Lynn, I'd like to try that now. | 57. Summary of group feedback with the explicit confrontation that the group would support a more assertive and complete Lynn. "On one hand, Lynn, we like you and your support, but on the other hand, we'd like to see you take more care of yourself and your needs." Again, note how the summary provides a pause for the group and a point where the direction can change.<br><br>Assertiveness training is an important psycho-educational and therapeutic strategy that is often taught in groups. Chapter 10 presents specifics of how this might be taught as part of group process. |

If the conflict management taught via assertiveness training is successful, we will see Lynn changing her behavior in the group (Level 2 on the OCS) and, hopefully, generalizing the change to the real world (Level 3). The group process here provides Lynn with the perspectives of several group members rather than just that of the leader. Individual therapy can accomplish much the same objective but misses the power of group observation and support.

Note the pattern of Shomari's leadership style. She used the following confrontation/challenge pattern:

1. *Intentional positive leadership.* Shomari had many possible alternatives ready for action as she observed the group.
2. *Listening and observation.* Shomari observed individual and group verbal and nonverbal behavior, with a constant eye for discrepancies, incongruities, and conflict.
3. *Confrontation and challenge.* Shomari summarized Lynn's internal conflict coupled with an emphasis on positive assets. She observed the results of the confrontation and, when appropriate, she moved to a strategy (assertiveness training) that might enable further change.
4. *Evaluating change.* Shomari noted Lynn's movement using the Observation of Change Scale from 1 (virtual denial of the issue and partial examination) to 2 (full encounter with group feedback and self-examination), which led her to 3 (assertiveness training to help generalization of behavior to the real world).

## Managing Conflict Among Group Members

Conflict also occurs between and among group members. Note how Shomari handles this type of issue in the following two transcript examples. You will note again the importance of intentionality—the ability to have multiple responses available, the ability to predict what might happen when a particular microskill is used, and the ability to flex and change as the leader observes what happens.

In the following excerpts, pay special attention to the actual confrontation process itself: summarizing the conflict using positive strengths as much as possible, focusing generally on support rather than attack, and observing how the group member responds. As the member responds, the intentional leader is aware that he or she has multiple possibilities for intentionally working with the infinite array of things that can happen in a group.

In this first transcript, Anthony, although often helpful, uses a "yes, but" style of communication, never quite agreeing with the group or an individual, and conflicts sharply with Camille.

| Transcript—Conflict Among Group Members | Group Process Comments— Direct, Mutual Communication |
|---|---|
| 70. *Lynn:* I feel better. I'll think about things all this week and perhaps next week, I'll work on this further and share more about how my style in the family is similar to the way I am here. I want to try assertiveness training too. | 70. Self-disclosure, focus on problem. |
| 71. *Anthony:* Yes, Lynn, I'm glad you are feeling better, but I kind of like you the way you are. I'm not sure you should listen to all this feedback. I know that this assertiveness stuff sometimes only increases the anger. | 71. Feedback and advice. We note a beginning challenge to the leader and Anthony has repeated his "yes, but" style. This is characteristic of group members who use blocking as a standard behavior in groups. He is also a "would be" leader. |

| Transcript | Process Comments |
|---|---|
| 72. *Camille* (heatedly, with anger): There you go again, Anthony. You are a really nice guy, but again and again I see you "yes, butting" all over the place. I'm getting fed it up with it. It is always your way of doing things. Try listening more; others see it differently from you. | 72. Feedback, focus on individual, here-and-now and there-and-then behavior connected in a pattern. Advice and direction. |
| 73. *Anthony* (angrily): Hey now, what's got into you? I'm only trying to help Lynn. How come you're such a know-it-all? | 73. The conflict becomes more apparent. |
| 74. *Camille* (louder): Help, smelp. You are laying one of your trips on us again. | 74. Reframing/interpretation. This idea may even be accurate and potentially helpful, but said in this way, not much is likely to happen in a positive direction. |
| 75.–80. (The issues escalate even further as the two continue to exchange insults. The tension in the room becomes thick.) | 75.–80. Shomari, as leader, is busy observing not only the combatants but also the other members of the group. They seem to be sitting back and merely observing. She senses that the majority of the individuals want to support Camille, but as the group remains silent, Shomari decides to intervene. |
| 81. *Shomari:* Hold on you two. You both have given so much to the group. If you are willing, I'd like to introduce a strategy that I'd really like you to try. It's called direct, mutual communication (DMC) and is a systematic listening and problem-solving method. Would you be willing to try this?<br><br>(Camille and Anthony agree, albeit somewhat unwillingly.) | 81. Structuring, positive assets. Direct, mutual communication (see Box 9.4) is a here-and-now strategy oriented toward conflict resolution through clear communication of messages from each participant. Shomari, as an intentional leader, could have used other conflict resolution methods. She selected DMC as it provides a way to resolve conflict in the here-and-now and is specific enough to be a teachable strategy that all in the group (including those who observe) can take home. |
| 82. *Shomari:* First, I'd like Camille to tell Anthony what she is thinking and feeling about the difficulty the two of you have. Anthony, your job is to listen silently to what she is saying right now, here, in the moment.<br>    After Camille has finished, Anthony, I'd like you to say back to her what she has said until she is satisfied that she has been heard. Keep at it until she feels understood.<br>    Then, Anthony, it's your turn. I'll say more about that later. | 82. Structuring. Note emphasis on here-and-now communication. The goal of this confrontation strategy is to help people listen to one another's opposing points of view. Once having heard the other fully and accurately, problem resolution becomes more feasible. |

*(continued)*

| Transcript | Process Comments |
|---|---|
| 83. *Camille:* Anthony, you really get to me. Just when the group starts moving, you always come in and change the flow. You never seem to listen. | 83. Camille gives Anthony direct feedback in a rather accusing fashion. Note that she generalizes his behavior with words such as *always* and *never*. |
| 84. *Anthony:* That's wrong, that's not what I . . . | 84. Anthony is clearly at Level 1 on the Observation of Change Scale at this moment. |
| 85. *Shomari* (interrupts gently): Anthony, it's your turn now, but before you go on, I want you to repeat back to Camille exactly what she said and then give her feedback on how you react to that. | 85. Shomari takes control through structuring and reminds Anthony of the task. She also empowers him by reminding him that he will get his full "airtime" to share his point of view. |
| 86. *Anthony:* OK, I'll try . . . Camille, I hear that I get to you and make you angry, you feel that I don't listen. Is that right? | 86. Anthony paraphrases and reflects Camille's feelings accurately. |
| 87. *Camille:* You hear me talking. | 87. Camille feels heard accurately. |
| 88. *Shomari:* Good, Anthony, now you can react to Camille. What do you have to say in response? How are you feeling at this moment? | 88. Structuring, open question, focus on the here-and-now. |
| 89. *Anthony:* Right now, I'm pretty angry. I'm doing my best and it really is unfair to treat me this way. Didn't you notice how I tried to help Lynn? | 89. Anthony speaks in the here-and-now and tries to explain himself. |
| 90. *Shomari:* Camille, before you respond, say back to Anthony what he just said until he feels heard. After he says OK, then you can add your own response. | 90. DMC conflict management stresses the importance of accurate listening as the first step. |
| 91. *Camille:* You heard me accurately, Anthony. You feel angry with me for what I said and feel I was unfair. I did notice you trying to help Lynn, but it seemed intrusive and patronizing to me. | 91. Camille accurately paraphrases and reflects Anthony's feelings. She shares her observations through feedback and her interpretation of what she observed. |
| 92. *Shomari:* All OK, but that last sentence. Hold that back until Anthony indicates you have heard him. | 92. Structuring. |
| 93. *Anthony:* OK, I think you heard me. I was trying to help, but I sure don't like being called patronizing and intrusive, especially when all I am trying to do is the right thing. That hurts. | 93. The couple is now moving more into the DMC process and Anthony is sharing what is going on with himself more openly. He has moved to Level 2 on the OCS. |

| Transcript | Process Comments |
|---|---|
| 94. *Camille:* Anthony, I hear you hurting a bit over what I said. That surprises me. I didn't think I could get through to you. You apparently are trying to do the right thing, but it just doesn't come across all that well. But I do appreciate what you are trying to do a bit more. | 94. Note that as members are heard in the here-and-now they tend to modify their position and develop increasing respect for the other. Camille is starting to change her opinion about Anthony. |
| 95. *Shomari:* Remember, Camille and Anthony, try to keep it in the here-and-now—be immediate! You're doing fine. | 95. Structuring, positive feedback. |
| 96. *Anthony:* I feel a little relieved. Camille, it seems to me that you are recognizing me for trying at least. How is it that I seem to be patronizing? | 96. Anthony self-discloses his feelings in the here-and-now and has moved to asking Camille for feedback, whereas before he was resisting it. |
| 97. *Shomari:* We'll continue the process until you both feel heard and then we'll evaluate where we are. My task in this process is to help you focus on the here-and-now, remind you to include both thoughts and feelings, emphasize the importance of hearing the other person to her or his satisfaction, and monitor turn-taking. Let's go on . . . | 97. Structuring, here-and-now emphasis. Note that group members by observing Anthony and Camille are learning the process of DMC themselves. |
| (Anthony and Camille continue to work in the here-and-now and both gain understanding and respect for the other. As their encounter ends on a positive note, Shomari asks the group members to provide feedback to both of them. She also asks them to comment on the direct, mutual communication strategy and how it might be helpful to them.) | Shomari again shows skilled leadership when she asks the group to reflect on what happened through feedback to the participants and commentary on DMC. Through this type of reflection, group members can absorb a deeper cognitive and emotional understanding of what has happened. |

The here-and-now immediacy of direct, mutual communication (DMC) in the group (also see Box 9.4) carries the expectation that careful listening and sharing of each person's position will lead to greater understanding and eventually facilitate resolution of conflict and difficulties. DMC is based on the belief that much interpersonal conflict starts with good intentions; if we can uncover those good original intentions, we can often (but not always) develop ways to communicate and work together more effectively. The structured direct exploration of thoughts and feelings promoted by DMC brings immediacy and power to the group. It is also a system that is clear enough that members can generalize it to their home settings as a conflict mediation strategy.

In the example presented here, Shomari encouraged the two angry members to talk to each other directly. A useful alternative would be for members of the group to provide Anthony with direct feedback on his behavior. In this case, Camille took on the work of the group. This itself is a behavior to observe. Some members, often very constructive, take on the task of helping the group work. In the process of doing good things as Camille did here, they allow other group members to sit back and not speak their minds openly. If Camille repeated this pattern over several encounters, it would become incumbent on the leader to point out the pattern and to help Camille look at what some might term a "rescue the group member's" style. Just as Lynn is trying to please and do the right thing, so perhaps is Camille, although her style appears quite different. However, Anthony is not yet off the hook, as the next transcript excerpt reveals.

| Transcript—Conflict Among Group Members | Group Process Comments— Surprise, the Wheel Turns to You! |
|---|---|
| 104. *Anthony:* I think I get the point. I'm trying so hard to help that I fail to listen where the person really is. Thanks to all of you, especially you, Camille. I've got a lot to think about. | 104. Self-disclosure. Anthony has changed his thoughts and feelings in the here-and-now. Will he be able to transfer this to a Level 3 change in the real world? |
| 105. *Rosalind:* Well, think a bit more. I'm not sure you have "got it" yet. It all seems a bit too smooth right now. | 105. Feedback, here-and-now. |
| 106. *Camille* (defending Anthony now): And, where are you coming from? | 106. Here comes Camille to the rescue? Is this a pattern for her? At the same time, she is providing a strong confrontation for Rosalind to deal with. |
| 107. *Rosalind* (hesitates and the group turns their full attention to her): What? . . . (pauses defensively) All I was saying is that Anthony seems to have put one over on us again. | 107. The group "wheel" turns and suddenly Rosalind finds herself at the center. Everyone in the group is staring at her. She is at Level 1 on the OCS. |
| 108. *Camille:* You know, Rosalind, you seem super-smooth yourself. | 108. Feedback, again negative, but highly challenging and confrontive. |
| 109. *Ramon:* Yes, you come across sometimes rather "high and mighty." You've seemed a little aloof from the group. | 109. More negative feedback in the form of a confrontation. |
| 110. *Shomari:* I hear a lot of negativity in the group right now. What's going on with us? And Rosalind, how are you reacting to that difficult feedback? (The last comment is said in a particularly supportive tone of voice.) | 110. Shomari shifts the focus to the group as a whole as she is concerned about scapegoating Rosalind. |
| 111. *Rosalind* (defensively): I thought Anthony got off pretty easy, but now everyone is looking at me. I don't like this. | 111. Self-disclosure, here-and-now. |

| Transcript | Process Comments |
|---|---|
| 112. *Anne Marie:* Rosalind, we've heard very little from you in this group. I think Ramon and Camille are telling you that you appear pretty smooth yourself. What are you feeling right now? | 112. Anne Marie has learned group skills and the importance of focusing on the here-and-now. Her comments are very similar to those that Shomari would have made earlier in the group. Anne Marie has confronted Rosalind on the same issues presented by Camille and Ramon, but her more gentle, supportive tone enables Rosalind to cope with it more easily. |
| 113. *Rosalind* (starts to tear up): I thought I was helping Camille, but then everyone now is focusing on me. I don't know what is happening. I just feel scared. | 113. Self-disclosure. Rosalind is very much in the here-and-now. She had appeared very controlling and distant in the past, but now that the focus is on her, she acknowledges her fear. |
| 114. *Shomari:* I think the group wants to understand and help. Camille was defending Anthony, which I think is terrific, given the problems they just had. (Now, she talks more quietly and gently.) I think Anne Marie and the others want to understand you a bit more. Would you like to share what's going on? | 114. Shomari summarizes the group process to this point, seeking to reframe each person's comment in as positive a way as possible. She is trying to help Rosalind accept and acknowledge the heavy feedback she is getting. She provides an open question, suggesting that Rosalind share, but only if she wishes. |
| 115. *Rosalind* (tears flow): Well, the real reason I came to this group is that my husband gets so angry at me—all the time. I thought if I came I could understand what is going on. Actually, he is pretty smooth and reminds me of Anthony.<br><br>(She continues to tell her story. As the group understands what is going on, they provide support and positive suggestions for dealing with a complex situation.) | 115. The positive reframing of the challenge to Rosalind by Shomari (and the supportive comment from Anne Marie) opens Rosalind so that she can share what is really occurring for her. |

In this case, the leader has allowed the wisdom of the group to prevail. Shomari has generated a working group that is able to encounter and challenge other members. The confrontation by Camille and Ramon was important and useful to the process but needed to be balanced by more supportive comments by Anne Marie and the leader. All together, the group pushes and supports Rosalind so that she can look at her behavior and what is going on in her world more openly.

## Managing Conflict with the Leader

Intentional group leaders anticipate that some group members are eventually going to challenge and conflict with them. They are constantly observing what is occurring between and among group participants. While leaders can never predict when they will be confronted, they need to be ready with multiple responses. Again, it is important to say that you as leader are not necessarily the target. Leaders represent authority, and many members have a history of problems with authority figures. You can expect that concerns over leadership and power will play themselves out in the group and often with you as a symbol of authority.

In the following transcript, Ramon challenges Shomari and seems to want to take over the leadership of the group. At first, she responds inappropriately, then notes her error and recovers quickly. Expect to make errors; no leader is perfect. The ability to recover from your mistakes is one of the most important skills you can master. You will also see some issues around termination and ending the group that are beginning to appear.

| Transcript—Conflict with the Leader | Group Process Comments— The Leader Makes an Error and Recovers |
|---|---|
| 192. *Shomari:* We've had a good session today and have about fifteen minutes to go What's happening for you all at this moment? | 192. Several challenging issues have played out in this third session. Anticipating termination issues, as the next session is the last, Shomari implicitly opens the issue. |
| 193. *Anne Marie:* I really appreciate what happened today. Although I haven't said much, I learned so much about what happens in groups in the way we all can work through our differences. | 193. Self-disclosure, focus on self and the group. Other group members nod in agreement. |
| 194. *Ramon* (with slight sarcasm): Yes, Shomari, you are a great leader. You're very skilled. You are super at focusing on others, but where are you? How come you share so little of yourself? | 194. Feedback, interpretation, open questions all focusing on the leader in a demanding confrontation. The group members look at Ramon and Shomari wondering what will happen next. |
| 195. *Shomari* (obviously surprised; her words stumble, her irritation at Ramon shows through her body language and vocal tone): Well . . . my job is to help the group find its own direction . . . | 195. Even the best leader is at a loss for words at times. Shomari makes the mistake of appearing defensive and allows Ramon to make her angry. Most often when a leader is attacked, it is because members are bringing in authority issues from outside the group. |
| 196. *Ramon* (interrupts and smiles): See, she isn't one of us; she's above, directing it all. See how defensive she is when I ask her to join us? Is this entire group bogus? Has anything really happened here? | 196. Ramon seems to want to take over leadership here. He observes Shomari's defensive behavior and uses this to attack her. It is critical that Shomari gather herself together and respond appropriately or she is in real trouble. |
| 197. *Shomari* (gaining more assurance): I think I understand, Ramon . . . you're angry at me because to you I look like I'm distant and apart . . . | 197. Most important here is that the leader is now responding nondefensively. She reflects Ramon's feelings and acknowledges some of his thoughts. |
| 198. *Ramon* (interrupts again, more angrily): There you go again; you aren't responding, you aren't here with us. You think we are puppets you can just manage. | 198. Here-and-now emotional response. Ramon blurts out his immediate perception of what has occurred in the group. |

| **Transcript** | **Process Comments** |
|---|---|
| 199. *Shomari* (clearly and firmly, but with respect for Ramon): You really are angry, Ramon. May I respond? It will take a moment. | 199. Rather than being put off by Ramon's outburst, Shomari becomes more calm. Effective leaders learn over time that if they maintain their equilibrium in the face of strong emotion, it is much easier to deal with difficult situations. Maintaining "one's cool" is half the battle of dealing with difficult situations. Firmness and a clear statement of what she is going to do are important here. |
| 200. *Ramon:* OK, what have you got to say? | 200. Ramon hears Shomari's firm statement and is willing to listen. |
| 201. *Shomari:* First, let me say that this is a great group and we've come a long way together. Ramon, you've been an important part of that process. Let me tell you a bit about my style. If the group is working effectively, I really prefer to let the group move on its own. This is a good group and so many of you have been helpful. It's made leading this group fun— | 201. Shomari wisely responds both to Ramon and the group as a whole. If she had responded to him alone, it could have been her versus Ramon. Making Ramon part of the group context enables her to say good things both about him and the others present. Note that Shomari constantly emphasizes the positives in Ramon and the group. |
| 202. *Ramon* (interrupts): But where are you, Shomari? | 202. Ramon eases up, but he is still aware that Shomari is acting as the leader. |
| 203. *Shomari:* Frankly, Ramon, I like you and the group very much. You have been very supportive to many members and offer a lot of understanding. At the same time, I haven't seen much of what's going on with you. You did say early in the group that you lost your cool on your job and that it was beginning to get you in trouble in the classroom, especially with difficult students. | 203. Shomari makes a genuine statement on how she feels toward Ramon and the group. She now feels able to throw the confrontation back to Ramon and link his current behavior in the context of what he said earlier in the group to what she knows about difficulties he has on the job. This linking is important in both reflecting meaning and interpreting a group member's behavior. |
| 204. *Ramon:* You're avoiding the issue and turning it back to me. | 204. Ramon notices what is going on! |
| 205. *Anne Marie:* Perhaps not, Ramon—you've been a wonderful support to all of us, but don't we have some responsibility to you as well? Often you seem to be there to take care of us. What could we do for you? We only have one more session. | 205. The wisdom of responding to Ramon in a group context shows here. Anne Marie comes in and says what Shomari might like to say, but coming from a group member at this moment, Ramon is more likely to hear what is happening. |
| 206. *Shomari:* Again, Ramon, I like you. We all like you. I could share more, but I wonder where you are now? | 206. Self-disclosure, expression of feeling and positive feedback. Shomari turns it back to Ramon with a question. |

*(continued)*

| **Transcript** | **Process Comments** |
|---|---|
| 207. *Ramon* (pausing, hesitantly): A flashback just hit me. I see you, Shomari, as much like my principal. He seems supportive and interested, but somehow I still feel alone. It really gets to me. | 207. Ramon is now responding to the positive approach of Shomari and Anne Marie. He starts making his own reframing and interpretation of the current situation, linking it to what is happening to him on the job. |
| 208. *Camille:* We're here for you, Ramon. | 208. A supportive group member joins in. We all need them! |
| 209. *Shomari:* And, sad to say, we've got to end in just a few minutes. I really appreciate your coming forth Ramon. Thanks for challenging me; perhaps I needed it. As I said, this is a great group and I love its flow. Would you be willing to explore this further in our last session, Ramon? It sounds a bit much for now. | 209. Often, critical issues appear near the end of a group session. Shomari openly acknowledges the value of Ramon's feedback, but then moves to the group as a whole before asking Ramon if he would like to continue this issue in the final meeting. <br><br> Leaders should always be aware that issues that occur in the final session or close to it may be the result of termination and closure issues among members. It is possible that Ramon is speaking for more people than just himself. |
| 210. *Ramon:* Well, I'll think about it. Maybe it will help. | 210. Still somewhat dubious, Ramon is nonetheless willing to think about things. Don't expect positive and complete resolutions immediately. |
| 211. *Shomari:* Thanks, Ramon . . . sometimes we have to end in ways that seem a bit incomplete. Let us all think about it this week. One thing for sure is that we have to end today and next week is our last session. What are some thoughts among the group as we end today? And how do we all feel about the fact that this group will end soon? | 211. Shomari moves toward termination of the group session and uses the final minutes to encourage group members to share what is on their minds. This provides an opportunity for all to think about the meaning of the group ending soon. |

Some group members save their issues until the end of the session or near the conclusion of a series of group meetings. It is a way for them to deal with their ambivalence about whether to talk about their concerns. They want both to share and to avoid sharing. In the example above, Ramon's challenge perhaps represented his indecision about what to do in the group. There are likely others with termination issues. Shomari was at first surprised and her initial response was weak, but she soon recovered and gained her composure. Your recovery skills when you make an error are sometimes the real test of your competence.

Intentionality demands that you have several ways to meet challenges to your leadership. In this case, Shomari responded only partially to Ramon's challenge, and her reference to Ramon's and the group's positive assets and strengths was probably a wise move. There are times, however, when you will need to respond completely and fully to a group member's challenge and it will be you and the confronting group member working it out in front of the group. In this case, your awareness of the principles of direct, mutual communication and here-and-now interaction can be useful.

In addition, recall the basic principles of effective confrontation:

1. Build intentionally on a positive base. If you have already treated the group member in a positive fashion and built inclusion into the group process, the chances for positive resolution are greatly enhanced. The confrontation becomes an opportunity for growth as much as or more than a challenge to be met. It may even be useful to reframe the confrontation from this positive viewpoint. For example, "Ramon, we are working here with real issues in the here-and-now. It gives both of us an opportunity to see if what we are doing here in this group works. Let us see what we can learn together."

2. Listen to what the confrontive group member has to say, for you may learn something useful. Observe discrepancies in the member and yourself throughout the group process. What you have observed earlier may be useful in working through a challenge.

3. Periodically summarize the differences between you and the member clearly and accurately; direct, mutual communication can be helpful in this process. Search out positive dimensions in the group member and the situation. Observe the reactions of the challenging group member and have available many alternatives that are potentially useful. Using the basic listening sequence, changing the focus of the discussion to contextual issues, reframing/interpreting the discussion, reflecting meaning, and all the influencing strategies may be useful.

4. Evaluate what occurs on the Observation of Change Scale. Consider yourself as well: Are you able to learn and grow from the challenge? As part of this, periodically video- or audiotape your sessions and obtain feedback from supervisors and colleagues.

## USING CONFLICT MANAGEMENT SKILLS WITH CHILD AND ADOLESCENT GROUPS

Elementary school-age and adolescent children and youth often face many difficult discrepancies and incongruities in their lives—teasing and bullying, family conflict and divorce, and conflict with peers and teachers. Increasingly, they are exposed to violence.

Most of the confrontation strategies presented in this chapter can be used directly with adolescents. However, expect a more egocentric attitude with the typical teenager, who focuses on self with an early formal operations style. While adolescents are often able to reflect, their reflections are generally from their own frame of reference, and seeing the perspective of others can at times be most difficult.

The cognitive-emotional style explored in this chapter presents a special problem when you are working with teens. They usually can reflect and think about things but often find it difficult to listen to others, particularly the leader who may represent adult authority. We suggest that you facilitate group discussion as to how the group views a situation. For example, if you are working with drug prevention and your adolescent group thinks that parents simply "don't get it," it will do little good for you or them if you present the adult view. The model confrontation statement could become, "You see it this way . . . and your parents see it that way . . ." Then encourage discussion of the adolescent frame on drugs and summarize what they have said. Follow this by asking them to describe or even role-play how their parents and other adults might view the situation. You are then in a position to summarize the two positions and ask the group what possible resolutions come to mind. This approach often helps adolescents see other perspectives, but you have encouraged them to find their own way of dealing with the situation.

Thus, a general rule of working with adolescent groups is to encourage them to take as much control as possible. They are usually quite good at giving feedback and can "call" and name phony or false behavior as well as most group leaders. Maintain a good sense of humor and encourage inclusion and constantly emphasize individual and group strengths.

Younger children will often have difficulty reflecting on what is happening, something that is required when groups are examining conflict through confrontation. Your language needs to be much more concrete and include experiential activities such as role-playing, art work, and games that will help children tell their stories and plan new actions. As mentioned earlier, reading aloud from age-appropriate books focusing on challenging life issues (friendship problems, divorce, teasing, etc.) is often an avenue facilitating problem solving and may enable them to tell their own stories more fully.

With younger group members, it is important to listen and comment on positive assets that the child has to cope with a difficult situation. Telling stories of children who successfully deal with difficult issues is often very helpful to children. They may not generalize or learn from others as quickly as adolescents and adults, but they often will comment on the parallels between others' stories and their own experience. And when a child mentions something that works, some children in the group may want to try the same thing themselves. Just as in adolescent and adult groups, children learn that they are not alone with their issues.

For both adolescents and younger children, peer mediation and conflict-resolution psychoeducational groups can be especially useful. Most mediation and conflict-resolution groups include a strong emphasis on listening and observing skills stressed throughout this book. The actual process of mediation and conflict resolution involves many of the influencing skills with a special emphasis on confrontation.

## MOVING TOWARD YOUR OWN LEADERSHIP STYLE

Confrontation skills have been presented here in a four-point model: (1) intentional positive leadership; (2) listening and observation emphasizing the search for discrepancies, incongruities, and conflict; (3) confrontation and challenge by summarizing the internal or external conflict while simultaneously emphasizing positive assets and strengths. Observe the results of confrontation and, when appropriate move to another strategy that might be more effective; and (4) evaluate the change.

Once again, think back on this chapter. What have you learned here? What points struck you as most important? What stood out for you? What would you like to work on in the area of improving your confrontation skills?

_____

_____

_____

_____

_____

_____

_____

_____

_____

_____

_____

## CONFLICT MANAGEMENT

### 1. Process Observation

There are two suggestions for process observation related to conflict management. The first involves observing individuals for styles similar to those listed in Box 9.1 that may lead to conflict in groups. Can you learn to spot the person who blocks, the person who seeks to please and smooth things over, the individual who intellectualizes? The individuals described in Box 9.1 are found in many groups. As you observe groups in operation, you will want to add additional personal styles to your own list.

Second, engage in conflict process observation using the categories delineated in Box 9.2. Can you identify key incongruities, discrepancies, and mixed messages internal to individuals, and between and among group members? Can you also find styles of conflicting with the leader?

In all of your observations above, pay special attention to the behaviors the leader engages in when faced with varying types of conflict. How effective is the leader you observe? What can you learn from her or him?

Summarize your observations here or in more detail in a formal report and analysis of the group you observe.

_____

_____

_____

_____

_____

_____

_____

## 2. The Fish Bowl

Box 9.1 lists various personal styles that can lead to conflict in a group. Place the names of each style in a hat or box and have prospective group members draw out the name and a brief description of the style. Each group member is to enact the personal style he or she obtains.

A volunteer leader has "the pleasure" of working with these difficult group members. Needless to say, the leader has the opportunity to practice skills of effective confrontation when faced with a group consisting of such difficult people.

An alternative exercise is to conduct the fish bowl, but only one or two members take on a selected style (for example, one member tends to be a blocker and another member tries to please others). The remainder of the group play themselves. This exercise is useful as it provides an opportunity to study how to work with difficult people one or two at a time.

## 3. Your Own Group Practice

The above exercise is repeated for your own practice in small groups.

1. Divide into groups of five or six. One person is to serve as leader and one is observer who focuses on the nature of conflict and the ability of the leader to cope with various issues. The remainder serve as group participants.
2. Define the topic for the small groups. For this practice exercise, it is suggested that individuals share issues of interpersonal conflict that they have outside the group. However, feel free to select topics of interest and comfort to you and the group.
3. Fifteen minutes should be used for the small groups. Allow five minutes for feedback from the observer. Finally, each small group can reflect on its own group process.

Where possible, add videorecording and practice to your work with attending skills and observation. You will always obtain very useful feedback on yourself and the group.

## REFERENCES

Carroll, P., & Wiggins, J. (1997). *Elements of group counseling: Back to basics.* Denver: Love.

Higgins, W., Ivey, A., & Uhlemann, M. (1970). Media therapy: A programmed approach to teaching behavioral skills. *Journal of Counseling Psychology, 17,* 342–346.

Ivey, A. (1971). *Microcounseling: Innovations in interviewing training.* Springfield, IL: Charles C Thomas.

Ivey, A., & Gluckstern, N. (1976). *Basic influencing skills: Participant manual.* North Amherst, MA: Microtraining.

Ivey, A., & Ivey, M. (1999*). Intentional interviewing and counseling: Facilitating client development in a multicultural society* (4th ed.). Pacific Grove, CA: Brooks/Cole.

Lieberman, M., Yalom, I., & Miles, M. (1973). *Encounter groups: First facts.* New York: Basic Books.

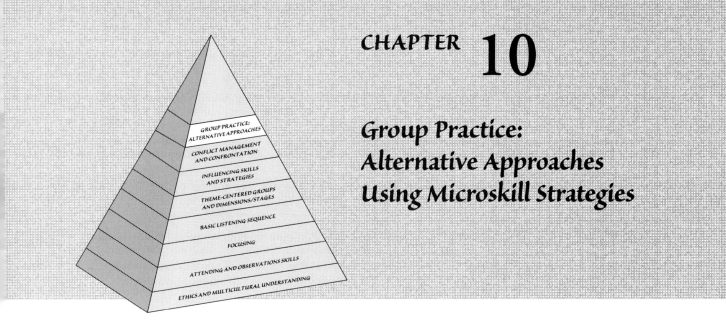

CHAPTER **10**

# Group Practice: Alternative Approaches Using Microskill Strategies

The pyramid, from top to bottom, reads:

GROUP PRACTICE: ALTERNATIVE APPROACHES

CONFLICT MANAGEMENT AND CONFRONTATION

INFLUENCING SKILLS AND STRATEGIES

THEME-CENTERED GROUPS AND DIMENSIONS/STAGES

BASIC LISTENING SEQUENCE

FOCUSING

ATTENDING AND OBSERVATIONS SKILLS

ETHICS AND MULTICULTURAL UNDERSTANDING

## CHAPTER GOALS

This book has thus far concentrated on the specific skills and strategies that you can employ with all groups. We have suggested that the five dimensions/stages of the group provide a platform for utilizing the microskills in effective practice. Theme-centered group interaction has been presented as an important framework for understanding and working with the complexities and challenges you will face in facilitating the majority of groups.

This chapter is designed to lead toward your future work in groups and presents some specifics to help you advance to the next step of leadership: implementing multiple orientations and practices in group work. The chapter presents several types of groups, outlining the specific steps you can take to facilitate a beginning group in each area. Some of the most important theories and practices of groups are summarized in this chapter. In addition, specifics for implementing several alternative systems of group work are described.

However, we should add a note of caution. Most of the group orientations summarized here will require further study on your part. For example, it would be inappropriate and unethical for you to engage in therapeutic group treatment without considerable further study and supervision. On the other hand, at this point you are likely quite able to run basic communication skills training and groups focused on assertiveness training. Here again, follow the clear ethical guidelines of group work as presented in "Before You Start." Suggestions for further reading and study are presented near the conclusion of this chapter.

In this chapter, seek to accomplish the following objectives of understanding and mastery:

▲ Define your preferred skills and strategies of group work and compare and contrast your leadership style with several approaches to group practice and theory.

▲ Develop a beginning understanding of how the skills and strategies of this book may be employed differentially among varying approaches and theories of group work.

▲ Utilize the constructs of some of these models to facilitate your own practice in groups. Special attention is given here to introductory work in task groups, assertiveness training, communication skills, and support groups along with related consciousness-raising groups.

## WARM-UP EXERCISE

The purpose of this exercise is to encourage you to examine your own preferences for facilitating groups. You will be asked to think back on this book and identify your favorite skills and strategies. These preferences represent an important part of your own leadership style. Then, you will have the opportunity to compare and contrast your emerging leadership style with alternative orientations to group work and theory.

Group leaders have personal preferences as to style and theory. One leader may favor the listening skills, focus entirely on individual counseling and therapy (and give little attention to group process), and tend to avoid confrontation. Another leader may be equally skilled in listening, but emphasize group process (almost to the exclusion of a focus on the individual), and be highly confrontational. Other leaders may adjust their styles to the varying types of groups they facilitate. Being able to use multiple microskills and strategies will facilitate your flexibility in professional practice. Box 10.1 shows different uses of microskills by leaders.

Building a personal style and theory of group leadership requires self-examination. This warm-up exercise asks you to think about the skills and strategies that you favor and have found most beneficial throughout this book. You are asked to review the skills and strategies of this book and then indicate those you believe necessary for successful group practice.

Please note the last column of Box 10.1. The boxes there are empty and you are asked to fill in and mark the skills and strategies you think are most important to group practice for you as a *leader*.

▲ If you think that the skill or strategy listed is most central to your thinking about group practice, darken the box ( ■ ).

▲ If you would use the skill frequently and still consider it important, darken half the box ( ◪ ).

▲ If you would use the skill rarely or infrequently, leave the box blank ( ☐ ).

**Box 10.1**  Leader Microskills and Strategies in Varying Groups[1]

| Microskills and Strategies | Structured and Psychoeducational Groups | | | | Theme-Centered Groups | | | Theory-Based Groups | | | | Integrative Styles | | |
|---|---|---|---|---|---|---|---|---|---|---|---|---|---|---|
| | Task and Decision Groups | Anger Management, Psychoeducational Groups | Assertiveness Training, Psychoeducational Groups | Communication Skills, Educational Groups | Gender Discussion Groups | Support Groups | Consciousness-Raising Groups | Psychoanalytic | Cognitive-Behavioral | Person-Centered | Existential-Humanistic | Multicultural Counseling and Therapy | Eclectic | Your Skill Preferences |
| **ATTENDING BEHAVIOR** | | | | | | | | | | | | | | |
| Listening | ▪ | ▪ | ▪ | ▪ | ■ | ■ | ▪ | ▪ | ■ | ■ | ■ | ▪ | ▪ | □ |
| Observing | ▪ | ▪ | ▪ | ▪ | ▪ | ▪ | ■ | ▪ | ■ | ■ | ■ | ■ | ▪ | □ |
| **FOCUS** | | | | | | | | | | | | | | |
| Group | ▪ | ▪ | ▪ | ▪ | ■ | ■ | ■ | ▪ | ▪ | ▪ | ■ | ▪ | ▪ | □ |
| Subgroup | ▪ | ▪ | ▪ | ▪ | ▪ | ▪ | ▪ | □ | ▪ | □ | ▪ | ▪ | ▪ | □ |
| Individual | ▪ | ▪ | ▪ | ▪ | ▪ | ■ | ▪ | ■ | ■ | ■ | ■ | ■ | ▪ | □ |
| Main theme | ■ | ■ | ▪ | ■ | ■ | ■ | ■ | □ | ▪ | □ | □ | ▪ | ▪ | □ |
| Leader | ■ | □ | □ | □ | □ | □ | □ | □ | ▪ | □ | □ | ▪ | □ | □ |
| CEC[2] | ▪ | ▪ | ▪ | ▪ | ■ | ■ | ■ | ▪ | ▪ | ▪ | □ | ■ | ▪ | □ |
| Here-and-now | □ | ▪ | ▪ | ▪ | ▪ | ▪ | ▪ | ▪ | ▪ | ■ | ■ | ▪ | ▪ | □ |
| There-and-then | ▪ | ▪ | ▪ | ■ | ▪ | ▪ | ▪ | ■ | ▪ | ▪ | ▪ | ▪ | ▪ | □ |
| **BASIC LISTENING SEQUENCE** | | | | | | | | | | | | | | |
| Open questions | ▪ | ▪ | ▪ | ▪ | ▪ | ▪ | ▪ | ▪ | ▪ | □ | ▪ | ■ | ▪ | □ |
| Closed questions | ▪ | ▪ | ▪ | ▪ | ▪ | ▪ | ▪ | ▪ | ▪ | □ | □ | ■ | ▪ | □ |
| Encourage/restatement | ▪ | ▪ | ▪ | ▪ | ▪ | ▪ | ▪ | □ | ▪ | ■ | ■ | ■ | ▪ | □ |
| Paraphrasing | ▪ | ▪ | ▪ | ▪ | ▪ | ▪ | ▪ | ▪ | ▪ | ■ | ■ | ■ | ▪ | □ |
| Reflecting feeling | □ | ▪ | □ | □ | ▪ | ▪ | ▪ | ▪ | ▪ | ■ | ■ | ■ | ■ | □ |
| Summarization | ■ | ■ | ■ | ■ | ■ | ■ | ■ | ■ | ■ | ■ | ■ | ■ | ■ | □ |
| **INFLUENCING SKILLS** | | | | | | | | | | | | | | |
| Listening | ▪ | ▪ | ▪ | □ | ▪ | ▪ | ▪ | ▪ | ▪ | □ | □ | ■ | ▪ | □ |
| Reframing/interpreting | ▪ | ▪ | ▪ | □ | ■ | ■ | ■ | ■ | ■ | ▪ | ■ | ▪ | ▪ | □ |
| Self-disclosure | □ | □ | □ | □ | ■ | ■ | ■ | □ | ▪ | ■ | ■ | ■ | ▪ | □ |
| Feedback | ▪ | ■ | ■ | ▪ | ■ | ■ | ■ | □ | ■ | ■ | ■ | ■ | ▪ | □ |
| Structuring | ■ | ■ | ■ | ■ | ▪ | □ | ▪ | □ | ■ | □ | □ | ▪ | ▪ | □ |
| Logical consequences | ▪ | ■ | ▪ | □ | ▪ | ▪ | ▪ | □ | ■ | □ | □ | ▪ | ▪ | □ |
| Reflecting meaning | □ | □ | □ | □ | ▪ | ■ | ■ | ■ | ■ | ■ | ■ | ■ | ▪ | □ |
| Confronting | ▪ | ■ | ▪ | □ | ■ | ■ | ■ | □ | ▪ | ▪ | ■ | ■ | ▪ | □ |

[1] ■ central use of skill or strategy,  ▪ frequent use,  □ occasional or infrequent use

[2] CEC = cultural/environmental context

You may not have fully mastered all the skills presented. The way you fill out the column represents your practical skill goals that will lead ultimately to a personal style and theory of group practice. What do you notice about your preferences?

_____

_____

_____

_____

You will also note that Box 10.1 presents several orientations to group practice and theory. Each system represented has a different focus on leader skills and strategies. What occurs to you as you compare your preferences, strengths, and abilities with some of the many possibilities for organizing and facilitating groups? Do you identify skills and strategies that you might want to develop further as you compare and contrast your preferences with the group orientation?

_____

_____

_____

_____

_____

_____

_____

_____

_____

_____

## COMPARISONS AND CONTRASTS AMONG ORIENTATIONS TO GROUP WORK

First, note some important commonalities among the approaches. Listening and observing are the foundations of all group systems. If you are able to listen and to observe what is occurring in your group, you have a strong beginning toward success. A second similarity is a focus on the group itself. This is, of course, logical and to be expected, but there are some "group" leaders who do individual therapy in the group with little attention to group process.

The next few paragraphs examine research that explored the interpersonal influence of the leader. Some people unfortunately prefer to ignore research findings because they have difficulty connecting them to real life. As you read the following few paragraphs, consider whether the study has any relevance to you. Completed before many of you were born, it may still have relevance.

Using the Ivey Taxonomy, Sherrard (1973) examined transcripts of three well-known group leaders—Robert Carkhuff (structured human relations training), Walter Lifton (person-centered training), and Carl Goldberg (encounter/sensitivity training) plus one "leader X" whose work was focused on the task of problem solving. The varieties of group leadership described are still in wide use.

The results of the study are interesting and in accord with predicted skill usage as presented in this book. As you read the following summary, you may agree that the data provide a clear indication that varying group leaders do indeed do differing things in the group. Review these key examples:

*Talk-time:* The number of sentences each leader used is fascinating and reveals marked differences in style: the structured human relations trainer spoke 52% of the time while the person-centered leader spoke 8% of the time and the encounter therapy leader 6%. The problem-solving leader spoke 33% of the time.

*Focusing:* The structured group leader focused leads 60% of the time on individuals and 20% of the time on the group. The person-centered leader focused 60% on the group and 15% on individuals while the encounter leader focused 90% of his leads on the group and none on the individual. As might be anticipated, the problem-solving group leader focused on the topic or theme 45% of the time while giving secondary attention to the group and individuals.

*Microskills and strategies:* The structured group leader used directives 40% of the time while sharing information 30%; 15% of his leads were reflections of feelings or paraphrases. The person-centered leader reflected feelings or paraphrased 40% of the time while the encounter leader interpreted or reframed group comments nearly 70%, reflected 20%, and used no questions. The problem-solving group leader used the most questions (30%) while sharing information about vocations 40% of the time.

In summary, you may note that your decision as to style of leadership will have a clear effect on what occurs in your group. If you talk a lot, your group members will have less time to explore their issues (but if you are training them in a special topic, this may be appropriate). If you focus on individuals, expect individual issues and concerns to predominate. If you focus on what is occurring in the group, the group is much more likely to think about themselves as a group. If you reflect feelings, your group is likely to explore the emotional dimension. On the other hand, if you spend most of your time on the theme or topic, facts and thoughts may be what is discussed in the group. You as leader have a very strong influence on what occurs in your group. Again, recall that members do not always respond as predicted.

All group leaders use the basic listening sequence, although they may emphasize different aspects of it. Summarizing is one of the most important skills and strategies available to leaders and it has been highlighted as central to all approaches. The summary, used effectively by the leader, brings together in an organized fashion what the group has said and done. It also serves as a punctuation that helps end a segment of the group and leads to the next step. It is a way to conclude the group and can be used at the beginning of the next group session to remind group members what happened last time.

Focusing, on the other hand, reveals more significant differences among group leaders' styles. Theme-centered groups balance the attention among individuals, the theme, and the group as a whole with secondary attention to other points.

A task group will focus on the theme or problem while psychoanalytic therapy groups may focus mostly on the individual. Multicultural counseling and therapy (MCT) and theme-centered consciousness-raising groups give prime attention to the cultural/environmental context. Person-centered groups as well as existential-humanistic groups will place major emphasis on here-and-now communication. This may be contrasted with the more there-and-then educational and task groups. The integrative multicultural counseling and therapy (MCT) group will focus on the cultural/environmental context.

All group leaders will use the basic listening sequence, but their emphasis on each skill or strategy may vary. Questions may be used relatively infrequently in existential-humanistic theory while they usually figure prominently in cognitive-behavioral work. Emphasis on feelings will be strong in psychoanalytic and growth and encounter groups while task and decision-making groups will use the skill less frequently.

Use of the influencing skills may vary widely. Interpretation is central to psychoanalytic work and leader self-disclosure is not to be expected. The existential-humanistic leader will engage in minimal interpretation/reframing while stressing feedback and meaning dimensions. Behavioral groups use many directives and provide considerable structure. Feedback will be important in all, but especially important in the existential-humanistic and person-centered theories.

There is extensive structuring in assertiveness training, communication skills workshops, and most psychoeducational groups. Theme-centered groups vary in their degree of obvious structure, but the plan is always present. Behavioral groups tend to be highly structured while psychoanalytic and existential-humanistic groups tend to vary in specific structuring procedures. Person-centered groups, especially those emphasizing interpersonal encounter, do have a structure—that of focusing on the here-and-now and primarily individual thoughts and feelings—but that structure emerges through the group process. These last groups really are as close to the unstructured concepts as one can find.

## ENCOURAGING USE OF SKILLS BY MEMBERS

Leaders will usually make an effort to encourage group members to apply different skills. All effective group leaders favor group members' listening and using the basic listening sequence. The facilitator of a consciousness-raising group will reinforce members who relate issues to cultural/environmental/contextual issues. Most group leaders will encourage more use of here-and-now conversation in the group, although it is especially central to person-centered growth groups and the existential-humanistic orientation. The existential-humanistic leader will usually encourage members who self-disclose and provide constructive feedback to others. The task group leader will generally support those members who provide clear ideas through structured opinions or self-disclosure.

In short, the leader often seeks to have members engage in the skills and strategies associated with each theoretical or practical orientation. It is not necessary for the effective leader to be a "superstar"; rather, the goal is to have a smoothly working group with all members participating. Leaders can sometimes become too impulsive and take power away from their groups by speaking too quickly.

## THE VALUE OF MULTIPLE LEADERSHIP STYLES

Although there are clear differences among the types of groups, most group leaders are competent with a number of leadership styles. Professionals often find themselves conducting an assertiveness training group one day, a therapeutic cognitive-behavioral group the next, and in the evening facilitating a consciousness-raising group. Their next session of the cognitive-behavioral group may find them drawing on some psychoanalytic or existential-humanistic methods as the group process moves in that direction for a time. The following week they may consult with a community agency on effective decision-making processes. The same professionals may themselves be involved in male or female support groups. They may meet with other group leaders in discussion groups where they explore new ideas in group theory and practice.

Leaders such as these have developed an eclectic style, integrating skills, strategies, and theories in their own unique manner. Over time they have become adept in the multiple possibilities of group work. But each of these professionals will have certain skills and strategies that they favor and that they will use in virtually all the groups they facilitate. Some professionals may be particularly skilled at linking here-and-now behavior in the group with there-and-then behavior outside the group. Expect these leaders to use that particular skill regardless of the theory or setting in which they work. Some leaders are particularly effective in obtaining positive feedback from their groups while others find exploring meaning a more productive strategy.

The orientation of multicultural counseling and therapy (MCT) to group work is eclectic. As an integrative theory, MCT also draws from previously existing methods. However, when an MCT group worker uses psychoanalytic or behavioral strategies and theories, these would be accompanied by an appropriate focus on the cultural/environmental context. Dream analysis, for example, might follow some traditional lines, but the dream would be interpreted within a cultural framework. Taub-Bynum (1984, 1992) talks about any single dream representing not just individual experience but also parts of family life and the cultural tradition. Thus, dream interpretation may involve reframing, but the new perspective also includes how the dream may represent multicultural issues.

An all-female assertiveness training or anger management group would be managed very similarly to one from the behavioral tradition. But the need for assertiveness might be presented within the framework of cultural sexism and/or racism. Anger management, in the behavioral tradition, is often seen as a problem of the individual. Issues of oppression and, once again, racism and sexism, would be included as appropriate parts of the MCT anger management group curriculum.

The last column of Box 10. 1 provides a place for you to review your own preferences and skills in group work. Are you moving toward a specific preference for your work in groups? Do you have a favorite theory or are eclecticism and multiple styles your preference? Once again, compare your rating of your own skill preference with the multiple orientations to groups. Which types of groups do your own skill preferences match most closely? Have you developed any goals for change? We suggested early in this book that all group work was multicultural. What are your thoughts on this matter now?

_____

_____

_____

_____

At this point, let us examine how skill sequences may be manifested in various orientations to group process.

## INTEGRATING MICROSKILLS WITH VARYING ORIENTATIONS TO GROUPS

How can skills and strategies be used with varying styles of groups? This section provides a beginning answer by presenting specifics of how you might facilitate an assertiveness training group, a communication skills training session, a task-oriented decisional group, and a consciousness-raising group. Step-by-step suggestions for each of these four approaches are discussed. The chapter will conclude with brief summaries of how microskills might appear in the remaining group orientations of Box 10.1.

The following pages will equip you with several important approaches to group practice. Part of determining your own style in group work is leading groups with varying goals and methods. Then, based on the skills and strategies presented in this text and your own practical knowledge, you will be prepared to plan a lifetime of learning in the richness of group work. You may want to review the introductory statements on ethics and multicultural issues in "Before You Start." We recommend that all group work begin with these central dimensions.

## STRUCTURED AND PSYCHOEDUCATIONAL GROUPS

A task group, often focused on decision making, is one of the most common groups. We all go to meetings. Presented in this section is one approach to this type of group. Structured psychoeducational groups come in many types, and three are described in some detail in this text: anger management (Chapters 8 and 9), assertiveness training, and communication skills workshops (this chapter).

Common to all of these is a high degree of structure and direction by the leader. The communication skills workshop has the most specific content: a strong educational focus on learning skills. The assertiveness training session is also highly structured but gives more attention to individuals. You have seen that the anger management sessions moved between structured exercises in the style of communication skills and assertiveness training and a less structured, theme-oriented group.

## Task and Decision Groups

"Task groups are usually developed to achieve either of two broad purposes: (a) to serve organizational needs through vehicles such as committees, task forces, delegate assemblies, and administrative groups of various kinds; or (b) to serve client or member needs, through means such as teams, treatment conferences, and social action groups" (Toseland & Rivas, cited in Conyne, Wilson, & Ward, 1997, p. 123). The Conyne, Wilson, and Ward text is an excellent resource for working with task groups in more depth.

You may lead task groups yourself or work with staff from businesses, churches, or government agencies who wish to learn how to manage effective task and decision groups. One, among many ways, to approach task and decision groups is presented in Box 10.2. There you will find a structured plan for a meeting that could be used in any of a variety of groups. Important in this particular task group is the positive asset search and encouraging each member to participate. The group members share their own stories of the problem or decision to be made. Hear each other out fully—no interruptions, please!

Think of a task or decision group as people who come together in a meeting in a school, community, or business to discuss and resolve a specific issue. Their theme is the concern at hand—developing a school budget, deciding to build a parking garage, or creating a business plan. Whatever the main issue, many of the principles of group leadership apply. Consider the following brief summary of how theme-oriented concepts can be applied to meetings in general. Structuring is useful throughout and summarizing differing points of view is essential.

Focusing is a particularly important skill of the leader in task groups. The theme is always the decision or task and needs to be the central focus, but individuals, subgroups, and the group as a whole need to be recognized. The cultural/environmental context is also vital as some groups will tend to think in insufficiently broad terms. Helping them see how the task is related to external issues and pressures outside the group can be essential. For example, the idea developed by the group may be fine, but is it politically acceptable to the community or to higher management?

Encouraging divergent thinking and brainstorming solutions can be especially helpful in the work phase. The unchallenged free flow of ideas is important. Even those that seem less effective need to be considered and listed as they later may enable the breakthrough of new concepts that work.

All the strengths and problems of group process can and will occur in task groups. You will find all the challenging members of the group outlined in Box 9.1 of Chapter 9. Thinking through how to work with difficult group members is a basic part of effective task group management and will be so in all the groups with which you work.

## Assertiveness Training

The word *assertive* may be defined as *positive confidence*. People who are assertive have trust in themselves and can handle multiple situations. Assertiveness is not being aggressive nor is it being overly passive; rather, it is a balance in which

**Box 10.2**    *A Task-Oriented Decision Group*

|  |  |
|---|---|
|  | The following model focuses on a meeting in which a group gathers to make a decision. Particularly important throughout this process is encouraging all the members to speak and share their ideas. |
| *Dimension 1: Initiating the Group—Rapport and Structuring—Goals (including Dimension 3: The Positive Asset Search)* | The meeting begins with recognition of each member. Some groups begin with all members sharing "what's new and good" in their lives. This could be especially useful if the topic to be discussed is conflictual. Humor and positive feedback can be helpful to relieve tension.

An agenda (the goals) is laid out by the leader, often on newsprint or written on a whiteboard. Before proceeding further, the leader asks members if the agenda is satisfactory and if they want to add anything. |
| *Dimension 2: Gathering Data—Stories and Dynamic Balancing of Focus (including Dimension 3: The Positive Asset Search)* | Each member is asked to share her or his view of the issue. The points of view are summarized by the leader and may be displayed on a whiteboard or newsprint. Here the ability to listen is central and, as appropriate, the leader encourages, paraphrases, and reflects or acknowledges feelings briefly. It is important that each member feel heard. Positive feedback, even if the leader disagrees, is useful.

The leader may summarize the individual stories of the problem or decision to be made and the larger story of similarities and differences among the group. Often when all members are allowed to make their views known and they feel heard, they are more likely to respond to conflict resolution. Furthermore, the careful listening required in this approach often helps the group see that their differences are not as large as previously imagined. |
| *Dimension 3: The Positive Asset Search* | With considerable data now developed, the strengths that the individuals and groups bring to bear on the problem or decision can be reviewed. Positive feedback and reframing/interpreting the situation in a more positive, doable fashion is to be encouraged. The leader's ability to summarize positives leading toward resolution of conflict and effective decision making can sometimes turn around even the most difficult group. |
| *Dimension 4: Working—Examining Goals, Sharing, Confronting, Restorying* | Dimension 4 is often the hard part. Individuals are encouraged to disclose their thoughts and feelings about the issue; differences are always treated in a positive way with respect by the leader. Only one person speaks at a time. Conflict management skills are vital here. Recall that challenging confrontation effectively requires careful listening to each person and to the pattern of the group.

You may find some members interrupting, changing the topic, or bringing in irrelevant data. Again, listen carefully and supportively, but keep the main theme and topic in your mind and before the group.

A useful concluding process for this phase is to ask each member to share her or his thoughts and feelings on the topic. If a vote is to be taken, save that until all have been heard. As necessary, restate or paraphrase each individual's contributions. At the conclusion of the sharing, summarize the group's comments and you may find that a new story has evolved. |
| *Dimension 5: Ending—Generalizing and Acting on New Stories* | After a difficult decision is made, people are often tired and want to leave. An essential last step is to follow up and see that specific individuals volunteer or appointed members are designated to complete necessary tasks. The agreed-upon conclusion needs to be summarized by the leader with thanks to and recognition of all, including those whose opinions did not prevail. Include specific plans to follow up on the action to be taken by participants. |

individuals act appropriately according to the context in which they find themselves. They are true to themselves and sensitive to others. Those who can gain the most from assertiveness training are people who allow others to "run over" them or people who "come across" as being too strong and indeed do invade others' space and rights.

An assertiveness training workshop is outlined in Box 10.3. As you review this example, note that clear structuring and the basic listening sequence are especially important in the beginning of the group. See how the leader seeks to involve each member early in a positive way, thus helping to develop feelings of inclusion and enabling each member to "buy in" to the group by saying something. As the group progresses, the influencing skills become more important, but listening is still essential.

The general focus of most assertiveness training groups is on the theme of assertiveness and on individuals and the group as a whole. The cultural/environmental context is also important in that the meaning of assertiveness varies among individuals and cultural groups. Assertiveness training with women has been especially popular and effective, but insensitive assertiveness training can be harmful if a woman is in danger of being abused at home.

When you are engaging in assertiveness training, you are usually directly addressing interpersonal conflict issues, and this must be done with care. Confronting discrepancies, incongruities, and differences is essential, but the mode of confrontation has to be adapted to each individual's situation and cultural background.

Some cultures require a different approach to assertiveness. Paniagua (1994, p. 51) comments:

> In many traditional Hispanic families, children and adolescents are not allowed to argue with their parents and respect toward the father is expected. In this case teaching assertive behaviors to manage family conflicts involving an adolescent and his or her parents (e.g., saying to a Hispanic father "You don't want me to date Juan, but I will date him anyway") may be seen as a violation of a fundamental cultural value, namely that properly respectful behavior toward the father is expected by all members of the family including his children and his wife.

The author also argues that Hispanic women need to be taught assertiveness carefully. Rather than the direct approach usually taught in Eurocentric assertiveness workshops, Comas-Diaz and Duncan (cited in Paniagua, 1994, p. 52) suggest:

> Instead of teaching a woman how to reject orders from her husband, a better approach would be to teach her to use certain words that acknowledge the authority of the husband (e.g., "With all the respect that you deserve, I feel/believe . . ."). This statement places the emphasis on *respect* toward the husband, which is then followed by the expression of assertive behavior ". . . that I would prefer to visit my family this week."

For acting-out children, adolescents, and adults, the pattern is often one of being too aggressive. The cultural demand for certain men to appear strong and have machismo needs to be addressed. This is usually best done through pointing out that being assertive may take even more strength, and that it is often easier to be macho.

**Box 10.3**    *A Beginning Assertiveness Training Session*

The following outline is typical of many assertiveness training sessions. Note that the primary focus is on individual issues and problems, and the group learns by listening to and observing others. Given enough time, each group member can go through all the steps. Confronting and resolving the conflict between present behavior and desired goal behavior is the major objective of this session.

*Dimension 1: Initiating the Group—Rapport and Structuring—Goals (includes Dimension 3: The Positive Asset Search)*

1.1. *Introduction.* Structure the group by welcoming them and asking them to divide into pairs. The pairs are to spend three minutes together and then they are to introduce the other person with an emphasis on that person's strengths.

1.2. *Mini-Lecture/Discussion/Goal Setting.* Ask the group to define assertiveness. Write down responses on newsprint or a chalkboard. (Use open questions plus encouraging, restating, and paraphrasing to each member with a summary of what the total group has said at the end.) Provide your own definition and relate it to what they have provided. Outline your plans for the session and encourage them to ask questions about what is to happen.

You have defined your goals for the session, but it is also useful to ask the total group to outline their own goals in a preliminary fashion. These group goals may be outlined in writing and individuals encouraged to think more specifically about their personal aims.

*Dimension 2: Gathering Data—Stories and Dynamic Balancing of Focus (includes Dimension 3: The Positive Asset Search)*

2.1. *Data Gathering.* Ask members to share stories, concerns, and issues around assertiveness. Use the basic listening sequence to draw out the facts, feelings, and organization of their stories and issues. Periodically summarize what individuals and the total group have said. The focus should be on individuals and the theme of assertiveness, but it needs to include commonalities and differences among group members. This will tend to be there-and-then discussion.

2.2. *What Was Done Right?* As each story, concern, or issue is presented, search immediately with the group for things, no matter how small, that the individual is already doing correctly. This may only be awareness of the problem, but that itself needs to be rewarded. We can best become assertive on a positive base of self-esteem and personal power.

*Dimension 4: Working— Examining Goals, Sharing, Confronting, Restorying (includes Dimension 3: The Positive Asset Search)*

4.1. *The Rational Response.* (If time is short, you may wish to omit 4.1.) Chapter 8, pages 187–188, briefly outlines rational-emotive behavior therapy (REBT) (Ellis, 1994,1995). Introduce Ellis's system by demonstrating it with a volunteer from the group. (Alternatively, you could provide a mini-lecture on the concepts and have group members work through the system in triads or groups of four, followed by a report-out). Note the A (the story)–B (faulty cognitions)–C (emotional consequences) of the person's story by using the basic listening sequence. The identification of issues is most successful if the observing group participates rather than simply watching while you as leader do all the work. Identifying faulty cognitions requires reframing/interpretation and feedback; C, the emotional consequence of not being assertive, requires sensitive reflection of feeling. Stop for a moment and summarize what has been said thus far and obtain feedback from the volunteer before going on to D (disputing). Disputing is clearly confrontation of the discrepancy between faulty cognitions and a more rational response to the situation. Again, think of the concept of "gentle challenge," although people who are too aggressive may need a strong confrontation to their behavior and thought patterns. The A phase tends to be there-and-then while B, C, and D are usually a balance of here-and-now and there-and-then with linkages.

Although Ellis did not stress strengths, you will find that most people respond more easily if you do a positive asset search and bring in their strengths periodically. In this session, we recommend moving on to E (examining the effect of disputation) and F (new feelings and behaviors) through behavioral role-plays.

4.2. *Behavioral Role-Plays.* Especially effective in assertiveness training is bringing there-and-then behavior into the here-and-now of the group. A volunteer is selected and shares her or his story with the group once again, being very specific as to what happened (the second exercise of Box 8.1 can be especially helpful here). The individual is then asked to role-play the situation with another volunteer from the group. After a satisfactory role-play demonstrating the lack of assertiveness (too passive or too aggressive) has occurred, the group and leader provide feedback and the person is asked to define behaviorally specific goals for change. The role-play is repeated using new behaviors; it may require several tries before the individual succeeds and reaches the goals that were established. When the individual changes behavior in the role-play, we are seeing Level 2 of the Observation of Change Scale.

Skills required here include clear structuring and directives as well as listening and observing skills followed by feedback. Examination of the logical consequences of continuing the behavior may be useful. One of the clear objectives of the leader is to have there-and-then behavior outside the group repeated (and then changed) in the here-and-now.

Group discussion follows a successful role-play and the rational and role-playing processes may recycle again and again.

*Dimension 5: Ending—Generalizing and Acting on New Stories (including aspects of Dimensions 3: The Positive Asset Search)*

Assertiveness training has as its goal the change of behavior, thought, and feeling outside the group. Unless the group members reach Level 3 of the Observation of Change Scale, the exercise is incomplete. Those who have examined the rationality of lack of assertiveness and have engaged in a role-play have a reasonable chance of behavioral transfer. But the leader needs to contract with the group members for specific actions and follow-up. Structuring and listening skills are particularly important for the leader in the following two exercises. The leader needs to reward positive movements toward change and encourage those more hesitant in the most supportive way possible.

5.1. A useful ending exercise is for group members to share what they learned during the session and then to indicate behavioral specifics of what they plan to do differently during the coming week. The leader seeks to have each member share concrete actions that he or she would like to attempt, even though they may not have been central participants in the discussions or role-plays. A particular strength of group process is that members can learn new behavior through listening and observing others.

5.2. Another useful but more general strategy you might bring in at the conclusion is to ask each member to respond to the question, "What stood out for you today? What might you remember during this coming week?"

As in all group work, be prepared for anything to happen. You may have a pre-set agenda to do assertiveness training, but something can occur in the group that may take precedence over your original plan. Your ability to be intentional is vital. If the situation is complex, it may best to state, "This is an assertiveness training session and I will talk to you about that issue after the group has finished."

## Communication Skills Training

Virtually all group leaders will at some point find themselves leading communication skills groups. The training of school or community peer counselors usually begins with some form of listening training. Management trainers in community or business organizations, AIDS volunteer training, and parent education are only three examples of the multiple possibilities. You will also find that counseling and therapy clients benefit from learning listening skills as part of group counseling.

Box 10.4 outlines a standard microskills communication workshop. You can use this workshop to teach attending behavior and observations skills, the basic listening sequence, or any of the more complex skills and strategies. If you teach a series of workshops, you will want to add other materials. You will find that videotape and audiotape practice is particularly helpful.

**Box 10.4** *Microskills Communication Workshop*

The following is a basic workshop that may be used for any of the communication skills described in Chapters 2 through 9. Videotaping or audiotaping the practice sessions can be very helpful.

*Dimension 1: Initiating the Group—Rapport and Structuring—Goals (includes Dimension 3: The Positive Asset Search)*

1.1. *Introductions.* Begin the group by asking members to form pairs and share something about themselves and their names with each other. Each pair is also to share their special needs and learning goals for this session. When each pair reports, start by asking each pair member to introduce the other person and notice something that the person did right in communicating to them. This exercise is particularly helpful in beginning the training group on a positive foot; the leader can write down the positive assets of the group members and post them in the room. You will find that many of the effective communication skills are already there in the room. Follow this by noting and writing down the specific goals and needs of the group members.

1.2. *Mini-Lecture.* Draw on the information already gathered as you talk about the outline of your communication skills workshop. Briefly outline what is to happen and encourage the group to ask questions. Talk briefly about the skill or skills to be taught in this session. As part of this introduction include information on individual and cultural differences and seek to make this an important part of group discussion throughout.

*Dimension 2: Gathering Data—Stories and Dynamic Balancing of Focus (includes Dimension 3: The Positive Asset Search)*

2.1. *What Listening Is Not.* Ask for two volunteers if you are focusing on teaching individuals; one person is to be the listener and the other the person seeking help. If you are teaching group microskills, obtain a volunteer leader and three or four members of the demonstration group. The task for the listener or group leader is to demonstrate ineffective listening skills. The person seeking help or the group members should continue to talk as well as they can. Usually about one or two minutes is satisfactory to make the point.

The exercise is often humorous and makes clear the opposite of what is desired. The ineffective list may be contrasted with the positive list generated earlier in Exercise 1.1.

2.2. *Mini-Lecture.* Drawing on the selected microskill(s) of Chapters 2 through 9, present the most important components of the skill(s) you have selected. Balance your presentation with discussion with your group. Be sure to point out what your group is already doing right.

2.3. *Live Demonstration or Videotape.* It often helps clarify the skill if you, yourself, demonstrate the skill live in front of the group. This provides further clarification and may facilitate discussion. Videotapes of the skills are also available (Ivey, Gluckstern, & Ivey, 1994, 1996).

*Dimension 4: Working—Examining Goals, Sharing, Confronting, Restorying (includes Dimension 3: The Positive Asset Search)*

4.1 *Practice Role-Play.* Divide your group into subgroups of three or four members. If you are teaching dyadic communication skills, one person is to be the listener, and the other the person seeking help; the remaining two observe the process and provide feedback. The listener is to practice the specific microskill emphasized in this session. Allow approximately five minutes for the role-play and another five minutes for feedback and discussion in the small groups.

If practicing group microskills, groups of five are recommended with one person as leader; the entire group will provide feedback to the leader. Remind the group members to focus on positive feedback and to keep suggestions, corrections, and negative feedback to a minimum.

Your role as facilitator is to move among small groups and provide feedback and specific suggestions and structure as needed. It is here that a constant search for strengths and positive assets can be especially helpful. Periodically, discuss the potential of individual and cultural differences in the skill with the subgroups and the larger group.

4.2. *Further Practice and Discussion as Needed.* Depending on the skill level of your group, one practice role-play may be enough. More often, it is wise to shift the roles so that each member has a chance to serve as listener or leader.

During or after the practice sessions, it is usually helpful to have process discussions of how things have gone. If there are audiotapes or videotapes, playing some of them to the larger group with discussion of the skills can be especially helpful.

*Dimension 5: Ending—Generalizing and Acting on New Stories (including Dimension 3: The Positive Asset Search)*

5.1. *Transfer to the Home Setting.* Try to obtain a specific contract for each group member to use the learned skill during the coming week. This may be done by listening to friends or family members and by visiting groups in the community and observing the group process, with special attention to the skills of the workshop. You may wish to share some of the process observation methods from the various chapters of this book.

Follow up the generalization plans or contracts at your next meeting. Make a special effort to reward the positive strengths of each member.

5.2. *"I Learned" Statements.* Close the group by asking each member to share one thing that he or she might remember most from the session. End the session with positive comments and thanks to the group members.

Note that your ability to structure and provide clear directives for your group members is important. You can add further structure by giving short presentations or mini-lectures. This psychoeducational group focuses primarily on the theme or topic of learning skills, with a secondary emphasis on individuals, subgroups, and cultural/environmental context. You may wish to review material on cultural differences in communication styles presented earlier in the chapter or multicultural chapters in Ivey, Ivey, and Simek-Morgan (1997).

The second central skill of this workshop is your ability to provide clear, accurate, and generally positive feedback to your group members. Summarizing what has occurred in the group as you transfer to the next dimension or stage is vital.

Listening to your group's special needs and desires for learning and observing their progress in skill development throughout the workshop is central.

All the microskills may be used at any time in the workshop, but the primary focus will remain on the theme of learning specific skills.

## THEME-CENTERED GROUPS

Theme-centered groups were introduced in Chapter 5 where we emphasized that one-third of the time is to be spent focusing on the individual, one-third on the theme, and one-third on the group. This is generally the most useful balance to have in mind, but many other possibilities for focusing need to be ready for use, particularly the cultural/environmental context. The theme-centered gender discussion group of Chapter 5 had some structuring by the leader, but the emphasis was on a much freer flow than was used in the structured psychoeducational groups discussed above.

The basic listening sequence is particularly important in theme-centered work. As the group progresses, you should periodically summarize what has occurred in the group. In the Chapter 5 gender-oriented group, the emphasis was on listening, with minimal attention to influencing skills. Two additional theme-centered groups are presented here: the closely related support and consciousness-raising groups. Support groups focus more on individuals; consciousness-raising groups focus more on cultural/environmental/contextual issues.

### Support Groups and Consciousness-Raising Groups

The most commonly functioning group today, outside of task groups and meetings, is the support group. If you check your home newspaper or community bulletin board, you will find notices of many different kinds of groups. Some will invite people to discuss their issues around multicultural matters of gender, sexual orientation, disability, ethnicity, or race. Trauma survivors have established many support groups, such as those for cancer survivors, war veterans, and people who have experienced rape, domestic violence, incest, or sexual abuse. There are men's groups, women's groups, groups for children of alcoholics, groups of psychotherapists who meet to discuss difficult cases, and groups of teachers or administrators in schools who gather to discuss common issues. The variety continues: parents without partners, groups for the elderly, caregivers who cope with parental Alzheimer's disease, and AIDS groups.

In the process of sharing, many support groups gradually become consciousness-raising groups. A consciousness-raising group examines personal stories but spends far more time examining contextual issues that may relate to their individual concerns. The group and its members develop a consciousness that their difficulties—for example, experiencing sexism in the workplace, surviving domestic violence, or living through a war—are not just personal problems. They become aware that external issues of a sexist society, the abusing partner, or the difficulties encountered in war are as much or more "the problem" than they are. Their consciousness changes. Before, the individual group members felt themselves almost totally responsible for their troubles; in the group they develop awareness that external reality—the cultural/environmental context—has been a major contributor to their individual issues. Box 10.5 outlines a framework for support and consciousness-raising groups.

**Box 10.5**   *Support and Consciousness-Raising Groups: A General Framework*

|  |  |
|---|---|
|  | Each group will be unique, but there are underlying general principles that you can employ and that will provide you with a beginning structure. Skills in theme-centered group interaction are basic for both consciousness-raising and support groups as they both focus on discussion around a central theme. Note that leaders in these groups generally use less formal structuring, although the leader needs to be ready to provide structure and assistance if the group starts wandering. |
| *Dimension 1: Initiating the Group—Rapport and Structuring—Goals (Includes Dimension 3: The Positive Asset Search)* | 1.1. *Introduction.* A positive introductory exercise is recommended such as those described in Boxes 10.2, 10.3, and 10.4. With support and consciousness-raising groups, it is important to identify strengths and positive assets so that each member feels comfortable and part of the group as soon as possible. One useful exercise is to ask members to meet in pairs, trios, or groups of four and identify strengths that each member brings to the group that might be useful to other members and the goals that each might have. |
|  | 1.2. The leader summarizes the purpose of the group. If it is a support group, comments around the value of sharing stories and issues can be given. The importance of positive feedback needs to be stressed. The same would be done for a consciousness-raising group, but the goal of cultural/contextual/environmental awareness and possible eventual action would also be stressed. Rules for that particular group are discussed, particularly around issues of confidentiality. |
| *Dimension 2: Gathering Data—Stories and Dynamic Balancing of Focus (includes Dimension 3: The Positive Asset Search)* | 2.1. Individuals share their stories and the leader uses the basic listening sequence to help them enlarge their understanding while simultaneously encouraging group members to take over more of the responsibility for listening and sharing. The leader encourages positive feedback and self-disclosure. The focus tends to be on the individual, but as the group progresses, particularly consciousness-raising groups, the focus will usually become more externalized. A domestic violence support group will often start with individual stories and a good amount of emotional expression. The focus needs to be appropriately balanced among the individuals in the group, the perpetrator of violence, other key family members, and issues related to the cultural/environmental context. Early on, it is often difficult for some self-blaming abused women to externalize issues. They may mistakenly think problems are their "fault." |
|  | 2.2. The leader can summarize the stories, pointing out commonalities and differences within the group. Depending on the type of group, the focus can also be initiated on contextual issues of oppression. |

*(continued)*

**Box 10.5 (continued)**

| | |
|---|---|
| *Dimension 3: The Positive Asset Search* | 3.1. Strength bombardment is a useful strategy to draw on. The leader explicitly suggests that the group focus on strengths in each person that might be useful in working with the central issue. The group itself should be considered a resource for strength. External resources for coping and dealing with issues can also be summarized. |
| *Dimension 4: Working— Examining Goals, Sharing, Confronting, Restorying (includes Dimension 3: The Positive Asset Search)* | 4.1. The structure of support and consciousness-raising groups often does not follow the linear step-by-step approach suggested here. Very likely, participants have already started examining their life goals as they told their stories and received feedback in Dimension or Stage 2. Confrontation of discrepancies often begins early. Thus, Dimension 4 is often a mixture of all the earlier segments of the group, and issues may recycle frequently. However, if this is your first attempt in this area, it may be wise to start with a more structured approach.<br><br>In consciousness raising, the focus usually can be expected to turn to external events and how outside issues are internalized in the person. The leader can be especially influential here by the way he or she supports and reinforces the focus of group members' comments. Reframing/interpretation becomes an important part of restorying and in helping members think in new ways about the group issues.<br><br>Expect many group members to repeat there-and-then behavior from their daily life in the here-and-now of the group. Both you as leader and the group members can be helpful in linking the there-and-then to the here-and-now.<br><br>The strategies of confrontation, examining logical consequences, and eliciting and reflecting meaning all can be helpful. |
| *Dimension 5: Ending— Generalizing and Acting on New Stories (includes Dimension 3: The Positive Asset Search)* | Support groups can usually be expected to end with a focus on how each individual group member can take home learning from the group, with the hope that it will lead to new action. In a domestic violence group, for example, one of the key actions may be that the abused woman will leave home for a safe house. However, several sessions with considerable support may be required before the woman takes action. At times, the group leader may have to intervene for the safety of the member, but generally, support group members will take the positive learning home in their own ways.<br><br>Consciousness-raising groups may also need to start planning for action. To accomplish this they may turn into a task-oriented group for a time. The ideas in Box 10.2 may be useful in this phase of their work. |

Some support groups move toward action—helping prevent the problems that brought them into the group in the first place. This has been especially apparent in the African-American community and in women's and gay/lesbian/bisexual/transgendered support groups. Vietnam veterans came together to work for understanding of their issues and to obtain adequate support from the government. As part of the restorying process, these groups learn that their individual stories have much in common. A larger joint story is built through group discussion, and the group may decide to move against societal lack of understanding and oppression.

### Focusing with support and consciousness-raising groups

The focus dimensions of the microskills paradigm may help explain the differences between support and consciousness-raising groups and why they are often so closely interrelated. Support groups are often formed to help *individuals* cope with the stresses of the job, the problems encountered as a single parents, the difficulties of women working and bearing the major responsibility of homemaking, or the widespread incidence of high blood pressure among African Americans.

As in all support groups, people tend to focus first on their individual challenges, problems, and concerns. They tell their stories in the group and receive positive feedback and support. Later they may use confrontation and challenge as appropriate to help members examine themselves and their relationship to the cultural/environmental context. As the consciousness-raising group matures, members often learn that they have a larger story in common. It is not just an individual woman's story; it is the larger story of all women. It is not just one person's experience in the Gulf War or in Vietnam; it is part of a larger story of all veterans. The focus turns from the individual to the larger cultural and environmental context.

Workers may decide that the problem lies with the demanding employer who has just downsized rather than with the employees. Single parents discover that their problem is not just "their problem," but that the community and schools are not organized to address their needs. Women discover that other women also have partners who do very little to help with the children or the house and that societal sexism is an issue that they all face. African Americans discover that their physical health issues may be a manifestation of their reaction to repeated instances of racism and discrimination.

Such groups may maintain a focus on individual needs, but they may also focus on environmental and community action to address issues of oppression and to seek change. Rape survivors join together to take back the night. A support group of elders in a retirement home may jointly discover that they all feel mistreated by the staff and come together to obtain their rights. Cancer survivors discover that insufficient research funds have been provided by the government and that certain doctors are not up to date on the latest methods. Support groups often become consciousness-raising groups that subsequently lead an action for societal change.

*Nonetheless, uniqueness remains.* Each support group, even though it may have the same general topic as other groups, will be totally unique. Gulf War veterans' groups share a common experience, but each member lived through circumstances different from those that happened to all other veterans—and each had a different life experience before the war. Groups of elderly people focused on hard-of-hearing issues will vary one from another. Children of divorce groups will also be different as each child has a different parental background, all with different stories affecting the here-and-now life of the family.

As a leader, the way you focus the group conversation will have much to do with the degree of consciousness-raising and action the group takes. This is a matter that can reappear in many groups. While indeed it may be desirable for women with breast cancer or African Americans with hypertension to take action against the medical system, they are first individuals in need. People must tell their stories in groups and obtain personal support to make it through the day or week. Too much social action may cause some members to leave the group.

At the same time, immense personal support can be gained among women who learn that sexism is the issue and that they are not crazy. Vietnam veterans have learned through group work that they have developed posttraumatic stress as a result of their war experiences and that they, too, were not crazy. A major function of support groups is to help their members learn that the things troubling them are shared by others and that external events are often the cause of internal distress. Learning through a support group that you are not alone, that you have been oppressed in some way, and that you alone are not responsible for your difficulties can be immensely valuable and freeing.

For the individual seeking support, is the concern internal or externally attributed? Even if the problem is caused by external issues, the individual still remains responsible for her or his actions and life. Thus, even the most externally oriented support of consciousness-raising groups still needs to attend to individuals and their special and unique thoughts, feelings, and behaviors. Support and consciousness-raising groups show us that we are not alone and they can guide us toward responsible action for change in ourselves and others.

### The importance of learning the life experience of those in support groups

Generalizations are difficult; nonetheless, there are general principles of support groups that the leader can employ. The first of these, of course, is to become informed about the special needs and life demands of those who come to varying support groups. If you are to work with low-income, single parents, you will need to conduct home visits, read extensively, and interview potential members and social workers. You will need to learn as much as possible before the group starts. You can seldom learn enough, but the more information you gather, the better prepared you are. If you are working with an issue with which you are not fully conversant, it is often wise to ask a person who has experienced the issue to work with you as a co-leader. Men working with a group consisting primarily of women, for example, are wise to ask for a female co-leader.

The story–positive asset–restory–action model works especially well in support groups. For example, alcoholics or substance abusers may share their stories in a group; they will tend to receive considerable support and feedback for telling their stories honestly. Group members will often disclose similar stories and similar emotions. The group itself becomes a major positive asset leading toward change. In the work phase, confrontation of discrepancies ("You say you don't plan to drink, but you still go into bars." "You're not telling it straight—you're not off drugs") can be especially powerful as a change strategy.

## THEORY-ORIENTED GROUP WORK

Box 10.1 presents four example groups that might be conducted from varying theoretical perspectives. Again, you must realize that you will need considerable further work before you attempt to lead these types of groups. Even so, a few highlights of each orientation are described with suggestions for where you might find additional information on the theory and its practice.

Listening and observation skills, conflict management strategies, and feedback are important in all these groups. However, you will find that each approach tends to use the dimensions or stages of the group somewhat differently from the others and that the degree of structuring will vary.

Psychoanalytic, cognitive-behavioral, person-centered, and existential-humanistic groups may tend to give the individual primary focus, with secondary attention to group process. As all four theories were generated out of individually oriented theory from counseling and therapy, this is not surprising. For the most part, cultural/environmental/contextual issues are not central to these theories. Nonetheless, the leader will still use group process to strengthen the underlying goals of the group and consider contextual issues from time to time.

Multicultural counseling and therapy groups draw from more recently developed theory and will give considerable attention to cultural/environmental/contextual issues and will tend to balance the focus among the individual, the group, and the cultural/environmental context.

## Psychoanalytically Oriented Groups

Central to these groups is how the past relates to the present. For example, a person with difficulties in the workplace or in personal relationships is expected to have a personal history from the past that might explain what is going on in the present. This linkage is for the most part unconscious, outside of the individual's awareness. Some psychoanalytic groups work rather directly on this relationship of the past to the present through member storytelling and discussion of their concerns; others may use more traditional psychoanalytic techniques such as dream analysis, free association, or an exploration of fantasy.

The leadership style tends to be relatively unstructured, but the group gradually learns what is expected of them as the leader will respond most often to theoretically appropriate member comments. The focus will be primarily on the individual with a balance of here-and-now and there-and-then emphasis.

Interpretation/reframing is the main skill used by the leader. The major goal of interpretation is to link the past to the present and to show how unconscious thoughts and feelings may rule current actions.

Psychoanalytic work has historically been considered inappropriate for minorities, but Duran and Duran (1995) use Jungian psychoanalytic theory with Native American Indians successfully. They find that the concept of myth making and the collective unconscious are helpful in bringing past cultural awareness to here-and-now issues. LaFromboise (1996) uses dreams in her work with Native American youth and her strategies have application with other groups as well.

## Cognitive-Behavioral Groups

Assertiveness training, ABC behavioral analysis, rational-emotive behavior therapy, and communication skills training are all cognitive-behavioral methods and thus you have had considerable opportunity to experience this type of group work.

Cognitive-behavioral therapy (CBT) is one of the major conceptual frameworks you will encounter in group work and has many methods useful in group practice.

Cognitive-behavioral therapy originally came out of behavior therapy with the specific emphasis on directly observed behavior. Primarily through the work of Albert Ellis (1994, 1995), the emphasis expanded to thoughts and feelings as well. More recently, CBT has expanded to include dimensions of the past related to the present and multicultural emphasis (Ivey, Ivey, & Simek-Morgan, 1997). It now is described by many as an inclusive integrative theory and perhaps could be classified in the integrative style column of Box 10.1.

CBT leaders use all the microskills according to their special interests, but generally they structure their groups more than other leaders. CBT usually has a clear agenda that is shared with its members. The skill of logical consequences is used by the group leaders frequently and they do not hesitate to encourage members in certain directions. However, each leader is different as is each group, and most group leaders today will use some CBT strategies, even though they may favor other orientations to group leadership.

Cognitive-behavioral therapy is used rather widely in multicultural situations, but as noted in some detail in the section on assertiveness training above, it needs to be adapted to the special needs of the group. LaFromboise's (1996) *American Indian Life Skills Curriculum* is developed primarily from a CBT base. While oriented to Native American Indians, this book has implications for many multicultural groups, including the White majority. It is highly recommended as a general reference for facilitating CBT groups.

## Person-Centered Groups

Carl Rogers in the late stages of his career discovered the power and importance of group work. He applied his individualistic person-centered theory to many groups and has had considerable influence on the field. His approach has essentially replaced the historically important T-groups and encounter groups. While we usually think of Rogers as individually focused, he did powerful work in promoting cross-cultural understanding in Ireland and other settings.

There is relatively little structuring in the person-centered group. Rogers (1970, p. 8) comments:

> Because of the unstructured nature of the group, the major problem faced by the participants is how they are going to use their time together—whether it be eighteen hours of a weekend or forty or more hours in a one-week group. Often there is consternation, anxiety, and irritation at first—particularly because of the lack of structure.

Despite the intervening thirty years, Rogers's comments remain as fresh and accurate as if they were said yesterday.

Listening and observing are central. The leader may pay special attention to individual and group emotions through reflection of feeling with minimal use of questioning skills. Self-disclosure and feedback are encouraged. Meaning issues often become important, at which time eliciting and reflecting meaning may be used by the leader. There is a strong here-and-now focus, and there-and-then talk is discouraged, although linkage between the two may occur from time to time.

The experience of a here-and-now person-centered group can be very powerful and challenging to group members. With an irresponsible leader, there is possibility for hurt and damage to fragile individuals. The here-and-now experience can be threatening. As such, it is recommended that you go into this work only after considerable experience and supervision. Nonetheless, the learning and training you can obtain from this type of group can be invaluable for you as a group leader. At some time in your group work, you will want to engage in this kind of experience.

Rogers's (1970) classic work, *Carl Rogers on Encounter Groups,* will be both fascinating and helpful in expanding your knowledge of groups. The encounter group has been used successfully in many multicultural situations, and Pack-Brown, Whittington-Clark, and Parker (1998) have adapted some dimensions of Rogers's concepts for African-American women with success. An important new resource in person-centered group work includes useful sections on issues of diversity and current practice (Lago & MacMillan, 1999).

## Existential-Humanistic Groups

Existential-humanistic leaders are concerned with helping members discover the meaning of being in the world. They are interested in moving behind thoughts, feelings, and behaviors to underlying concerns and the purpose of one's life. There is a strong emphasis on personal freedom and choice. Corey (1995a, p. 93) comments on the role of group members:

> Members always have a part in the group process. They look at who and what they are; they clarify their identity and make decisions concerning how they can achieve authenticity. Members decide what they will explore in the group, as well as how they want to change. They define their personal goals.

The existential-humanistic approach is very similar to the person-centered in that a leader will provide minimal structure, there is a strong here-and-now focus, and self-disclosure and feedback are vital skills. The goal of this type of group is different, however, and linkage between there-and-then and here-and-now becomes more central. Eliciting and reflecting meaning is perhaps the most important strategy of the leader, and he or she will encourage group members to do that on their own as much as possible. Logical consequence strategies may appear as the individuals examine the results their choices may have. Skilled confrontation strategies become especially vital in this type of work as we are often working with issues of real personal depth.

As in person-centered groups, the existential-humanistic system can produce casualties; for this reason especially, it needs experienced leadership. Spirituality often becomes important in the existential-humanistic approach as religious and spiritual matters often underlie meaning concerns. Simultaneously, spiritual conflict can produce serious crises of meaning. Yalom (1995) is often considered the expert on existential-humanistic group work. The model was expanded to include spiritual dimensions by Clement Vontress (1995; also see Ivey, Ivey, & Simek-Morgan, 1997, for elaboration of his ideas). Vontress talks about the *uberwelt,* the area beyond our immediate experience. He incorporates dimensions of multicultural experience and spirituality in his work. It has been pointed out that underlying meaning and existential concerns are multicultural and spiritual issues.

## INTEGRATIVE GROUP WORK

Integrative group leaders tend to draw their methods, skills, and strategies from multiple orientations to groups. Most likely, you will find a type of group you feel more comfortable in leading and you will generate your own approach and theory of group practice. Three approaches to integration are presented here: multicultural counseling and therapy, eclectic, and your own developing style.

### Multicultural Counseling and Therapy Groups

The introductory pages of this book, "Before You Start," presented the idea that all group work is in some way multicultural. The exercise with the list of multicultural issues was designed to help you see that cultural issues are virtually always present in any group discussion. Multicultural counseling and therapy (MCT) is a comprehensive integrative theory that gives central attention to the cultural base of all counseling and therapy practice, individual or group (Sue, Ivey, & Pedersen, 1996). MCT is often called the fourth theoretical force in counseling and therapy (psychoanalytic is termed first force; cognitive-behavioral, second force; and person-centered and existential-humanistic, third force). Thus, MCT is both a theory in itself and a system of integrating multiple approaches to groups.

Consciousness-raising groups, women's or men's support groups, a task group focused on developing access for the handicapped, an assertiveness training group for those who experience domestic violence, an existential group discussing the meaning of being gay in a predominantly heterosexual world are all part of the MCT movement. Thus, as you review the strategies and skills of MCT in Box 10.1, note that all skills and strategies are used, but the cultural/environment/contextual focus stands out as consistently central.

Specific group orientations are now being generated for group work with members of varying cultural backgrounds. *Images of Me: A Guide to Group Work with African-American Women* (Pack-Brown, Whittington-Clark, & Parker, 1998) is particularly important. Based on Afrocentric theory, it outlines group stages and processes with specifics and ways to adapt traditional group methods to African-American women. Even though this book is specifically directed to one cultural group, it still has considerable value for anyone working with African-American men or those who seek to develop new ways to bring diversity into groups. Furthermore, the structure and ideas of this book should lead to further expansions of MCT theory in culture-specific counseling.

Duran and Duran (1995) and LaFromboise (1996), previously cited, are two other important sources for culturally centered group work. Overviews of multicultural counseling and therapy theory and practice are available in Sue, Ivey, and Pedersen (1996) and Ivey, Ivey, and Simek-Morgan (1997). The latter work provides some specifics for feminist consciousness-raising groups and a general practice for psychotherapy as liberation, building on the model of Paulo Freire (1972). Freire's *Pedagogy of the Oppressed* has become a central theoretical work for consciousness-raising, and A. Ivey (1995) provides specific structures and microskill strategies for implementing Freire's work in individual and group practice.

## USING VARIOUS ORIENTATIONS WITH CHILD AND ADOLESCENT GROUPS

The in-depth approach of psychoanalytic, person-centered, and existential-humanistic styles is not generally suitable for children and young adolescents. However, all the other groups presented in this chapter can be adapted for work with young people. Older teens often enjoy and profit from person-centered growth groups under an experienced leader.

For example, support groups are very effective for children and adolescents who may be experiencing divorce in their families. The sharing of stories will often appear very similar to what is seen in adult groups. Leaders need to be sensitive to individual differences. Some children will ramble and need help in focusing their stories—paraphrasing what they say often helps. On the other hand, children can say anything and may reveal inappropriate information in the group that should be restricted to individual work. With younger children, the leader needs to take a more active role, introducing group activities other than talking that may be more suitable. Particularly helpful are artwork, therapeutic games, and theme-related books (e.g., those exploring how other children feel about teasing or parental divorce).

In a similar fashion, adolescents benefit greatly by sharing concerns in small groups. The issue may be dating or social relationships or it could be living with an alcoholic or abusive parent. The same general guidelines for storytelling and sharing as discussed above with younger children should be followed. Teens are more likely to understand the limits of confidentiality, but the leader needs to monitor degrees of openness carefully. Gay and lesbian teenagers are particularly vulnerable for depression and suicide. Group work in which they share their problems and concerns can lead to satisfaction and pride in their sexual orientation and facilitate development of self-esteem.

Communication skills training and workshops can be useful for children and teenagers, not only in teaching them social skills of conversation with others but also in helping them develop skills as peer counselors or mediators. If you are working in schools or communities, the value of peer counselors cannot be overstated. Students not only learn the skills; they also can often relate better to their peers than to adults. This has frequently been useful for some acting-out students. Box 10.4 on communication skills workshops can be adapted for use with children and teens.

The cognitive-behavioral orientation is generally suitable, but adaptations must be made to meet the language style and experience of the age group. For children, sessions should be shorter and it is best to focus on a single concept. Children and teens often enjoy assertiveness training. Children and adolescents are unlikely to sit still for the highly structured decision and task group suggested here, but some of the principles may nonetheless be used. Young people need to make decisions and work on tasks just as adults do.

Adolescents respond to the multicultural orientation and consciousness-raising approaches surprisingly well. While you must adapt your style to the age of the group, you'll find young women very interested in feminist consciousness-raising issues (sometimes even as early as grade school), young children very interested in their multicultural identities, and a surprising tolerance and interest in general multicultural issues. Ernest Washington of the University of Massachusetts has had great success with cultural identity groups in elementary school. Often you'll find older members of elementary school classes as well as students from middle schools and high schools becoming involved in social action and seeking to change the atmosphere of their school setting and classrooms or the community.

## ADDITIONAL REFERENCES TO THEORY AND PRACTICE

For further study in theory and practice of specific theories, you can examine basic texts such as Corey (2000), Gladding (1999), and Yalom (1995). These books will introduce you to theory and refer you to other specifics of managing theoretical persuasions effectively. Conyne, Wilson, and Ward (1997) provide a comprehensive view of the world of group work for advanced students.

A cutting-edge text is *Images of Me: A Guide to Group Work with African-American Women* (Pack-Brown, Whittington-Clark, & Parker, 1998). While this book specifies strategies for a specific cultural group, its insights and procedures are invaluable for any group leader. It can help you understand multicultural issues and it gives you ideas for working with many types of cultural groups. For an extremely useful set of structured exercises for people of all races and ethnicities, we have repeatedly recommended the excellent *American Indian Life Skills Curriculum* (LaFromboise, 1996). One of the most useful theoretical articles will be Ogbonnya (1994), who describes the person as community. Ogbonnya stresses that we are not alone; our whole being reflects the communities and cultures within which we have been raised and live.

Books of structured exercises can be useful, particularly if you are working within the cognitive-behavioral tradition. The following are especially recommended.

Carrell, S. (1993). *Group exercises for adolescents.* Newbury Park, CA: Sage.
> This book, cited earlier, covers many central issues for teens such as identity, sexuality, and anger. Coupled with the *American Indian Life Skills Curriculum* mentioned above, you will have a solid library for work with adolescents.

Davis, M., Eschelman, E., & McKay, M. (1995). *The relaxation and stress reduction workbook* (4th ed.). Oakland, CA: New Harbinger.
> This is perhaps the clearest book on cognitive-behavioral exercises. It includes relaxation training, thought stopping, cognitive analysis, and a broad selection of widely used methods. The book focuses on stress management, but virtually any structured or psychoeducational group you facilitate can benefit from the ideas presented here. Anger management workshop ideas can be found here.

McKay, M., Davis, M., & Fanning, P. (1997). *Thoughts and feelings: Taking control of your moods and your life.* Oakland, CA: New Harbinger.

The author describes a variety of exercises including stress inoculation, relaxation, and imagery. This book will be particularly helpful in groups working with depression and other mood-based issues. The exercises are easily adapted to a wide array of day-to-day issues faced by all of us.

For further work in the microskills and strategies, the following may be useful:

Daniels, T., & Ivey, A. (In press). *Microcounseling.* Springfield, IL: Charles C Thomas.

Ivey, A., Gluckstern, N., & Ivey, M. (1994). *Basic influencing skills.* North Amherst, MA: Microtraining Associates. (Includes videotape and book)

Ivey, A., Gluckstern, N., & Ivey, M. (1996). *Basic attending skills.* North Amherst, MA: Microtraining Associates. (Includes videotape and book)

Ivey, A., & Ivey, M. (1999). *Intentional interviewing and counseling: Facilitating client development in a multicultural society.* Pacific Grove, CA: Brooks/Cole.

Ivey, M. (1999). *Counseling children: A microskills approach.* (Videotape and Instructor Guide with Transcript). North Amherst, MA: Microtraining Associates.

These books and videotapes define the basics of the microskills approach in detail and can be useful as you plan and design your own training programs in communication skills.

The following books by Paul Pedersen will be useful for multicultural group work:

Pedersen, P. (1997). *Cultural-centered counseling interventions.* Thousand Oaks, CA: Sage.
This book describes the implications of making culture central, rather than marginal, to the counseling process. Each chapter includes useful group exercises.

Pedersen, P. (2000). *Hidden messages in culture-centered counseling: A triad training model.* Thousand Oaks, CA: Sage.
Group dynamics requires us to understand the multiplicity of interacting roles/identities/cultures to which each individual belongs at the same time. This book defines Pedersen's influential triad training model, which provides highly useful culturally based exercises for many types of group work.

Pedersen, P., & Ivey, A. (1993). *Culture-centered counseling and interviewing skills.* Westport, CT: Greenwood.
This book begins with a major exercise—developing a synthetic culture laboratory for small groups ranging from twelve to forty members. The exercise demonstrates the power of culture to shape individual and group behavior. Microskills concepts are presented in the context of culture-centered counseling and therapy.

## MOVING TOWARD YOUR OWN LEADERSHIP STYLE

The essence of eclecticism is drawing from as many methods as the situation may demand. Box 10.1 illustrates this point in that all skills and strategies are balanced. In truth, any leader who uses an eclectic approach will tend to favor some skills and strategies over any other. The more you become aware of your own preferences and personal style, the closer you will come to a theory-based integrative approach.

Thus, we are asking you once again to review the exercise at the beginning of this chapter and note which skills you prefer and compare and contrast them with the various orientations to groups presented in Box 10.1. You now have had the opportunity to consider at least briefly several orientations and theories of group leadership. Have your skill preferences changed? Which systems appeal to you most?

_____

_____

_____

As you evolve and gradually develop more experience in groups, you will start to see yourself developing certain preferences in the life of the group. You will note these best by audiotaping or videotaping your group leadership style. You also want to receive feedback from group members and as much supervision as you can obtain. Coleading groups can be quite useful. Over time, you may find yourself developing a preference for a certain type of group and using a consistent pattern of skills.

When you find consistency of group leadership behavior on your part, it indicates that you are developing your own theory of groups at an implicit level. The question you need to ask yourself at that time is, "Am I really using the theory, skills, and strategies that I believe in?" This will help make your implicit theory explicit and clear. You may want to continue in the path you have taken, or you may prefer to change your pattern of skill and strategy.

In short, what you actually do in groups in terms of your choice of skills and strategies is your real theory of group practice. We all want to examine whether what we do achieves our theoretical ideal. *"Does your real match your ideal?"*

Once again, think back on this chapter. What have you learned here? What points struck you as most important? What stood out for you? What would you like to work on in developing your own style of group leadership?

_____

_____

_____

_____

_____

_____

_____

_____

_____

## PRACTICING MULTIPLE ORIENTATIONS TO GROUP WORK

### 1. Process Observation

This chapter has suggested that different groups have varying uses of skills and strategies. By this point in your work, you have been asked to observe several different types of groups. What have you already noted about differences in skill usage among the varying groups you have visited?

Summarize your observations here or in more detail in a formal report and analysis of the groups you have observed.

_____

_____

_____

_____

_____

_____

_____

### 2. The Fish Bowl

Select one of the four group orientations presented in the boxes of this chapter (task group, assertiveness training, communication skills, and support or consciousness-raising group) and practice this in front of others. If task, support, or consciousness raising is selected, the group should select the topic on which they wish to work.

If time permits, have different group members present workshops on each of the microskills and strategies of this book using the basic communication skills workshop design described in Box 10.4.

### 3. Your Own Group Practice

For group practice we suggest that you take one or more of the four group orientations discussed in the fish bowl exercise and practice them here.

1. Divide into groups of five or six. One person is to serve as leader and one as observer. The remainder serve as group participants.
2. Define the topic for the small groups. For this practice exercise, it can be any one of the four orientations presented in the boxes of this chapter. If task, support, or consciousness raising is selected, the group should select the topic on which they wish to work.
3. Fifteen minutes should be used for the small groups. Allow five minutes for feedback from the observer. Finally, each small group can reflect on its own group process.

Where possible, add videorecording and practice to your work with attending skills and observation. You will always obtain very useful feedback on yourself and the group.

# REFERENCES

Carkhuff, R. (1971). Demonstration protocol. In G. Gazda, *Group counseling: A developmental approach* (pp. 249–266). Springfield, IL: Charles C Thomas.

Carrell, S. (1993). *Group exercises for adolescents.* Newbury Park, CA: Sage.

Conyne, R., Wilson, F., & Ward, D. (1997). *Comprehensive group work: What it means and how to teach it.* Washington, DC: American Counseling Association.

Corey, G. (1995a). *Student manual for theory and practice of group counseling* (4th ed.). Pacific Grove, CA: Brooks/Cole.

Corey, G. (1995b). *Theory and practice of group counseling* (4th ed.). Pacific Grove, CA: Brooks/Cole.

Corey, G. (2000). *Theory and practice of group counseling* (5th ed.). Pacific Grove, CA: Brooks/Cole.

Daniels, T., & Ivey, A. (In press). *Microcounseling.* Springfield, IL: Charles C Thomas.

Davis, M., Eschelman, E., & McKay, M. (1995). *The relaxation and stress reduction workbook* (4th ed.). Oakland, CA: New Harbinger.

Duran, E., & Duran, B. (1995). *Native American postcolonial psychology.* Albany: State University of New York Press.

Ellis, A. (1994). *Reason and emotion in psychotherapy.* New York: Birch Lane.

Ellis, A. (1995). Changing rational-emotive therapy to rational-emotive-behavior therapy. *Journal of Rational-Emotive and Cognitive-Behavior Therapy, 13,* 85–90.

Freire, P. (1972). *Pedagogy of the oppressed.* New York: Herder and Herder.

Gladding, S. (1999). *Group work: A counseling specialty* (3rd ed.). Columbus, OH: Merrill.

Goldberg, C. (1970). *Encounter: Group sensitivity experience.* New York: Science House.

Ivey, A. (1995). Psychotherapy as liberation. In J. Ponterotto, J. Casas, L. Suzuki, & C. Alexander (Eds.), *Handbook of multicultural counseling.* Beverly Hills, CA: Sage.

Ivey, A., Gluckstern, N., & Ivey, M. (1994). *Basic influencing skills.* North Amherst, MA: Microtraining Associates.

Ivey, A., Gluckstern, N., & Ivey, M. (1996). *Basic attending skills.* North Amherst, MA: Microtraining Associates.

Ivey, A., & Ivey, M. (1999). *Intentional interviewing and counseling: Facilitating client development in a multicultural society.* Pacific Grove, CA: Brooks/Cole.

Ivey, A., Ivey, M., & Simek-Morgan, L. (1997). *Counseling and psychotherapy: A multicultural perspective.* Boston: Allyn & Bacon.

Ivey, M. (1999). *Counseling children: A microskills approach.* (Videotape and instructor guide with transcript.) North Amherst, MA: Microtraining Associates.

LaFromboise, T. (1996). *American Indian life skills curriculum.* Madison: University of Wisconsin Press.

Lago, C., & MacMillan, M. (Eds.). (1999). *Experiences in relatedness: Group work and the person-centered approach.* Ross-on-Wye, U.K.: PCCS Books.

Lifton, W. (1972). *Working with groups.* New York: Wiley.

McKay, M., Davis, M., & Fanning, P. (1997). *Thoughts and feelings: Taking control of your moods and your life.* Oakland, CA: New Harbinger.

Ogbonnya, O. (1994). Person as community: An African understanding of the person as an intrapsychic community. *Journal of Black Psychology, 20,* 75–87.

Pack-Brown, S., Whittington-Clark, L., & Parker, W. (1998). *Images of me: A guide to group work with African-American women.* Boston: Allyn & Bacon.

Paniagua, F. (1994). *Assessing and treating culturally diverse clients.* Thousand Oaks, CA: Sage.

Rogers, C. (1970). *Carl Rogers on encounter groups.* Pacific Grove, CA: Brooks/Cole.

Sherrard, P. (1973). *Predicting group leader/member interaction: The efficacy of the Ivey Taxonomy.* Unpublished doctoral dissertation, University of Massachusetts, Amherst.

Sue, D., Ivey, A., & Pedersen, P. (1996). *A theory of multicultural counseling and therapy.* Pacific Grove, Ca: Brooks/Cole.

Taub-Bynum, E. (1984). *The family unconscious.* Wheaton, IL: Quest.

Taub-Bynum, E. (1992). *Family dreams.* Ithaca, NY: Haworth Press.

Vontress, C. (1995). *The philosophical foundations of existential-humanistic perspective: A personal statement.* Unpublished manuscript, George Washington University, Washington, DC.

Yalom, I. (1995). *Theory and practice of group psychotherapy* (4th ed.). New York: Basic Books.

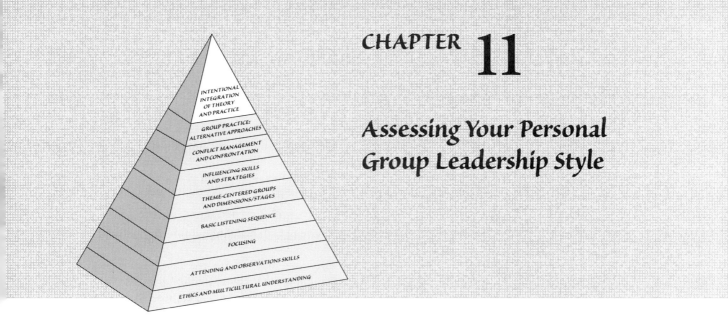

CHAPTER **11**

# Assessing Your Personal Group Leadership Style

The pyramid levels, from top to bottom, read:

INTENTIONAL INTEGRATION OF THEORY AND PRACTICE

GROUP PRACTICE: ALTERNATIVE APPROACHES

CONFLICT MANAGEMENT AND CONFRONTATION

INFLUENCING SKILLS AND STRATEGIES

THEME-CENTERED GROUPS AND DIMENSIONS/STAGES

BASIC LISTENING SEQUENCE

FOCUSING

ATTENDING AND OBSERVATIONS SKILLS

ETHICS AND MULTICULTURAL UNDERSTANDING

## CHAPTER GOALS

Chapter 10 began and concluded by asking you to assess your personal preference for varying skills and suggested that you start the process of identifying orientations and theories to group work that appeal to you. This chapter extends these ideas and asks you to engage in three important tasks involving self-assessment and the detailed examination of your group leadership style.

> In this chapter, seek to accomplish the following objectives of understanding and mastery:
>
> ▲ Assess your personal skill level with the several skills, strategies, and dimensions/stages discussed in this book.
> ▲ Review and assess your personal skill level with the process observation approaches and instruments presented throughout this book.
> ▲ Audiotape or videotape yourself with a group, develop a transcript of your work, and complete a process analysis on what you are actually doing in a group session.
> ▲ Review the concept of intentionality and how it relates to group practice and your future work.

## ASSESSING YOUR SKILL LEVEL

It is easier to be flexible and intentional if you have many alternatives for action. The more skills and strategies you have mastered, the greater will be your possibility for success as a leader. Remember the one set of skills you can fall back on when all else fails: the basic listening sequence. Mastery of the ability to listen (and observe) is fundamental to intentional group work.

The following form lists the skills and strategies of this book with their expected influence on group members. Again, recall that the predicted effect of consequences does not always occur and be ready to flex intentionality when surprises happen. Four levels of mastery or competence are presented and defined here: classification, basic, intentional, and teaching. Rate yourself on each skill or strategy for your mastery level.

*Classification Mastery.* You are able to identify the skill, strategy, or concept through process observation. You are aware of possible cultural differences that might relate to this skill.

*Basic Mastery.* You are able to engage in the skill, strategy, or concept as you facilitate your own group. You also know what to expect group members to do when you use this skill or strategy. You can use the skill appropriately with different cultural groups.

*Intentional Mastery.* You can use the skill, strategy, or concept in multiple ways. If the group does not respond as you predict or anticipate, you can revise your use of the skill or change to another appropriately.

*Teaching Mastery.* This is an objective you can plan for the future. Most group leaders at some point will teach communication skills. It will be useful if you gradually develop the ability to teach basic group skills to others. You are likely to be engaged in training peer counselors, community volunteers, parents, business people, and many other groups in the basic skills of listening and influencing. For specifics on how to teach a basic communication skills workshop, see Chapter 10, Box 10.4, on teaching microskills.

| Skill, Strategy, or Concept and Intentional Prediction of Its Effect in a Group | Level of Mastery (C, B, I, or T)[1] | What Will You Do If and When Prediction Fails? |
|---|---|---|
| 1. **Attending Behavior** <br> Culturally Appropriate Listening (by the leader): Observing group members with awareness of individual and cultural differences <br><br> Expected consequence: The leader is able to demonstrate culturally appropriate visuals, vocals, verbals, and body language. The leader is able to observe attending behaviors in group members and use the observations as a foundation for applying listening and observing skills and strategies. Group members will talk freely and respond openly, particularly around topics to which attention is given. The leader can observe nonverbal and verbal styles and use these to engage the group members more fully. <br><br> [1]C = Classification; B = Basic; I = Intentional; T = Teaching | | |

| Skill, Strategy, or Concept and Intentional Prediction of Its Effect in a Group | Level of Mastery (C, B, I, or T) | What Will You Do If and When Prediction Fails? |
|---|---|---|
| **2. Focusing**<br><br>2.1. Focusing (Pacing and Leading)<br><br>Pacing<br><br>Leading<br><br>Expected consequence: The leader is able to "walk with" the group and its members, listening to them where they "are" and is also able to lead them toward other focuses and emphases as appropriate. Group members will talk more freely and respond openly, but they will also follow the leader interventions in other appropriate directions. Focusing provides structure and structure provides safety for members to discuss topics that would otherwise be difficult or dangerous.<br><br>2.2. Focusing (Topic Aspects)<br><br>Individual<br><br>Subgroup<br><br>Group<br><br>Main theme (Problem or issue)<br><br>Group leader (Yourself)<br><br>Cultural/environmental/contextual issues (moral, spiritual, or religious, economic or social, family, community, multicultural context)<br><br>Expected consequence: The leader is able to focus on specific dimensions in the group, both pacing and leading in all areas. Group members and the leader are able to focus their discussion on multiple issues.<br><br>2.3. Focusing (Time Dimensions and Linking)<br><br>Here-and-now<br><br>There-and-then<br><br>Linking here-and-now to there-and-then thoughts, feelings, and behaviors and helping members find patterns and similarities among their lives.<br><br>Expected consequence: Participants will discuss their issues in the here-and-now or the there-and-then in ways that correspond to the focus of the leader. If links (relationships, parallels, patterns, or similarities) are suggested by the leader, these links will be discussed—and may lead to new insights in thoughts, feelings, and behavior. | | |

*(continued)*

| Skill, Strategy, or Concept and Intentional Prediction of Its Effect in a Group | Level of Mastery (C, B, I, or T) | What Will You Do If and When Prediction Fails? |
|---|---|---|
| **3. Basic Listening Sequence**<br><br>3.1. Open Questions<br>Expected consequence: Participants will answer open questions in some detail.<br><br>3.2. Closed Questions<br>Expected consequence: Participants will give short answers.<br><br>3.3. Encourage/Restatement<br>Expected consequence: Participants will be encouraged to keep talking about the same subject, particularly when encouraged by the leader in a questioning tone of voice.<br><br>3.4. Paraphrasing<br>Expected consequence: Participants will feel heard. They will tend to move on and not repeat the same story again. If a paraphrase is inaccurate, it provides the participant with an opportunity to correct the leader. If a questioning tone of voice is used, the participant may elaborate further.<br><br>3.5. Reflecting Feelings<br>Expected consequence: Participants will go more deeply into their emotional experience. They may correct the reflection with another word. A focus on group general tone and feeling can be useful.<br><br>3.6. Summarization<br>Expected consequence: Participants will feel heard and often learn how their stories are integrated. Particularly useful is summarizing the group's stories so that varying thoughts, emotions, and behaviors of the group to that point can be integrated, thus facilitating a more centered discussion that builds on past work in the group. The summary provides a more coherent transition from one session or topic to the next.<br><br>**4. Dimensions/Stages**<br>4.1. Initiating the Group—Rapport and Structuring, Establishing Goals<br>Expected consequence: The group members will feel at ease with each other, know what to expect, and have goals for everyone's participation. | | |

| Skill, Strategy, or Concept and Intentional Prediction of Its Effect in a Group | Level of Mastery (C, B, I, or T) | What Will You Do If and When Prediction Fails? |
|---|---|---|
| 4.2. Gathering Data—Stories and Dynamic Balancing of Focus<br>Expected consequence: The group will share their stories, concerns, and issues and eventually be able to focus on multiple perspectives on these data. The group is also writing a combined story even as the members are telling or listening to each other's stories. | | |
| 4.3. The Positive Asset Search<br>Expected consequence: Each group member will feel identified as a valuable contributing member with positive strengths. This dimension can be treated as a separate phase or integrated throughout the group process. When the work of the group begins with the positive resources already available and builds on them, the accomplishments of every group member are validated, giving each one hope for the future. In the absence of a positive attitude and hope, change becomes extremely difficult and slow. | | |
| 4.4. Working—Examining Goals, Sharing, Confronting, Restorying<br>Expected consequence: Through group experience, goals may change. "If you don't know where you are going, you are likely to end up somewhere else." Members work through their issues, experience both conflict and trust as the group moves toward more depth, and may restory their issues. Members may move in positive directions on the Observation of Change Scale. Movement toward action begins. | | |
| 4.5. Ending—Generalizing and Acting on New Stories<br>Expected consequence: If all stages are completed successfully, expect movement toward change in behavior, thought, and feelings outside the group. | | |
| 5. **Influencing Skills**<br>Expected consequence: Special note—All the influencing skills may lead to reframes, new ways of thinking, and behavior changes. | | |
| 5.1. Basic Listening Sequence and Focus<br>Expected consequence: Effective listening can lead to restorying on the part of group members. | | |
| | | *(continued)* |

| Skill, Strategy, or Concept and Intentional Prediction of Its Effect in a Group | Level of Mastery (C, B, I, or T) | What Will You Do If and When Prediction Fails? |
|---|---|---|
| 5.2. Reframing/Interpreting<br>Expected consequence: The group or group member discovers another perspective on a story, issue, or problem. The perspective can be generated by a theory or simply by looking at the situation from a new viewpoint. | | |
| 5.3. Self-Disclosure<br>Expected consequence: Brief self-disclosure by the leader may encourage group members to self-disclose in more depth. | | |
| 5.4. Feedback<br>Expected consequence: Group members obtain the perspectives of the leader or group members on thoughts, feelings, and behaviors and this may lead them to make changes in their own behavior. | | |
| 5.5. Structuring<br>Expected consequence: Group members will listen to and follow the directives, opinions, and structures suggested by the leader. | | |
| 5.6. Exploring Logical Consequences<br>Expected consequence: Participants will discuss their issues in the here-and-now or the there-and-then in ways that correspond to the focus of the leader. If links (relationships, parallels, patterns, or similarities) are suggested by the leader, these links will be discussed—and may lead to new insights in thoughts, feelings, and behavior. | | |
| 5.7. Eliciting and Reflecting Meaning<br>Expected consequence: Group members will discuss their stories, issues, and concerns in more depth with a special emphasis on deeper meanings and understandings. | | |
| 5.8. Confronting<br>Expected consequence: Group members will confront discrepancies and conflict with new ideas, thoughts, feelings, and behaviors and these will be manifested in observable change. | | |

Summarize your observations of your present skills as a group leader at this point. Where do you see your strengths? What skills and strategies do you need to work on more fully? Where might you need special supervision?

_____

_____

_____

_____

_____

_____

_____

_____

_____

## ASSESSING AND REVIEWING PROCESS OBSERVATION SKILLS

Skills and strategies of the microskills are essential to competent and effective group leadership, but we hope that you have become aware of the equal importance of observing carefully what is occurring in your groups. We have emphasized observation and process analysis throughout.

The next form is a summary of the major process evaluation methods presented in this book. You may wish once again to evaluate yourself for level of mastery of these various observation methods and instruments.

The intentional group leader will constantly be observing what is occurring in the group. There are many process observation systems beyond those presented in this text and each system provides a new perspective for understanding what is happening. Over the years, multiple ways of considering process in the group will become an automatic part of your style. In the early stages, it is important to engage in just one type of process observation at a time. With experience in group practice, you will become more sensitive to your groups and be able to use that knowledge at an intuitive level. Making process observation a central part of your skill repertoire is necessary to your effectiveness and professionalism over time.

As part of process observation, you need to observe other groups in operation, but it is also extremely helpful to audiotape or videotape your own work from time to time and then apply various process observation systems to your own practice. In addition, from time to time ask some members of your group to sit outside the group and provide process observation to both you and the group itself. In the early stages of your career as a leader and when in doubt about what is occurring in a group, seek supervision and consultation. This is the only ethical thing do.

| **Observation System and Page Location** | **Level of Mastery** |
|---|---|
| Attending behavior process instruments<br>    Who talks to whom? (Charting conversational patterns in a group) See page 51.<br><br>    Who interrupts and how often? See page 52.<br><br>    Checklist for 3Vs + B. See page 52.<br><br>Focusing observation. See page 67.<br><br>Basic listening sequence and Ivey Taxonomy. See page 104.<br><br>Theme-centered process observation. See page 115.<br><br>Integration of skills group checklist. See page 122.<br><br>Observation of Change Scale. See page 163.<br><br>Process observation of structuring in groups. See page 200.<br><br>Conflict process observation. See page 211.<br><br>The Ivey Taxonomy. See page 268. | |

As you review the systems listed in the form, think about where you stand in terms of your skills as a process observer. What are some of your next steps?

_____

_____

_____

_____

_____

_____

## EXAMINING YOUR OWN GROUP PRACTICE

Throughout this book, we have presented transcripts of groups dealing with various issues around skills and strategies in group work. It is now appropriate that you examine your own style as a group leader through audiotaping or videotaping a full group session. Nowhere can you learn better what and how you are doing than by examining one of your group sessions in detail.

Then, develop a transcript of the group session. Present your work in two columns similar to the format used in Chapter 6 (see page 137) and throughout the book. In the first column, list each leader and group member statement. Use the second column for process observation and classification of the skills applied by both you and group members.

Developing a transcript is time-consuming and challenging, but it will provide accurate information about yourself and your abilities in groups. There is often a large gap between a person's ability to do well on an examination and that same individual's ability to demonstrate that he or she can affect a group positively. Developing and examining transcripts can help you close any gap that may exist for you.

As part of this process, you might team up with a partner or a small group. Each of you can review the other person's transcript and provide additional insights and suggestions for the future. Peer supervision of group work and practice can be invaluable for both your beginning and long-term work as a group leader.

Review the material on prescreening and ethics in the "Before You Start" section at the beginning of the book. Obtain permission from each group member before audiotaping or videotaping a session. In prescreening and as the group starts, inform your group members that the recording equipment can be turned off if they wish. This will happen very seldom if you have prepared the group for the taping and you, yourself, are comfortable with it.

At the end of your group, ask your group members to write a brief, informal evaluation of your work. Develop your own assessment instrument or use the questions here:

*Evaluation of Group*
What did you personally learn?

What did you like best about this group?

What would you like to have seen done differently?

*Evaluation of Leader*
What did the leader do right?

What might the leader have done differently?

Please use the reverse side of the paper to make any additional comments or suggestions.

When transcribing the group session, be sure to change participants' names and disguise any identifying information. As you make the transcript, identify the dimensions and stages of everyone's comments.

You may wish to consider the following questions after you have classified and made process comments on the group:

1. What skills and strategies do you use most frequently? Do you see yourself demonstrating different levels of competency or mastery in some skills or strategies compared to others?
2. Do you see an evolving theoretical orientation or personal style? How does your actual skill usage compare to various group orientations presented in Box 10.1?
3. Discuss the five dimensions or stages of the group. Did you cover each? To what level of effectiveness?
4. Discuss the multicultural issues in your group. Recall that every group has multicultural issues, even though they may not be apparent immediately.
5. What did you note among your group members on the Observation of Change Scale? Did you have an impact on members? If possible, conduct follow-up and look for change and generalization of behavior from the group at Level 3.
6. Summarize feedback from your group members. What stands out for you from their comments?
7. Summarize observation and feedback from peers and supervisors.
8. What are you most pleased with about your work? What would you most like to change in the future?
9. Where are you going next in your group work?

## INTENTIONALITY: A REVIEW

Intentionality demands that you have multiple responses and leadership skills to respond to the many things that can happen in any group. As has been indicated throughout this book, the intentional leader can expect certain things to happen in a group if he or she uses specific skills and strategies. For example, if you ask an open question that focuses on the here-and-now, you can expect the group member to respond in the here-and-now at greater length than if your question were closed. If you confront effectively, expect change in group members' response on the Observation of Change Scale—both during the group and in transfer of learnings to daily life.

Remember, however, that member responses don't always occur as predicted. An open question focused on the here-and-now may be met with silence, or the group may talk in the there-and-then, avoiding your intent. While we can make general predictions of what will happen, people and groups often don't respond as we expect. Multiple interventions on your part and even several sessions may be required before you see significant change in some group members.

Therefore, true intentionality means that the group leader realizes things won't always happen as expected and will be ready to use other skills and strategies when the first (and second and third) intervention doesn't work. However, skilled intentional leadership almost always leads groups to talk in the here-and-now (if that is your objective) and resolve conflict. It may take time, patience, and experience; each group is different from every other.

Effective group leaders of all kinds demonstrate intentionality. Think of your favorite heroes in social, political, military, or any other sphere of activity. They are willing to commit and act decisively, but they are also able to change direction and style as they observe the results of their actions.

Intentionality is also important in working with various orientations to groups. You may start a psychoeducational group with a highly structured agenda, but within the first session, you realize that the group wants to be more theme oriented and discuss things in more detail than your time plan allows. Will you switch your plan and "go with the group" or will you continue your own agenda? At times, either choice could be correct—or wrong. Intentionality will require you to take risks and then learn from the errors that will inevitably occur.

Multicultural issues and cultural empathy underlie all forms of intentionality. We might coin a new term for your consideration—*multicultural intentionality.* Multicultural intentionality emphasizes competencies in group work as in the central dimensions of the *Diversity Competencies for Group Workers* (see page 31). Multicultural intentionality may be defined as:

1. *Awareness*—becoming aware of your own multicultural heritage, recognizing your own biases and the limits of what you can do.
2. *Knowledge*—possessing and gaining knowledge of multicultural groups and the workings of oppression, recognizing that some traditional approaches to group work may be inappropriate or need adaptations for varying multicultural groups. This is a continuing lifelong issue, one that the competent group leader is always learning as he or she becomes more proficient in dealing with it.
3. *Skills*—possessing and constantly gaining expertise in group work and its multiple orientations, developing appropriate skills to work with differing cultures, and actively seeking to prevent and eliminate prejudices, biases, and discrimination.
4. *Humility, confidence, and recovery skills*—being aware that one does not always have the answer, that one can correct mistakes, and that one is confident in her or his ability to adapt, change, and learn. It is not your errors, but your ability to recovery from them gracefully, that is most important.

As you move forward and work in more depth with all the multiple possibilities in group work, enjoy the process. Group work is important and will only become more influential in a world needing connections and understanding. Good luck in your journey of movement and intentional transformation.

# GLOSSARY

This glossary provides definitions for some of the most important concepts used in this book. It does not provide definitions for every term. You will want to supplement this basic glossary with a list of your own central ideas, their definitions, and their meanings to you. In addition, you may want to refine some of the definitions here as you gain experience in group leadership. This is part of defining your own leadership style. Ultimately, *your* definitions, not ours, will determine how you practice group leadership.

**ABC:**   The behavioral ABC sequence is a process of analysis that examines *observable* antecedents, behaviors, and consequences. What happened before the incident, what were the actual behaviors, and what was the result? ABC is related to **ABCDEF** (below) but emphasizes observable events—things that can be seen, heard, and perhaps even counted.

**ABCDEF:**   Albert Ellis' REBT sequence examines A, the objective facts (similar to ABC above); B, the person's beliefs about A; C, the emotional consequences of A; D, disputing irrational thinking; E, effect of disputation; and F, new feelings and behaviors. The emphasis in ABCDEF is more on internal cognitions—thoughts and feelings—but still includes aspects of the more observable, countable dimensions of ABC.

**anger management:**   Anger can have a positive or negative effect on the group, depending on how it is managed. Anger management is a skill-based, theme-centered process that teaches group members to express their negative feelings in constructive ways toward accomplishing appropriate and meaningful change.

**attending:**   Some people are more aware of their surroundings than others. Attending is the ability to pay attention to the multiple and complicated dynamics going on in the group as a whole and among its individual members at the same time.

**attending behavior:**   The skills of effective group leadership depend on paying attention to what is going on in the group. Attending behavior requires close observation of the "3 Vs + B" dimensions:   visuals, vocals, verbal following, and body language.

**awareness:**   Some of us pay more attention to our culturally learned assumptions than others. Awareness requires the identification of assumptions made by ourselves and those around us. Leaders must be aware of assumptions that help them better understand culturally learned behaviors in the group as the first stage of multicultural competence.

**basic listening sequence:**   The process of effective listening has been organized into components using the microskills pyramid. The basic listening sequence involves using microskills designed to draw out the group member's story, concern, or issue. They include questioning, encouraging, paraphrasing, reflecting feelings, and summarizing.

**behavior change:** Just as group members influence the group's behavior, the group will influence the behavior of group members. Behavior change identifies new ways of achieving an objective that seem more effective and/or efficient than previously used ways.

**body language:** How we stand and/or sit tells others a lot about what we are thinking and feeling. Communication occurs both verbally and nonverbally, and our movement or body position may send a message quite different from our verbalizations.

**closed questions:** Closed questions can be answered by a word or short and specific response. Closed questions are often used to fill in specific information gaps or to encourage group members to talk less.

**community genogram:** A community genogram is a drawing a person makes to show her or his relationships within the community of origin or the community of residence. The individual develops in a family and community within a culture. Genograms drawn by group members showing some of the main facts of their family and community history will help the leader understand the context of their individual issues.

**confidentiality:** Confidentiality refers to protecting the integrity of other group members by not sharing information about those group members with persons outside that particular group. Most groups do not have the protection of legal confidentiality so the ethical obligation to keep information confidential is particularly important.

**conflict:** Disruption, challenges, and disturbances can occur in groups. Discrepancies, incongruities, and contradictions are indicators of conflict in the group relationship. Conflict is a potentially positive and/or negative process in groups as the members explore alternative explanations of their different perceptions. Conflict provides an opportunity for learning.

**conflict management:** Conflict cannot always be resolved or eliminated and sometimes provides a valuable or painfully necessary element in a relationship. Conflict management is the process of observing individual and group conflict, as when the group leader is being challenged, and reframing the conflict into an asset that can lead to a positive resolution.

**conflict resolution:** Some conflict is unnecessary and can be eliminated or resolved through clarification. Conflict resolution is a process of reconciling two individuals or groups among whom disagreement is evident and unproductive and where the differences are typically eliminated by one side giving in to the other. Effective conflict resolution aims toward a "win-win" strategy whenever possible.

**conflict with the leader:** As group members define their individual role in the group they may be expected to challenge the leader. Conflict with the leader is a phenomenon in which the group may vent their frustrations by directing their anger directly or indirectly at the leader as a target of opportunity, an action that may or may not be deserved.

**confrontation:** Confrontation is a group of microskills oriented toward a "win-win" approach to managing individual and group conflict. Confrontation is not a direct or harsh challenge but a more gentle skill that involves listening to the group member carefully and respectfully and then helping the group member examine the situation more fully with a supportive but firm challenge.

**consultation:** When we don't know the answer to a problem we seek out someone who does know the answer. Consultation means giving or receiving advice from some other person based on that person's specialized expertise.

**contact hypothesis:** The saying "the more we get together the happier we will be" is not always true. The contact hypotheses predicts that group interaction under favorable conditions will have a positive consequence but under negative conditions will have a negative consequence and that spontaneous contact usually occurs under unfavorable conditions until or unless the favorable conditions for contact have been arranged.

**context:** Some cultures put a higher emphasis on context than others. In a high-context culture, all behaviors are interpreted differently depending on the surroundings, and the relationships between members are emphasized. In a low-context culture there is a more abstract and "one size fits all" perspective where the same guidelines are applied across all situations.

**contract:** By joining a group, each member has implicitly or explicitly entered into a contract. This contract is an agreement among group members/leaders regarding expectations each member has for each other member participating in the group.

**corrective feedback:** When someone gives you good advice it is wise to listen carefully. Corrective feedback is information given back to a leader or group member on something that can be changed and is based on the positive asset search.

**cultural empathy:** All group work is multicultural according to the broad definition of culture. Multicultural issues underlie the verbal and nonverbal behavior of all group members. Cultural empathy requires developing an understanding of each member's multiple cultural groups, based on ethnicity, race, sexual orientation, and so on, and requires constant attention for personal growth and group cohesion. (See also **multicultural.**)

***cultural/environmental/contextual issues:*** The surroundings of the group itself and of each group member have a strong influence on the group activity. The synonymous use of culture with environment and context describes an overlapping and broadly defined web of significance that combines the backgrounds of each and all group members in a single group context.

***culture of the group*** (*also see* group mind): Each group itself becomes a "microculture" in that it is unique and not likely to be repeated elsewhere. Many group leaders talk of the specific and unique cultures developed in each group. The culture of the group is a reflection of the interaction between and among leaders and group members with the past and present contexts within which they live.

***dialectics of change:*** Groups change in response to each new situation. The dialectics of change refers to how every move stimulates a countermove. The dialectics of change describes how group members and leaders influence one another moving from a thesis to an antithesis toward a new synthesis of the group's identity.

***dimensions:*** In the holistic interpretation of groups it is important to understand that the individual group member, the group as a whole, and the topic being discussed will have multiple simultaneous levels or dimensions that constantly recycle as the group develops over time. The five holistic, recycling dimensions are initiating the group, gathering data, making a positive asset search, working, and ending. Each dimension will require a different set of microskills and strategies.

***direct, mutual communication (DMC) strategy:*** Direct mutual communication is a systematic listening and problem-solving method that helps us understand conflict and differences in a safe and mutual manner. Direct mutual communication involves listening to each other's story, repeating back to the person what was said as completely as possible, noting the other person's feelings and thoughts about your response, and then allowing the other person to respond using the same formula.

***directives:*** Directives are specific directions, suggestions, or advice that focus on a change in behavior by individuals or groups in order to achieve desired outcomes. An example of a directive would be to tell someone to "do" something. Directives are more effective if used sparingly and with caution.

***discrepancies:*** Discrepancies are mixed messages in verbal and/or nonverbal behavior, between group members, and/ or between the group and the leader. Discrepancies are two messages that seem incompatible with one another in their explanation of a behavior, event, or conclusion when one element contradicts the other.

***dual relationships:*** Each individual is connected with other individuals in more than one role relationship. We treat people differently according to each of those different roles. There are possibly negative consequences for one or both individuals when those role relationships overlap. Having dual relationships makes it hard to know if you are speaking with another group member as a classmate, family member, roommate, boy/girlfriend, or supervisor.

***dynamic balancing:*** The dynamics of a group need to be adjusted artistically and flexibly rather than in a rigid manner. Dynamic balancing is a concept developed by Ruth Cohn describing how the focus moves from individual to group to theme discussion in the group process, with one-third of the group time being focused on each of the three elements.

***empathy:*** Empathy is the ability to perceive a situation from the other person's perspective. We sometimes impose our own sympathetic feelings on others rather than recognizing their unique feelings. The goal is to see, hear, and feel the unique world of the other.

***encouragers:*** Encouragers are key words, nonverbals, restatements, phrases, or sentences intended to indicate support and positive feelings or to help a group member say more about a topic, thought, or feeling Most people respond more completely and comprehensively when they are in a friendly and supportive environment.

***feedback:*** Feedback is a skill used in both basic attending and more advanced influencing microskills. The function of feedback is helping the individual group members and/or the leader identify how they are being perceived by others on a particular topic or activity. Effective feedback follows specified guidelines.

***fish bowl:*** Structured exercises help group members observe and debrief the group process in a systematic way. The "fish bowl" is a standard group exercise in which a smaller number of members—like fish in a bowl—interact in a prescribed manner; the other group members surround them, reporting back what they observe.

***focusing:*** The leader and/or group members frequently attend to one particular element of the group at a time. Focusing involves intentionally concentrating the energy of group members individually and/or collectively. Focusing may center on the individual, the topic, the other people, the family, mutual relationships, the group leader, cultural/environmental issues, or other elements.

**foundational skills:** The microskills framework suggests that microskills such as attending, observing, and the basic listening sequence are the substructure on which group process develops. Influencing and other more advanced group skills build on these foundational skills of listening.

**goals:** Each group has an implicit or explicit agenda to accomplish. The particular goals or objectives to be accomplished by individual group members or through group activity are formally or informally part of each group's agenda. Goals are the end-point outcomes identified by individuals and groups as the optimal consequence of and rationale for getting together.

**group:** Most of what we learned came from the groups to which we belong. Groups are gatherings of individuals who recognize their joint membership for completing a task or process, celebrating a relationship, or sharing involvement in some kind of mutual activity.

**group counseling:** Counseling can be provided to individuals or groups of individuals. When counseling occurs in groups, the focus of activity is on the psychological well-being of the group members both individually and collectively from an educational or psychological perspective. Group counseling requires the combined effort of all members and not just the leader.

**group empathy:** Leaders need to understand the "group mind" or the feelings the group as a whole has toward itself and the topic under discussion. Group empathy is a process of responding to the group members individually and/or collectively from their unique perspective without imposing your own interpretation.

**group mind:** (*also see* culture of the group): The group mind is difficult to define precisely but represents the group in action. Each group develops its own identity and "personality." This unique element in each group provides the basis of understanding and consensus for group decisions. The nature of the group mind can at times be facilitative, at others conflictual and distracting from achieving group goals.

**group psychotherapy:** Psychotherapy can be provided to individuals or through groups. Group psychotherapy is provided when groups focus on the psychological well-being of the group members individually as well as collectively from a healing perspective. Group psychotherapy requires the combined effort of all members and not just the leader.

**group work:** People can be helped individually or in groups. Group work is the professional practice of helping others in a formal group context in which the leader takes responsibility for guiding group members toward educational and/or therapeutic goals.

**here-and-now:** Describing events in the present tense tends to make those descriptions more concrete and verifiable than speculating on the past or the future. Here-and-now provides a focus on the present activity of a group or the discussion in the present of some past or future activity.

**holistic group perspective:** Each group is complex and dynamic in the various dimensions that emerge and are recycled as the group develops. The holistic perspective is a recognition that all aspects of the group are related to one another in a complex network. No single part of a group situation can be completely understood until all other points of the holistic context have been considered.

**"I" statements:** What each of us says about ourselves tells others a lot about us. Those statements beginning with first person singular said by group members and the frequency with which group members use the first person singular will tell the leader a lot about the feelings of individual group members. Questions asked by leaders of members often hide or disguise underlying "I" statements.

**incongruities:** Incongruities are mixed messages in nonverbal behaviors that may be internal to a single group member, between or among group members, or between the leader and group members. Incongruities may seem incompatible with one another and unconventional in how they relate to one another in ways that "don't fit," requiring further clarification.

**influencing skills:** The influencing skills are found in the microskills group pyramid. Influencing skills include the basic listening sequence, reframing/interpretation, exploring logical consequences, self-disclosure, feedback, and giving information, advice, opinions, instruction, suggestions, and directives. Influencing skills seek to change or influence the individual and/or collective activities of group members in a particular direction and with specified outcomes predicted. Again, the intentional group leader is aware that predictions are not always successful and so is ready with alternative skills and strategies as needed.

**integrative styles:** Although there are clear differences among the varying groups, most group leaders today vary their styles. Skilled group leaders incorporate ideas from a variety of theories and perspectives in an intentionally eclectic style, depending on the needs and abilities of their different groups.

**intentionality:** A well-trained group leader will be able to anticipate opportunities. Intentionality is being purposive rather than "accidental" in taking a particular action with anticipation of the probable consequences of that action. The intentional leader will have many possibilities for effective leadership. If one skill or strategy does not work, another is available.

**interpersonal influence:** We continuously influence others whether we want to or not both by what we say or do and by what we do not say or do. Interpersonal influence refers to the impact every person in the group has on every other person, recognizing that the quiet person may influence or be influenced as well.

**Ivey Taxonomy (IT):** Allen Ivey developed a structured framework for microtraining that matches a leader's comment with microskills, anticipated results, area of focus, and time orientation. The IT is based on extensive research about each microskill resulting in data-based predictions about the consequences of using each microskill with intentionality, although the predicted results do not always occur. Be prepared to flex intentionally and have another response ready if the first one "doesn't work."

**key words:** Key words are often the constructs by which the group member organizes his or her world and therefore have important underlying meanings. Certain words appear again and again in the group member's description of different situations. Assisting a member to explore the facts, feelings, and meanings underlying those key words may help the member and others to better understand the situation.

**leadership:** Each group will depend on one or more members to take the initiative in organizing their activities. Leadership includes those activities by the formal or informal group leader(s) or group members who take responsibility for guiding others in the group to bring about a positive change toward accomplishing the group's goals. However, it is also possible that a group member can lead the group in less useful directions.

**leadership style:** Each group leader will develop a unique and special style. Leadership style is a recognition that each individual develops a unique perspective for working with groups to achieve a purpose or goal-related activity and that what works for some does not work for others.

**leading:** An effective group leader will anticipate where the group is headed. Leading involves providing the initiative for changing the direction of group activity, supporting group members, and interpreting the meaning of previous group activities.

**linking:** Every element in the group is related to every other element. Linking is the skill used by the leader and/or group members to see the relationships between individual members' perspectives or between the views of any one member and the group as a whole, bringing together both the here-and-now and the there-and-then.

**listening:** Listening is basic to the foundation microskills. The messages others send and the messages we receive may be quite different as we filter the messages through our own biased perspective. Listening is being able to articulate accurately what was said, felt, and meant by the individual or group.

**logical consequences:** Sometimes experience is the best teacher. Logical consequences refers to those things that happen predictably in response to an appropriate or inappropriate behavior by an individual or group and how those consequences can result in learning something important.

**mastery:** Mastery can be classified into several levels. Classification mastery means you are able to identify the skill. Basic mastery means you are able to demonstrate the skill. Intentional mastery means you are able to use the skill and change skills if the first attempt fails. Teaching mastery means you are able to teach the skill to others.

**microskills:** Allen Ivey developed a hierarchy of microskills that combine to define the competencies of skilled counselors, therapists, and group workers. These specific and concrete verbal and nonverbal counseling skills or behaviors are important in leading a group effectively and intentionally. The major microskills and strategies are listed in the Group Skills Pyramid.

**multicultural:** All groups are multicultural in the broad application of culture, which includes ethnographic, demographic, status, and affiliation variables. Because all behaviors are learned and displayed in a cultural context, accurate assessment, meaningful understanding, and appropriate intervention require that each behavior be understood in its cultural context.

**multicultural counseling:** The authors consider all group work, whether structured, counseling, or psychotherapeutic, to be multicultural. More specifically, each group member comes from a wide range of culturally different backgrounds (listed in "Before You Start"). There is a need to recognize that members and group leader share similarities in some aspects of their cultural backgrounds but are different in other aspects.

**multicultural knowledge:** Some of us know more facts and information about cultures than others. Multicultural knowledge is a comprehensive and meaningful understanding of the facts and information about our own and other people's cultures so that we can better understand the behavior of ourselves and others as the second stage of multicultural competence.

**multiple dimensions of focus:** An effective leader will be able to focus on several aspects of the group at any time. The multiple dimensions of focus recognizes that the group leader and group activities will be focused on many different dimensions, topics, or processes at the same time, combining information from past, present, and future perspectives.

**narrative model:**   We teach and learn through telling stories or listening to the stories of others. The narrative model as presented here is an approach that presumes communication is primarily the telling and hearing of stories or narratives. The leader can identify positive assets in each story and through restorying can help the member discover a positive meaning in each story.

**nonjudgmental:**   It is important for group leaders to suspend judgment about what the group member says or does and to avoid fixing blame. Being nonjudgmental requires providing the group member a summary of what has been said or done in a nonjudgmental manner without taking sides.

**nonverbal process observation:**   It is important to observe the nonverbal cues of the group leader and/or members carefully. Through nonverbal process observation of the group leader or member's body language, it becomes possible to more accurately interpret what the group leader or member is saying and how others in the group are reacting even when they are silent.

**Observation of Change Scale:**   Groups and group members respond to change in a variety of ways. The Observation of Change Scale measures responses to conflict or change from denial, to full consideration, to generalization of the complicated factors contributing to that conflict or change.

**open questions:**   Open questions typically cannot be answered briefly and require a longer or somewhat complicated response. Open questions are often used to encourage group members to talk more.

**oppression:**   Prejudice plus the power to implement discriminatory practice. Conscious oppression appears as deliberate acts designed to harm and/or unfairly favor a group. Unconscious oppression occurs when an exam is scheduled on a Christian, Jewish, or Muslim holy day, an employer talks to men while ignoring women on the staff, or a business owner forgets to provide handicapped access.

**pacing:**   "Being with" and empathizing with each member of the group, pairs and subgroups, and the group itself. Pacing is another way to describe listening that builds trust—we listen to the stories and narratives of the group and walk with them. Effective pacing is active and can lead to individual or group change.

**paraphrasing:**   A paraphrase feeds back to the member the essence of what the person has just said by shortening and clarifying the comments. Paraphrasing is not parroting but is using some of your own words plus the important main words used by the speaker.

**person as community:**   All group members bring a "community" of significant past relationships into the group with them. The person as community is a recognition that each of us is a summary of our past relationships and experiences, which we accumulate and which influence our contemporary behaviors.

**personal styles:**   Each group member will develop her or his own style of functioning in the group. Typical group member roles may be either positive or negative, such as life crisis participant, passive or active member, active contributor, informal leader, fighter, follower, intellectualizer, analyst, interpreter, or "idea" person as discussed in the book.

**positive asset:**   Individual group members have strengths and positive assets that will help them accomplish their goals. Positive assets are those implicit or explicit characteristics of the person or group that provide a meaningful resource to accomplish the group's or individual's purpose.

**power:**   Each person or group has a greater or lesser access to power. Power is the ability to influence self and others in a particular direction at a particular time in a particular way. Power may have positive or negative consequences, depending on how it is used. Power refers to the energy or resources for accomplishing individual and/or group goals.

**process observation:**   Process observation is defined in two ways. Persons sitting outside the group observe what occurs and provide feedback to other group members. Often the process observer uses a formal system to categorize some aspect of group behavior, such as who talks after whom, group structure, and so on. When the leader or member observes what is going on in the group while simultaneously participating in the group, that is also process observation.

**process-oriented groups:**   A process group is often focused on the way in which decisions are made as much as or more than the decision itself. A process-oriented decision group is focused on skill building or exploring the more emotional effect that members have on one another. Some examples of process-oriented groups might include person-centered training groups and aspects of male or female consciousness-raising groups.

**rapport:**   The "good feelings" of a positive relationship are very important to the success of a group. Rapport refers to the positive feelings that group members have toward one another and/or the group leader, which encourage trust, accurate communication, and the capability of the group to work out difficult issues.

**recovery:** Being successful depends on what one does or says after having made a mistake in the group. Recovery skills include the ability to utilize a mistake or accident as an opportunity for increasing trust, rapport, and/or accomplishment by responding in an empathic and meaningful manner.

**recycling** (*also see* holistic group perspective): Groups are complex and dynamic as they develop over time. Recycling refers to focusing on an individual and/or group process when the same topic or idea may appear again. Individuals and groups tend to repeat patterns of behavior. Recycling also refers to the five dimensions in that issues concerning initiating, gathering data, searching for positive assets, working, and ending may appear at any time in group practice.

**reflecting feeling:** Feelings and emotions are implicit in the group member's words and behaviors. The purpose of reflecting feeling is to make these implicit, sometimes hidden, emotions explicit and clear to the group member.

**reflecting meaning:** The relationship between and among behaviors, thoughts, feelings, and their underlying meaning structure provides a context for the leader to understand a group member's behavior. Reflection of meaning is concerned with finding the deeply held thoughts and feelings underlying life experience and reflecting those deeper meanings back to the group member for validation.

**reframing/interpreting:** There are many different ways of interpreting a past or present experience. Reframing provides the group member with an alternative frame of reference from which to view life situations and generate new stories.

**restatements:** People respond more openly and honestly when they feel they are being understood. Restatements involve repeating back to individual group members what they have said, using their exact words. Restatements provide clarification and validation to the person that her or his message has been heard as intended.

**restory:** We remember the most important stories in our life from which we learned who we are and what we can do. Through restorying individuals have the ability to reframe, reinterpret, or redefine the stories of their own background that have influenced them and make those stories into positive learning experiences.

**right to pass:** Each group member has rights that must be recognized. Right to pass is a recognition that group members may appropriately take a more passive role in the group's activities without pressure from other group members to take a more active role.

**screening:** Individuals are selected for membership in a group activity based on specific characteristics of those in-

dividuals. A major goal of screening is to help ensure that a group "works," has members who are interested in the goals of the group, and is able to work toward those goals.

**self-disclosure:** Group leaders and especially members take a big risk when they disclose something private about themselves. Self-disclosure is the process in which an individual member or leader takes the risk of revealing something about herself or himself that would be otherwise considered private so that the group can benefit in some way.

**skills:** Some of us are better able than others to change ourselves and those around us to fit the changing situation of each cultural context. Skills are the ability to make appropriate changes based on accurate awareness and meaningful knowledge to take the right action at the right time in the right way as an important part of multicultural competence.

**sociogram:** Group members interact in repeating patterns. The sociogram is a visual representation of how individual group members interact with one another and whether the interactions are reciprocal; they illustrate each member's role in the group activity.

**stage theory:** Most books on groups have typically described the group as going through a series of four or five stages in a linear and somewhat rigid fashion, one stage at a time. In the holistic approach used in this book, stages recycle again and again so that the ending of one aspect is the beginning of something else. While groups are always different at their beginning from their ending, the developmental changes tend to be more complicated than stage theories imply.

**stages of group development:** Varying theorists have generated several methods of defining sequential stages. This book takes a holistic perspective in which we emphasize the complex and dynamic "dimensions" of the group at any one time more than the sequence of stages. The stages of group development refer to a structure of planning, initiating the group through rapport and structuring, gathering data through stories and a balanced focus, making a positive asset search, working to examine goals, restorying the group members' activities, and ending the group by generalizing what was learned toward generating new stories.

**stereotyping:** As we learn from our experiences, we develop expectations about other groups of people. Stereotyping occurs when your mental expectations of other specific individuals or groups are more important than the actual behaviors of each individual or the group itself for making your decisions.

**storytelling:** Each of us learns and teaches through stories about our own and others' experiences. Individuals learn through recognizing patterns of activity that help them

No.

*Glossary*

understand, describe, and explain those stories, their meanings, and their consequences.

**structured groups:** Some groups have more specific organization and direction than others, avoiding or eliminating ambiguity wherever possible and providing clear guidelines about what the member can expect of the group or what the group can expect of the individual members. Structured groups have a preset agenda directed toward a specific task, activity, or purpose external to the group.

**structuring:** Structuring skills of directives, suggestions, and instruction are explicitly designed to make things happen in the group and they influence what occurs directly, often immediately. Structuring skills influence the group to follow strategies and actions suggested by the leader.

**structuring strategies:** Building the structure of a group can best be done in an orderly plan based on intentional strategies. Structuring strategies are reasonable explanations of how future behavior can build on past behavior in a systematic process to the advantage of individuals and the group itself.

**task-oriented decision groups:** A task group, often focused on decision making, is one of the most common groups. A task-oriented decision group is focused on a particular activity or population. An example of task-oriented decision groups is a committee meeting to decide on the use of computers in a school.

**theme-centered group:** Ruth Cohen developed a model for combining a focus on the individual, group, and topic at the same time. A theme-centered group is organized to focus on a particular topic, population, activity, or social issue as the more frequently salient feature in which the "I" and the "we" interact with the topic or "it." This is a basic model useful in all topic-centered groups.

**there-and-then:** Our recollections of the past and expectations for the future tend to be less than accurate as we filter our memories to fit our own needs. There-and-then perspectives put distance between the group expectations and a particular event or activity that will occur in the future, occurred in the past, or occurred some place outside the group. At the same time, it is important to provide linkage between here-and-now and there-and-then, thus maximizing transfer of learning from the group to the real world.

**thought-stopping:** Thought-stopping is a technique of interrupting the discourse at selected points to focus on the internal dialogue or thinking that was going on at a particular point in time. Members may snap a rubber band on the wrist and say "Stop" to themselves when thinking a negative thought and then substitute a positive thought, for example.

**Three Vs + B:** Acronyms make complicated ideas easier to remember. This acronym of visual, vocal, verbal follow-

ing, and body language summarizes the main points of attending.

**trust building:** Trust is essential to the success of a group. Trust building involves effective pacing and listening, which is especially important at the beginning of a group experience to make the group a safe place in which to take risks.

**verbal following:** Each culture teaches its own verbal and nonverbal language. Verbal following is being able to pay attention to what the group members are saying and responding to some central theme on which the group is focused.

**visual process observation:** How a group leader or group members use their eyes is a significant clue to what they are thinking and feeling. Visual process observation is a recognition of how eyes can gather information both by what they see and how the eyes are seen to be used by others.

**vocal process observation:** How a group leader or group members use their voice is a significant clue to what they are thinking and feeling. Vocal process observation is a recognition of the information you can gather about a person by that person's loud/soft, slow/fast, smooth/rough vocal qualities.

**warm-up exercises:** It is useful to bring the group up to speed before starting. Warm-up exercises are activities for generating interest and energy among group members at the beginning of a session through group-building interactions.

**wheel:** Sometimes the group leader is tempted to conduct therapy with group members while the rest of the group looks on. The "wheel" is a strategy in which the group leader focuses therapeutically on each group member in turn, going around the group like the spokes of a wheel.

**White privilege:** White members of the dominant culture do not always recognize the traditional advantages they have unfairly had over others. Being a member of the White dominant culture results in the enjoyment of certain advantages in a culturally biased society. White privilege is a recognition that membership in any dominant culture group offers certain advantages not normally available to members of minority culture groups who do not also share membership in the dominant culture group.

**worldview:** Each of us views the world differently. We depend on culturally learned guidelines to interpret what we can expect of others and what they expect of us in a variety of different contexts. The dimensions typically used to define worldview include the view of human nature as good or bad; one's relationship with others; one's relationship to nature; one's orientation toward the past, present, or future; and the mode of human activity.

# NAME INDEX

American Association for Marriage and
  Family Therapy, 18
American Counseling Association, 5, 11
American Group Psychotherapy
  Association, 18
American Psychological Association, 18
Amir, Y., 83
Association for Specialists in Group
  Work, 11*ff*, 22, 30, 31

Bach, G., 116
Bednar, R., 20, 183
Bloch, S., 20
Bohn, M. (*see* Ivey, M.)
Brain, L., 96
Brown, L., 75
Brown, M., 75
Burlingame, G., 38, 57, 80

Carkhuff, R., 66, 241
Carrell, S., 102, 197, 262
Carroll, P., 205
Cline, R., 171
Cohn, R., 25, 107, 111, 114, 116, 117,
  119, 122, 132
Commission on Rehabilitation
  Counselor Certification, 18
Conyne, R., 245, 262
Corey, G., 3, 71, 117, 120, 183, 259,
  262
Corey, M., 183
Cox, J., 55
Crouch, E., 20

Dagley, J., 55
Daniels, T., 20, 132, 263

Davis, M., 262
Dies, R., 68
Dreikurs, R., 186
Duran, B., 257, 260
Duran, E., 257, 260

Ellis, A., 187*ff*, 248-249, 258
Eppinger, S., 55
Epston, D., 30
Eschelman, E., 262

Fanning, P., 262
Freire, P., 261
Fukuyama, M., 82
Furhiman, A., 38, 57, 80

Gazda, G., 55, 116, 117, 119
Gladding, S., 262
Gluckstern, N., 55, 216, 251, 263
Goldberg, C., 66, 241, 262
Grey, L., 186

Higgins, W., 216

Ivey, A., 5, 20, 25, 36, 41, 66, 83, 85,
  118, 121, 132, 156, 163, 170,
  182, 184, 187, 188, 193, 203,
  214, 215, 216, 251, 251, 258,
  259, 260, 263
Ivey, M., 5, 27, 36, 41, 66, 83, 85, 118,
  121, 132, 163, 170, 182, 184,
  187, 188, 193, 203, 214, 215,
  251, 252, 258, 259, 263

Jongsma, A., 197
Jordan, J., 116

Kaplan, S., 116
Kaul, T., 20, 183

LaFromboise, T., 102, 197, 257, 258,
  262
Lago, C., 259
Lieberman, M., 209
Lifton, W., 241
Locke, D., 82

MacMillan, M., 259
MaKay, M., 262
McInnis, W., 197
McIntosh, P., 4
McKay, M., 262
Miles, M., 209
Miller, J., 116
Morran, K., 171
Myrick, R., 55

National Academy for Certified Clinical
  Mental Health Counselors, 18
National Board for Certified
  Counselors, Inc., 18
National Council for Credentialing
  Career Counselors, 18

Ogbonnya, O., 83, 262

Pack-Brown, S., 118, 119, 120, 172,
  174, 260, 262
Paniagua, F., 247
Parham, T., 121
Parker, W., 118, 119, 120, 172, 174,
  260, 262

# SUBJECT INDEX

ABC, 182–183, 187, 257, 279
ABCDEF, 187–188, 190–192, 279
Abuse (*see* Multicultural groups and issues, life experience context)
Action (as part of restorying), 32–33 (*see also* Storytelling)
Adolescent groups (*see* Child and adolescent groups)
Afrocentric perspective, 83, 118, 119
Age (*see* Multicultural groups and issues, demographic context)
AIDS (*see* Multicultural groups and issues)
Alcohol-related issues, 30, 70, 127, 252
"Am I crazy or is this really happening?" 172–174, 188 (*see also* Feedback)
Anger management groups, 180*ff*, 203, 219*ff*, 243, 244, 262, 279
Assertiveness training, 223, 243, 245, 247–250, 257, 261
Assessing skill level, 267*ff*
Attending behavior, 39–42*ff*, 90, 114, 133, 268, 279 (*see also* Body Language; Verbals; Visuals; Vocals)
Awareness, 31, 277, 279

Basic listening sequence, 25, 62, 81*ff*, 88, 155, 158–161, 133–134, 135, 188, 241, 242, 270, 279
Basic mastery, 268
Behavior change, 280
Bereavement groups, 127
Bias (*see* Multicultural groups and issues, life experience context)
Biracial individuals, 82

Bisexual individuals (*see* Multicultural groups and issues; Oppression, heterosexism)
Body language, 40, 43, 48–50, 96, 184, 211–212, 280

Cancer (*see* Multicultural groups and issues, life experience context)
Captive group, 114
Challenging group members (*see* Personal styles and behaviors of group members)
Checkout, 88, 93, 184
Child and adolescent groups, 55, 75–76, 99, 101–102, 127–128, 175, 197, 233–234, 261
Circular questions, 185
Classification mastery, 268
Client-centered therapy (*see* Person-centered groups)
Closed questions, 280 (*see also* Questions)
Coercion and pressure (*see* Ethical issues)
Cognitive-behavioral groups, 166, 185, 243, 257–258, 259, 261 (*see also* Anger management groups; Communication skills groups/workshops; Social skills groups)
Communication skills groups/workshops, 242, 244, 250–252, 257, 261 (*see also* Social skills groups)
Community (*see* Multicultural groups and issues, demographic context)

Community genogram, 83, 84–87, 101, 185, 280
Concreteness, 184
Confidentiality (*see* Ethical issues)
Conflict, 280 (*see also* Confrontation)
Conflict management, 27, 61*ff*, 280 (*see also* Confrontation)
Conflict resolution, 280 (*see also* Confrontation)
Confrontation, 123, 125, 135, 203*ff*, 247, 272, 280
Consciousness-raising groups, 23, 188, 197, 242, 243, 252–256, 260
Consequences (*see* Logical consequences)
Consultant, 11, 17, 43
Consultation, 280 (*see also* Ethical issues)
Contact hypothesis, 83–84, 280
Context, 280 (*see also* Multicultural groups and issues)
Contract, 280 (*see also* Ethical issues; Sample group contract)
Contradiction (*see* Discrepancies)
Corrective feedback, 156, 174, 242, 280 (*see also* Feedback)
Counseling groups (*see* Group counseling)
Cultural empathy, 280 (*see also* Empathy; Multicultural groups and issues)
Cultural/environmental context, 281 (*see also* Focusing)
Cultural identity groups, 262
Cultural intentionality, 28–30 (*see also* Multicultural intentionality)